"With brilliance and brio, William Boelhower provides the emergent field of Atlantic studies with the prospectus that it has been waiting for. Arguing for trialectical engagements of history, geography, and literary studies, with trans-, cis-, and circumatlantic soundings and groundings, he maps current positions and plots future directions. No better guide could be hoped for."

KENT MATHEWSON, Fred B. Kniffen Professor of Geography and Anthropology, Louisiana State University

"This book provides a timely and beautifully written genealogy and future vision for the Atlantic studies paradigm. Bringing together theories and methods from the fields of history, geography, and literary and cultural studies, William Boelhower calls for research on the Atlantic world that dares to be multidisciplinary, transnational, multilingual, and multiscalar."

NICOLE WALLER, author of *Contradictory Violence: Revolution and Subversion in the Caribbean*

"William Boelhower gets right to the heart of what makes Atlantic studies vital to contemporary critical thought, but also cogently lays out the challenges facing those who would first dip their feet into its breaking waves. As capacious as it is complex, Atlantic studies is fortunate to have Boelhower as a guide."

MICHAEL J. DREXLER, coeditor of *The Haitian Revolution and the Early United States: Histories, Textualities, Geographies*

Atlantic Studies

.

Atlantic Studies

PROSPECTS AND CHALLENGES

William Boelhower

Louisiana State University Press
Baton Rouge

Published by Louisiana State University Press
Copyright © 2019 by Louisiana State University Press
All rights reserved
Manufactured in the United States of America
First printing

Designer: Barbara Neely Bourgoyne
Typeface: Adobe Caslon Pro
Printer and binder: LSI

An early, shorter version of chapter 2 was published as "The Influence of Atlantic Studies on American Literary Scholarship," in *Oxford Handbook Online* (New York: Oxford University Press, 2016), copyright © 2016 Oxford University Press. Reproduced with permission of Oxford University Press through PLSclear.

An early version of chapter 6 was published as "Cartographic Practices: Depicting the *Mundus Novus* and the New Oceanic Order," *Yearbook of English Studies* 46 (2016): 21–36, copyright © 2016 Modern Humanities Research Association.

Library of Congress Cataloging-in-Publication Data
Names: Boelhower, William Q., author.
Title: Atlantic studies : prospects and challenges / William Boelhower.
Description: Baton Rouge : Louisiana State University Press, 2019. | Includes
    bibliographical references and index.
Identifiers: LCCN 2019009853 | ISBN 978-0-8071-7163-9 (cloth) | ISBN 978-0-8071-7294-0 (pbk.)
Subjects: LCSH: Atlantic Ocean Region—Historiography. | Atlantic Ocean Region—
    Intellectual life—Research. | Atlantic Ocean Region—Maps—Research.
Classification: LCC D210 .B58 2019 | DDC 909/.09821072—dc23
LC record available at https://lccn.loc.gov/2019009853

The paper in this book meets the guidelines for permanence and durability of the Committee on Production Guidelines for Book Longevity of the Council on Library Resources. ♾

To Franca Bernabei

Contents

Illustrations

Acknowledgments

The evolution of this book is in itself a complementary story. In the midst of a larger collective of European scholars interested in comparing multiethnic cultures and societies in Europe and Africa with those of the Americas, five of us sensed the need for a cross-disciplinary periodical that eventually became the interdisciplinary, Routledge-sponsored journal *Atlantic Studies,* the first issue of which saw the light of day in 2004. As part of that founding group of editors, I later moved from the University of Padua, Italy, to a teaching position at Louisiana State University, where I was offered the opportunity to form an Atlantic studies program with colleagues from the departments of geography and anthropology, history, comparative literature, and English. Before the state (and the university in its wake) suffered from a reeling economic crisis, an enthusiastic interdisciplinary group of us were able to generate a number of well-financed collaborative initiatives that included an international symposium on Atlantic studies and a speakers forum that brought to campus scholars such as Walter Johnson, Marcus Rediker, and Adam Rothman. Our local interdisciplinary cadre included Kent Mathewson, Craig Colten, and Andrew Sluyter (geography); Gaines Foster, Paul Hoffman, and Mark Thompson (history); John Lowe, Solimar Otero, Angelita Gourdine, Keith Sandiford, and Jerry Kennedy (literature and cultural studies); and Adelaide Russo and Christian Fernandez-Palacios (comparative literature). I mention them one by one because our weekly meetings often blossomed into extremely intense and fruitful discussions about the conceptual and cross-disciplinary dimensions of Atlantic studies, its overly charged ideological and Anglo-American formation better known as the "Atlantic Community," and the development of a number of seminar curricula that would truly express a humanities-wide sensibility. Out of this flurry of guests and encounters came the Routledge volume of essays *New Orleans in the Atlantic World: Between Land and Sea* (2010). Having been so tenaciously in the front lines of Atlantic studies initiatives, I was eventually awarded an Atlas Research Grant by the Board of Regents of the State University System of Louisiana, which I employed to work on the writing of this book. I also benefited from the research and travel funds that came with my designated Robert Thomas and Rita Wetta Adams Professorship. In addition to the speakers and my colleagues mentioned above, I would like especially to thank a number of other colleagues for having invited me to present parts of this book project to their graduate students and departmental colleagues: Dan Walden (Baylor), Mauro Peressini and Ratiba Hadj-Moussa (University of Ottawa), Gordon Hutner (University of Illinois, Urbana), Carmen Birkle (Marburg, Germany) and Nicole Waller (Potsdam, Germany), Stephen Fender, Maria Lauret, and Richard Follett (Sussex, England), Simone Francescato (Ca' Foscari University, Venice).

This book has greatly benefited from discussions on the Atlantic studies paradigm with a variety of individuals, above all the following: Vera Kutzinski, Kent Mathewson, Andrew Sluyter, Solimar Otero, Femi Euba, Mark Thompson, Dorothea Fischer-Hornung, Nicole Waller, Richard Follett, Neil Safier, Maria Lauret, Paul Hoffman, Christian Fernández-Palacios, and the dearly missed Susan Manning. I have also drawn inspiration from the work of Carlo Ginzburg, Sanjay Subrahmanyam, Walter Johnson, Marcus Rediker, Natalie Zemon-Davis, Margaret Cohen, and David Armitage. Still others inspired and incited me through conversations, criticism, and encouragement: Gary Boelhower, Susan Griffiths, Myriam Chancy, Adelaide Russo, Keith Sandiford. For her comments and suggestions on the book as a whole, I wish especially to thank Franca Bernabei, who read various versions of the manuscript and offered invaluable observations and criticism. I also benefited from the patient editing of George Roupe, whose eagle eye helped to improve the book's readability. The personnel at LSU Press were a delight to work with. I would like especially to thank acquisitions editor James Long, a superb guide with a passionate love of literature, and senior manuscript editor Catherine Kadair, who admirably and judiciously oversaw the final stages of preparing the book for publication.

Atlantic Studies

Introduction

Over the last twenty years or so, Atlantic studies has developed into a recognized and increasingly attractive research field in universities around the Atlantic. As part of a larger epochal shift in the academy, its rise has shared in the energy released by the call to rejuvenate an entire area of study, the old *mare nostrum* of the Atlantic world. Expressing a broad humanistic curiosity while having no exclusive departmental attachments, Atlantic studies scholars have drawn freely from the important new stimuli of cultural, postcolonial, and subaltern studies. In doing so, the field has evolved into a thriving cross-disciplinary engagement characterized by innovative research and new themes and opportunities it often shares with a generation of historians committed to renewing an inherited tradition of imperial, colonial, and military histories of the Atlantic world. Historians, cultural studies and literary scholars, journal editors, and publishers have produced enough work in this new field to warrant a backward glance at its genealogy, conceptual patterns, and exemplary texts and, equally important, to identify its prospects and challenges. While fostering interdisciplinarity and promoting a more inclusive pantheon of Atlantic subjects (and in the process, having to refine the very notion of human agency), atlanticists have mined or invented new archival sites even while exploring familiar cachets in a more critical light. This inchoate exuberance, springing largely from forays into the black Atlantic, has led significantly to new narrative and perspective approaches and, over the last two decades, to a specifically Atlantic studies sensibility.

This sensibility was not born from the head of Jupiter. Already in the late 1970s cultural studies intellectuals such as Raymond Williams and Stuart Hall redefined the work of cultural analysis thanks in large part to their reading of the prison notebooks of the Italian Marxist Antonio Gramsci, who gave culture a central role in the politics of the class struggle. What they found particularly useful were Gramsci's concepts of hegemony, the important role of organic intellectuals, the national-popular, and other related categories such as historic bloc, civil society, and more generally his philosophy of praxis.[1] In these same years Gayatri Chakravorty Spivak, then an emerging postcolonial intellectual, used Gramsci's concept of the subaltern, via the historian Ranajit Guha and his history collective, in her influential essay "Can the Subaltern Speak?"[2] Also and perhaps even more so than Stuart Hall, Edward Said was deeply influenced by Gramsci's work, not only for the Italian's elaboration of the role of intellectuals but also for his practice of embedding political and cultural analysis in geography. For this reason Said frequently singled out Gramsci's essay "Some Aspects of the Southern Question" as an explicitly geographical model of cultural analysis.[3]

While first-generation postcolonialists such as Spivak and Homi K. Bhabha contributed greatly to illuminating the complexities of subjectivity and identity formation under colonial regimes, they also deployed deconstructionist close reading of colonial and postcolonial literary texts to do so. Holding teaching positions in major universities, these intellectuals helped those on the margins of empire to write back, as they systematically uncovered the horrors and bad habits of Western imperialism. After the rapid rise of postcolonial critique, shelves of history celebrating the "benign and civilizing effects" of European rule abroad were turned into evidence against an epoch of one-sided historiography. As Edward Said noted about the post-colonial onslaught in his book *Culture and Imperialism,* "An immense wave of anti-colonial and ultimately anti-imperial activity, thought, and revision has overtaken the massive edifice of Western empire, challenging it, to use Gramsci's vivid metaphor, in a mutual siege."[4]

Standing on the shoulders of cultural and postcolonial studies intellectuals, a new cadre of atlanticists (both historians and scholars in other disciplines) began to take shape by the early 1990s. This came about as scholars inevitably sought to embrace a broader horizon of interest and involvement, beyond the ultimately reductive binary logic of metropole and colony that drove so much of the best postcolonial critique. To be sure, this tensive relation between European nations and their colonies has remained an important conceptual level in Atlantic studies perspectivism.[5] But other lines of inquiry were needed to appreciate the full significance of more elusive notions such as diaspora, hybridity, creolization, "biocapitalism,"[6] cosmopolitanism, wild weather, and oceanic mobility. Such concept formations could more fruitfully be examined by focusing on a single place (the cisatlantic perspective) or, at the other extreme, by tuning in to a previously uninflected supranational dimension characteristic of multiple modernities and processes of global interdependency (the circumatlantic perspective). At a certain point, scholars found themselves repeatedly coming up against this dilemma of multiple levels of engagement reaching both below and above the transatlantic relation typical of early modern colonialism. It is in response to this heuristic challenge that a defining feature of Atlantic studies emerged: the paradigmatic consciousness of having to keep multiple ways of looking in mind when deploying any one of them. This perspective complexity has generated an essentially ecological sensibility. Space and geography, place and territory, contextual identities and diasporic subjects, events, contingencies, interculturality, circulation, and mobility came to define the research parameters of Atlantic studies. Equally important, each perspective line assumes—even requires—different sets of disciplinary expertise. Herein lie the prospects and the challenges of Atlantic studies, both of which inform the making of this new sensibility's exemplary texts. I will return to these issues later (in chapters 1 and 2), before proceeding to offer a number of test cases involving Atlantic studies themes and interdisciplinary approaches.

Perhaps a telegraphic way to capture the innovative turn of Atlantic studies with respect to its cultural predecessors is to mention a few of the exemplary texts of postcolonial critique, all of which have a relatively different focus and agenda. Published in 1978, Edward Said's *Orientalism: Western Conceptions of the Orient* quickly became a foundational source for an explosive critical movement. Although he surprisingly did not discuss the West's construction of its own scene of origin in Greek culture via the important work of intellectuals such as Johann J. Winckelmann, Ernest Renan, Gabriel Bonnot de Mably, Louis de Jaucourt, and Anne-Claude de Caylus, Said early on performed a timely autopsy of an important branch of European knowledge by looking through the other end of the civilizational telescope. In other works Said announced what quickly became part of the agenda for cultural and postcolonial studies by quoting once again from Gramsci: "The starting-point of critical elaboration is the consciousness of what one really is, and is 'knowing thyself' as a product of the historical process to date, which has deposited in you an infinity of traces, without leaving an inventory. . . . [T]herefore it is

imperative at the outset to compile such an inventory."[7] Like other postcolonial intellectuals, Said, then installed at Columbia University, chose to start
with himself and his own status as "exile."

The work of drawing up an inventory of traces in the colonial subject was
most brilliantly carried out by Homi K. Bhabha in his book *The Location of
Culture*, published in 1994. Schooled in French critical theory (he frequently
cites Roland Barthes, Claude Lefort, Jacques Lacan, Jacques Derrida, Jean
François Lyotard, Michel Foucault, and others), Bhabha assembled or borrowed a series of discursive concepts in order to produce microstructural
insight into the postcolonial subject's condition: mimicry, stereotyping, the
Other (othering), hybridity, difference, doubling, metonymy, and race, to name
the most prominent.[8] Having opened up and enlarged the endosemiotic dimensions of subjectivity for postcolonial critique, he made any direct return
to the naïve, uncomplicated subject impracticable not only for cultural studies
scholars but also for a new generation of historians of the Atlantic world.
Along with Gayatri Chakravorty Spivak, whose work is equally steeped in
French thought of the 1970s–1980s,[9] Bhabha taught a generation of enthusiastic scholars how to tease out postcolonial meanings in the interstices of canonic literary texts and archival documents of British imperial culture. He and
Spivak often did this with wit and great sophistication, proving immensely
influential in the shaping of postcolonial discourse analysis.

At the same time, Bhabha's and Spivak's textualist emphases and their
overloaded use of critical jargon have made their work largely unpalatable
for historians and occasionally for scholars in the field of cultural studies. But
there was another more accessible vein of colonial critique coming from African and Caribbean intellectuals, who were often directly involved in the politics of decolonizing their home societies. I am thinking above all of the work
of Aimé Césaire, Albert Memmi, Frantz Fanon, Ngũgĩ wa Thiong'o, Wole
Soyinka, Édouard Glissant, Sylvia Wynter, Wilson Harris, Erna Brodber,
and Kamau Brathwaite, to name a few.[10] These writers wrote with a different
spirit and a different audience in mind. The postcolonial critics mentioned
above, all academics, were primarily interested in cultural and theoretical
aspects of colonialism, and this differentiated them from an older generation
of African and Caribbean intellectuals and writers, who had a broader and
deliberately ad hoc agenda derived from the actual circumstances of colonial
rule in their countries.[11]

Exposed to the thematic permutations of the aforementioned schools and currents but focused on a specific area with its own conceptual interests and genealogy, scholars and historians of the Atlantic world formed a different front. Above all, there was the core issue of slavery and the slave trade that fueled the plantation system in the Americas, giving rise to the capitalist world system and differently invested modernities. Along with the slave trade linking an increasingly imperial Europe to the west coast of Africa and the Americas (the port cities of Brazil, the Caribbean archipelago, the colonies of North America), a host of related issues arose, such as migration, the killing off and removal of indigenous peoples, the extraction and circulation of all kinds of raw materials, commodities, cultigens, and printed matter, the advent of revolutionary ideas and talk of human rights, and a progressive tally of technological improvements (such as instruments to determine longitude and later on the telegraph, the railroad, and the steamship) that helped to establish the so-called oceanic order. Indeed, of central importance to atlanticists is the Atlantic Ocean itself as a unique interpretive space—a critical space that comes fully to light only by our becoming familiar with the complementary role of maps and ships in creating a specifically circumatlantic world.[12] I use the word "only" advisedly, because of the critical interface not only between maps and territories but also between a more flexible set of cartographic practices and texts of all kinds (travel reports, letters, ships' logs, histories, journals, as well as novels and poetry dealing with exploration, settlement, empire, slavery, abolitionism, migration, piracy, revolution, gender, and other salient Atlantic themes).

As an American poet once declared, "I need to understand how a place on the map is also a place in history."[13] This need to interweave history and geography in order to understand either one of them is as old as the two disciplines themselves and comprises another open challenge for Atlantic studies. John Smith, the disciplinarian and self-promoting savior of the Virginia colony in 1607–8, expressed this same requirement a bit more vividly: "As Geography without History seemeth as carkasse without motion, so History without Geography wandereth as vagrant without a certaine habitation."[14] Maps have not always been considered important documents for understanding how the Atlantic world was invented, nor have they been sufficiently appreciated as exemplary texts in themselves. This is because we still need to acquire cartographic fluency.

In order to underscore the status of maps as integral Atlantic texts and archival sites, I have dedicated the third part of this book exclusively to cartography and mapping practices. But mental mapping and geographical tactics also inform the case studies of part II. In part III, chapter 6, after discussing what Vespucci's *Mundus Novus* (New world) actually meant at the beginning of the sixteenth century, I offer a full discussion of three major European world maps depicting the dawning presence of the Atlantic world. No other discursive genre can match these highly newsworthy documents as early modern acts of scenario visualization. Following this exercise in close reading, chapter 7 formalizes the three signifying functions of maps as these are encoded by the cartographic signs of line, word, and image. To be sure, maps are remarkably composite documents inasmuch as they mix not only art and science but also different cultural media. In the burgeoning Atlantic world of the early modern period, they were people's Smartphones, by which they could see where they were going, inscribe brief messages, and provide snapshots of memorable scenes and events. Today, of course, these early maps are not only indispensable archival resources but also important documentary witnesses to those first intercivilizational encounters that took place along the edges of the Western Hemisphere. Now that most of these Atlantic-world maps can be viewed and studied on the Internet, it is my hope that Atlantic studies scholars will begin to integrate them more fully into their research horizon.

Throughout this book, maps and mapping practices provide the key to Atlantic studies ecology and its exemplary texts. Indeed, in themselves they stand as *figures of thought:* material and cultural emblems not only of European overwriting but also of the indelible traces of indigenous dwelling. As screens of archeo-geography, they provide us with a more allusive and yet embodied sense of the challenges of an Atlantic studies sensibility than rival concepts such as system, unit of analysis, or structural complexities based on an assemblage of trade routes, port cities, colonial settlements, and boundaries. As I discuss in chapter 1 of this book, the danger of imposing the concept of system on the Atlantic world—as several prominent scholars have done—is that it implicitly converts territory into a unity or becomes unilaterally another word for order, hierarchy, and envelopment. But as my preliminary analysis of Cotton Mather's 1702 map of New England in chapter 6 suggests, maps remain intrinsically *tabulae* (tables, workspaces) or, to put it more effectually, open fields in which well-argued causes are often indistinguishable from mere connections and relations. Mather's settlement map provides an excellent introductory key to reading Hawthorne's classic story of colonial

Boston. What the map visualizes and makes immediately evident is that New England had expanded into a considerable territory with a network of roads and towns that vaunt new possibilities of travel, circulation, and future growth. In short, the map was meant to be a form of colonial boosterism.

But does a reinforcement of cultural homogeneity and political order also follow, as Mather wants to claim? Not at all. Hawthorne's fugitive heroine, Hester Prynne, proves to be a disruptive go-between as she moves along and frequents Boston's streets and outer limits. It would be interesting to diagram her various trajectories to see just how mobile she is. But the author has chosen to keep this diagram an open secret. Rumor has it that her nocturnal itineraries are frequent, contingent, and indiscriminate. They defy the city's order and hierarchy. In this activity Hester could serve as a fitting figure of contingent history or even what Sanjay Subrahmanyam has called "connected history."[15] She cannot know or control whom she will meet in her countless excursions: her ex-husband, her lover, an indigenous American, or perhaps the town's governor, each obviously belonging to a different office or order of reality. The most important encounter in Hawthorne's story, Hester's and Dimmesdale's love tryst, occurs before the narrative begins so that we have no image of it, as if to suggest that many such encounters simply cannot be captured in a coherent scheme of narrative order.

Random forms of connectivity such as those represented by Hester help to illustrate the map genre as an intrinsically open field, in which the very idea of Atlantic-world encounter "connects any point to any other point, and its traits are not necessarily linked to traits of the same nature; it brings into play very different regimes of signs, and even nonsigns."[16] This is certainly true of oceanic encounters between slave ships, privateers, imperial navies, and merchant ships in the Atlantic world from the sixteenth to the nine-teenth century. In an obvious sense, networks of roads and places (and sea routes and port cities) remain relatively flat, contingent, and open. Encounters along them are nomadic as much as they are potentially hierarchical. In their instructive use of the concept of rhizome, Gilles Deleuze and Felix Guattari have noted that "[h]istory is always written from the sedentary point of view and in the name of a unitary State apparatus, at least a possible one, even when the topic is nomads. What is lacking is a Nomadology, the opposite of a history."[17] Much has changed since 1987 when these words were written. For the Atlantic studies sensibility can specifically be characterized by its comprehensive embrace of the oceanic order and its monitoring of outlaw traffic, incidental wild weather, and ineffectual amity lines among European nations. As we shall see, several notable Atlantic exemplars by scholars such as Marcus Rediker, Peter Linebaugh, and Siân Rees have been written from an "offshore" perspective.[18] As for political order and cultural homogeneity in Hawthorne's colonial Boston, one need only attend the narrative's market day to appreciate the ethnic and racial "chaos" of a thriving Atlantic port city: gold-earringed sailors, indigenous Americans, ministers, adulterers, dancing children, merchants, and shoppers of all purse sizes.

Mental mapping and topographical tactics often pivot on some adverbial particle like "here." In two of the case studies of part II, Shakespeare's Caliban and Frederick Douglass's heroic slave make use of this ostensive (or deictic) function when arguing the sovereign right to inhabit freely a Caribbean island or the right to revolt on the unconquerable waters of the Atlantic, respectively. Not to be confused with mimesis, the discursive use of *evidentia* (description) in these two case studies is implicitly a form of testimony. It is for Caliban just as much as for Madison Washington, the leader of the uprising aboard the slave ship *Creole* in 1841. In both instances, their authors resort to this quintessential axiom of cartographic practice: "Method of this work: literary montage. I have nothing to say only to show."[19] It is precisely this emphasis on visualization and location that anchors agency to the human body and theory to practice. This kind of entanglement also has led to considerable methodological inventiveness among Atlantic scholars. Given the skein of perspectivism woven by the Atlantic world itself, different perspective lines often require discrete forms of interdisciplinary knowledge.

In my three case studies, each of the texts chosen has provoked a different method: Shakespeare's *The Tempest* is fully interwoven with questions of geography, ethnography, critical race studies, and Gramsci's concept of subalternity; Hawthorne's *The Scarlet Letter* with matters of anthropology and gender; and Douglass's "The Heroic Slave" with claims deriving from historiography and the definition of archive. I have sought to read all three narratives with an Atlantic studies sensibility. More to the point, it is this unique cross-disciplinary horizon—with its remarkable set of exemplars, by Marcus Rediker, Joseph Roach, and Paul Gilroy, to name three forerunners—that pushed me to choose and read my authors in a new light. Curiously, the abundant scholarship on the *Creole* mutiny and Douglass's narrative "The Heroic Slave" splits neatly along disciplinary lines, with historians on one side and literary scholars on the other. There is little or no dialogue between the two, as if the two "events" (the historical and the literary) were totally unrelated. And yet the disciplines of history and literature were once inseparable twins, sharing many of the same narrative tools and modes. I am now convinced that Douglass himself saw the two disciplines as conspiring sisters. For that matter, Madison Washington (the name of Douglass's heroic slave) is the offspring of both. My case study of his efforts is somewhat longer than the other two cases because I was determined to overcome this scandalous disciplinary divide.

While Atlantic studies has emerged in reaction to an older field of Atlantic history, it is also true that many current Atlantic historians have been wholeheartedly committed to the interdisciplinary habitus they share with Atlantic studies scholars—to such a degree that they have revolutionized the writing of history in the process. For example, if we consider the vexed matter of agency and the often extremely nuanced processes of subject formation, we now find Atlantic historians often using a rich interdisciplinary palette. Proof of this is a line of work begun by Walter Johnson, *Soul by Soul: Life inside the Antebellum Slave Market* (1999), and Marcus Rediker, *The Slave Ship: A Human History* (2007), and continued by Edward E. Baptist, *The Half Has Never Been Told: Slavery and the Making of American Capitalism* (2014); Sowande' M. Mustakeem, *Slavery at Sea: Terror, Sex, and Sickness in the Middle Passage* (2016); Daina Ramey Berry, *The Price for Their Pound of Flesh: The Value of the Enslaved, from Womb to Grave, in the Building of a Nation* (2017); and in a slightly different key, Kay Wright Lewis, *A Curse upon the Nation: Race, Freedom, and Extermination in America and the Atlantic World* (2017).[20]

What characterizes this new Atlantic studies/history is the willingness of its authors to cite sources that history departments once discouraged. Thus, in explaining his own modus operandi, Edward Baptist writes, "In this book, some of the vignettes told from the perspective of enslaved people incorporate not only the specific content of the historical documents cited, but also details from other sources, as is the custom with *evocative history*. By drawing upon a wide variety of sources, I attempt to provide a richer depiction of the landscape, work practices, and cultural practices of the time and *a more intimate portrait of the enslaved African Americans whose experience is the center of this history*" (my emphases).[21] As we shall see below, in part I, Marcus Rediker certainly helped to make this widening of horizons not only possible but acceptable, both by his choice of subject matter and by his insistence on redefining the notion of historical document.

At the turn of the twenty-first century several prominent historians, in an effort to promote the revival of interest in Atlantic history, sought to develop concepts and shape an agenda around the well-known tradition of Anglo-American relations. In this same period still other historians began to draw from the themes and approaches of cultural studies, particularly in the area of slavery and African diaspora studies. As scholars in the fields of history, geography, cultural and literary studies, and comparative and foreign language literatures found themselves investigating shared themes such as the slave ship, processes of creolization, the inhumanity of slave auctions, life on a Caribbean sugar or cotton plantation, sexual abuse and the commodification of the slave body, and early travel reports, diaries, and slave narratives, they also learned from each other and developed new methodologies across traditional disciplinary lines. This exciting aura of revival also affected a higher level of theoretical debate regarding interdisciplinary entanglements, new themes, and new archival sources. Chapter 1 reviews and evaluates the important views of Bernard Bailyn and David Armitage on Atlantic history from the beginning of this century, as well as the debate that ensued. Battle lines were also drawn over what kind of history should be written, with Braudel's concept of "total history" still a haunting presence. At the same time, other historians were already exploring new interdisciplinary approaches to the Atlantic world in a larger circumatlantic context. In particular, Marcus Rediker and Peter Linebaugh seemed to find fellowship with the research efforts of Joseph Roach and Paul Gilroy. The publications of all four immediately became important exemplars in the creation of a new Atlantic studies sensibility.

In chapter 2, while tracing the growing interest that Atlantic historians such as Rediker and Linebaugh have shown in the methodologies and themes of cultural studies, I will offer a synoptic genealogy of the initial phase of what has now become a full-blown Atlantic studies sensibility. This genealogy, which begins with an extended examination of David Armitage's influential essay "Three Concepts of Atlantic History," identifies a core of now widely recognized studies that we might call Atlantic-world exemplars, since they have helped notably to provide a direction to this burgeoning cross-disciplinary formation.

The chapters of part II, featuring case studies of three well-known literary texts, have a decidedly more practical vein representing some of the cross-disciplinary challenges of the new paradigm. Each of these texts presents an elusive, embattled, and emphatically subaltern subject having the social status of a marginal figure. But in an Atlantic studies perspective, they become iconic representatives of a refurbished Atlantic pantheon: Shakespeare's Caliban, Hawthorne's antinomian colonial rebel Hester Prynne, and Douglass's Madison Washington—like Toussaint Louverture, another black Spartacus of the Americas. I have chosen these cases for the ways in which they can instruct us about issues of intersecting geocultural scales. As we trace the effects of these scales in our three texts, we end up inevitably having to acknowledge new spatial and cultural dimensions that confound the boundaries between text and context. When taken together, these case studies suggest new ways of reading according to a specifically Atlantic studies ecology. In each of them, narrative facts are transformed into ecofacts, point of view into view from a point, and interpretation into a form of place wisdom with circumatlantic implications. In short, mental mapping and chorographic practices thoroughly inform the reading habits deployed here.

After Robert Ralston Cawley identified the many American references in Shakespeare's *The Tempest* in his classic essay "Shakespeare's Use of the Voyagers in *The Tempest*" (1926) and after postcolonial writers and playwrights such as George Lamming and Aimé Césaire began to rewrite the play according to their own cultural agenda, the allusiveness of Shakespeare's last play has been exploited to advance any number of circum-Caribbean and circumatlantic themes.[22] Building on these critical perspectives, this chapter reads *The Tempest* in terms of the various cartographic and ethnographic practices informing it. In the discursive context of a case study, the rhetorical figure of *evidentia* (narrative description or evidence) in *The Tempest* serves to characterize the speech and character of Caliban, a subaltern Caribbean islander dispossessed of his territory by Prospero, the exiled Duke of Milan. Caliban's inflated use of a local figure of speech gradually merges with the judiciary notion of testimony as the Creole slave's eloquent speech performances offer persuasive evidence against the Italian usurper's own foundational narrative. By chorographing the island in speech after speech, Caliban's mental maps of it succeed in convincing us that it is indeed "his" island, although the concept of private property is not the issue here. The kind of place wisdom and knowledge of the island habitat that he possesses qualifies him to represent all those anonymous indigenous guides that helped the first European explorers and settlers to gather indispensable information for future colonization schemes.

By identifying the ecological grid informing the play's prospective representation of Hegel's master-slave dialectic, Caliban becomes an exemplary witness to a foundational script of British colonialism and in the process turns Shakespeare's island romance into an ethnographic and political site. Seen metaphorically as a mock trial in which master and slave, defendant and plaintiff, present their respective stories about ownership of the island, Caliban's case can be said to rest on his love of "scamels." Taken at first as a mere sign that appears fleetingly in one of the slave's descriptive flights, the word "scamels," when joined with still other hidden delights of the island, reveals an entrenched habitus and a sense of place that Prospero, a Renaissance magus, cannot equal. In the end, the rebellious Caliban becomes conscious of his subaltern status and conspires to take the island back from his former master, whom he now calls a tyrant. In doing so, he goes beyond the spontaneous desire to rebel and at the very end of the play emerges as a historical personality, fully conscious of the effects of his entanglement with the dethroned Italian duke.

Hawthorne scholars have often pointed to the symbol of the rosebush growing near Boston's prison door when looking for an initial clue to the symbolically rich character of the adulterer and heroine Hester Prynne. But there is another insignificant plant alongside it that provides an even more allusive entry into her agency, namely apple of peru and its intriguing circumatlantic whereabouts. It is apple of peru—alias, Love Apple or Jamestown weed—that captures a new dimension of Hester's legendary work in colonial Boston. For this work, not unlike the medicinal effects of apple of peru, becomes a key to the gift spirit circulating in Hawthorne's romance. What is more, through Hester's agency the romance genre is transformed into a gendered ethnographic narrative, in which city form and colonial ideology are seriously (though covertly) undermined. This protofeminist activity, already anticipated more expansively on colonial maps showing the network of roads leading in and out of Boston, is due to an increase of individual and social circulation that Hester quietly epitomizes as she moves among the city's womenfolk and beyond the city limits.

Not enough has been said about the diplomatic rites—known as gift diplomacy—that indigenous peoples in the Americas exercised when dealing with European colonizers. And yet, thanks to the agency of the banned Hester Prynne, the gift principle is represented not only as rivaling colonial Boston's patriarchal theocracy but invoking a new social contract and alternative (albeit informal) economy percolating from below. Hester is shifty and hard to pin down. She seems to have multiple identities. While being an English immigrant like the majority of her fellow Bostonians, she is also very "American." In effect, she is essentially *in between* and promiscuously *among* people, very much like the apple of peru at the city's prison door. Similar to those indigenous peoples flanking Boston to the west, north, and south, she is in part nomadic. She seems always on the move, at all hours, circulating invisibly around and beyond Boston. She identifies as an indigenous "American" in rejecting Boston's transcendent hierarchies, its vertically arranged dualisms and allegorical way of thinking about territory, governance, and gender. Above all, she is "American" in setting up an informal economy based on the gift principle.

In my case study of Frederick Douglass's narrative "The Heroic Slave," the intersection of geocultural perspectives necessarily traps the researcher in an abysmal archival dilemma involving many different kinds of documents. This dilemma forced Douglass, as it forces us, to foreground the theme of black historiography. In the heated ideological climate of white supremacist antebellum America, Madison Washington—a hero of the *Creole* mutiny of 1841—was immediately denounced as a murderer and a mutineer by the proslavery press and then just as quickly removed from the public record. The documents in the public record, primarily the white sailors' depositions, were irremediably slanted. But in 1852 Douglass found ways to bring Madison Washington back to life, and he did so brilliantly by redefining the very notion of what a historical document is. The need to overhaul our understanding of archives has become a major defining feature of the new Atlantic studies paradigm.

Texts like "The Heroic Slave" have now become central sites of cultural debate, as have any number of other subjects that were once deemed marginal in narrow national contexts. Besides the depositions of the *Creole*'s white sailors, we also have those of the British officials from Nassau, where the black insurgents forced the *Creole* to land. These depositions tell a completely different story of what happened and remind us that the *Creole* mutiny was an Atlantic-world event. Douglass, of course, portrayed Madison Washington as a transatlantic hero, but until recently scholars have read his narrative as if it were merely a part of United States literature. My own reading of "The Heroic Slave" repositions it firmly in its circumatlantic context, while underscoring its investment in black historiography and a redefinition of archive.

The first chapter of part III probes into the origins of the Atlantic world in the early modern period. It does so by relating these origins specifically to the new expertise that went into the mapping of this world and the development of a generic set of cartographic practices. This new order of imperial visualization advocated the spatially oriented sensibility that informs the various reports, relations, and travel literature of the late 1400s and 1500s. Chapter 6 discusses the mapping of the Atlantic Ocean and the rise of the Atlantic world, which is coterminous with the emerging image of Vespucci's *Mundus Novus* as historical concept and absolute metaphor. In addition, I analyze three stunning European world maps of the early 1500s that first depicted the Atlantic world—those by Martin Waldseemüller, Juan de La Cosa, and Alberto Cantino—and discuss such notions as Bernard Bailyn's "marchland" and gift diplomacy as these conditioned intercivilizational contact between Spanish colonizers and indigenous peoples. European *mappaemundi* had a premier role in projecting confidential visions of empire across a newly emerging, ocean-dominated world. As such, they also tell us about European intentions in the initial phases of colonial expansion. Functioning as both mirror and theater, these world maps are as full of pathos as they are of a new mathematical hubris and princely power. Considered as primal scenes, these documents also rely on a set of practices that helped to forge their unique prestige, reliability, and power to persuade.

Building on the historical and analytical insights of the previous chapter, here I take a close look at cartographic practices and strategies in an attempt not only to explain how maps work analytically but also to outline what I refer to as the cartographic semiosphere. This semiosphere embraces competing representational modes that range from recording (map as *speculum* or mirror) to producing (map as *theatrum* or theater) the world; it pivots on the key notion of *figura* (figure), which is fundamental to both cartography and narrative composition. In order to elaborate the defining functions of cartographic semiosis, I discuss and illustrate its three representational systems of image, word, and line, and conclude by examining two central genres involved in the ideological genesis of the Atlantic world, namely utopia and *naufragium* (shipwreck).

Given the prominent role of maps in Atlantic studies, it is important that we explore how they work in their own right, as signifying documents having a unique kind of resourcefulness intrinsic to that cross-disciplinary sensibility advocated herein. This same signifying activity is caught between two figures (*figurae*) that once expressed the cultural and existential extremes of circumatlantic trafficking—namely, those complementary sixteenth-century genres of utopia and *naufragium,* both having strong cartographic affinities.[23]

Recently, due primarily to the rise of world history and global history, Atlantic studies scholars have begun to decenter the geographical space of the Atlantic world by recognizing the ways in which its seas and economies and peoples are also connected to the larger world of the Indian Ocean, Southeast Asia, and the archipelagos of the Pacific and Pacific Rim. It is not surprising, therefore, that more emphasis is now being placed on circulation, cultural interaction, and exchange among people involved in linking distant places.[24] In closing, I will discuss the influence of two innovative forms of history writing that are particularly useful for Atlantic studies scholarship: namely, Sanjay Subrahmanyam's "connected history" and global microhistory. In both instances, biography has become a paramount vehicle for bringing multiple scales and encounters together in a single life. In his critique of Hegel's lectures on world history, Ranajit Guha also points out the need to recover large chunks of colonial historicality that imperial historians excluded from their high-flying accounts of European empire building. This call for a history of everyday life finds a corresponding interest in recent Atlantic studies scholarship on the gendered slave body, the Irish coffin ships, and other forms of mobility studies.

I

PROSPECTS AND GENEALOGY

I

Atlantic Studies Prospects
Complexities and Singularities, Flows and Places

As I began preparing a series of six lectures on "The New Atlantic Studies" for faculty and students at Louisiana State University in Baton Rouge, I suddenly felt as if I were in Kafka's Prague, where jokes about professors and umbrellas were once in vogue. In his book of essays *Le rideau*, the Czech novelist Milan Kundera tells a story about Albert Einstein, who taught for a brief period at the University of Prague. Einstein had just finished his weekly lecture and was about to leave the classroom when he heard a student calling after him, "Professor, you better take your umbrella, it's raining out." Einstein thoughtfully considered the umbrella standing in a corner of the classroom near him and then replied to the student, "You know, my dear fellow, I often forget to take my umbrella with me. That's why I have two of them. One I keep at home, the other here in the classroom. Of course, I could take that one over there because, as you very correctly observe, it's raining out. But in doing so, I would end up with two umbrellas at home and none here at the university." And having made his point, he walked out into the rain without an umbrella.[1]

Not so many years ago, scholars who were involved in the cross-disciplinary process of reconceptualizing study of the Atlantic world as it has been narrated in countless administrative and colonial histories of the various European empires undoubtedly had their umbrellas in the right corners, but as they passed from an inchoate paradigm to experiment and practice, they ventured forth without the tutelage of an attendant set of examplars. My purpose here is simply to track the development of the new interdisciplinary framework and its inaugural spawn of case studies. Bearing out Thomas Kuhn's observations on the history of science as a series of paradigm shifts, perhaps the major obstacle to the formation of this new Atlantic studies field has been the restrictive departmental protocols of a wary academy. For example, a graduate student in Atlantic history or geography once had to fight to get approval for a dissertation project drawing significantly from the discursive resources of cultural or postcolonial studies. It may now surprise us that a text-type like the slave narrative was once off limits for historians of slavery. On the other hand, literary scholars seemed totally unaware of what has become a quintessential Atlantic-world genre, in part because they often worked with a narrow sense of 'serious' literature and ignored the fact that cultures themselves are discursive texts.

As I will discuss in chapter 2, plunging into the often unpredictable currents of multidisciplinarity has now become a necessary part of a distinct Atlantic studies challenge. Indeed, the geographical corners of the Atlantic world—Europe, Africa, and North and South America—make for an apparently clear-cut oceanic and maritime world picture. But when it comes to embracing this space as an entangling web of cultural, geographical, and historical connections extending across, around, and beyond the Atlantic; when it comes to charting innovative research within this regime of intersecting spaces and crossing traditional disciplinary lines in order to do so, the wide-ranging results may at first seem far from delineating something as conceptually hard-edged as a new paradigm. In this chapter, therefore, I will try to address some of the conceptual issues that have emerged in the formation of an identifiable Atlantic studies sensibility by reviewing in particular the reflections of several prominent Atlantic historians. An exposition of their views will help to clarify the challenges that the first generation of Atlantic studies scholars have had to address and that continue to characterize study of the Atlantic world as a burgeoning cross-disciplinary matrix. In the process, I will also consider the initially wary relationship between Atlantic historians and Atlantic studies scholars as both have sought to articulate what the circumatlantic *novum* and its accompanying theoretical prospects might entail.

As I mentioned above, at the heart of this incipient quest there looms what may seem a largely insurmountable problem: I am referring to the traditional separation of academic disciplines, their often rigid institutional protocols and degree requirements, and the slim possibilities of creating multi- or interdisciplinary cooperation among Atlantic historians, geographers, sociologists, anthropologists, folklorists, archaeologists, cultural studies and literary scholars, and more generally, Atlantic studies scholars. In the spirit of Kuhn's notion of a paradigm shift, allow me to recall a famous academic precedent, worth citing here because of its astonishing achievements: I am referring to that exhilarating intellectual adventure that lasted from 1956 to 1972 in Paris, when the historian Fernand Braudel was president of the fifth section of the École Pratique des Hautes Études, then a rather modest institute without the power to confer degrees equivalent to the other faculties and that therefore had little weight to throw around in the academic community.[2] But within five or six years and perhaps even because of its rather low prestige, Lucien Febvre, Fernand Braudel, and a handful of others were able to put together one of the most stimulating centers of the social sciences in Europe, if not the world. In that short time, they handpicked a stunning variety of young researchers and scholars—some without a degree to their name—not only from France but from all over Europe. With a great nose for excellence, Braudel hired during his presidency such scholars as Roland Barthes, Claude Lévi-Strauss, Alain Touraine, Jacques Le Goff, Maurice Godelier, Jacques Lacan, and from outside of France, Lucien Goldmann, Julien Greimas, Ruggiero Romano, Étienne Balazs, Krzysztof Pomian, Clemens Heller, and others.

The cross-disciplinary spirit that reigned at the École might best be summed up by these words, which Lucien Febvre wrote in July 1956:

> *Science* is the sum of notions considered as valid in a given epoch and transmitted to students through university courses or by means of books on science. . . . *Research* distances itself from science by preceding it. Researchers do not organize the terrain conquered. . . . They precede Science of which they make up the vanguard. . . . Research sets as its goal the task of conquering the *new*. The scope of Science is to organize the knowledge that has already been acquired. . . . Given this premise, Research is not taught in the current sense of the word "to teach." It is not the product of a method or of a *recipe*.[3]

Febvre underlined four words in this passage: *science, research, recipe,* and *new.* They will help to guide us across the new territory that Atlantic historians and Atlantic studies scholars have begun to map out as they balance research, pedagogy, and a new cross-disciplinary sensibility. Needless to say, innovative research and the traditional divisions among university departments often find themselves at odds. Paradigm shifts inevitably trigger power struggles and resistance within the academic community.

It should be said right off that while research in Atlantic history has a rather long and onerous genealogy to its credit, particularly in the areas of empire and colonial studies, the idea of it as a formal disciplinary area has only consciously taken hold in the last two decades or so.[4] Currently, with the rise of the new Atlantic studies matrix, universities on both sides of the Atlantic have begun to offer regular courses and degree minors in Atlantic history and Atlantic studies. In addition, there are more than a handful of book series and academic journals hosting new research on this "highly critical space, centered not on a single nation or land mass but on a new cosmopolitan interchange of ships and peoples, cultures and texts, ideas and tools"—as the journal *Atlantic Studies* put it in the editorial statement of its inaugural issue in 2004.[5] In line with the architecture of paradigm change, there are also conferences, societies, a remarkable set of exemplars, and an identifiable community of scholars adhering to Atlantic studies as a prestigious new research area. As a result, we now have an identifiable spectrum of theories, concepts, methodologies, themes, and disciplinary standards in the service of Atlantic-world research.

Bernard Bailyn points out in his book *Atlantic History: Concept and Contours* (2005) that historians who began to discuss the existence of an Atlantic "world" after World War II often argued that there was a shared civilization, common cultural values, and democratic institutions among the countries bordering the Atlantic Ocean. This so-called *world* was projected as another Mediterranean civilization, and the ocean was envisioned as an inland sea or *mare nostrum*. Even today, albeit in a totally different spirit, atlanticists frequently appeal to world and hemispheric maps portraying the maritime world of the Atlantic Ocean as an identifying banner of the new paradigm. This choice of cartographic labeling brands D. W. Meinig's *Atlantic America, 1492–1800; The British Atlantic World, 1500–1800,* edited by David Armitage and Michael J. Braddick; *Slavery and the Rise of the Atlantic System,* edited by Barbara L. Solow; Bernard Bailyn's influential *Atlantic History: Concept and Contours;* and periodicals such as the Leiden-based *Itinerario,* the European-based *Atlantic Studies,* and the international journal of *Comparative American Studies.*[6] The practice is extremely popular and symptomatic of the new paradigm's political will and sense of investment. In effect, one of the foundational appeals of Atlantic studies as a new matrix was codified in this remark by the cultural geographer Donald Meinig: "Although areas will vary greatly in their significance for particular topics, the geographer works with the full map at hand."[7] In our case the full map, the defining image, is one having as its center the Atlantic ocean, implying thereby the enabling function of circumatlantic circulation. In order to follow up on Meinig's point, in part III of this overview of the burgeoning moment of Atlantic studies, I will devote two chapters specifically to the role of cartography and its extended heuristic resources. The first focuses on the stunning visual emergence of the Atlantic world on European world maps, while the second considers the close alliance between cartographic practices and narrative reports charting the push across *Mare Occidentalis,* as the Atlantic Ocean was called at the beginning of the sixteenth century.

The advantages of choosing an early modern world map centering on the Atlantic Ocean to announce or identify the ecological vocation of one's research are obvious enough, but never more so than in Werner Sollors's ingenious mapping of the travels of Olaudah Equiano, a formerly enslaved African, who first published his now canonic autobiography in 1789. Like all such maps, Sollors's makes the critical space of the Atlantic world visible in a single glance.[8] Its unique *coup d'oeil* is so effective that it would not be far-fetched to call Equiano's autobiography a narration of place-names and the map a periplus of his travels.[9] Circumatlantic texts such as Equiano's inevitably seem organized less on the basis of chronology than on a random number of moves and stops in social and geographical space.[10] Contemporary atlanticists—historians, geographers, ethnographers, and literary scholars alike—now agree on considering Equiano's autobiography an exemplary Atlantic text, given the way his cosmopolitan life was typically structured by chance encounters; the whims of weather, war, and race; and the life-and-death importance of learning how to pilot boats of all kinds (he mentions these: wherry, punt, drogger, hoy, sloop, frigate, snow, privateer, schooner, man of war).[11] The narrative's largely circumstantial structure makes it easier to understand why his autobiography also embodies many of the difficulties that emerge in speaking of its coherence in terms of an Atlantic *system*—one with a new "framing notion"[12] based on daunting grand-scale patterns of looped circumatlantic itineraries. There are enough trials and traumas to think otherwise.

Some seventy years ago, in a period of frenzied ideological debate, a number of major historians and political scientists went so far as to apply the term *human community* to the Atlantic zone and referred to it as "a single great cultural area" with an inner structure and logic of its own.[13] Today, such Cold War claims seem willful, to say the least. If we consider a fractionary life like Equiano's, so singular and random in its extravagant sequence of fortunes and misfortunes, we are immediately faced with a number of conceptual and methodological challenges. The idea of coaxing out an integrated and integral Atlantic world from his autobiographical adventures seems at first sight a thankless task. Of course it is equally true that the careers of many a black sailor in the eighteenth century proved a very distinct, and often distinguished, option for members of an oppressed race.[14] The attempt by historians and cultural studies scholars to recount the sea-tossed existence of these sailors has brought to light heuristic questions that are as subtle as they are disruptive. Perhaps the most obliging issues the lives of these pioneers of the black Atlantic raise are these: Just whose Atlantic are we talking about? And this immediately leads to another: Depending on the lively dance of geographical scales, how many Atlantic worlds—and in what languages and dialects—are there on any given occasion? One might be tempted to fall back on this familiar defense of life in a pluriverse: to each their own milieu! But then would it still be possible to build a paradigm that would sit historians, geographers, and cultural studies and literary scholars around the same table? The point is, the new Atlantic studies regularly convenes a shifting set of national and international scholars skilled in different disciplines and working in different languages and archives.

Equiano's endlessly looping travels do clearly indicate that in his day the Atlantic was an increasingly busy network of sea lanes and traffic for not only merchants, soldiers, officials, missionaries, sailors, botanists, scientific explorers, abolitionists, and reformers but also Amerindian and African slaves, indentured servants, prisoners, outcasts, and migrants of all kinds. As the historian Bernard Bailyn points out: "By mid-century [the eighteenth] 1,000 ships a year were involved in England's transatlantic traffic, 459 ships across the Atlantic to transport colonial goods. No less than 3,500 vessels were engaged annually in the Atlantic wine trade, moving out from six nations . . . to the Azores and the Canaries where they took on cargoes for delivery in 104 ports in Europe, Africa, and North and South America."[15] The Dutch historian Victor Enthoven's statistics on the number of ships and people (sailors, soldiers, and passengers) going from the Netherlands to the western colonies during the period 1600–1800 are equally impressive. "For the better part of the seventeenth century in excess of two-hundred ships left annually for the Atlantic," he says, estimating that there was a total of 36,000 voyages for the two-century period.[16] As for enslaved men, women, and children shipped from the coasts and islands of Western Africa to various parts of the Americas between the sixteenth and nineteenth centuries, Barbara L. Solow estimates the number to be an almost unimaginable eight million. Millions of others died at sea during the Middle Passage.[17] With such numbers in hand, Solow observes, "What moved in the Atlantic in these centuries was predominantly slaves, the output of slaves, the input to slave societies, and the goods and services purchased with the earnings on slave products."[18]

If for the sake of commerce alone, we decided to lump together these countless human bodies under the mystifying label of cargo as the slave traders regularly did, arguing that everything ends up in the ship's hold anyway, then yes, we can readily see that the Atlantic rapidly became an anesthetized "cohesive communication system," as Bailyn calls it.[19] The historians Horst Pietschmann and David Armitage also employ the notion of "system" to bolster their argument for a specifically oceanic or circumatlantic history.[20] As Armitage writes in his theoretically inspired essay "Three Concepts of Atlantic History," "Circum-Atlantic history is the history of the Atlantic as a particular zone of exchange and interchange, circulation and transmission." In addition, "The European achievement was to link these subzones together into a single Atlantic system."[21] Certainly, by the mid-nineteenth century, once steamships began their regularly scheduled transatlantic crossings, sea travel took on a new significance and created a potentially enforceable oceanic system.[22] But in the age of sail, Atlantic circulation could only be called a system by armchair metropolitan officials. Ship captains having to rely on the winds and currents of an always fickle weather system and challenged by predatory corsairs and rebellious tars hardly thought in such heady terms. While they may have followed acknowledged sea routes, the trajectories they traced on maps speak more of an adventure than a routine. This is especially true when we turn our attention to the ships' cargo and passengers, those rudimentary elements of Atlantic state and empire building. Of course, one could cite the many edicts of imperial courts and navies to argue that European governments in the eighteenth and nineteenth centuries were quite successful in taming the circumatlantic zone for lawful trade and thereby conclude that this "mare nostrum" was indeed a system. But a top-down, core-centered approach does not come close to reflecting the real Atlantic, which was more a Darwinian world of force and predation than a realm of international law. As Guy Chet observes in his book *The Ocean Is a Wilderness: Atlantic Piracy and the Limits of State Authority, 1688–1856,* the British Atlantic was a Wild West: "The ocean did not become a British sea."[23]

Armitage and Michael J. Braddick point out in their joint introduction to *The British Atlantic World, 1500–1800* that the "synoptic" approach to "the Atlantic experience as a whole" also has as its subject "a social system, with permeable boundaries, created by the interactions of migrants, settlers, traders, and a great variety of political systems."[24] Armitage, one of the first Atlantic historians to attempt an explicit historiographical definition of his field, has in effect theorized what he calls a three-dimensional approach to the Atlantic world, which seeks to articulate a multiscalar and multiperspective vision. Nevertheless, his model also harbors an unsounded risk. Once we convert circumatlantic history into a *system*, then it seems that we are virtually obliged to give equal emphasis, as in fact Armitage, Bailyn, and others end up doing, to "studies of connection, identity, and solidarity."[25] In truth, Atlantic history is much more than that. It also has a dark side. But if we accept the concept of system as the defining characteristic of circumatlantic mobility and ecology, how can we avoid enforcing a tautology: by starting with system we will inevitably end up finding it. The Oxford historian Sir John Elliott seems to have been thinking along similar lines when, in his afterword to the essay collection cited above, he added this dissenting note: "[B]y and large Atlantic history is always likely to remain a history framed more in terms of connections than of comparisons. . . . An Atlantic history conceived in terms of connections, though, also has its problems, not the least of which is the space over which connections are traced."[26] *System* tends to cast aside anomalies, singularities, unconnected experiences, and disconnecting forces. It also unwittingly shares in the cultural capital accruing to it from systems theory in sociology and the hardly forgotten ultrarationalist certitudes of 1960s–1970s structuralism.

The point is, the term goes well beyond the confines of historiography. If the Atlantic world is to be envisioned as a *system*, then we need to be apprised of its unspoken implications and its chronological transformations. Is it meant to be an overall model, or are we to understand it simply as an "absolute metaphor"—a figurative and not an analytical concept?[27] The issue is ultimately ideological and concerns the very reasons why one decides to write one kind of history rather than another. Although Britain ruled the waves during much of the nineteenth century, the royal navy and its shifting set of allies heroically failed to suppress slave-trade smuggling around the Atlantic. The species of causality or connectivity inherent in the circumatlantic world perceived as a system risks being circular in that everything is apparently deduced from the system as such. There is movement and exchange in Armitage's Atlantic system, but it is always for the sake of contributing to Bailyn's "coherent communication system" mentioned above. Given the implicitly theoretical claims of this 'historiographic' construct, how can we not end up looking for evidence of coherence, control, adaptability, self-maintenance, and, to use a favorite systems word, autopoeisis?

One might rightfully wonder, where is the other half of circumatlantic history, the half we might label antisystemic? What about all those chthonic place-names on early modern maps of the Americas? Undoubtedly, a string of such names is worth more than any historiographic theory. And what about the half that deals with singularities, silences, gaps, traumas, a branded Fon or Mendi worker on a cotton or sugar plantation in Brazil or Haiti or Louisiana? What about such "negative" forces as hurricanes, droughts, pirates, slave revolts, and shipwrecks? What about wars of independence and local applications of ideas about human rights? The danger in using the metaphor of system to explain the historical and cultural vicissitudes of the circumatlantic world is that there is a compelling social-science tendency to reduce processes to normative states, if not to static conceptual schemes.[28] In an attempt to focus on the processual nature of social reality, Norbert Elias sought to study what he called the "figurational dynamics" of a culture or civilization.[29] By figurations, he meant "networks of interdependent human beings, with shifting asymmetrical power balances."[30] It is the reworking of this figurational scale that informs two of the case studies included in part II as examples of interdisciplinary accounts of characters who defy or are even invisible to the guardians of imperial systems.

Undoubtedly, Amitage has developed a very stimulating, albeit at times cursory, scheme for a comprehensive approach to Atlantic history, which he articulates in a tripartite (Braudelian-like) typology: (1) circumatlantic history as an integrating history of circulation and exchange; (2) transatlantic history as comparative (or international) history between empires, nations, metropoles and their peripheries, or even between regions and cities; (3) cisatlantic history as local history—the history of a single island, city, or region—studied within the contributing contexts of the other two narrative economies.[31] Armitage also seems to suggest that this tripartite division is ordered into integrated but essentially different historiographic levels, although it is not clear if—and to what extent—the latter are also meant to stand for different *kinds* of history writing and different sets of skills, as they certainly did for Braudel.

While Armitage does not directly acknowledge Braudel in elaborating his scheme, he is obviously indebted to him, if only to the extent that his own three-dimensional project is aimed at reducing Braudel's tripartite historiography to a constructive methodology cleansed of any geographical determinism. It is significant, too, that Armitage does not care to incorporate or at least flag Braudel's multidisciplinary acumen and curiosity, which brings us back to the vexed problem of academic protocols that I mentioned at the beginning. Of the three scales of history, the circumatlantic is undoubtedly salient inasmuch as it functions as the "systemic" driving force behind the other two, the transatlantic and the cisatlantic. But Armitage may be promoting an undeclared agenda that has haunted the rise of Atlantic history from the very outset and that Bernard Bailyn has recently outlined for us in his brief study of its conceptualization. In his preface to the essay collection *The British Atlantic World, 1500–1800,* Bailyn names what I take to be the Holy Grail of this line of largely post–World War II history, namely "the entire inter-hemispheric civilization."[32] *Civilization* is certainly the most ideologically charged and frequently invoked concept in Bailyn's compact narrative of the rise of Atlantic history. But he uses it in the singular and is not entirely clear what he intends by it. There is no mention of Lucien Febvre's important essay on the concept of civilization (1973), of Jean Starobinski's more recent philological study (1983), or of the current work on civilizational analysis by macrosociologists such as S. N. Eisenstadt (2004).[33] Today, Atlantic studies scholars are conscious of living in a pluriverse, if you will, and use the plural form of civilization when talking about the peoples around the Atlantic world.

The conventional narrative plotting of this so-called Atlantic civilization is utterly linear and follows this diffusionist, Eurocentric sequence: scene one— the Mediterranean sea and its civilization (factor in ancient Greek political culture, the Greek ideal, and Fernand Braudel's unavoidable *The Mediterranean and the Mediterranean World in the Age of Philip II*); scene two—the voyage outward along the west coast of Africa and then out across the Atlantic Ocean to a *Mundus Novus* (consult the narratives, chronicles, and compendia of Columbus, Vespucci, Ramusio, Oviedo, de Bry, the Hakluyts, Purchas, and so forth); scene three—through exploration, colonization, and the rise of the African slave trade, the Atlantic becomes Europe's new *mare nostrum,* a vast internal ocean (see the many European imperial histories of colonization and settlement, the rise of European empires, the making of the "West" and of the modern world system, and the epoch of transatlantic political revolutions); scene four—the firm taking hold of Western civilization and the making of an Atlantic Community (consider the effects of the two World Wars, the Cold War, and the division of the world into clearly defined ideological blocks). Roughly speaking, this familiar script provides the plotline for many early and even a few current Atlantic-world narratives—for example, Samuel Huntington's—and more importantly its major category, *civilization*, remains caught in the net of an antiquated ideology.[34]

David Armitage, Sir John Elliott, Bernard Bailyn and others mention Braudel's book on the Mediterranean, but they do so for the sole purpose of assailing his alleged geographical determinism.[35] They have no interest in sifting through his overall method of juxtaposed levels and differently gauged temporal rhythms to see if there is something that can be salvaged from it for the good of Atlantic historiography and, if you will, methodological literacy. It should be said that no matter what one's antipathies might be—whether as historian or literary scholar—no one casts a bigger shadow over the new paradigm's considerable prehistory than Braudel, for whom the category of civilization was a fundamental heuristic framework. The essay "Notes sur la définition de civilisation" (1913) by Emile Durkheim and Marcel Mauss not only had a major influence on Braudel's historiography (especially his book *Le monde actuel* of 1963) but also has become a canonic reference for scholars of civilizational analysis.[36] While Bernard Bailyn, William O'Reilly, and others have rightly criticized the uses to which early historians of the Atlantic world put the category of civilization, a diffusionist model of "the West" still lingers. As David Armitage declares: "[T]he Atlantic was a European invention," which is an evident throwback to the very ideology of early post–World War II Atlanticism that evoked the word *civilization* in the first place.[37]

From one end of the telescope, the Atlantic world may well be a European invention—as early *mappaemundi* and travel reports seem to suggest—but if so, this statement must be paired with a further query: How were *Europe* and the *European* invented? Otherwise Armitage's claim simply repeats the reductionist perspective typical of moments of civilizational expansion and contraction, when cultures are more focused on identity and boundaries than on dialogue and openness. As the sociologists Said Amir Arjomand and Edward A. Tiryakian point out, "The holistic conception and reification of a civilization typically occurs in civilization encounters."[38] If therefore the

Atlantic world as a new oceanic order was a European invention, it is equally true that "Europe" was an invention of the Atlantic world. The many different peoples of this world compelled the Spanish, Portuguese, Dutch, French, and English explorers and colonizers to look at themselves from the outside—that is, from the shores of western Africa, the Caribbean islands, and the southern and northern continents of "America."[39] In doing so, these peoples over time formed such notions as *Europe, the West,* and *Western Civilization.* This observation also seems to capture the gist of Paul Gilroy's polemical comment in *The Black Atlantic* in which he notes, "A concern with the Atlantic as a cultural and political system has been forced on black historiography and intellectual history by the economic and historical matrix in which plantation slavery—'capitalism with its clothes off'—was one special moment."[40]

Among Atlantic historians Bernard Bailyn, particularly in his book *Atlantic History,* has been the sharpest critic of Braudel's epochal historiography. It is worth reviewing his objections in the light of current attempts to imagine new, Braudelian-inspired ways of studying the Atlantic world. In an opening salvo Bailyn observes: "For Braudel's *The Mediterranean and the Mediterranean World in the Age of Philip II* is disaggregative—taking apart in three dimensions of time, not putting together, the elements of a world. It is conceptually meta-historical not historical, based on a formulation essentially epistemological not historical."[41] Apart from playing down Braudel's more fundamental investment in the notion of civilization, Bailyn chooses not to consider Braudel's revolutionary historiography and its epistemological implications for study of the Atlantic world, particularly the French historian's indefatigable interest in multidisciplinarity. Of course Bailyn has a declared penchant for a linear rather than a layered history of the Atlantic, which would seem to preclude a multiscaled and structurally complex approach to it. It is interesting to note that elsewhere Bailyn proposes an enchanting image of history writing that seems to adopt the figural historiography articulated by the Dutch historian Johann Huizinga. Here is Bailyn: "I decided . . . to try to carry throughout that entire part of the book . . . a single literary image, an image of the progressive clarification of an immensely detailed panoramic painting, like the exquisitely detailed backgrounds of fifteenth-century Flemish pictures. . . . I felt that, in the end, the whole panorama would be revealed."[42] Nevertheless, not only does Bailyn prefer to accent the narrative side of history at the expensive of social science inflections but he seems to advocate a middle-ground form of history, without any philosophical or social science deviations. For no matter how large and complex the Atlantic world may be, he says, "it too is comprehensible as a story in itself."[43] In his second salvo against Braudel he says: "The problem is not to lump together the whole of the Atlantic world in the early modern period in order to describe in abstract terms its persistent strata, its layers. The task, I believe, is the opposite: to describe not the abstracted, meta-historical structural elements but the phasing of the development of this world, its motion and dynamics—to grasp its history as process."[44]

In his summary assessments of Atlantic history, Bailyn also invokes the vexed notion of "complexity." And he is right in doing so, for it is "complexity"—and not necessarily the concept of civilization—that challenges current attempts to elaborate a specifically Atlantic-world sensibility. Bailyn recognizes that "the Atlantic world was multitudinous"[45] and that the variations are enormous, but it is in the face of this very scenario that he articulates his own wager: "Yet in the evolution of this protean world there was, I believe, despite all the complexities, at least in rough terms, a common morphology, and a general overall pattern, however fluid and irregular, of development and change—a pattern that transcends and subsumes the familiar stories of national rivalries for primacy in the Atlantic."[46] If I understand the gist of these observations correctly, what we have is the substitution of a historically tainted *civilization* for an ideologically sublimated "world." Admittedly, that world is complex and has a "common morphology" and an "overall pattern." The reason Bailyn enthuses over the work of the American geographer Donald Meinig and its relevance to his own Atlantic project is because Meinig, who invests in Wallerstein's world-system analytic, understood the fundamental role of geography in introducing—and giving ballast to—the kind of terminology Bailyn uses above. In order to *world* a somewhat elusive Atlantic communication system into a complex morphology, one needs geography. But Bailyn ultimately backs away from geohistory, leaving its challenges for Meinig. Indeed, the geographer cites Bailyn to effect on the title page to the second part of *Atlantic America, 1492–1800:* "[T]he problems it [the "single story" of the peopling of America] involves lead naturally beyond history itself to other disciplines as they relate to history: anthropology, demography, and particularly, cultural geography."[47] Already at the outset of the sixteenth century, circumatlantic circulation included an inseparable cargo of plants, animals, commodities, peoples, skills, languages, races, and ideas. It has been the task of Atlantic studies not only to embrace the cultural constellations this mélange produces in endlessly shifting forms but to develop contingent cross-disciplinary methodologies as the need arises.

As Meinig notes in his preface to *Atlantic America, 1492–1800*, "Geography, like history, is an age-old and essential strategy for thinking about large and complex matters."[48] According to him, these two disciplines are not only complementary but interdependent. That is why at the outset of his book the geographer quotes Braudel and draws upon several of his major works to shore up his own project. Braudel is the inventor of geohistory and, perhaps even more crucially, what is called *total history*. There is yet another pivotal instrument that atlanticists seeking to come to terms with the notion of complexity cannot help being interested in, and that is *scale*. Here is a further observation from Meinig: "Such an attempt to envision an Atlantic World ensnares us in an even larger web and leads us logically to the necessity of seeing it as only part of a scale ever in our minds."[49] While the words are from Meinig, the scholar who first theorized a dialectic of scales for history and nuanced these into "a confluence of methods" is Braudel.[50] The very idea of a dialectic of separate but interacting levels—each with its unique methodological solicitations—takes on the status of a fundamental scene of inquiry, which we might formulate as follows: Which scale do you need to focus on in this specific situation, and what methodological literacy is required for its successful rendering? Scale jumping is nothing if not highly self-conscious. Having cast out the embracing category of civilization and having opted instead for an abstract entity called *system*, atlanticists could do no better than foreground the nimble but critical play of scales.

Let us return once again to the historical genealogy of Atlantic history as it emerged in the 1940s and '50s, for it now seems markedly ethnocentric in outlook and implicitly informed by what the geographer J. M. Blaut has referred to as the supertheory of diffusionism.[51] According to this once-influential theory, the modern world has a single permanent center, Europe or the West, from which all significant cultural, economic, and political ideas have sprung. Europe is the center, the "Inside," while the rest of the world is the periphery or the "Outside." Particularly in the early modern period, the argument goes, Europe proffers and the rest of the world receives. According to Blaut, this expression of "spatial elitism" is "the colonizer's model of the world."[52] As postcolonial scholars and intellectuals have pointed out, Europe's (and the West's) world-spanning achievements—familiarly known as the linear emergence of the modern capitalist world system—were made possible because of the colonization of the Americas and plantation slavery in the Caribbean, Brazil, the British colonies in North America, and Southeast Asia. Colonization is a code word for the exploitation of African and Central and South American gold, silver, manpower, and cultural know-how.

In truth, the European world system cannot be explained satisfactorily on the basis of causes originating exclusively from within Europe. Conquest, colonization, and extraction of resources (both human and nonhuman) in the Americas and Africa went hand in hand with the progress of European world hegemony. Causally, the two can hardly be separated. There are of course other strictly endogenous factors making up the Eurocentric model of the world. They include the emergence of modernity, the cultural Renaissance in early modern Europe, the rise of nation-states, the ideology of progress, and the episteme of modern rationality.[53] Most of the vintage history of the so-called Atlantic Community up to and including the Cold War, quietly embraced this Eurocentric vision of the world. One of the most urgent tasks of the new Atlantic studies, therefore, has been to question—rather than take for granted—this model of Europe as a unified and unaccompanied agent of modernity. There is still much to be done. For a perceptive overview and bibliography of "America's" leverage of transatlantic public diplomacy in post–World War II Europe and the shaping of American studies, see George Blaustein's *Nightmare Envy and Other Stories: American Culture and European Reconstruction*.[54]

But let me suggest why Braudel remains an important predecessor for Atlantic studies scholarship. Deeply influenced by the geographers of his day, in particular the work of Vidal de La Blache and Friedrich Ratzel, Braudel went on to revolutionize history by exploding the unitary concept of time. After 1949, the year the first edition of his book on the Mediterranean civilization was published, history would henceforth be measured primarily in terms of its synchrony of different times. Furthermore, these multiple times were to be construed as "time-spaces" so that now the two dimensions were made to work in tandem. Here, then, lies the core of the Braudelian revolution; to dismiss him for geographical determinism is like throwing away one's canteen in the desert. What Braudel does in *The Mediterranean* is give us three distinctive readings of the same geocultural area. In the first reading (or level) he talks about the Mediterranean's geography, its weather, the seasons, the crops, the soil. In the second he turns his attention more closely to the collective history of the peoples living there, their economies and cultures. In the final reading, he looks at the faster-paced political and military history of the Mediterranean. Each of these clusters of elements represents a different kind of history (structural, conjunctural, and "événementielle"—this last dealing with chains of events), and Braudel tries to describe the various rhythms of the grouped topics, all of which when taken together represent a new kind of total history.[55]

Note that what has led to the consecration of Braudel's work as a classic in its field is the very fact that he provided no definitive formal explanation as to how the three parts (and three levels) of his study were connected.[56] They were simply held in tension as three layered views of a composite intercivilization. This creative tension, though, is also caused by another of Braudel's notable strengths: namely, multidisciplinarity. For example, he would argue that just as one should not resort to the same concept of time when studying radically different phenomena, so we should not rely on only one kind of disciplinary expertise for them. Let us briefly consider an example of how Braudel's law of levels translates into narrative. When in his powerful autobiography *Twelve Years a Slave* (first published in 1853) Solomon Northup takes time out to explain systematically how sugarcane and cotton were planted, cultivated, and harvested, he is talking about the slow, cyclical history of a typical Louisiana slave plantation along Bayou Boeuf (chapters 12 and 15).[57] But when he recounts the emotionally dramatic moments of his liberation, we are caught up in the tumbling world of events and a speeded-up temporal rhythm, not to say heartbeat. In addition, the two narrative moments exhibit two quite different kinds of skills. As the inventor of a totally new approach to the writing of history, Braudel above all was curious about these sliding scales of duration and wrote history in terms of them. And since for him history was always geohistory, he also talked about strata or levels, which requires the historian to be a true polymath. The most important consequence of this new kind of history, though, was that it produced a holistic vision. Braudel had an expansive sense of the phenomenological richness of the human scene that resulted from a radical recognition that historians inevitably must begin and end with the world in all its plenitude.

What then is this *world* that Atlantic historians, and now a more critically savvy tribe of Atlantic studies scholars have been trying to catch in their narrative nets? In the end it is this category—understood both as *globus* and *mundus*—that atlanticists of all stripes have been trying to come to terms with, even when they do not directly ponder over the genealogical significance of the category itself. For our purposes here, we might simply ask, how do we as atlanticists equip ourselves to acknowledge and cross multiple Atlantic worlds? These questions undoubtedly deserve to be addressed more exhaustively. But we can do no better than to start with the Atlantic as *globus*, a highly volatile and visual construct developed mainly by the art and science of early modern cartography.[58] While I will dedicate the last two chapters to this critically undertheorized narrative genre in part III, here I would like to review some of the immediately useful implications of the concept of total history.

Above all, Braudel asks us to begin from a specific site, and this site is not something already there or given but is a fully human—historicized—construct. Secondly, atlanticists should be open potentially to all suggestions from the various arts and sciences as we find ourselves having to bring different kinds of phenomena together in a single narrative formation. This formation also includes multi-media deep mapping (the grounding of layers of various kinds of knowledge on a single cis-atlantic site) and spatial narratives or spatial framing in general. Basically, "total history" can be understood as a coded label corresponding to the world represented as a pluriverse, and this pluriverse is inveterately caught up in Atlantic processes that are often both intra- and intercivilizational. In effect, it is through an awareness of the latter processes that we find ourselves compelled to develop an ecological frame while also welcoming the hypothetical probings of microhistory and the allusive, circumstantial details of the case study. There are many kinds of spaces in the Atlantic world and, as one historian has recently argued, each requires its own special sort of consideration: histories of localization focus on space as a distribution of places; environmental histories, on habitat and landscape; histories of localized identities, on space as region. Notions of space also underpin constructs like territoriality, diaspora, borders, and social discontinuities.[59]

It is worth noting that at one point in his essay on Atlantic history, David Armitage expresses the same essential doubt about its promise that Sir John Elliott raised in his afterword cited above. "In short, what makes Atlantic history a novel approach to genuine problems rather than just a license for superficiality or an apology for imperialism?" Armitage asks.[60] By "license for superficiality" he may be alluding to the fact that the genealogy of Atlantic history remains weighed down by an often heinous colonial record as well as by a relatively narrow understanding of its discursive vocation. Since Armitage's breakthrough essay, Atlantic studies scholars have militantly avoided further "apolog[ies] for imperialism," primarily by embracing different kinds of previously unpresentable sources, formerly unworthy subjects and themes, complicated intersecting scales, and cross-disciplinary forms of scrutiny. As for pursuing synthetic schemes of narrative history and its "license for superficiality," today's atlanticists seem very conscious of the need to explore the fault lines of a triumphalistic imperial outlook and the well-sifted documents of empire. In the process, these scholars have also become more willing to foreground and reflect upon the categories informing their research, precisely because like modern-day speleologists they often find themselves having to invent new approaches as they plumb the undiscovered caverns of official Atlantic archives.

Within the context of the paradigm shift of Atlantic studies I have been discussing here, the *circumatlantic* is truly a different space than that mapped by the old comparatist, transatlantic legacy, for it is firmly ocean-based and supranational.[61] A good example of an attempt to theorize human mobility in terms of an essentially fluid kind of relationality in the Caribbean archipelago (the Atlantic world in microcosm) is provided by the novelist Édouard Glissant, who in his book *Poétique de la relation* has refocused our attention on the subtle, rhizomatic workings of Atlantic-world creolization and opacity.[62] In this world of islands, in fact, identities are typically hybrid and circulation dominates, as he himself points out: "We move along the surface, across the expanse, weaving our imaginative pattern, and not filling holes with knowledge."[63] Qualifying his penchant for a history of systems, Bernard Bailyn has encouraged atlanticists to pay more attention to "large-scale spatial orbits," noting that "Atlantic history is the story of a world in motion."[64] Balancing *flows* and *patterns* against a veritable *system* may also remind social science students of Manuel Castells's trilogy on the network society, where he makes a fundamental distinction between the "space of flows" (produced by informational technology networking) and "the space of places" (embracing historically rooted experience).[65] For our purposes, in the oceanic order of the Atlantic world, flows and places have generated a presiding dialectic of

circulation and resistance, translation and interference, continuity and interruption, movement and stasis, an expansive diffusion of signs and a subject-
bound hermeneutics. This dialectic has found corresponding research conduits
in the digital humanities and information technologies now revolutionizing
archival research and the very notion of historical evidence and articulation.
Indeed the new Atlantic studies sensibility has emerged in tandem with the
advance of cyberspace and digital interconnectivity—where, for example, the
challenge of combining nomothetic forms of causality with more nuanced
humanistic concepts of connection and relationship have led to innovative
and more hypothetical forms of research on the Atlantic world.

Atlanticist attention to spaces of flows—diasporic phenomena, circumatlantic trade, the rise of the capitalist world system, the circulation of rights
discourse, migrations, piracy, slave smuggling—is now complemented by studies of sites of memory, which have stirred up considerable interest among
historians and cultural studies scholars, to the point that memory has often
gotten the upper hand over history based on traditional archival documentation.[66] This process was undoubtedly due to the emergence of dozens of
holocaust survivor memoirs (for example, those of Elie Wiesel, Primo Levi,
and Robert Anselme) and the oral testimony of those who survived the Nazi
death camps. The historian has now become a mnemon, reminiscent of the
"memory-bearer" of ancient Greek city-states, as well as a judge and a "vicarious witness."[67] To some extent, this role change has also affected historians and scholars of the African diaspora, the Middle Passage, and the
slave-fueled plantation system of the Atlantic world. In fact, renewed interest
in the slave narrative and fictional rewritings of it (referred to as neoslave
narratives) have proliferated alongside—and in dialogue with—scholarship
documenting the Shoah. Thus, we now have any number of works like Walter
Johnson's microhistorical study of slave auctions in *Soul by Soul: Life inside
the Antebellum Slave Market* and Mark Reinhardt's case study of a fugitive
slave woman's convulsive decision to murder her children in *Who Speaks for
Margaret Garner?*[68]

Traditionally, Atlantic historians had only rarely, and then reluctantly,
ventured beyond the fences of their academic training, careful to avoid both
the ideological precepts of an explicit philosophy of history (Marx's classless
society, the myth of progress, or Hayek's free market) and the social-science
probes of anthropology and sociology. As a result, they paid a formidable
price when it came to handling both broad cultural issues such as "global

civilizational ascendancy" and "civilizations as networks of prestige and at-traction"[69] and intensive forms of historicality such as the gendered slave body and the terrors of the slave ship that microhistorians have begun to study. Since the concepts of civilization and interculturality are so undeniably central to study of the circumatlantic world, neglect of them is not only astonishing but ultimately self-defeating. So far even historians who have done much to promote the field of Atlantic history have been rather modest in describing the emergence of a truly cross-disciplinary Atlantic studies formation even as they helped to shape debate within it. Thus it comes as no surprise that an Atlantic historian such as Sir John Elliott, known for his work on comparing the Spanish and British empires in the early modern period, has remained skeptical about "the degree to which large elements of the history of peoples who live around the Atlantic basin can be compressed within a conceptual framework of this magnitude."[70]

The daring that is missing among scholars who have chosen to remain within the borders of their own disciplinary traditions can be found in the often groundbreaking experiments of scholars in cultural studies, postcolonial studies, cultural geography, and the social sciences. For that matter, in her sur-vey essay "A Long Atlantic in a Wider World" the historian Donna Gabaccia scolds American studies scholars for not as yet having created a disciplinary sensibility that would help them go beyond the confines of the nation-state. As she points out, "Atlanticists in all disciplines would be well advised to venture more often across disciplinary boundaries in their readings." Gabaccia also concedes that "[l]iterary and cultural studies of the Atlantic have proved occasionally influential (consider particularly the work of Paul Gilroy) but still deserve more space in the interdisciplinary dialogue."[71] In the following chapter on Atlantic studies genealogy I will discuss a number of exemplary contributions that have helped to give rise to the paradigm shift that Gabac-cia has called for. In a moment of heightened rhetorical appeal in his essay on Atlantic history from 2002, David Armitage himself notes: "Like the Atlantic itself, the field is fluid, in motion, and potentially boundless, depending on how it is defined; . . . Atlantic history—whether circumatlantic, transatlan-tic, or cisatlantic—pushes historians towards methodological pluralism and expanded horizons. That is surely the most one can ask of any emergent field of study."[72]

Interestingly, these prophetic observations came at the very end of Armit-age's provocative essay, in which he mentions both Paul Gilroy's *The Black*

Atlantic and Joseph Roach's *Cities of the Dead: Circum-Atlantic Performance.* But, as we shall see below, Armitage himself did not go on to suggest how one might incorporate their multidisciplinary skills and curiosity into a broader as well as more complex theoretical agenda. The reason for this is quite simple. Both Gilroy and Roach, who have taken a literary and cultural studies approach to the Atlantic, turn the rather imperious concept of system inside out by focusing on the heavily connotated categories of diaspora, cultural hybridity, and archival sites of performance. In doing so, they offer approaches to the circumatlantic and cisatlantic worlds that make ample room for silence, loss, dispersal, discontinuity, interference, interruption, the random, the fleeting gesture, and the singular—all potentially antisystemic forces or modalities spawned by the capitalist world system of the early modern period.

The two books by Gilroy and Roach (and one could also include here the work of authors such as C. L. R. James, Eric Williams, Philip Curtain, Édouard Glissant, Sylvia Wynter, Kamau Brathwaite, Peter Hulme, Marcus Rediker, Mary Louise Pratt, Orlando Patterson, John K. Thornton, Paul Lovejoy, Michel-Rolph Trouillot, Sibylle Fischer, Walter Mignolo, and Jorge Cañizares-Esguerra, to mention a few) have become flashpoints for Atlantic studies scholars, mainly because of the boldness with which they have crossed traditional disciplinary lines and poached freely from the shelves of history, anthropology, geography, ethnography, political philosophy, literature, and so forth. Due to their wide-ranging but also microhistorical interests, Rediker, Gilroy, and Roach in particular have led the way in exemplifying a constructivist approach to the Atlantic world reminiscent of the inventive practice of bricolage, where one learns each time to work with what one is able to collect, often beyond the traditional archives of empire. As the Italian philosopher Enzo Melandri once quipped in his massive study of analogy, *La linea e il circolo,* "[E]very theory can be taken as a symptom of an underlying disfunction in society and the theory's value is generally proportionate to its capacity to act therapeutically: that is, to eliminate its own reason of being, of existing as theory."[73] Here, of course, we are talking not about theory but about something much broader and undefined—something like a new research paradigm, in the sense that these scholars, intellectuals, and writers, although working within traditional academic fields, share a refreshingly open, cross-disciplinary state of mind.

Returning to David Armitage's essay of 2002, wherein he outlines his three loosely sketched concepts of Atlantic history, we should note that when taken all together they are meant to "offer the possibility of a three-dimensional history of the Atlantic world." He further claims that "it may be the only one that can be construed as at once transnational, international, and national in scope."[74] But his apparent reluctance to foreground the relationship between research skills and the actual scaling of his highly intriguing "three-dimensional history" amounts to a missed opportunity. And yet both Armitage and Braddick place such a heavy accent on the complexity and interdependence of the exchanges that went into forming the Atlantic world that they feel obligated to append this cautionary note: "[T]o try to capture them simultaneously with a sensitivity to change over time is a daunting task." Perhaps to compensate for this humbling prospect, they then suggest how we might yet hope to channel this fluid oceanic order: "Finding routes into this complexity is easier, however, since there are many individual connections which can be followed."[75]

To sum things up, on one side we have routes, itineraries, and trajectories and, on the other, a marshaling system or network that turns all of this motion into a highly stratified visual scenario pictured through the synoptic modernity of a sixteenth-century Atlantic-world map. Any appeal to individual connections, though, seems inevitably to invoke a commitment to the relational dynamics of singular trajectories and a mosaic of multiple modernities. If given its due, such an appeal certainly can help us to embrace the important function of witnessing to the casual forms of contact that the concept of system tends routinely to integrate or more cunningly, cover over. Nevertheless, such instances of singular testimony and cultural contingency may equally embody an unresolved or irreducible enigma, a case that resists all systems, raising vital questions instead of providing vindicating answers. For the kind of contingent history that "individual routes" often represent can lead just as easily to asyntactic and asymmetrical forms of suspension and interruption as to the confirmation of an Atlantic system. I will have more to say about this in part II, where I will present three cross-disciplinary case studies, each with its own figurational dynamics.

2

A Brief Genealogy

From Atlantic History to Atlantic Studies

Dating back to the turn of the twenty-first century, the scholarly field of Atlantic studies has established a noteworthy genealogy, with a creative multidisciplinary horizon and a familiar province of interrelated themes and practices. Over the last two decades, this field has witnessed a paradigm shift as historians, geographers, and cultural studies scholars have begun to fashion new forms of cross-disciplinary literacy. University curricula now feature Atlantic-world themes in a variety of disciplines, and major academic presses have inaugurated book series devoted exclusively to this revived but also significantly renewed area-studies domain—a domain that was once the acknowledged preserve of historians of empire and colonialism. Along with popular Atlantic studies course offerings, new anthologies and manuals aimed at student needs have also sprung up. In addition, there are annual conferences and a variety of panels within established academic organizations that regularly solicit papers on such themes as the African diaspora, the Middle Passage, the red (socialist) Atlantic, transatlantic abolitionism and feminism, the neoslave narrative, creolization, piracy, the Irish coffin ships, and so forth. Such topics have engaged scholars from across the humanities and social sciences and have led them to broach not only new themes but also innovative approaches to them.

Equally important, this flourishing academic activity has generated a core of exemplary texts that in turn have spawned similar kinds of cross-disciplinary and multilingual scholarship and new uses of old archival sources. Also we now have a number of prestigious journals such as *Atlantic Studies: Global Currents* that are devoted specifically to interdisciplinary approaches to the Atlantic world and its wider relations. For constructive purposes, in this chapter I will try to weave these diverse threads into a more coherent genealogical pattern, one that helps to illuminate the emergence of a new Atlantic studies paradigm, in the popular sense explored by Thomas Kuhn in *The Structure of Scientific Revolutions* (1962).[1] Indeed most of the features mentioned above—research field and a set of accompanying practices, exemplars, university curricula and degree programs, publishing houses, journals, and academic conferences—are very much a part of Kuhn's concept of paradigm.

It should be said that Atlantic studies owes much to the historical investigation of both slavery and the slave trade and the cultural-philosophical study of modernity, what Immanuel Wallerstein in 1974 called the modern world system.[2] While this debt is formative, the significance of Atlantic studies is evidently due to its scopic fusion of the two fields of study—slavery and modernity—as these socioeconomic formations played out across the same oceanic sea routes and ports of the Atlantic world. As I will discuss below, this fusion was brought about by the cultivation of hermeneutic interests that broke down traditional disciplinary fences. Inevitably, the study of life under slavery and the effects of the African diaspora in the postcolonial era required a new sensibility and renewed forms of humanistic acuity from scholars located throughout the Atlantic world.

Noteworthy works that have contributed to the formation of the thematic core of Atlantic studies include a rich gamut of titles: Eric Williams's *Capitalism and Slavery* (1944), Philip D. Curtin's edited volume *Africa Remembered: Narratives by West Africans from the Era of the Slave Trade* (1967) and his monograph *The Atlantic Slave Trade: A Census* (1969), David Brion Davis's *The Problem of Slavery in Western Culture* (1966) and *The Problem of Slavery in the Age of Revolution, 1770–1823* (1975), Eugene D. Genovese's *From Rebellion to Revolution: Afro-American Slave Revolts in the Making of the Modern World* (1979), Orlando Patterson's *Slavery and Social Death: A Comparative Study* (1982), Sidney Mintz's *Sweetness and Power: The Place of Sugar in Modern History* (1985), Robin Blackburn's *The Making of New World Slavery: From the Baroque to the Modern, 1492–1800* (1997), David Eltis's coauthored *The Transatlantic Slave Trade: A Database on CD-ROM* (1999) and his *The Rise of African Slavery in the Americas* (2000).[3] Needless to say, the scholarship on slavery studies is now too vast to summarize here; nevertheless, it is the abundance of this research as a whole that has allowed for a more sophisticated discussion of such cultural notions as diaspora, the Middle Passage, creolization, bondage and freedom, rebellion and resistance, the master-slave relation, reform and abolition, and related issues touching upon the status of the modern subject, universal human rights, republicanism, gender, sexuality, and the often unspeakable horrors of the slave system.

It is worth noting that as early as 1967, several years before novelist Arna Bontemps's inclusion of Olaudah Equiano's Atlantic autobiography in *Great Slave Narratives* (1969), the historian Philip Curtin considered autobiographical narratives like Equiano's to be important historical documents, thereby anticipating the post-Shoah shift in interest to oral history, testimony, and trauma. By the end of the twentieth century, Equiano's autobiography had become an exemplary Atlantic world text, leading to the discovery of a host of similar testimonies, some of which Henry Louis Gates Jr. and William L. Andrews later collected in their anthology *Pioneers of the Black Atlantic* (1998).[4] Likewise, Harvard sociologist Orlando Patterson provided a broad, comparative analysis of slavery not only as a historical institution but also as a dialectic of internal relations.[5] Note that besides drawing his analyses from the field of history, he also relied heavily on the insights of anthropology and sociology.

As for Atlantic historians, a few prominent scholars at the outset of this century—Donna Gabaccia, David Armitage, Bernard Bailyn, Alison Games, Jack Greene, Philip Morgan—began to acknowledge the innovative work of a handful of scholars from cultural, literary, and geographical fields who were instrumental in the development of Atlantic studies as a cross-disciplinary project, thereby sounding the call for a renewal in the writing of history.[6] In her oft-cited lead article in the first issue of the journal *Atlantic Studies,* which began publication in 2004, Donna Gabaccia noted, "Literary and cultural studies of the Atlantic have proved occasionally influential (consider particularly the work of Paul Gilroy) but still deserve more space in the interdisciplinary dialogue."[7] Published in 1993, Gilroy's *The Black Atlantic: Modernity and Double Consciousness* quickly became a central exemplar for Atlantic studies scholars across the humanities. As will be discussed in more detail below, Gilroy's major insight was to envision the "Black Atlantic" as "a Counterculture of Modernity,"[8] an aperçu that first became apparent thanks to him. In the words of Gabaccia, "Interest in the 'black' Atlantic has also generated the most interdisciplinary work, from the anthropology of Mintz to the seminal writings of Paul Gilroy."[9] She also cites the pioneering work of Peter Linebaugh and Marcus Rediker on the "red" Atlantic.

In his important attempt to set forth a preliminary frame for the refashioning of Atlantic history, in which he seeks both to clarify its conceptual opportunities and to posit its creative tensions beyond the so-called white Atlantic, the intellectual historian David Armitage called to his side Joseph Roach's *Cities of the Dead: Circum-Atlantic Performance* (1996) and Paul Gilroy's *The Black Atlantic,* both of which quickly emerged in the late 1990s as persuasive Atlantic exemplars.[10] Specifically, Armitage cited Roach to describe what the focus of "Circum-Atlantic history" might profitably be: "Accordingly, '[t]he concept of a Circum-Atlantic world (as opposed to a transatlantic one) insists on the centrality of the diasporic and genocidal histories of Africa and the Americas, North and South, in the creation of the culture of modernity.'" Setting this abysmal thematic burden as his major task, Armitage noted that circumatlantic history would have to be attuned to "everything around the Atlantic basin" and therefore would have to envision it as "a single . . . system" based on forms and patterns of circulation and, within them, subzones of exchange and movement that went well beyond the binary politics between nation-states and European metropoles and their colonies.[11] Above all, the historian insisted that this particular concept of Atlantic history—as we have already seen, he proposes three: transatlantic, circumatlantic, and cisatlantic—is transnational, not just international. To make his point he then calls on a British cultural studies scholar and a theater scholar from Tulane University: "In the words of Paul Gilroy, the Atlantic was a crucible of 'creolisation, métissage, mestizaje and hybridity'; out of that crucible of identities emerged what Roach has called an 'interculture . . . along the Atlantic rim.'"[12] As I will discuss more fully below, Armitage's leap forward hails as an appropriate response to Donna Gabaccia's earlier plea for more interdisciplinary boldness among historians, since issues of culture and identity are now included as major research themes across the humanities.

Another historian, coming from the field of working-class history, has contributed significantly to the Atlantic studies paradigm by broaching a topic closely related to modern circumatlantic identity, mobility, and protest. In his prizewinning book *Between the Devil and the Deep Blue Sea,* published in 1987, Marcus Rediker set out to write history from the bottom up by focusing on the nomadic "proletarian" figure of the deep-sea sailor during the period 1700–50. The seaman, in the author's words, "toiled among a diverse and globally experienced body of workingmen, whose labors linked the continents and cultures of Europe, Africa, Asia, and North and South America."[13] Building on Wallerstein's notion of the modern world system—with its core, periphery, and semiphery zones—Rediker discussed not only trade commodities such as tobacco and sugar but also the slave trade connecting England, West Africa, and the Caribbean. That said, his ultimate theme was the collective life of sailors as embattled wage laborers during the rise of British capitalism. As he also recounts, life on the high seas was very much a multiracial and multinational experience, the ship being a synecdoche of Atlantic modernity. This book and the one he later coauthored with Peter Linebaugh, titled *The Many-Headed Hydra: The Hidden History of the Revolutionary Atlantic* (2000), led to the identification of a specifically "red" (proletarian) Atlantic constellation.[14] Although both of these books have become popular exemplars for atlanticists, primarily because of their focus on forgotten forms of agency and their interdisciplinary élan, Rediker's next study, *The Slave Ship: A Human History*, published in 2007, proved equally important for Atlantic studies.[15] For the first time we were provided with an in-depth anatomy of this infamous racialized vehicle of the capitalist world system.

Some nineteen years earlier, Paul Gilroy had already drawn attention to the ship in *The Black Atlantic* when he wrote, "I have settled on the image of ships in motion across the spaces between Europe, America, Africa, and the Caribbean as a central organising symbol for this enterprise and as my starting point." For him, the ship was "a living, micro-cultural, micro-political system in motion."[16] But besides a brief appreciation of the ship in Martin Delany's mid-nineteenth century novel *Blake; or, The Huts of America*, Gilroy made little operative use of his "central organising symbol." In the notes to *The Black Atlantic*, we do find references to Rediker's "brilliant book" *Between the Devil and the Deep Blue Sea* and appreciation of an early coauthored essay by Linebaugh and Rediker titled "The Many-Headed Hydra,"[17] but he passed up the opportunity to discuss the Middle Passage and other accounts of ships in Olaudah Equiano's autobiography, which he cites for other reasons. Nevertheless, as Werner Sollors points out in his introduction to the 1789 version of *The Interesting Narrative of the Life of Olaudah Equiano, or Gustavus Vassa, the African, Written by Himself*, the autobiography is very much "a memoir by a seaman."[18] In those same years, Michel Foucault made a trenchant comment on the ship as a heterotope, which quickly became an essential intertext for Atlantic studies scholars, both literary and historical. Given its allusive appeal and brevity, I quote it here:

Think of the ship: it is a floating part of space, a placeless place, that lives by itself, closed in on itself and at the same time poised in the infinite ocean, and yet, from port to port, tack by tack, from brothel to brothel, it goes as far as the colonies, looking for the most precious things hidden in their gardens. Then you will understand why it has been not only and obviously the main means of economic growth . . . , but at the same time the greatest reserve of imagination for our civilization from the sixteenth century down to the present day. The ship is the heterotopia par excellence.[19]

In Rediker's *The Slave Ship*, the Middle Passage, British capitalism and colonialism, the carceral society of the plantation, transatlantic abolitionism, and millions of African deportees all converge to make the slave ship the single most powerful icon of the Atlantic world. Rediker's anatomy of this "heterotopia" also capably implemented Gilroy's symbol of the ship, only now as both a material and a cultural system. Embedded in the black Atlantic as the counterculture of modernity, Rediker's slave ship provides us with a traumatic vortex of circumatlantic memory. In an attempt to explain the spirit behind the writing of *The Slave Ship*, Rediker chose to quote these words from Aimé Césaire's *Notebook of a Return to the Native Land:* "My mouth shall be the mouth of those calamities that have no mouth, my voice the freedom of those who break down in the solitary confinement of despair."[20] By regularly bringing together merchants, sailors, pirates, slaves, ships, empire, and race in the fluid space of the Atlantic world in all of his work, Rediker has done much to identify a set of major figures, themes, and methodological challenges that are now a constitutive part of the Atlantic studies archive. His ongoing probes into various genealogical sites of circumatlantic history make each of Rediker's books, including his recent *The Fearless Benjamin Lay: The Quaker Dwarf Who Became the First Revolutionary Abolitionist*, another restored tessera of Atlantic studies possibilities.[21] But his way of doing history has not pleased everyone in the academy.

The historian David Armitage pointed out in his review of *The Many-Headed Hydra* that the book's methodology "has little in common with the traditional political histories of the white Atlantic [the Anglo-American, northern Atlantic connection] and more with the cultural studies of the black Atlantic, especially Paul Gilroy's account . . . of the Atlantic as the crucible of a modernity defined by upheaval and dispersal, mass mobility, and cultural hybridity."[22] A historian of ideas unfamiliar with the mimetically elusive levels of narrative representation plied by Linebaugh and Rediker, Armitage expressed little sympathy for the *kind* of project under review, for he goes on to say that it is really not social history at all but literary history with a Marxian narrative structure.[23] Mostly an investigation of the anglophone Atlantic, Linebaugh and Rediker used a surprising variety of sources, including testimony, poetry, drama, pamphlets, trial data, and political debates. Faced with the inherent difficulties involved in reconstructing the flickering agency of slaves, pirates, sailors, servants, market women, indentured servants, and common laborers, the authors often found themselves using modernist narrative techniques such as juxtaposition and metalepsis to narrate the impulsive rebelliousness of their collective subject. In the end, Armitage laments, they offer little more than a bricolage of fragmentary sources and motifs and a mosaic of set pieces. Today, of course, this reads as high praise. While the reviewer admits that *The Many-Headed Hydra* makes for a compelling and enjoyable story, he also states that such eclectic archival trawling cannot be taken seriously as a legitimate form of documentary history. In short, for Armitage what was wrong was the approach, its promiscuous juggling of sources. Acting as watchdog for a more acceptable kind of middle-range academic history, Armitage assigned *The Many-Headed Hydra* to the then inchoate, muddling world of Atlantic studies: "In the end . . . they do not provide a reliable model for a new kind of Atlantic history."[24]

Armitage's review helps us to identify the period shift from a traditional narrative form of Atlantic history to the new Atlantic studies paradigm. His critique is important not because of its local quibbling over some of Linebaugh and Rediker's readings and perceived evasions but because of its discontent over the book's experimental articulation of an Atlantic-world poetics based on levels of *aisthesis* (sensory representation) and agency considered beyond the purview of academic history. Since, however, this same poetic boldness also informs Rediker's subsequent books *The Slave Ship* and *The Amistad Rebellion: An Atlantic Odyssey of Slavery and Freedom* (2013), both of which recount quintessential Atlantic world sites, it is worth commenting further on the disciplinary disjunction noted here. Apparently aware that an increasing number of historians of the modern period and of post-Shoah history were investing in new social science, microhistorical, and interdisciplinary methodologies, Armitage ended his review with this tip of the hat: "Anyone seeking inspiration for a multicolored, multivalent, and multinational history of the Atlantic world—in much the same period, and treating many of the same themes—would be better advised to read the theater historian Joseph Roach's brilliant (but, among historians, little known) *Cities of the Dead: Circum-Atlantic Performance* (1996), whose texts are better chosen, readings more credible, and juxtapositions more truly revealing than those making up *The Many-Headed Hydra*."[25] Needless to say, by citing both Gilroy and Roach in his review, Armitage was calling on his fellow historians in Atlantic history to embrace the new literary turn informing Linebaugh and Rediker's book.

Only a year after his review of *The Many-Headed Hydra*, Armitage published his pivotal essay "Three Concepts of Atlantic History" (2002), which I have already discussed at length in the preceding chapter. This essay marked a succinct attempt to identify, classify, and connect the various perspective forces that had already begun to rally young historians of colonial North America, the Age of Revolution, and British and European imperialisms. Given the increasing importance of race, identity, and ideas within these topical periods, not a few among the emerging generation of historians showed familiarity with postcolonial scholarship and the writings of Edward Said, Benedict Anderson, Stephen Greenblatt, Peter Hulme, Paul Gilroy, Mary Louise Pratt, Michel Foucault, Judith Butler, and others outside the discipline of history proper. In his essay of 2002 Armitage again mentioned *The Many-Headed Hydra*, but now as an exemplar of the red Atlantic and without attaching any reservations. More importantly, he identified Joseph Roach's *Cities of the Dead* as the source for one kind of his threefold typology of Atlantic history, namely the "Circum-Atlantic" one.[26] In the process he also acknowledged what Eliga H. Gould later termed the "literary turn" in Atlantic history.[27] In his description of the circumatlantic, Armitage identified it primarily as a circulatory system characterized by motion and fluidity, which, although apparently boundless, has generated a polycentric "rim" (a term he draws from Roach). Looking back over the rapid development of cultural histories of the Atlantic, Eliga Gould confirmed Armitage's advocacy of this diasporic space, over and above the political and economic dimensions of metropolitan cores and colonial peripheries: "[T]he work of literary scholars played an important role in conceptualizing the early modern Atlantic as a sort of 'imagined community,' one sufficiently coherent to merit analysis in its own right."[28]

If we take a closer look at Roach's reading practices in *Cities of the Dead*, the conceptual clarity of what a specifically circumatlantic perspective might look like becomes considerably enhanced. For Gilroy, this perspective line was transparently thematic: the African diaspora and its accompanying issues of identity and double consciousness, race, and national belonging. For Roach, self-consciously positioned in the Gulf of Mexico's city of New Orleans, Louisiana, the circumatlantic stands for a much broader "oceanic interculture" composed of the contributions of many peoples: "Bambara, Iroquois, Spanish, English, Aztec, Yoruba, and French."[29] In effect, Roach, a theater critic then at Tulane University, studied genealogies of performance and sites of memory in two circumatlantic rim cities, New Orleans and London, over a stretch of time running from the eighteenth century (Alexander Pope's *Windsor-Forest,* Henry Purcell's *Dido and Aeneas,* Shakespeare's *Macbeth* staged with Mohawk Indians as the witches) to the end of the twentieth (New Orleans's Congo Square, slave auctions, Mardi Gras, Storyville, jazz funerals). While the confluence of readings and the range of critical notions that Roach draws upon add up to a tour de force of Atlantic-world literary and anthropological engagement, he locates circumatlantic interculture in well-rooted behavioral vortices that become "boundless" only through processes of surrogation and memory.

Roach's forays into eighteenth-century London stage performances reveal the manifold ways in which, as Felicity A. Nussbaum puts it, "the empire penetrated Britain."[30] This climate of infiltration hovers over such notable works as Shakespeare's *The Tempest,* Aphra Behn's novel *Oroonoko* (and Thomas Southerne's stage adaptation of it), and Daniel Defoe's novel *Robinson Crusoe,* all of which have become canonical circumatlantic texts. The very idea of an "oceanic interculture" as a hypothetical unit of analysis also has given way to a critical practice that can readily be called contingent or connected history, in which two quite different works such as Equiano's *The Interesting Narrative* and Defoe's *Crusoe,* roughly close in time and plying the same seas, provide a critical interface for considerations about race and freedom in a far from homogeneous modern world. By juxtaposing these two works, literary critic Laura Doyle has recently sought to bring into a dialectical relation both Anglo-Atlantic and African-Atlantic traditions.[31]

In short, it is the geocultural perspective of the circumatlantic that licenses such facings in the name of an open-ended archive of themes irrespective of their relevance to a red, green, black, or white Atlantic tenure or to a north, south, east, or west Atlantic location. Similar juxtapositions have also been (and should be) extended to gender and linguistic divisions in such genres as the slave narrative, the captivity narrative, sentimental and gothic fictions, and travel literature.[32] In her sweeping study *Freedom's Empire* (2008), which builds on the results of her essay, Doyle identifies what she calls "the liberty plot" in early Anglo-Atlantic novels and autobiographies.[33] In an original move, she locates the origins of this ur-plot in eighteenth-century English and American historiography (David Hume, Catherine Macaulay, David Ramsay, Mercy Otis Warren), which consistently celebrated the Anglo-Saxon legacy of freedom. Having established this correspondence between early history writing and the rise of the novel, Doyle deftly broaches her central argument: how the themes of liberty and rights became racialized—and then racist—in modern Atlantic-world English fiction and memoir.

It is not implausible that David Armitage was still drawing from his reading of Roach's *The Cities of the Dead* when he posited what for him is the most practicable type of Atlantic history, namely "Cis-Atlantic." Here one can find the routes-roots configuration innervating all of Roach's sites of memory. Of this kind of history, Armitage muses, "[I]t may prove to be the most useful as a means of integrating national, regional, or local histories into the broader perspectives afforded by Atlantic history, both as an example of oceanic history and as a fashionable mode of historical inquiry in the English-speaking world."[34] We should note that cisatlantic history—and cisatlantic literary scholarship—is above all the history of a particular place understood as a crossroads for circumatlantic and transatlantic trajectories, and by place we also can intend a particular institution, object, piece of music, text, or local practice.[35] What a circumatlantic perspective adds to the study of a particular place, life, or practice is preeminently a form of attention that recognizes the porousness and fluidity of borders, sites, limits, and statuses. It also questions the mute interests behind narratives of descent and the mythologizing ploys of genealogy. Apart from conceptual distinctions, therefore, it seems impossible in practice to separate the two kinds of Atlantic figuralism discussed above. As the sociologist Pierre Bourdieu once declared, a point of view is a view from a point.[36] Indeed, if a viewpoint claims to be from everywhere, it is in fact from nowhere.

Compared to the cisatlantic perspective, the circumatlantic is not a standpoint but an ecology. While Atlantic circulation vivifies and enriches interest in local place, it is local place that provides forms of agency with a purchase it otherwise would not have. I will return to this point below, when discussing a select number of exemplary cisatlantic literary studies. The point I want to make here is that only when taken together do the circumatlantic and cisatlantic viewpoints generate the perspectivism that makes for a specifically Atlantic approach to history, literature, and culture. In effect, once he has introduced all three concepts of his threefold typology—the third he calls "Trans-Atlantic history"—Armitage then suggests that when taken together, these concepts "offer the possibility of a three-dimensional history of the Atlantic world."[37] Although he remains tentative here, it is precisely this three-dimensionality that proves most promising for the creation of a full-blown Atlantic studies heuristic. For by fostering a triple form of historicity in terms of a law of shifting epistemic levels and scales, Armitage implicitly recognizes the multiform representational tensions characterizing the Atlantic world. As a result of these shifts and tensions, no one perspective—neither the circumatlantic nor the cisatlantic nor the transatlantic—can be considered absolute or exclusive. The adherent tensional condition of Atlantic studies perspectivism makes it so that all three representational levels appear radically constructive and competitively interdefined.

As an example of this tension, we can consider the case of Frederick Douglass, who until quite recently was read wholly within the restrictive confines of US culture, even though the eighteen months he spent touring Ireland, Scotland, and England as an abolitionist speaker (1845–47) proved to be an intellectual turning point for him. As Paul Giles points out in his groundbreaking, Atlantic-keyed essay "Narrative Reversals and Power Exchanges: Frederick Douglass and British Culture," the radical revisions Douglass made to the 1855 version of his autobiography were largely due to the positive tensions brought on by his new transnational outlook.[38] After his highly successful experience in Great Britain, Douglass reconsidered the Emersonian pattern informing his 1845 narrative by adopting a more reflective, ironic style, which Paul Giles attributes to his "comparative consciousness."[39] In effect, *My Bondage and My Freedom* is beset with an ideological tug-of-war between a newly adopted form of constitutional patriotism and a transnational standpoint bolstered by British abolitionism and Chartist reformism.

Written in 1852, under much the same historical and ideological conditions as the revised autobiography, Douglass's narrative "The Heroic Slave" equally embraces the interconnected spaces of Armitage's three-dimensional perspectivism: the cisatlantic, the circumatlantic, and the transatlantic.[40] Impressed by the 1848 revolutions in Europe and evidently buoyed by the pervasive Zeitgeist of an ever-advancing circumatlantic freedom, Douglass decided to retell the extraordinary but forgotten historical event of the *Creole* mutiny of 1841. With the effects of the new Fugitive Slave Law (1850) stirring up an outrage in the northern and western sections of an increasingly divided nation, his timing could not have been better. As the newspapers first told it, the slave Madison Washington and eighteen other black revolutionaries took command of the slave ship carrying them from Richmond, Virginia, to the auction block in New Orleans, and they had the ship brought to the British-controlled island of Nassau, where the governor eventually told the 135 slaves they were free. Taking only a few liberties with the historical facts, Douglass had the narrator-historian report the words Madison Washington spoke to the first mate, who acts as the only live witness to the revolt. In his quarter-deck declaration to the latter, Washington links the freedom of the Atlantic Ocean with his own spirit and justifies the revolt by citing the fathers of the American Revolution and the spirit of 1776. Here again, Douglass deploys a nationalist-cum-transatlantic perspective to persuade his readers in 1852 that violence had now become a legitimate option for the millions of slaves in the US South and their abolitionist supporters in the North. While the story's push came from the ever-looming spirit of revolutionary Haiti and its black Spartacus, the pull came from an Atlantic-propelled spirit of liberty already installed in the British-governed Bahamas and other West Indies possessions. From the very outset, the new Atlantic world paradigm helped systematically to reframe previously national readings of texts such as Douglass's *My Bondage and My Freedom* and "The Heroic Slave." I will return to a further consideration of the latter in a separate chapter in part III.

Armitage's "Trans-Atlantic" history is the one requiring least annotation. In fact, it represents the rather well-trodden path of comparative history, especially imperial and colonial, carried a step forward in the late 1960s by scholars such as Jack P. Greene, Bernard Bailyn, and J. H. Elliott.[41] Greene and Bailyn were instrumental in launching graduate courses in Atlantic history at Johns Hopkins University and Harvard, respectively. In the mid-1990s, Bailyn spurred interest in Atlantic history among young scholars when he launched the Harvard International Atlantic History Seminar (1996–2007), which produced more than four hundred papers over the years.[42] Building on his own substantial scholarship and the results of the Harvard seminar, Bailyn wrote what he meant to be a timely description of the field, *Atlantic History: Concept and Contours* (2005). But in comparison to the more inclusive horizon promoted by the journal *Atlantic Studies,* his vision—which I have discussed at length in the previous chapter—appeared parochial and did not address issues related to interdisciplinarity, multilingualism, the tensive fluidity of shifting scales, and the sheer variety of Atlantic geocultures. With Bailyn specifically in mind, the historian Alison Games noted, "The comparative absence of Africa in conceptualizations of the Atlantic is a consequence both of the dominance of Atlantic history by historians of the North Atlantic and of enduring Eurocentrism."[43]

If transatlantic history can be said to trace a road across the Atlantic, then a full-blown Atlantic studies turns that same vector into a three-dimensional crossroads connecting four continents. Perhaps more alive than historians to the cultural, racial, and linguistic complexities besetting the colonial and early national period of North America, the Caribbean, and the United States, literary scholars at the beginning of the new century increasingly sought to turn the study of "American" literature inside out. The paradigm shift they helped to enforce was based on a very simple Atlantic studies perception: "American" literature could not be set apart. It belonged to a binding network sustained by the busy traffic that connected people, commodities, and ideas on both sides of the Atlantic, along a north-south hemispheric axis and re-gionally among the Caribbean islands. Nor could European explorers and colonists have survived and flourished without creating cultural, trade, and military networks with the various indigenous peoples of the Americas.[44] In short, the old chestnut of American exceptionalism and the diminished rewards of national introspection now seemed outmoded in an increasingly interconnected world.

The paradigm shift I am talking about can be captured in a synthetic over-view of a handful of scholarly texts that have become recognized exemplars of the new Atlantic studies vision of US literature, a vision that has now become a dominant force in reshaping curricula and introducing new literary histories and cultural studies. Above all, the three-dimensional horizon of Atlantic perspectivism has led to a new interest in the role that geography and cartog-raphy have played, particularly in the shaping of colonial and early national literatures. Indicative of this geocultural sensibility is Paul Giles's *The Global Remapping of American Literature* (2011), which is an extended meditation on the geographer D. W. Meinig's efforts to place the United States within a spatial context he called Atlantic America.[45] As Meinig notes, geography and history are complementary and independent: "This relationship is implied by such common terms as space and time, area and era, places and events—pairs that are fundamentally inseparable."[46] Giles discusses mental maps and their relation to actual maps and invests his concise analyses of literary texts with an ecological sensibility. A heightened awareness of Atlantic America leads Giles radically to revise the old genealogy of American literary history based on a process of "retrodiction," whereby colonial and Augustan American literatures were read from the decades-strong exceptionalist perspective incarnated in F. O. Matthiessen's classic *American Renaissance* of 1941.[47]

Giles sets out to reevaluate such writers as Richard Alsop, Timothy Dwight, Ebenezer Cook, and William Byrd II by considering them in the light of a highbrow-lowbrow republicanism based on burlesque, travesty, and an ironic sense of cultural geography. We are now a far cry from the mythologizing tendencies of the American landscape that once argued for a national culture based on an original, ahistorical relation with nature. Giles also discusses Henry Wadsworth Longfellow's interest in the work of George Catlin and Henry Rowe Schoolcraft. Indeed, in one chapter calling attention to the many traces of Mississippi valley mound culture in early national literature, he corrects the notion that the indigenous peoples had no past. In line with his atlanticist framework, Giles also discusses the geographical visions of the antebellum southern slaveholding class, which ambitiously dreamed of incorporating Cuba, parts of Central America, and the lands taken from Mexico in an all-embracing cotton empire—a mental geography that Matthew Pratt Guterl has called the "American Mediterranean."[48] In an earlier book, *Transatlantic Insurrections: British Culture and the Formation of American Literature, 1730–1860* (2001), Giles often brilliantly pairs writers such as Samuel Richardson and Benjamin Franklin, Thomas Jefferson and Laurence Sterne, Nathaniel Hawthorne and Anthony Trollope, and Edgar Allen Poe and Olaudah Equiano with the express purpose of getting us to rethink literary history and creative allegiances. Few scholars of the British transatlantic literary exchange have Giles's grasp of the literatures in question. At one point, for example, he points out that Mary Rowlandson's captivity narrative, which was extremely popular in Britain in the early years of the eighteenth century, helped to creolize the novels of Samuel Richardson.[49]

Working in the wake of Gilroy's black Atlantic, Brent Hayes Edwards, in his thoroughly researched and rigorously conceived book *The Practice of Diaspora: Literature, Translation, and the Rise of Black Internationalism* (2003), studies periodical print culture, anthologies, and the connections among black intellectuals in Paris, New York, London, and elsewhere between the two world wars in order to identify and restage the significant cultural phenomenon of *internationalisme noir* / black internationalism. Shelves of celebratory commentary have already been dedicated to the vogue of African and African American music, art, and literature in 1920s Paris, New York, and Berlin, but Edwards is the first to formalize the conceptual dimensions of this undertheorized cultural formation as a multiscalar effort involving preeminently the work of translation, correspondence, and radical political initiatives. Edwards offers not only detailed commentary on the polyvocal poetry of Langston Hughes, the Martinican René Maran's internationally influential novel *Batouala* (1921), French interest in Alain Locke's watershed anthology *The New Negro* (1925), and Claude McKay's plotless novel *Banjo* (1929) but also provides a comprehensive survey of the often short-lived but always vibrant journals produced by African, Caribbean, and African American intellectuals—for example, Marcus Garvey's *Negro World;* W. E. B. Du Bois's *Crisis;* Charles S. Johnson's *Opportunity;* Paulette Nardal and Joseph-Léo Sajous's *Le Revue du monde noir, Les Continents,* and *La Dépêche africaine;* Tiemoko Garan Kouyaté's *La Race Nègre* and later *Le Cri des Nègres;* and George Padmore's *Negro Worker.*

All of these periodical organs invested in the cultural work of translation as the groups that formed around them embraced transnational black cultures and anticolonial movements advocating Pan-Africanism and support for the Negro worker. Edwards deploys Stuart Hall's concept of articulation (difference within unity) and his stress on ideology (which Hall takes from Antonio Gramsci) to describe the complex set of scales at work in the formation of black internationalism. Implicitly, Edwards focuses on the tensive relation between the three conceptual dimensions of the circum-atlantic (the diasporic circulation of ideas and peoples), the international (relations between New York and Paris), and the cisatlantic (above all, Paris as a cosmopolitan hub). Each of these dimensions requires a quite different perspective and alignment. Given the theoretical ambitions of Edwards's project, it seems unfortunate that he has not read Gramsci, whose overhauling of Marxism took place in the years between the two world wars. Gramsci's university thesis was on linguistics, and his view that every language expresses a peculiar worldview suggests how germane his philosophy of praxis and deep interest in translation/translatability are to the cultural and political formation of black internationalism. Such Gramscian categories as subalternity, war of position, hegemony, the role of organic intellectuals, cosmopolitanism, and popular culture, to name a few, would have helped to tether Edwards's cultural discussions more firmly to political theory. That said, we owe a great deal to him for having so painstakingly identified and reframed such important phenomena as the Harlem Renaissance and the vogue of African culture in Paris in terms of an Atlantic studies perspective having global ramifications.

While a growing number of scholars have now begun to investigate the north–south axis of cultural exchange in the Americas, Anna Brickhouse's *Transamerican Literary Relations and the Nineteenth-Century Public Sphere* (2004) was especially influential, and for obvious reasons.[50] Brickhouse introduces her project by discussing the 1826 Congress of Panama, which, under the leadership of Simón Bolívar, sought "to form a hemispheric political coalition against imperial threat from Europe" and wrest the colonial territories of Cuba and Puerto Rico from Spanish control.[51] Article 27 of the congress's Treaty of Perpetual Union also called for an end to the slave trade in the Americas. Starting from this opening event, Brickhouse points to "the first flourishing of a hemispheric consciousness" and what she calls a "paradigm shift" toward "an inter-American cooperative system."[52] Generously acknowledging her vast critical debts, she names the work of Paul Gilroy, Joseph Roach, and Paul Giles, but also that of Lois Parkinson Zamora, Vera Kutzinski, Walter Mignolo, and Michael Dash, to name the most prominent. Focusing on Spanish-, French-, and English-language cultures and steeped in Latin American and Caribbean history, Brickhouse calls for recognition of a "transamerican renaissance"[53] in place of the narrow American Renaissance that Paul Giles also targeted. The time period of her own historically dynamic renaissance is roughly the same as that of F. O. Matthiessen, but now the physical and cultural geography demands a much broader horizon and set of linguistic skills.

Brickhouse's insistence on an implicitly three-dimensional hemispheric, cisatlantic, and circumatlantic perspectivism also leads to an equally rich interdisciplinary use of history, geography, and literature. Her cultural and geographical visitations carry her to Cuba, Haiti, Boston, Mexico, New Orleans, Paris, and elsewhere as she discusses various literary coteries and journals such as *Revue des colonies* (1830s–1840s) and the *North American Review* (especially its early interest in Latin America and Haiti). Also an advocate of contingent history, Brickhouse convenes in one interpretive site works such as Harriet Beecher Stowe's *Uncle Tom's Cabin* (1852) and Pierre Faubert's play *Ogé, ou Le préjugé de couleur* (1856), Frances Calderón de la Barca's *Life in Mexico*, Hawthorne's "Rappaccini's Daughter," the anonymous historical novel *Jicoténal*

(1826), James Fenimore Cooper's *The Last of the Mohicans* (1826), and W. H. Prescott's *History of the Conquest of Mexico* (1843).[54] If these tensive encounters prove startlingly fresh and surprising, their rationale is well grounded in the paradigm shift Brickhouse evokes in her prologue. Sibylle Fischer's *Modernity Disavowed: Haiti and the Cultures of Slavery in the Age of Revolution,* which was also published in 2004, shares not a few of the same texts and geographies discussed by Brickhouse, only now the author more exclusively focuses on the theme of slavery as the countermemory of modernity.[55] Again, Fischer's sites of memory include Haiti and Cuba, but her critical aim is also to correct Gilroy's overemphasis on culture in theorizing the black Atlantic.

Citing the work of such historians and sociologists as David Brion Davis, Eugene Genovese, Orlando Patterson, Robin Blackburn, and Michel-Rolph Trouillot, Fischer, a professor of literature and romance studies, discusses "the conflictive and discontinuous nature of modernity in the Age of Revolution," a phenomenon she refers to as "a disavowed modernity."[56] Devoted, like Brickhouse, to the Atlantic studies *forma mentis,* Fischer explains the aims of her book as follows: "It is an attempt to think about literature, culture, and politics transnationally, as forms of expression that mirrored the hemispheric scope of the slave trade; to think what might have been lost when culture and emancipatory politics were finally forced into the mold of the nation-state."[57] Again, Fischer's interests introduce a new cast of cisatlantic and transatlantic poets, novelists, revolutionaries, and intellectuals: Gabriel de la Concepción Valdés (known asPlácido), José Antonio Aponte, Gertrudis Gómez de Avellaneda, Félix Tanco y Bosmeniel, Domingo del Monte, Toussaint Louverture, Léger-Félicité Sonthonax, Henri Christophe, and Cirilo Villaverde. Inevitably, her discussion also relates antislavery culture to the events of the French Revolution, the *Amis des Noirs,* and the way in which European events and ideas resonated locally, in the sugar islands of Haiti and Cuba. We are also reminded that women's rights movements first gained strength as women became actively and internationally involved in abolitionist societies and other reform movements in England and North America during the period 1830–60. Fischer notes that it would be interesting to study "the links between the struggle against slavery and sexual subordination" inasmuch as women in the suffrage movement were quick to adopt the emancipatory language of antislavery to their cause.[58] According to Fischer, the fact that such links have not been studied is due in part to the disciplinary fragmentation and disciplinary hierarchies of academic scholarship. But a few years later, the essay collections *Women's Rights and Transatlantic Antislavery in the Era of Emancipation* (2007) and *Transatlantic Women: Nineteenth-Century American Women Writers and Great Britain* (2012) dealt with those very links.[59]

As the scholarship reviewed here unanimously demonstrates, the new Atlantic studies paradigm is now increasingly multilinguistic and cross- and interdisciplinary. To be sure, the critical configurations of our Atlantic exemplars are also the direct result of a whole new ecology of cultural themes. Sean X. Goudie's *Creole America: The West Indies and the Formation of Literature and Culture in the New Republic* (2006) will serve as a representative cisatlantic text for a number of closing observations.[60] To stage the issue of Creole nationalism and the young nation's ambiguous ("paracolonial") relation to the West Indies, Goudie discusses at length the political and cultural projects of two representative Creole nationalists, Benjamin Franklin and Alexander Hamilton (who was born on the Caribbean island of Nevis). In the early years of US nation building, an ideological battle developed between those who envisioned a commercial nation based on hemispheric and transatlantic trade and those who favored Jefferson's vision of an agrarian nation whose future lay in westward continental expansion.

Both parties were eager to define the cultural process of ethnogenesis, and both had to come to terms with the hopelessly entangled relations between the sugar-rich, slave-run West Indies and the new nation's claims to be an empire for liberty. It is in this overheated context that Goudie, an English literature scholar, speaks of the "New Republic's creole complex" and the popular perception that white Creoles from the West Indies were degenerate.[61] To elaborate these issues, he discusses Edward Long's *A History of Jamaica* (1774) and Bryan Edwards's *The History, Civil and Commercial, of the British West Indies* (1810) and provides a number of illuminating hemispheric readings of well-known authors and texts—in particular, Olaudah Equiano's autobiography *The Interesting Narrative*, Benjamin Franklin's *Autobiography*, Philip Freneau's "West Indies" poems, Charles Brockden Brown's *Arthur Mervyn*, and Cooper's *The Last of the Mohicans*. In addition, he introduces us to several rediscovered works that are specifically relevant to the themes of Creole identity, Creole degeneracy, and, more broadly, the Creole complex: J. Robinson's once popular play *The Yorker's Stratagem; or, Banana's Wedding* (1792) and Leonora Sansay's epistolary novel *Secret History; or, the Horrors of St. Domingo* (1808).

What brings these texts into conversation with each other is precisely

Goudie's theme, which, along with the African diaspora, presents another major interdisciplinary site of the new scholarship. The history, ethnography, and theory of creolization has become a critical flashpoint for linguists, anthropologists, historians, and cultural studies and literary scholars.[62] As exemplary circumatlantic sites, port cities like New Orleans continue to be conspicuously unique and, quite literally, *eu*-phoric (producing an excess of self-reflexive commentary), as Rien Fertel's *Imagining the Creole City: The Rise of Literary Culture in Nineteenth-Century New Orleans* (2014), Catharine Savage Brosman's *Louisiana Creole Literature: A Historical Study* (2013), and the essay collections *New Orleans in the Atlantic World: Between Land and Sea* (2010) and *New Orleans and the Global South: Caribbean, Creolization, Carnival* (2017) promptly confirm.[63]

Of course the theme of creolization extends well beyond the cisatlantic/hemispheric context of South America, the Caribbean archipelago, and the new US republic. It was the historian Ira Berlin who first pointed to the circumatlantic breadth of the creolization process.[64] Commercial, kinship, and cultural networks between the West Indies and the new republic of North America were undoubtedly part of a larger circumatlantic world, where Creole ambivalences already characterized the fluid processes of all kinds of exchange coming together in singular encounters. Names, strategies of recognition and survival, roles and professions, fortunes and reputations, all could become liquefied in the interstitial zones between metropole and colony, center and periphery, and beyond the international divisions of state apparatuses.

The choice of exemplars I have discussed here recounts some of the formative moments of the new atlanticist milieu of literary and historical scholarship, all of them salient and representative. It should be said that within the context of this interdisciplinary perspectivism interest has grown in other significant themes accompanying the paradigm shift outlined here: transatlantic print and reprint cultures, translation histories, commodity studies, oceanic studies, abolition and reform interests, science and natural history studies, travel, and the rich vein of single-author studies—including Atlantic figures such as Toussaint Louverture, Alexander von Humboldt, Margaret Fuller, Giuseppe Garibaldi, Simón Bolívar, José Martí, Harriet Beecher Stowe, Lajos Kossuth, Harriet Jacobs, Ellen Craft, Sarah Forten, Sarah Parker Remond, Julia Griffiths, Frederick Douglass, and Harriet Martineau. Many of these special-focus areas are at the initial stages of elaboration and promise to enrich the current Atlantic paradigm for decades to come. Interestingly, after it grew into a major quarterly journal during its first ten years, the editors of *Atlantic Studies* have recently decided to add a new descriptor to its title: *Global Currents*. This addition marks the journal's intention to dialogue with Pacific Rim and Eurasian studies (which has recently become a complementary area-studies domain), world history, and world literature studies.

As for global (or world) history, it has become one more dimension complicating the horizon of the now seemingly retrogressive study of national literatures proper. In the last few years we have had a global history of the birth of the modern world, of the "empire of cotton" and an equally vast study of the "transformation of the world" during the nineteenth century.[65] Besieged by their own disciplinary crisis, comparative literature scholars have also sought to reinvent their programs by embracing the study of world literatures, although the problems this scopic challenge has raised have yet to be clarified.[66] The tensions of a three-dimensional, multilingual perspective alertness characterizing the best scholarship of the new Atlantic studies paradigm seem for the moment to be sufficiently comprehensive and ecologically responsive to the ever-changing needs of humanist criticism.

II

CASE STUDIES ACROSS THE HUMANITIES

3

Caliban's Scamels

From Shakespearean Romance to Ethnographic Site

> The storyteller's cry comes from the rock itself. He is grounded in the depths of the land; therein lies his power. . . . Purify the breath until it reveals the harsh taste of the land: bring breath to the death of rocks and landscape.
>
> —ÉDOUARD GLISSANT

When I was a boy spending summer vacation on my grandfather's farm not far from the township of Eden, Wisconsin, my uncles used to delight in telling about a New Yorker who got lost one day and ended up—only God knows how—on the dusty backroads of Eden township. When he came to a crossroads and spotted a farmer leaning on a fence nearby, the New Yorker eased his Cadillac Eldorado to a stop, rolled down his window, and hollered out in Newyorkese, "Hey, Mistah! Will this road here take me in the direction of Milwaukee?" The farmer looked at the driver and his car for a while, as if trying to believe his eyes, and then drawled out, "Can't say as I know that it does." The driver thought a bit and then snapped back with, "Well, then, can you tell me if it continues on straight south?" Removing a stone from his field, the farmer replied, "Nope, I'm afraid I can't." Staring at him now in disbelief, the New Yorker challenged the farmer again, "Well, then, can you at least tell me what's the next town down this here road and how far away it is?" The farmer blinked a few times, looked over his field of hay, and then concluded, "I guess I can't help you there either." At his wit's end now, the New Yorker shot back, "You sure don't know a hell of a lot, do you?" To which the farmer replied, "Maybe I don't, but I ain't lost either."

Having driven off the highway grid of his Rand McNally atlas, the New Yorker was certainly lost. The farmer's field did not mean a thing to him or, for that matter, to anybody in Milwaukee. In accordance with what was under his feet, the farmer might very easily have replied, "Son, if you don't know where 'here' is, ain't nobody can tell you." But that is beside the point. The farmer and the New Yorker represent profoundly divergent points of view and inhabit two completely different scalar worlds. On one hand we have the cruising cosmopolitan confiding in what are supposed to be the smooth cross-country transparencies of his road map and on the other we have a farmer absorbed in the small but dense cosmography of Eden township. It is not necessary to point out that chorography (local mapping) and continental road atlases express opposing kinds of attachment to the territory. And when it comes to the underlying issue of the above anecdote—namely the ethnography of dwelling and horizon of continental travel—such scanning practices express apparently irreconcilable economies of representation.

Arguably, much of early modern Atlantic-world literature can be read as a struggle to join together the constraining novelties of local, indigenous living and the more abstract privileges of European colonial law. This same divergence characterizes the standoff between Prospero, *The Tempest*'s cosmopolitan traveler, and Caliban, totally immersed in his native island. In this dual perspective, representation is physiognomically beset with the need to recount two different sources of sovereignty: that which springs from a form of *jus publicum europaeum* (a colonial order of white European subjects) and makes for a loosely defined "us" and that which springs from living in a given "New World" territory, such as a Caribbean island, inhabited by indigenous peoples who draw their identity from their ancestors and the land where they have always lived. Thus we have two quite different categories: one an abstract *nomos* based ultimately on written legal codes and the other an *ethnos* defined by custom and oral traditions. In Shakespeare's play *The Tempest*, these two contrasting categories indicate different ways of claiming possession of the (Caribbean) island. Each of these categories also serves as a source of sovereignty, even though both derive from the same fiction: the people (or *populus*). As an entity, the people express a rather undefinable reality the extremes of which are (1) the people as politically represented by the procedures of government—thus, a formal fiction based on relations of proportion and law—and (2) the people as a cultural and qualitative entity shored up by local traditions, language, customs, beliefs, daily practices, and a shared place of dwelling, whether it be a roughly defined territory, an island, or even a township that has taken root in a New World territory and has begun to draw its settler identity from the land.

But getting back to the example of my Wisconsin farmer, I think it is easy enough to lose our patience with him even if we are not from New York. While not an idiot, he is nevertheless "idiographic" in the way he daily moves about and reads his world from field and woods to barn and house. Had he cared to, he easily might have conceded some information to the New Yorker, even if in chorographic form. For example, he might have suggested, "What you'll be wanting to do is get on the big interstate. To get there, all you gotta do is just go down past that culvert—see that slight rise in the road up ahead?—until you come to Johnson's farm; turn left there and follow his cornfield all the way down to Van Hoorn's pond on the right. You can't miss it. There you'll see a sign announcing next week's annual county fair. Go just a stone's throw past it until you come upon two big oak trees. Take the road that runs between them and stay on that until you find what you're looking for." So much for chorography and its richly descriptive, highly personal expertise: "You can't miss it." There is, of course, much more to be said about this procedure of spatial immersion, which more directly addresses the strictly ethical and political themes of the kind of sovereignty informing Shakespeare's play.

The peculiar noetic difference between being a cosmopolitan spirit like Prospero—who quite naturally feels that he has every right to act as lord and ruler of the relatively "empty" island he happens upon—and an entirely local fellow like Caliban—an indigenous islander who was once quite snug and happy among his wild berries and succulent clams—describes in nuce a topological hermeneutic characterized by two distinct kinds of knowledge and two contrasting ways of relating to one's surrounding environment. As *The Tempest* proves, only Caliban's sensibility expresses the work of thick description and vertical connectivity. The chorographic information the Wisconsin farmer decided to hold back, probably realizing that it wouldn't help the New Yorker anyhow, is quite similar to the kind of local knowledge that Caliban excels in. Note how the farmer's unspoken directions are based on topographical features in the landscape: a summer crop, places associated with specific people, a couple of trees, and a sign involving an upcoming local event.

This unconfessed instruction also suggests a vertical weaving of different kinds of information that generate a topology of deep travel, if you will. We have to be familiar with the landscape, literally immersed in it, to be able to decode its tidings. On the other hand, had he cared to reply in the spirit of surfaces (such as that inscribed by a Rand McNally roadmap), the farmer might have given directions that would have made the New Yorker feel as if he were still in the same country he was in before he got lost: "Take the next left you come to, go a mile and then turn right. That'll put you on I-94, the interstate." Nothing to it. Anybody who can drive a car would be able to follow such advice. But existentially speaking, knowing where "here" is involves us in an altogether different spatiality requiring a local mind and not a little ethnographic schooling. Prospero, for example, has little or no connection to "his" island's environmental whereabouts. He has none of Caliban's local knowledge. Indeed, as he notes to Miranda, they could not survive without their slave's help.

In Shakespeare's day a huge canopy with gold signs symbolizing the heavens hung over the stage of London's Globe Theater. It was a *Theatrum Mundi*. *Theatrum Mundi* or *Orbis* was also a favorite title that the Dutch cartographers Willem Blaeu and Abraham Ortelius gave to their monumental atlases of the known world in the early 1600s. The theater as world and the world as theater nicely captures the two-way metaphorical passage that informs the economy of representation in Shakespeare's play *The Tempest* and forces us to ask, which island—in the play—are we dealing with? The island as a stage for a stunning but ultimately conventional romance or the island as a recently discovered geographical site enchanting in its own right? As Leo Marx wrote in his classic study *The Machine in the Garden*, *The Tempest* stands as a prologue to US literature, as it prefigures the design of many well-known American fables.[1] Of course, we have come a long way since 1964, when Marx first published his book. Since then, what Houston Baker has called "the venerable Western trope of Prospero and Caliban"[2] has become a kind of expanded showcase for framing postcolonial literatures across the Americas, while Calibanic literature now represents any displaced indigenous voice.[3] Elaine Showalter in her book *Sister's Choice* has traced a tradition of women's versions of the play, calling it "Miranda's Story."[4] But in her important essay "Beyond Miranda's Meanings: Un/Silencing the 'Demonic Ground' of Caliban's Women," the novelist and critic Sylvia Wynter focuses on the primacy of "race" to counter white feminism's conceptualization of the category "woman."[5] In *The Tempest* Miranda becomes the mimetic norm of Caliban's desire only because there apparently are no black women on the island. Nevertheless, it should also be said that Miranda is Italian/Mediterranean more than she is European. In other words, her "racial" characteristics may already be represented as a brew of cultural and physical signs. It depends on the casting.

Perhaps one of the most successful recent reworkings of the play in the US literature is Gloria Naylor's novel *Mama Day*, published in 1988, where Miranda is portrayed as a black conjure woman living on the island of Willow Springs off the coast of South Carolina and Georgia.[6] In 1987 in her novel *No Telephone to Heaven*, Michelle Cliff created a startlingly new and three-dimensional Miranda figure in her protagonist Clare Savage, and in 1992 the Caribbean writer Marina Warner also published a narrative version of the play titled *Indigo; or Mapping the Waters*, which is prefaced by a map of the island and a genealogical chart.[7] Warner's multigenerational, ocean-spanning novel orchestrates a polyphony of female voices (those of Xanthe, Sycorax, Miranda, Ariel) sidelined by Shakespeare and colonialism. In *Mama Day*, too, we are immediately provided with a map of Willow Springs and a genealogical chart to underscore the importance of deep travel in the text. What is more, it is from the central position of the island's cemetery that the story winds back to its origin. Referring to the tombstone of Bascombe Wade (the novel's absent Prospero), Mama Day says, "[T]here's a story behind that." And then continues:

> Bascombe Wade used to have the whole island before he deeded it over to his slaves. Said he fell under the spell of a woman he owned—only in body, not in mind. . . . But she got away from him and headed over here toward the east bluff on her way back to Africa. And she made that trip—some say in body, others in mind. But the point is that he lost her. He kept a vigil up here at Chevy's Pass—he's keeping it still. And when the wind is right in the trees, you can hear him calling and calling the name that nobody knows.[8]

In the novel as a whole, genealogy is used to pull back the veil from a typical story rooted in American slavery and the slave narrative. As was true for Caliban in Shakespeare's play, listening to signs like the wind becomes of central importance for Mama Day. Both she and Caliban are deeply immersed in the arcane secrets of their quasi-mythical worlds and show that they have the power to communicate with spirits. Here is Mama Day talking about the island to George, a visitor from outside:

Now sea life, birds, and wood creatures, they got ways just like people. 'Cepting they live in the sky, the earth, the tides. So who better to ask about their home? You just gotta watch 'em long enough to find out what's going on. She tells him what part of that forest she uses in the fall, summer, or spring. Differences in leaves of trees, barks of trees, roots. The tonics she makes up, the poultices, the healing teas. There's something in here for everything, she tells him, if a body knows what they're doing.[9]

Mama Day is a conjure woman, and her power comes from her knowledge of the woods. Even in her eighties she knows how to move about it in the dark. "But younger, the whole island was her playground: she'd walk through in a dry winter without snapping a single twig, disappear into the shadow of a summer cottonwood, flatten herself so close to the ground under a moss-covered rock shelf, folks started believing John-Paul's little girl became a spirit in the woods," the narrator recounts.[10] Mama Day's knowledge is not from books; it is local knowledge gained from experience, a form of "toposophy" or place wisdom. Steeping herself in chorographic expertise, she treats Willow Springs not as mere geography but as an ethnoscape imbued with ancestral patterns and values.

"This Bare Island": Place as Theory

The St. Lucian poet Derek Walcott promoted the same kind of cultural maneuvering in his Nobel Prize acceptance speech, "The Antilles, Fragments of Epic Memory": "Then the noun the 'Antilles' ripples like brightening water, and the sounds of leaves, palm fronds, and birds are the sounds of a fresh dialect, the native tongue. The personal vocabulary, the individual melody whose metre is one's biography, joins in that sound, with any luck, and the body moves like a walking, a waking island." And a bit further on: "It [history] is there in Antillean geography, in the vegetation itself. The sea sighs with the drowned from the Middle Passage, the butchery of its aborigines . . . , and even the actions of the surf on sand cannot erase the African memory. . . . [T]hey are there to be read, and if properly read, they create their own literature."[11] Walcott's entire speech is in this vein: a moving paean to his native island, an exercise in cultural archaeology where the island's sites seduce the writer with its themes and ultimately possess him so that he becomes a walking version of it.

With Naylor and Walcott in mind, let us now turn to Shakespeare's island in *The Tempest*. In what sense can it be appreciated as a primal scene of a larger circumatlantic world? If we look at the sources, it is clear that there are actually two islands and two conflicting representations of it. There is certainly the island of romance, the island as literary locus and part of the standard rhetorical system of Western culture.[12] So, for example, we have echoes of Virgil and Spenser and Sidney. This island is a *locus amoenus,* a brave new world with goodly creatures in it. It is Prospero who rules over it and puts the romance plot through its familiar metadramatic paces. Among other things we have a happy shipwreck, the revenge motif, final reconciliation, and marriage of the young heirs at the end. Prospero is given back his dukedom, he abandons his magic—throwing his book away—and at play's end leaves the "bare" island for northern Italy.

This handling of the island was a familiar one for Shakespeare's audience, with the capacity to tame any intruding actualities, such as the relatively new phenomenon of hurricanes in the Caribbean. Rhetorical islands are generally more fun than real ones. Thus when we examine the normative structure of romance in terms of its spatial syntax in the play, we cannot help asking how that syntax affects the status of the other island, the "real" one, which is abandoned to Caliban once Prospero decides to return to Italy, the one located in the Bermuda islands, as reported by William Strachey in his "True Reportory of the Wrack," dated July 15, 1610.[13] *This* island was known to sailors as one of the dreaded Devil's Islands and was directly related to John Smith's Virginia colony in North America. Prospero himself is too obsessively absorbed in his revenge plot to notice anything immediately around him and remains rather stationary throughout the play, letting Ariel and Caliban do his bidding. He is never the mouthpiece for descriptions of the island, though in the epilogue he does let escape:

> Now my charms are all o'erthrown,
> And what strength I have's mine own
> . . . .
>   Let me not
> . . . .

dwell

In this bare island by your spell

. . . .

Now I want

Spirits to enforce, art to enchant. (5, epilogue, 1–14)[14]

It is only when he is left to himself, without his magician's staff, that he confesses to being overcome by a bleak pessimism that evidently extends to his rarely observed surroundings. All told, in Prospero's eyes the island remains nothing more (or less) than a stage and is never anything but "bare." This attitude is quite conventional.

Then there is Gonzalo, who mentions that Prospero found his dukedom "In a poor isle" (5.1.213). Earlier it is Gonzalo who famously notes, "Here is everything advantageous to life" (2.1.49). And again: "How lush and lusty the grass looks! How green!" (2.1.52). This leads him to paraphrase rather closely a part of Montaigne's essay "Of the Cannibals" where he envisions on the shipwrecked island an ideal society without rulers: "Had I plantation of this isle" (2.1.144) it familiarly begins. Most of Gonzalo's descriptions seem indebted to Golden Age rhetoric and the soothing tradition of pastoral drama. Neither he nor Prospero gives us any specific details that would suggest that the island is something more than the conventional literary island of romance. And yet, through the spatializing strategy of hypotyposis the island is surely set up as the play's central locus; the rhetorical figure of hypotyposis—painting things in such a vivid and energetic manner that the play itself becomes a living scene—expresses the concrete form of the island's own energy, whether literary or historical.

What happens, therefore, if we take the locus of the island as its own evidence? What happens if we remain loyal to *it*? Turn our gaze on it *as* a singular geographical locus, a theme that outlives and goes beyond the brief diachronic maneuverings of plot to engulf the spatial syntax of the island as a very specific kind of rhetorical inscription? This, to be sure, is the donnée Prospero ignored, thereby making hypotyposis itself the play's best kept, but open, secret. Since the island itself, however, is nothing but the descriptive traces left by the partial and often interrupted excursions of Caliban's speech, we need to focus on the very physiognomy of these traces and expose them as the place of the island's own eventfulness. To do so is to consign the normative conventions of romance as inscribed in a rather cosmopolitan form of surface travel to an equally alert sense of ecocriticism. That is, we might begin by imploding the island locus, looking at it from the different positions of its descriptive excursions and not from the descriptively silent center of Prospero's cave.

Let us look at the island as geographical site, therefore: the island seen under the close-up gaze of a vertical hermeneutic, with the kind of place wisdom working in Gloria Naylor's novel *Mama Day* and Derek Walcott's Nobel Prize speech. I am talking here about immersion or deep travel, about letting ourselves become enchanted by the charming energy of the rhetorical figure itself, whose task is to paint in such a vivid fashion as to make the scene come alive. For Prospero, remember, the island is "bare," and as Gonzalo adds, "poor." But is it so? Both of these adjectives are meant to have a desemanticizing effect aimed at reducing the island to a dead thing—a cliché. By judging it empty and bare, they are, in effect, involved in a cover-up. To see what they are trying to conceal, we need only blow up (in the photographic sense) the literary locus until its secret depths—its details—come into view. In this case toposophy (place wisdom) means simply following the cross-world, rhetorical energy of hypotyposis. The island's history—inscribed in the struggle between Prospero and Caliban—can be found in the way it belongs to place.

Once again, there are two islands in *The Tempest* (Prospero's and Caliban's), making the locus twice true: as literature and as an actual geographical place. While Prospero rules over the conventions of romance, the subaltern Caliban witnesses to the actualities of Caribbean geography. So it is Caliban's position we must recover in order to follow the political fault line between the two islands. That the island locus consists of more than one spatial syntax, that it is the space of a heterology, is already evident in Gonzalo's suggestive use of the word "plantation," with its connotations of master/slave, European/native, colonizer/colonized dichotomies. The very name Caliban is an anagram of the word *cannibal* or some form of the word *Carib*. When Caliban suggests that perhaps Stephano and Trinculo came from the heavens (2.2.137), we are reminded of a similar view expressed by the indigenous people when they first met Columbus and his crew.[15]

It goes without saying that Prospero insists too much on his version of what took place when he first arrived on the island not to make us suspect that there may be another side to this primal but suppressed scene, namely Caliban's. In his violent partiality Prospero seems to fulfill the role of colonial historian, with all the straightforward fervor that role requires. Thus when

Ariel first appears on stage, we hear Prospero raise his voice in a rage: "Thou liest, malignant thing! Hast thou forgot / The foul witch Sycorax" (1.2.2.255–56). Prospero, it seems, must continually indoctrinate this island spirit against its inextinguishable desire for freedom: "I must / Once in a month recount what thou has been, / Which thou forget'st" (1.2.262–63). In the first reference we have to Caliban, we learn that he is Prospero's slave. As Miranda is told:

> We cannot miss him: he does make our fire,
> Fetch in our wood, and serves in offices
> That profit us. What, ho! slave! Caliban!
> Thou earth, thou! speak. (1.2.313–16)

When Caliban first speaks, we learn that he explicitly accuses Prospero of being a usurper, giving us at the same time a glimpse of the island's spatial order:

> For I am all the subjects that you have,
> Which first was mine own King: and here you sty me
> In this hard rock, whiles you do keep from me
> The rest o' th' island. (1.2.342–45)

It is a "styed" and indispensable Caliban who throws out suggestive hints undermining Prospero's story of foundation and helps us to see the island lovingly as an ethnoscape (a native dwelling site). If, then, Caliban is our "natural" key to the island's hidden agency, we can do no better than take Prospero's advice when he commands, "Thou earth, thou! speak" (1.2.316). In truth, it is initially as "earth" that Caliban introduces us to the island's special scenography, its real and enchanted geography. Later, as he watches the Europeans sail off from the island, he has learned to appreciate the epiphanies of a larger Atlantic world. We need not be told twice that for him the island is anything but a backdrop for scenes of world-historical adjustment. He and he alone establishes a semiotopic channel (a place endowed with signifying power) for getting in touch with this multidimensional site that English sailors—bewitched by its novelties in the early 1600s—hailed as Devil's Island. And when we too, as spectators, become immersed in its seductive singularities, then like Strachey's tars we can reexperience its enchantments in the form of an archaeo-geography, if you will. Since the island is a divided field of restricted spaces, and those directly under Prospero's jurisdiction are left blank, perhaps we should start from the unregenerated perspective of Caliban "the islander," as Trinculo calls him (2.2.37), and his rich and sensuous appreciation of his homeplace.

A Lesson in the Rhetoric of Topographia

It is, after all, a matter of life and death, of ecological stewardship versus a form of administrative law, of pursuing one's sovereign happiness versus undergoing colonial sanctions. Prospero knows he cannot do without his slave, as Caliban reminds him in that opening scene:

> and then I lov'd thee,
> And show'd thee all the qualities o' th' isle,
> The fresh springs, brine-pits, barren place and fertile:
> Curs'd be I that did so! (1.2.337–40)

Frank Kermode glosses that "brine-pits" suggests "he showed how to distinguish between useful and useless resources."[16] If we wish to reconstruct this canceled scene pertaining to the play's prehistory, we must imagine Caliban leading Prospero around the island as he points out its sundry "qualities." In the context of this descriptive work, showing means making him (and us) *see* the island. Such a script calls for an exercise in *topographia,* and in keeping with it, the longer the list of qualities the more pregnant the excursion. It is important therefore not to forget this rather summary allusion to their initial tour quoted above when we are entertained with Caliban's more fervent lists later on in the play. Here Caliban must have sensed that Prospero would not be moved by such an untimely cultivation of this geo-rhetorical figure. In short, the native need not waste his time in recalling the scene, unless of course his intention was to expose just how deep his own wound went.

When Caliban meets up with Stephano and Trinculo (2.2) and decides to switch his allegiance to them in the hopes of overthrowing Prospero and regaining his freedom, we have a Caliban whose imaginative powers are truly enchanting. Echoing his earlier encounter with Prospero, he aims to win over his newly met friends with this promise: "I'll show thee every fertile inch o' th' island" (2.2.152). This exercise in *showing* introduces us to the classical colonial script of seduction and intimates why so many of Sir Thomas Gates and Sir George Sumner's men in Strachey's account of "the wracke" went native on Devil's Island. Finding paradise at the tips of their fingers, they no longer needed the shield of English authority to enhance further the palpable intimations of a New World sovereignty. As Strachey notes, "[I]n Virginia, nothing but wretchednesse and labour must be expected, with many wants, and a churlish intreaty, there being neither Fish, Flesh, nor Fowle, which 'here' . . . at ease, and pleasure might be injoyed: and since both in the one, and the other place, they were (for the time) to loose the fruition both of their friends and Countrey, as good, and better were it for them, to repose and seate them where they should have the least outward wants the while."[17]

Some of the men on Devil's Island were so charmed by this tropical "here" that they moved to another part of the island and set up their own more relaxed colony; others conspired to overthrow Gates's rigid rule. Arguably, Strachey's "True Reportory" is most captivating in those parts where it assumes a simple chorographic posture and gives an unadorned account of the island's climate and riches. It is in his long descriptive passages that we are still able to imagine what the Bermudas were like at the beginning of the seventeenth century. Through an inadvertent site analysis of the varieties of plants and fish and fowl and of the climate and soil and the island's position, Strachey gives us a fine example of green archaeology, of what paradise was really like when given a local habitation and a name.

Now here is Caliban, not only as initiated insider but also as master of ceremonies for Trinculo's and Stephano's excursion around the island:

> I'll show thee the best springs; I'll pluck thee berries;
> I'll fish for thee, and get thee wood enough.
> . . . .
> I prithee, let me bring thee where crabs grow:
> And I with my long nails will dig thee pig-nuts;
> Show thee a jay's nest, and instruct thee how
> To snare the nimble marmoset; I'll bring thee
> To clustering filberts, and sometimes I'll get thee
> Young scamels from the rock. Wilt thou go with me? (2.2.165–77)

We know the answer without even having to guess. So Stephano says, "O brave monster! lead the way" (2.2.193). It must be acknowledged that Caliban is not given very many lines in the play, but still, several of his speeches have become set pieces of Shakespearean eloquence. The above excursion in hypotyposis is a fine example of it. As place sense transmutes into place power under Caliban's spell, Prospero's "bare island" proves not so bare after all. Underneath the literary locus of the island as platform for romance lies a secret island belonging to Caliban.

Getting young scamels from the rock is the work of a local, place-centered intelligence and skill. Caliban is teaching us not only how to "see" the island (which introduces the matter of deep travel and an ecocritical sensibility) but also how to appreciate it (which involves us in the ethics of dwelling). In the passage quoted above he puts us in the position of imagining a preconquest scene, what life was like on the island before the coming of Prospero and the spatial order of the plantation. Part of the animus of the above description surely derives from the fact that through its rhetorical spell Caliban is able to project himself forward into the spatially present past, to a happier time when there was no Prospero. Thus he insists with his fellow conspirators, "As I told thee before, I am subject to a tyrant, a sorcerer, that by his cunning hath cheated me of the island" (3.2.41–43). The energy of hypotyposis illustrates how the ingathering force of topographical minutiae and local habit is tantamount to clenching the revolt around a secret landscape.

To paraphrase the implicit sense of Caliban's descriptive excursion into this site's ethico-political base: this island, the one I am describing, is mine. If you help me get it back, it will also be yours. Apparently, at this point he has gone well beyond a merely spontaneous or instinctive impulse to rebel as he maneuvers to convince Trinculo and Stephano to help him topple the tyrant. In short, he is no longer politically naïve inasmuch as he has become actively aware of his subaltern status. Caliban's desire to break with Prospero suggests, in the words of Antonio Gramsci, "the progressive consciousness of his own historical personality."[18] Only at the end will Caliban be able fully to achieve such a consciousness and broach a new beginning: "What a thrice-double ass / Was I, to take this drunkard for a god! / And worship this dull fool!" (5.1.297–99).

The very names that haunt the foregoing descriptive passage with their presence also reveal a poetic function behind Caliban's rhetorical doings, and it is this same *poiesis* that Walcott evoked in his Nobel Prize acceptance speech when he talked rather astutely of "cherishing our insignificance," by which he meant learning to revel in the local names, such as the names of Antillean trees: "laurier canelles, bois-flot, bois-canot—or the valleys the trees mention—Fond St. Jacques, Mabonya, Forestière, Roseau, Mahaut . . . all songs and histories in themselves, pronounced not in French but in patois."[19] If such names allure, it is because of the stories that attach to them.

For African American writers like Toni Morrison, "The act of imagination is inevitably bound up with memory."[20] Caliban's voice resonates, takes on heft, through the spatial syntax of site-specific names that recall the moment of their bestowal. His, not Prospero's, island belongs to more than one world or, as the literary critic Ruth Ronen would say, "has a cross-world identity."[21] Caliban is able to unblock *The Tempest's* buried scene of origin precisely because his descriptive work is site-dependent. The energy he invests in hypotyposis evokes a scene that is moving enough to plunge both him and us into the nurturing conditions of Strachey's Devil's Island. His unique descriptive competence suggests a local *poiesis* that he alone is able to entertain us with. If then Prospero is the magician of romance, surely Caliban is the poet of place, claiming for himself the prototypical standpoint of the native writer in cisatlantic cultures. But let us study more closely how this obtains.

The best springs, berries, fish, crabs, pig-nuts, the nimble marmoset, hazelnuts, young scamels from the rocks. The name *scamels* alone would be enough to hold us. In seeking to trace the moment of the word's baptism, Stephen Orgel places it in the same company of borrowings as *Setebos*. Thus he derives its source from Antonio Pigafetta's account of Magellan's circumnavigation, *Il primo viaggio intorno al mondo* (First voyage around the world, 1519–22), where there is mention of small fish *"fort scameux"* (very scaly).[22] Frank Kermode and others suggest the word most likely refers to "sea mels," a variant of which is "sea-mew," which brings us back to Strachey's account of native methods of bird catching on the rocks in his "A True Reportory of the Wracke."[23] Showing his own awareness of mystic-sounding site names in his travel book *Cape Cod*, Henry David Thoreau holds forth on a now extinct form of oyster, the *"Escaille,"* that was indigenous to Wellfleet Harbor in Massachusetts Bay, explaining that the Indians settled the area because of the presence of this abundant food source. Picking through the "many traces of their occupancy," he also found a lot of arrowheads and bones of animals and then proceeds to trace down the story of the Wellfleet Harbor oyster:

> Champlain in the edition of his "Voyages" printed in 1613, says that in the year 1606 he and Poitrincourt explored a harbor (Barnstable Harbor?) in the southerly part of what is now called Massachusetts Bay . . . and there they found many good

oysters, and they named it "*le Port aux Huistres*" (Oyster Harbor). In one edition of his map (1632), the "*R. aux Escailles*" is drawn emptying into the same part of the bay. . . . Also William Wood . . . in his "New England's Prospect," published in 1634, spoke of "a great oyster-bank" in the Charles River, and of another in the Mistik, each of which obstructed the navigation of its river.[24]

Some local truth such as this is surely behind Caliban's enthusiasm for scamels. If Sir Thomas Gates's conspirators hoped to stay in the Bermudas instead of going on to the Virginia colony of Jamestown, where starvation and anarchy ruled, it was very much due to the abundance and tastiness of its scamels, whether they be shellfish like Champlain's foot-long shoe horns or especially sweet and tender fowl. Here is Strachey's incredible tale of how they caught "Sea-Meawe":

> Our men found a prettie way to take them, which was by standing on the Rockes or Sands by the Sea side, and hollowing, laughing, and making the strangest out-cry that possibly they could: with the noyse whereof the Birds would come flocking to that place, and settle upon the very armes and head of him that so cryed . . . and so our men would take twentie dozen in two houres of the chiefest of them; and they were a good and well relished Fowle, fat and full as a Partridge.[25]

In her celebrated poem "Diving into the Wreck," Adrienne Rich warns us that when it comes to exploring scenes of origin, "The Words are purposes. / The words are maps."[26] If anything, *The Tempest*'s mystic scamels and Champlain's "*Escailles*" are indexical signs. Like oysters, the names themselves are attached to a site. Caliban, therefore, plunges us into the geography of his island by transforming Prospero's literary locus into a site-specific praxis. Through his confident use of local knowledge, *The Tempest* is no longer seen as a locus of romance but as an ethnographic site, no longer a theory of place but place itself as cisatlantic theory.

In presenting us with different versions of the island, Prospero and Caliban are, in a sense, rival historians. Insofar as he superimposes generic conventions on "this bare island," Prospero exposes himself to Siegfried Kracauer's critique of the general historian: "Whenever [such generalizations] are removed from their native soil and made to sustain alien contexts, they may become dumb and no longer echo the meanings that led to their formation."[27] It is Caliban who penetrates the alien context by describing the island from within—as a singularity—and it is from within the scenographic site of his descriptive circling that we are led back to a local archaeomythology, a rival scene of sovereign belonging.

As Kracauer points out, "The belief that the widening of the range of intelligibility involves an increase of significance is one of the basic tenets of Western thought."[28] In effect, Caliban's island is Devil's Island because his descriptive blow-up of it hurls us through the global symbolism of the colonial world map and into the disjunctive ethnosophy of a specific Caribbean site. And when dealing with such local cunning, particularities—and they alone—count. *The Tempest* proclaims two versions of the truth: Prospero's from above and outside, Caliban's from below and within. Without his book and "spirits to enforce," the magician of romance says, "My ending is despair." But by now the island itself has charmed us as it once did the first English colonists. Looking over his hometown of Kingston, Jamaica, of an early dawn morning, the antihero of Orlando Patterson's novel *An Absence of Ruins* observes:

> What ancient civilisation flourished here long, long ago? How clever and resourceful they must have been to have made houses as durable as these out of the sides of empty cod-fish barrels. Who were the men that ruled them? Were they of another race, of another culture? How great and ingenious they must have been to create a mosaic of streets such as these. And in the same grid pattern as the Romans, too. Look, there are even gutters, part of their drainage system. I wonder what kind of refuse these gutters drained away? The waters of how many Rabelasian baths; the vomit of how many sumptuous feasts?
>
> There is a past here. There must be a past here. My city goes back a thousand years. If you dig deep you will find the relics of even more ancient times.[29]

This ethnographic frame of mind informs not only the narratives of the authors I have discussed here but also the work of a significant number of writers belonging to the African diaspora. C. L. R. James, Wilson Harris, Derek Walcott, Jamaica Kincaid, Sylvia Wynter, and Erna Brodber immediately come to mind. In short, no matter how synoptic early modern world maps were, they were only as good as the place-names scattered across their surface. For Atlantic-world scholars, imploding sites and writing microhistories about them has become a necessary form of testimony.

George Lamming opens his book *The Pleasures of Exile* with an essay titled

"In the Beginning," which in turn begins with this well-known passage from
The Tempest:

> Be not afeard; the isle is full of noises,
> Sounds and sweet airs, that give delight, and hurt not.
> Sometimes a thousand twangling instruments
> Will hum about mine ears; and sometimes voices,
> That, if I then had wak'd after long sleep,
> Will make me sleep again: and then, in dreaming,
> The clouds methought would open, and show riches
> Ready to drop upon me; that, when I wak'd
> I cried to dream again. (3.2.133–41)[30]

As we have seen above, Caliban is the only character in the play who really
knows the island inside out. It is his "primordial attachment" to its geography
that explains the workings of Caliban's local mind and the form of attention
required to become schooled in it.[31] If in Shakespeare's canon only *King Lear*
rivals *The Tempest* in its sonorous highs and lows, it is also true that listening to noises and voices is an essential part of the colonized Caliban's art of
survival. For this local sense of things the most insignificant object or sound
might easily become of absolute importance, might easily allow him to slip
away into another place. Awareness of singularities and of course an existential familiarity with the space of *here* are essential to Caliban's liberation. If
we wish to join the native's chorographic company, George Lamming argues,
the particulars of "here" are equally essential to our own liberation from the
Prospero syndrome.

The Eye and Light of History

Here is Lamming's own little autobiographical anecdote, meant to clarify the
metropolitan/colonial distinction with which every West Indian is imprinted
at birth:

> Some years ago I was a guest in the house of an English family. Their son was
> asked to entertain me with conversation until his mother arrived. His first ques-

tion was: "Where are you from?" I replied, "The Caribbean"; and proceeded to talk about my particular island in relation to the others.

Suddenly he said: "Excuse me."

I thought he had gone to the lavatory. But when he returned, he set about spreading a great carpet of paper over the floor. Without explanation or apology, he simply said: "Now let's see where we are talking about." He had brought his map.[32]

Cultural identity always involves us in genealogical entanglements (our family name and grandparents) and spatial emplotment (where we were born and grew up). For the exile suffering from a sense of placelessness, the issue of his or her lost *here* is now transformed into "Where are you from?" While the burden of connecting these two spatial adverbs—here and where—must be left to history and storytelling, the boy's map neatly serves as the proper topographic surface for *seeing* into and positioning Lamming's Caribbean identity. In a simple stroke the boy is now ready to submit the unstated but more obvious question "who are you" to the jurisdiction of a very peculiar "carpet of paper," with its place-names and lines and sites. Lamming can now close in on his point: "That boy was no more than nine years old. If he can preserve that spirit of curiosity and concreteness, his generation will save West Indians and others the torture of adult experience. It is to the spirit of that boy that we shall address our discourse, and since I shall call on West Indian children to reply to that spirit, I must ask you to accept the use of legend. How and where is the Caribbean?"[33]

The kind of competence Lamming is encouraging us to acquire is very special indeed. Although perennially undervalued as cultural texts, maps display a very composite and dynamic form of signification that is absolutely essential for a people's or a country's self-knowledge. As the myth of Daedalus—one of cartography's foundational stories—suggests, maps are capable of offering us a total or synoptic view of inhabited space in a way that no other cultural document can. And this same view also stirs our desire to go into the territory. With his map in front of him, Lamming's nine-year-old says, "Now let's see where we are talking about." According to Lamming, what we are talking about must proceed from the boy's cartographic *where*. Position comes first. These preliminaries taken care of, the Caribbean becomes visible in a coup d'oeil: a green scattering of islands of various shapes and names over an indigo sea. For possessing such awesome power once reserved for the gods alone, a comprehensive map of the territory was, in classical Greece, rightly called an *autopsia*—literally, seeing with one's own eyes.[34] At the beginning of Willem Blaeu's *Theatrum Orbis Terrarum sive Novus Atlas* of 1635 the reader is advised, "Geographiam vero oculum & lumen Historiae vocant" (geography is truly called the eye and light of history).

It is necessary to insist that we cannot have one without the other, history without geography. As both eye and light, geography is time made visible. With this sense of emplotment in mind, it comes natural for us to inquire about the role the cartographic gaze plays in conditioning the content and mode of the writing not only of history but also of fiction and drama. "How and where is the Caribbean?" Lamming asks, once his country's map has become the deep image for whatever storytelling he will get done while away in England's metropolis. Holding this theory—in the etymological sense of *seeing*—of the Caribbean steadily before his eyes, and indeed as a basis of his oeuvre, we can appreciate why the "culture image"[35] of Lamming's novels depends on his ability to make the map's sites speak. For all of that, Caliban's own place wisdom, like Lamming's in his essay "In the Beginning," began with the ethical space of a beckoning *here:* "Be not afeard; the isle is full of noises,/Sounds and sweet airs, that give delight, and hurt not/Sometimes a thousand twangling instruments/Will hum about mine ears; and sometimes voices." In *The Tempest,* this autochthonous beckoning represents the neglected terrain of political rights as well as the insuppressible source of a spontaneous demand for justice, solidarity, and community.

4

Apple of Peru, Hester Prynne, and Colonial Boston

When, at the outset of the eighteenth century, colonial Boston's Cotton Mather published his comprehensive narrative of New England church history, *Magnalia Christi Americana,* he chose to preface it with "An Exact Mapp of New England and New York."[1] What immediately catches the viewer's eye is an impressive scattering of colonial towns—a good hundred of them—each marked with the icon of a steepled church. In the map's western portion, along the "Conecticut" (*sic*) River and going from south to north, one finds familiar English names such as Lime, Seybrook, Hadham, Midleton, Wethersfield, Hartford, and Winsor, ending in the far north with Northampton, Hadfield, Swanfield, and then Squakheag (it too with a steeple). But the viewer's eye is inevitably attracted to the vicinity of Boston, where the steeples and names increase in density the closer they are to "The Chief Town of New-England, and of the English America," as Mather calls it in book I.[2]

The map indicates that a traveler starting out from Hartford could go by a well-marked road from there to Mendon, then to Medfield, and on into Boston. A lower road connects Lime to London and London to Manchester. From there it is possible to reach Boston via such towns as Warwick and Milton. Both roads run deep into the territory and through what the cartographer still considered Indian country ("Nipnak Country" and "Country of Naraganset"). Few Indian place-names remain on Mather's map, and these generally denote rivers or other natural features but rarely towns. There remain two tribal choronyms (regional place-names) in the heart of New England's dominions—those mentioned in parentheses above—but there are no further signs of an actual Native American presence. All told, this map portrays a land that has been ethnically cleansed. But an equally pressing problem loomed: not a few of the colonists under New England rule were becoming restless and, with an endless territory to the west, some were even slipping away—"going native," so to speak.

Evidently, Mather wanted the viewer to behold how thoroughly a land of unlikeness had been converted into one great Christian and British similitude. The map's vaunt is quite evident: one space, one people, with the steeple icons suggesting the kind of bond holding the towns together against a stigmatized wilderness associated with an overwhelming indigenous presence. In the *Magnalia* Mather talks about "the Angel of Boston" and quotes Ezekiel 48:35 to indicate the foundation of New England's political unity: "The Name of the City from that Day shall be, THE LORD IS THERE."[3] What the French philosopher Michel Serres once wrote about the founding of Rome applies well to Mather's colonial utopia: "Attraction and power vary with volume. This power is a capacity to attract, to absorb, finally to subsume the multiple."[4] Where names were placed upon the land, a peculiar English clarity appeared. Building around the name meant clearing the way, quite literally establishing a common ground among people living in harmony. This is what founding a colonial town like Boston was all about. Cartographically speaking—for Mather chose *this* type of document to begin his *Magnalia Christi Americana*—ethnogenesis is basically about names and the relation between them and the places they represent. As it was with Thomas More's map of Utopia, so it was meant to be with Mather's map of New England.

Maps are as inextricably linked to narration as narratives are to exploration of space. In truth, Mather's map has nothing to *say*, only something to *show*. Points of arrival and departure, the place-names are there for all to see, each representing an initial act of foundation. They are not only the connecting words of New England, visible signs of its cultural homogeneity, but also an allusive display of beginnings, the colony's linguistic primitives of sorts. All the big issues regarding this territory, Mather knew, ultimately referred back to this visual archaeograph of first intentions. By 1702 place-names like Boston were not only British and American but also transatlantic bywords. Indeed, in the imperial context of Europe Mather's map bore a world-historical dimension.

Thus Mather writes, "Upon that Miraculous Rescue of the Town, and of the whole country, whose Fate was much enwrapped in it, there follow'd that Action of the Prophet Samuel, which is this Day to be, with some Imitation

Repeated in the midst of thee, o BOSTON, Thou helped of the Lord."[5] The "remarkable and memorable . . . time" Mather recalls is when Samuel saved the town of Ebenezer (meaning "A Stone of Help") from destruction. As New England's prophet, Mather hopes once again to signal Boston's redemption by allegorical application. The method is substantive, the map of New England a *paysage moralisée*.

Though "Boston" has an Atlantic-world ring to it on Mather's map, it is also intractably local, a fact Mather implicitly acknowledges in tracing names to the scene of their origin. The frame for this interpretive practice is the following central passage from book II, "Lives of the Govenours":

> But, Reader, let us now take up our Old Oars with all possible Respect, and see whether we can't still make use of them to serve our little Vessel. But this the rather, because we may with an easie turn change the Name into that of Pilots.
>
> The Word GOVERNMENT, properly signifies the Guidance of a Ship. . . . New-England is a little ship, which hath Weathered many a Terrible Storm; and it is but reasonable that they who have sat at the Helm of the Ship, should be remembered in the history of its Deliverances."[6]

Mather deploys the familiar classical trope of the ship[7] because as scenes of commencement the towns represent for him so many safe landings or harbors. Similar to many early modern records, the *Magnalia* charts its narrative between the impulses of utopia and *naufragium* (shipwreck). While he begins with the metaphor of piloting a ship, he talks about New England history as a drama of appropriating the land. The spatial order he refers to is preeminently telluric. However, this turning to the local scene implicitly makes available a different kind of inquiry that cannot but undermine the linear ordering of history so familiar to the Judeo-Christian tradition informing the *Magnalia*. By moving inside the clarity of the name as a singular time and place, Mather potentially faces a broken temporality and an indigenous archaeomythology. If Boston stood for history, then the wilderness to the west stood for unredeemed nature.

In other words, in spite of Mather's original intentions, the *Magnalia*'s introductory map also functions as a form of involuntary memory. It displays the foundational sites not only of an expanding population of English settlers and of a process of colonial ethnogenesis but also of a scenario of intercivilizational conflict and removal. The names on the land open up a recursive space that remains internal to the cartographic celebration of a European people's expansion and dominion. There, where the word *clearing* usually meant the sweeping away of Amerindian life and culture, we inevitably come upon a record of founding deeds. In the light of such a mise-en-scène of an indelible geography of now forgotten traces, New England becomes not only one cultural space but many; not a smooth signifying (semiotopic)[8] surface, but a territory of uncanny and varying registers; not a world-historical event but a story culled from the stuff of local legends and indigenous traces. This bimodal capacity of the place-names and the modes of sign production characterizing them are clamorously presented on the eastern edge of the choronym "Country of Naraganset" in Mather's map.[9] There the viewer finds a town twice named, "Eastham or Namset."

The place-name Namset does not appear in John Huden's *Indian Place Names of New England,* but the choronym "Naraganset" does. According to Huden, it means "at the small narrow point."[10] As signs of local knowledge, such place-names as Namset raise gnawing questions and help to nourish instruction formed by such disciplines as archaeology, geography, history, mythology, and ethnography—all convened to shore up the cultural dimensions of the English colonial presence. Place-names like "Eastham or Namset" spatialize this type of cross-disciplinary questioning and even presuppose it in deferring to those cartographic stratifications that preserve a form of nearness to the past. Such is the theory-forming response the map as memory theater stages. "[T]hat is what the meaning of history comes to: scenes," Michel Serres says, adding, "[s]cenes, and thus sites, from which to see representations."[11]

It goes without saying that Mather had a deeper reason for recounting those glorious days in which the ship of New England weathered many terrible storms—and for spelling out the illustrious line of governors at its helm—than that of celebrating the triumphal "history of its Deliverances." Already at the time of his *Magnalia Christi Americana,* the ship metaphor itself served to indicate troubled waters, for the political and cultural grip of allegory on American space was rapidly slipping away. Mather, therefore, may have decided to return to historical foundations in order to react to the critical moment through which New England was passing. By 1709, with the publication of his jeremiad *Theopolis Americana,* his sense of "the Land of Unwalled Villages" was stridently vivid.[12]

The streets of New England's towns were running free: "It is but an easy metonyme, to make the STREET, signify the men that fill the Street."[13] The towns, it seems, were no longer able to control the coming and going of the people or, more importantly, their doings and desires. Thus, at the beginning of his address Mather exhorts, "The *Street* be in thee, O New-England; The interpretation of it, be unto you, O American Colonies."[14] Men and women, it seems, were living beyond themselves and their means. Usury was a common practice and immorality rampant. "They won't take in a reef of their sails tho' they are on the point of suffering ship-wreck," Mather complains. In the following passage he keeps up the biblical comparison, but with a show of considerable exasperation: "Ah, how will the Golden City cease to be such . . . except that flood of iniquity be dried up! A flood, which the dragon has cast out of his mouth, to devour the church in the wilderness!"[15] Certainly, his congregation still harbored a chilling vision of the Atlantic flood that the founding generation suffered in that first winter of their arrival. Mather's metaphor was undoubtedly fitting, but it remained snagged in allegory. Given the Puritans' backsliding, it was time to counter with an evocation of Boston's utopian beginnings. For Mather's Holy City was already an allegory in ruins, and on his map the names of church-steepled English towns also represented its scattering. It was time to return to beginnings and account for the very process of scattering.

In his first major romance, *The Scarlet Letter*, Nathaniel Hawthorne returned to the foundational moment of colonial Boston to tell the story of a free-spirited, slightly "Americanized" woman named Hester Prynne, who passes from the untamed spaces of the forest to the patriarchal order of Boston without acknowledging their difference. In the marketplace, she and her "mystic symbol" (the scarlet letter *A*) are as prodigal as "the swarthy-cheeked wild men of the ocean" and "the wild" Indians. As for her daughter Pearl, whose "native audacity" betrayed "a nature wilder than . . . the wild Indian," her every action presages Boston's ruin.[16] At the very outset, Hawthorne's narrator slyly associates Hester with a quintessentially Atlantic-world plant, apple of peru. Again and again, we see her and her love child Pearl out of doors, walking down a forest path, pausing in a meadow, sitting near a running brook, or passing through the marketplace of Boston in the wee hours. Ordered by the town magistrate to wear the letter *A*, adulterous Hester is free to circulate at all hours, like an unbefriended stray. But Hester's narrative brings us to the heart of the trouble of Mather's Boston, for she emblematically expresses a new, peculiarly Atlantic freedom—a freedom that Hawthorne exposes by exploring the heteronomic spaces of Mather's map and imploding its dominant scale of zipped-up English towns. In this case study of Boston's utopian generation, Hester Prynne exemplifies the leveling restlessness of the Atlantic world, and Hawthorne alludes to this theme by associating her ever so artfully with a plant common to the Americas but originating in Peru. For us, it is both a minimal and maximal sign encrypted in the scarlet *A* Hester is compelled to wear at all times. By following it around in Hawthorne's romance, we come to realize that Hester, too, is a creature of the Atlantic world.

There is a passage in Herman Melville's novel *Moby-Dick* that alludes to the suppression of heterodoxy during the English colonial period and the sense of a haunted land to which this has led. It is worth quoting in full: "If hereafter any highly cultural, poetical nation shall lure back to their birthright, the merry May-day gods of old; and livingly enthrone them again in the now egotistical sky; on the now unhaunted hill; then be sure . . . the great Sperm Whale shall lord it."[17] Almost overtly, the old "May-day gods" and the "egotistical sky" betray Melville's close familiarity with his friend Hawthorne's work; while the phrase "on the now unhaunted hill" recalls to mind John Winthrop's glorious vision of the city on a hill as well as the incipit of *The Scarlet Letter* proper, where we are told about Boston's utopian foundations—and how the town became unhaunted.

The title of chapter 1 of Hawthorne's masterpiece is "The Prison-Door" and it is with the activity of opening and closing that stories of utopia inevitably begin.[18] As William Bradford recounted the process in his history *Of Plymouth Plantation,* first the unattended soil was claimed and taken over, and then it was properly divided up. Like More's narrator Hythloday in *Utopia,* Hawthorne's narrator does not recount the initial scene of takeover. But it goes without saying that the land had to be seized before it could be distributed among the settlers and put to the plow so that in time wild nature would be transformed into a reflection of the colonists' new spatial and political order. One portion was set aside for a cemetery and another for the prison. At this point Hawthorne's narrator adds an almost negligible geographical aside: "In accordance with this rule, it may be safely assumed that the forefathers of Boston had built the first prison-house, somewhere in the vicinity of Corn-hill" (38). By this we are led to think that perhaps the prison site was once a field where local Indians grew or stored corn. (In *Mourt's Relation* of 1622, we are told of how the *Mayflower* pilgrims availed themselves of the natives' corn fields when they first landed off Cape Cod.) So even if the descriptive place-name Corn-hill remains, religious orthodoxy eventually ruled "on the now unhaunted hill."

Another of *The Scarlet Letter*'s inadvertent signs suggests that Boston had not yet completely banished "the merry May-day gods of old," for the prison's perimeters are still seedy with burdock, pigweed, "apple-peru," a wild rose bush, and other "unsightly vegetation" (38). Such a list of "weeds" discloses the sensibility of an Atlantic-world colonial gardener, but it also implies that no matter how sacred the rage for order may be, the task of weeding is evidently futile. First the place-name Corn-hill, now an allusion to a flower supposedly originating in South America and named "apple-peru." Of course, we have no way of knowing what Hawthorne had in mind by including this specific flower in his list, but *The Scarlet Letter* is a romance and not a novel. Such details of "the prison's perimeters" are hardly gratuitous. Perhaps, through a metonymic ploy the narrator merely wanted to associate his wayward heroine to undomesticated, if not exotic, surroundings. Closer investigation indicates that apple of peru was also known as the equally common plant called jimson weed (*Datura stramonium*), a corruption of "Jamestown-weed"—the latter name deriving from a mass poisoning of British soldiers in Jamestown, Virginia, in 1676. Supposedly, they added apple of peru leaves to their salad and suffered the consequences.

For a brief period in the sixteenth century, apple of peru was popularly considered an aphrodisiac–thus its name *Poma amoris,* or love apple.[19] Further investigation of the plant's history only deepens its circumatlantic presence. While this member of the nightshade family is very likely a native of Peru, the original home of the tomato family, it also has many common names that lead elsewhere: devil's apple, devil's weed, mad apple, devil's trumpet, stink weed, and jimsonweed. Pertaining to the tomato family because of the form of its fruit, "apple-peru" was frequently associated with the devil. Indeed, it not only produces attractive purple flowers but is also hallucinogenic. If ingested, it can cause nightmarish visions and temporary sickness. In folk medicine it has been used to treat madness, epilepsy, and melancholy.[20]

For atlanticists, "apple-peru," which *The Scarlet Letter*'s narrator pointedly includes among the identifiable weeds around colonial Boston's prison door, serves as a fitting emblem of Hester's character. Botanists point out that the plant is anthropogenic and multiplies quickly in man-made habitats or waste areas. When cultivated, apple of peru is called angel's trumpet, thereby confirming the reigning colonial dichotomy between the "wilderness" as the devil's territory—apple of peru as devil's trumpet—and the New England town as God's presence in North America. What makes Hester such an interesting character is that she straddles the threshold between town and wild nature throughout Hawthorne's narrative; associated metonymically with "apple-peru" as she is led from the prison to the scaffold in Boston's central square, she is both devil's trumpet and angel's trumpet. The ambiguity surrounding her is a quintessentially Atlantic-world twist.

In his now classic study *Essai sur le don* of 1925, a book so central to inter-civilizational encounters in the circumatlantic world, Marcel Mauss sought to identify "a heuristic principle" in archaic societies that could penetrate to "the hearts of the masses" (of his day) and understand their "common interest."[21] This principle, which took the form of the gift, had to embrace "'total' social phenomena," where "everything intermingles in them."[22] The gift principle enabled Mauss to explain what binds these societies together and allows them to live in civil accord. In an important rereading of Mauss's essay, the anthropologist Marshall Sahlins argued that the gift economy was nothing more than a peaceful means of fighting war. He further notes, "The primitive analogue of social contract is not the State, but the gift."[23] In North America, Native American peoples used gift diplomacy in an attempt to make European settlers their allies, if not to incorporate them into their polity.

Without an understanding of the gift's "system of total services"[24] it may be impossible to fathom the haunted colonial and imperial histories of Africa and the Americas. Mauss explains his sense of the gift perspective as follows:

> [W]e shall arrive at conclusions of a somewhat archeological kind concerning the nature of human transaction in societies around us, or that have immediately preceded our own. . . . As we shall note that this [gift] morality and organization still function in our own societies, in unchanging fashion and, so to speak, hidden, below the surface, and as we believe that in this we have found one of the human foundations on which our societies are built, we shall be able to deduce a few moral conclusions concerning certain problems posed by the crisis in our own law and economic organization.[25]

The immediate importance of this archaeological delving lies in its illumination of the formal relations between primal intercivilizational scenes of early modern colonial history (like that between Columbus and the Guanahani discussed in chapter 6) and later foundational narratives such as Hawthorne's

The Scarlet Letter. By looking at temporally distant moments as different strata of a common set of practices, Mauss sought to overcome the evolutionary view that premodern societies are merely outdated throwbacks of their more progressive counterparts of today. As Mauss suggests, the gift is a morphological constant that is as relevant to contemporary society as it once was to the Kwakiutl and Tlingit peoples of the American Northwest or Powhatan's federation around Chesapeake Bay. In *The Scarlet Letter* Hawthorne chose to revisit the founding moment of colonial Boston from his own perspective rooted in Jacksonian New England. He juxtaposed the two moments, making them spatially rather than linearly related. For that matter, Hester Prynne belongs as much to Puritan Boston as she does to the Boston of Hawthorne's day. As Mauss claims, the gift impulse is "hidden, below the surface" in every one of us and remains an essential feature of contemporary society.

The aim of Mauss's *Essai* was quite modest. He simply wanted to know what it is that compels people not so much to give but to give in return. It is true that he referred to the gift principle as a spirit—adopting the very names given to it by those in the societies he studied: *hau, mana, kula.* At one point, when discussing the Maori idea of *hau,* he even describes it as an atmosphere.[26] In modern societies the realm of gift exchange is distinct from the realms of the market and the state but just as important. Apart from the object that is put into circulation, what is risked in the gift economy is nothing less than one's identity.[27] To illustrate this crucial distinction, let us now return to Hawthorne's *The Scarlet Letter,* where the three realms of the market, the state, and the gift all lay claim to the letter *A* that Hester Prynne is condemned to wear as an outward sign of libidinous free love or, if you will, adultery. These conflicting and often overlapping claims also involve various attempts to control the symbolic order of the letter itself, which provides us with a forceful example of the method of the total social fact and the gift as saturated object.

At the beginning of his essay, Mauss insists: "In these 'total' social phenomena . . . all kinds of institutions are given expression at one and the same time—religious, juridical, and moral, which relate to both politics and the family; likewise economic ones, which suppose special forms of production and consumption, or rather, of performing total services and of distribution. [And one should also mention] the aesthetic phenomena to which these facts lead, and the contours of the phenomena that these institutions manifest."[28] The symbolic order of Hawthorne's scarlet letter is, I shall argue, coextensive with the workings of the gift economy outlined above. As a gift tale, his romance not only foregrounds the thematic of solidarity and intermingling (whereby even the threshold between town and wilderness becomes indistinct) but does so in such a way as to undermine the economy of salvation commonly attributed to the Puritan narrative of New England's origins.

Hester Prynne first appears in the second chapter of the romance, titled "The Market-Place." Chapter 1, "The Prison-Door," establishes the theme and setting of the political realm of law and order so essential to an always troubled colonial outpost. Hester emerges from the prison and appears in the midst of the crowd, which the narrator surveys and overhears even before Hester is brought onto the scene. Setting in this romance is intrinsically encoded with the town's fundamental order, although it cannot defend itself from such aggressive and self-sowing weeds as apple of peru. Also, this introductory presentation of the multitude—"a whole people" (49)—is in keeping with the collective (or anti-individualistic) structure of identity in Puritan society. This structure is further confirmed by the spatial layout of the scene, which is ordered vertically and reflects the authoritarian disposition of male power in Boston in the 1640s. It also reflects the confining space of community that encircles Hester as she walks through the crowd. Hester is led from the weedy site of the prison to a raised scaffold that is part of "a penal machine" (44), the purpose of which is to promote "good citizenship" (44). The beadle leads her there with the words "Come along, Madame Hester, and show your scarlet letter in the market-place!" (43).

The site of exchange and intermingling par excellence, the marketplace is the space most tightly controlled by the Puritan fathers assembled on the balcony of the meetinghouse directly above the scaffold where Hester stands. A "living sermon against sin" (49), she is the object of everyone's gaze, "a sad spectacle" (48) but "not without a mixture of awe" (44) and fascination. Overwhelmed by the scene, Hester casts her eyes down on the scarlet letter, and when she touches it to convince herself that her infant and her shame are indeed real, "all else had vanished!" (46). So while the crowd makes a spectacle of Hester, Hester makes a spectacle of the scarlet *A*. She dramatically invests her identity in its iconographic force and through it apparently gives herself up fully to the ritual of banishment and the role of scapegoat. The narrator, too, indulges in the scene's religious potential: "Had there been a Papist among the crowd of Puritans, he might have seen in this beautiful woman, . . . with the infant at her bosom, an object to remind him of the image of Divine Maternity" (44). The image of herself that Hester presents to the crowd is recognizably that of the Madonna with child of Christian tradition, but it is now totally secular.[29]

As so often happens in Hawthorne, we are immediately presented with the other side "of that sacred image of sinless motherhood," for here "there was the deepest sin in the most sacred quality of human life" (44). In fact, Hester's scarlet letter confirms the fact that her maternal body "remains a constant factor of social reality."[30] Hester, therefore, represents a complex spectacle of the colony's evolving tensions. She is both the ideal and the bad mother, religious and cultural icon as well as a natural and erotic one—apple of peru at the prison door. But in spite of such interminglings, the spectacle of the letter *A* points unambiguously to the political sphere that assigns Hester to her banished status—namely, that of the timeless figure of *homo sacer* or the segregated realm of bare life.[31]

In *The Scarlet Letter* Hester and Dimmesdale, the minister who is responsible for punishing her, are correlative figures. In the penultimate chapter, which narrates Dimmesdale's final agony on the scaffold as a form of *passio Christi* and depicts Hester in the supportive role of the Virgin Mary, we can construe them as competing for our attention—in the same way that Thomas Aquinas considered the Virgin's power as rivaling that of Christ's.[32] What Aquinas says of Jesus's mother also holds true of Hester and her relation to the ever popular Reverend Dimmesdale: "She possessed extraordinary gifts but could not use them publicly since it would detract from Christ's teaching."[33] In addition, as the philosopher Giorgio Agamben points out, "[T]he sovereign is the one with respect to whom all men [here, all women] are potentially *homines sacri,* and *homo sacer* [here Hester] is the one with respect to whom all men act as sovereigns."[34] As Hawthorne's narrator puts it, "The very law that condemned her . . . had held her up, through the terrible ordeal of her ignominy" (59). In the first scene in the marketplace, Hester is included in the juridical order of Boston only in the form of her exclusion. Lovers, Agamben notes, are often thought of as sacred "because they have separated themselves from other people in a sphere beyond both divine and human law."[35]

In Puritan Boston, Hester's bare life—her "natural life" (49)—must be politically and culturally controlled. In a telling passage the narrator clarifies the juridical effects of her holy (*sacer*) status: "With her native energy of character, [the world] could not entirely cast her off, although it had set a mark upon her. . . . Every gesture, every word, and even the silence of those with whom she came in contact, implied . . . that she was banished, and as much alone as if she inhabited another sphere . . . than the rest of human kind" (63). The ban leveled against her—and potentially against all women in Puritan Boston—marks her with the status of victim. According to the logic of sacrificial exchange,[36] Hester will buy back her purity through her long-suffering labor in the community (61). At one point toward the end of the romance, she says to Dimmesdale, "Surely, surely, we have ransomed one another, with all this woe!" (181).

At the end of Hawthorne's narrative, in fact, Hester returns from abroad to her old house on the outskirts of the town, and the narrator hints that by doing so she is acknowledging a cosmic order that does not allow for flight. But she has crossed the Atlantic at least three times and tried to get Dimmesdale to run off with her. Her transatlantic mobility and undaunted behavior identify her with the unruly European multitudes who began pouring into the Americas in the sixteenth century. Moreover, her life on the outskirts suggests she remains more "American" than colonial Puritan. *The Scarlet Letter*'s investment in an archaic form of the gift economy may help to account for the circular ending of Hester's life and the claim that she has internalized the Puritan model of the economy of salvation, but the motives of obligation and debt do not sufficiently explain Hester's complex relationship to the scarlet letter. For Hawthorne also superimposes a more recent cultural order on his romance, to which we can trace two other gift motives that also direct her actions—giving freely and spontaneously, and disinterested giving. Taken together, these four gift motives (obligation, interest, donation, disinterested giving) make up what Alain Caillé considers the gift circle's paradigmatic options.[37] Their coming together in Hester helps to explain the symbolic complexity of the gift principle in Hawthorne's romance. Banned from Boston's community of saints for having given her love freely to Dimmesdale, she continues to give spontaneously and freely, the very same way that Native Americans often did in their dealings with the English colonists.

In order to take up the second set of motives—giving freely and without interest—let us first consider the matter of the letter *A*'s color. In a scene where everyone from the governor and the clergy to the assembled crowd are dressed in "sable simplicity" (61), Hester sports a beautifully decorated scarlet *A* "surrounded with an elaborate embroidery and fantastic flourishes of gold thread" (42). Apart from a brief treatment of it in "The Custom-House," where the letter first comes to light, the romance's well-known theme of art originates from this passage and strikingly captures the disinterested energy of self-donation that Hester expresses through it. When she appears with the scarlet letter in public the first time, her attire "made a halo of the misfortune and ignominy in which she was enveloped" (43). But Hester's embellished *A* also hides a subversive, antinomian will.

As the gossip going around about Hester increases, the letter's meanings begin to multiply. It comes to stand for the badge of her suffering, her ability, her art, her charity, her mercy, her angelic nature, and, inevitably, "the general symbol . . . of woman's frailty and sinful passion" (59). But while Hester's spirit may seem subdued in public, "the faculties of animal life remained entire" (53). It is this animal life that she must sacrifice to the patriarchal and theological order of Boston, and from within this order the scarlet letter represents a sacrificial offering of her own "animal" blood, the blood of her "lawless passion" (120). To be sure, the scarlet letter stands for more than the economy of sacrifice, as Hester herself will bear out. And we have already noted that apple of peru acts as a metonym for her own potentiality. (Toward the end, she expresses her eagerness to escape back to England or even westward, into the American wilderness, if Dimmesdale will agree to join her.)

Hawthorne borrows from the genre of hagiography (the lives of saints) in order to place Hester's vertiginous spirit both within and outside of the cultural confines of Puritan theocracy. Not only is it rumored that she wears a halo, but "her daily shame would at length purge her soul, and work out another purity than that which she had lost; more saint-like, because the result of martyrdom" (61). The golden thread around the scarlet letter seems almost naturally to entwine the reader in Jacobus da Voragine's ever popular *Legenda Aurea*, perhaps the most famous devotional treatise of saints' lives ever printed. By mentioning several times that the scarlet letter was embroidered "with gold thread" (46), the narrator posits Hester as a figure belonging to Voragine's hallowed lives. But the "American" Hester is larger than the narrator's (or Cotton Mather's) allegorical machinations. Her spatial wanderings and dwelling place put her in a different world altogether. As rumors about her activities in the city begin to emerge through gossip and innuendo, we are also faced with a symbolic order that gathers around the letter *A*.

Already in the first scene set in the marketplace, when the Reverend Dimmesdale is confronted with Hester's refusal to name the father of her child, he is forced to marvel, "Wondrous strength and generosity of a woman's heart!" (53). As Françoise Meltzer has noted, "A successful saint does not overcome the body; he or she uses it as a pure vehicle for expressing *caritas*, if it means self-sacrifice, through what Voragine continually refers to as 'the crown': martyrdom."[38] In this sense Hester's dramatic act of self-exposure on the scaffold represents the stuff of a golden legend. The narrator insists more than once, "She was patient,—a martyr, indeed" (64); although he also adds, "The vulgar . . . had a story about the scarlet letter which we might readily work up into a terrible legend" (66). It is impossible to limit Hester's boundless significance to Puritan orthodoxy.

As hagiography, her story can be divided into two narrative threads: the time of trial and the time of glorification. In the first scaffold scene Hester is put on trial and made into a public spectacle. The narrator says she is "outlawed" (143) and condemned to live a life of grinding atonement. Accepting her abjection, Hester apparently submits to an economy of salvation based on sacrifice. But as "the symbol of her calling" (117), the scarlet *A* also endows her with "a new sense"—"it gave her a sympathetic knowledge of the hidden sin in other hearts" (65). The time of glorification, therefore, begins from the very moment of her first appearance on the scaffold and runs parallel to the temporality of trial. These two times overlap and reinforce the structural split in the *A* itself. In effect, the letter symbolically connects the order of appearance (Hester's daily life in and around colonial Boston) to a literally outstanding order of Being (beyond Puritan governance). The letter's legendary power derives not only from the relation between these two orders but also from their difference.

According to Michel de Certeau, "Saints are individuals who lose nothing of what was initially given to them."[39] Hawthorne's narrator understands this but, as his conservative comments in the conclusion indicate, he does not want to accept it. The butt of gossip both early and late in the romance, Hester's legendary reputation is the effect of the political and gendered codes that envelop her. The gossip of the women gathered in the marketplace in the opening scene is both negative and positive, depending on where they stand in relation to Boston's theocratic order: "She hath good skill at her needle, that's certain . . . , but did ever a woman before this brazen hussy, contrive such a way of showing it! Why, gossips, what is it but to laugh in the faces of our godly magistrates, and make a pride out of what they . . . meant for punishment?" (43). But a younger companion sees things differently and "whispers" this objection: "O, peace, neighbors, peace! . . . Not a stitch in that embroidered letter, but she has felt it in her heart" (43).

If we read such gossip as a further allusion to the script of Hester's martyr-dom, then the scarlet letter must also be construed as stitched in blood. But in the genre of hagiography, "[blood] is a metaphor for grace" (276). As a whole, the above gossip alludes to both the time of trial (of scorn and humiliation) and that of glorification. Both conform to the representation of Hester's life as that of a New World saint's. But if hagiography is above all based on a discourse of virtues, then it is a very peculiar notion of grace that leads to Hester's incoronation. For as the gossips in the marketplace have indicated, Hester's grace has to do with her special way of showing it. Her outstanding order of Being may not have anything to do with Boston at all; instead, it may represent the desires, reveries, and intentions of an invisible community of women both inside and outside of Boston's city limits: in short, a community of "American" women removed from their mother country, England.

As we have seen on Mather's map of New England, Boston's fundamental order manifests itself in the political, economic, and cultural control of space. All of these factors intersect in the symbol of the scarlet letter and lead to its splitting—not unlike the multiple meanings of apple of peru. Thus, the *A* stands for the reassertion of the magistrates' authority, a marked form of cir-culation in economic space, and a censored libidinous identity within Puritan society. Living on the edge of town, she straddles the threshold between the North American wilderness and British colonial culture. Under such con-ditions the scarlet letter undoubtedly represents Boston's severe patriarchal order. Hester lives with a ban over her head; she is silenced and without sov-ereignty. The narrator himself defines her as set apart when he says, "It [the letter *A*] imparted to the wearer a kind of sacredness, which enabled her to walk securely amid all peril" (118). In other words, within the space of the city, she is without place, without identity, and without rights. And yet, for this very reason—the reason of her "lawless passion" (120)—the scarlet letter be-comes "her passport" (143), allowing her to go wherever she wills, at all hours of the day and night. Marked with a ban, she can legitimately represent "the whole race of womanhood" and ask its fundamental question: "Was existence worth accepting, even to the happiest among them?" (120).

The question is ontologically radical in that it concerns nothing less than women's subaltern "position" (120) or, depending on one's point of view, non-position in colonial Boston's patriarchal society. Hester's own standpoint is manifest, she had "a home and comfort nowhere" (120), and this leads her to contemplate suicide. Expressing Boston's point of view, the narrator remarks,

"The scarlet letter had not done its office" (120). Indeed, for Hester the scarlet letter is "the token, not of that one sin, for which she had borne so long and dreary a penance, but of her many good deeds since" (118). On one hand, these good deeds seem to make her a "guarantor of the community";[40] on the other, they unite her to "a mystic sisterhood" (65) embodying transgressive desires, liberating laughter, and subversive thoughts. Apparently, this circle is "mystic" because there is little concrete evidence that such a sisterhood exists. When the narrator tries to describe it, he uses such words as "sympathetic throb," "electric thrill," and "momentary glance" (65). The evidence for this sisterhood is ultimately based on gossip and nightly visits to the sick. It has nothing to do with the Puritan economy of salvation. The narrator considers this sisterhood politically impossible, but he represents it all the same, as discursively manifest through Hester's golden legend. Hagiography, therefore, becomes the conduit for the symbolic power not only of the gift economy but, more specifically, of the pure gift—a form of giving that does not expect anything in return.

As I have been arguing, *The Scarlet Letter* illustrates a symbolically split foundational narrative that characterizes the central dilemma of Puritan culture in colonial North America. In this context, it also asks us to reflect deeply on the nature of Hester's gift. In his book *Donner le temps* Jacques Derrida argues that if the gift appears, then it is already not the gift spirit itself, but something else, something given. John Caputo and Michael Scanlon sum up Derrida's position as follows: "The gift is this impossible thing, or no thing, which we love and desire, in which we hope, for which we maintain a daily faith."[41] The pure gift is "a faith in the gift to come."[42] Ultimately, the gift is an event, an "experience of the impossible," Derrida would say, and it is precisely because of this impossibility that "we go on dreaming or thinking of pure hospitality."

The legend that has grown up around Hester and her scarlet letter is essentially a popular legend, namely a legend whose authority comes from the people and exists essentially in oral form. In *The Scarlet Letter* the narrator mostly weaves this legend out of "gossip," and this gossip—essentially a form of "we-speak" among women—concerns the *res gestae* of Hester as she circulates gracefully through the community, helping and sympathizing with those who summon her out of need. The narrator may freely interpret these charitable acts but their authority undeniably derives from their legendary status. When he first comes upon the letter in the introductory chapter, "The

Custom-House," he certifies the skill that went into its making by deferring to women of his acquaintance: "[T]he stitch (as I am assured by ladies *conversant* with such mysteries) gives evidence of a now forgotten art" (27, my emphasis). Even the foolscap sheets written by the old surveyor Mr. Pue, which are now the source of the narrator's own revived narrative gifts, are said to be based on the "oral testimony" (28) of old people who remembered Hester Prynne in their youth. In these same sheets Mr. Pue provides particulars not only about Hester's life but also about her "conversation" (28).

The narrator is also forthright in confessing his own hedged relation to what he essentially defines as a gift tale: "[B]ut how it was to be worn, or what rank, honor, and dignity, in by-past times, were signified by it, was a riddle" (27–28). All this mystery surrounding the scarlet letter's status leads him to call it a "mystic symbol" (28), which is his equivalent to what Mauss, with equally fuzzy charm, would later call the gift spirit. But it should be noted that both symbol and spirit are very much rooted in local place, in a town pinched in between a daunting Atlantic Ocean and an endless "wilderness" inhabited by Native American peoples. As Certeau helpfully points out, the life of a saint is a composition of places and conventionally originates in a founding place that has become a liturgical site.[43] Hester's Boston is the foundational center of colonial New England. Her saintly life and the mystical circle of women it alludes to concern a truth that is a place. On the other hand, a saint's life is above all a spiritual place, whose "meaning is a place which is not a place."[44] This is a fitting analogue for the paradoxical status of the pure gift. Hester's "mystic sisterhood" is a nonplace in Boston, although gossip informs us that it takes place.

Rumor and gossip confirm the effects of Hester's good works, although we can only infer this horizon of donation from a habitus widely attributed to her. If she has gained the reputation of being a sister of mercy, it is because she has presumably been circulating as one. She goes around the city freely and at all hours, and this performance of her office describes what is in effect a gendered gift circle. The "mystic sisterhood" is founded on intimate knowledge of the human heart to which her office has apprenticed her. The rounds she makes as a sister of mercy describe an invisible circle, and we have no reason to deny that this circle represents a covert sisterhood of women who share Hester's apple of peru status. As Certeau reminds us, "The Life of a Saint is inscribed within the life of a group."[45] You cannot have one without the other. Legend is a form of spiritual credit pertaining to the general economy of giving, receiving, and giving in return. It, too, implies a community of women. For Boston's patriarchs, the common name of "apple-peru" is undoubtedly devil's trumpet, but for Hester and her mystic sisterhood, it is also angel's trumpet. For that matter, it is the women who traditionally traffic in folk medicine based on wild plants. Apple of peru, when used as a medicine, is psychoactive. It can turn mere friendship into free love.

And what about surveyor Pue's mention of "particulars"? We are given only scattered snippets of gossip and no actual presentation of Hester's encounters as a sister of mercy. Thus her virtues (like those of apple of peru) are truly hidden. But "gossip" should not be belittled. It also represents an agency and a formal locus. The conversation that we can impute to Hester recalls the root meaning of the Latin word *conversatio*, from the past participle *converso*, the iterative form of *converto* (meaning *I frequent*, or *I often turn to*). Originally, the word conversation meant simply to get together or frequent a common place. As Rocco Ronchi points out, "To converse means to inhabit a common place. Only those who feel they share a common dwelling can, in fact, talk among themselves in a free and courteous manner."[46]

In the days of Voragine's medieval saints, *conversatio* evoked the totality of those things that perennially held a social group together: a common place, shared habits, and a way of being together that took for granted not only words and gestures but also desires and expectations.[47] If we read Hester's golden legend pragmatically, according to Mauss's total social fact, then we must expect the scarlet letter's office to embrace heart, mind, body, and hearth. Hearth, it should be noted, is the originary space of the vernacular—*vernaculum* meaning "relative to slaves born in the house"[48]—which indicates common usage and is therefore used only within the domestic sphere. In Mauss's words, such total services represent an intermingling: "Souls are mixed with things; things with souls. Lives are mingled together, and this is how, among persons and things so intermingled, each emerges from their own sphere and mixes together."[49] Here, it should be said, Mauss is talking about the gift circle as a manifest economy, while we began our discussion by entertaining the nonphenomenality of Hester's gift circle.

In effect, all four of the gift motives mentioned above inform the office of the scarlet letter. If Hester is juridically an outlaw in Boston but still able to circulate freely and gain access to its private homes and public buildings, it is because she has no rights while atoning for the sin of adultery. But as the rumor of a "mystic sisterhood" implies, the gift spirit also has a subversive side to it, which the narrator refers to as a form of knowledge or empathy. Empowered by the symbolic order of the scarlet letter, which feeds off of the biopolitical fact of her banishment, Hester is able to read other people's minds and hearts. These minds and hearts belong to "an already existing, available pool of outsiders"[50] who, along with Hester, hold open a space for the future refounding of Boston as a site of recommencement. It is, in part, Hester's mystic sisterhood that must have frightened Cotton Mather into writing his grand *Magnalia*. While waiting for this community of outsiders to emerge as insiders, we must settle for apple of peru growing outside Boston's prison door.

By means of the special power of the scarlet letter, Hester is able to gain access to a space of different subject(ive) possibilities beyond those culturally sanctioned by a Puritan theology of sacrifice. This space, too, pertains to Hester's golden legend and to the letter *A*, where wild nature and gardened culture converge to create a complex symbolic structure. Such knowledge as Hester's represents the gift in all its purity and a gift circle that remains largely invisible to patriarchal eyes. This gift spirit links the crisis embodied in the scarlet letter to a general societal crisis represented by the "mystic sisterhood" that prophetically redesigns social relations as Puritan Boston then knew them.[51] In the city that has banned her, the nonplace of Hester's gift practices is paradoxically a discourse of place. In Boston everything she does seems to turn into gossip. For this reason Hawthorne uses a scenic approach to Hester's gifted life. As Wittgenstein notes, "There are, indeed, things that cannot be put into words. They make themselves manifest. They are what is mystical."[52] Culture creates not only its own internal organization but also its own kind of external disorganization.[53] And it is this supposedly unstructured, nonsignifying space that intimates the space of another sign system, that of Hester's "golden love" (184), which radiates well beyond the confines of that troubled colonial town described by Cotton Mather in *Magnalia Christi Americana*. And so we return to where we began, to Hester's "mystic badge" (174–75) and apple of peru at the prison door.

5

"A Refugee from History"

Douglass's Heroic Slave in the Atlantic World

For the horrors of the American Negro's life there has been almost no language. The privacy of his experience . . . is only beginning to be recognized in language. . . . [T]he truth about the black man, as a historical entity and as a human being, *has* been hidden from him, deliberately and cruelly; the power of the white world is threatened whenever a black man refuses to accept the white world's definitions.
  —James Baldwin, *Down at the Cross*

Now a well-known part of Frederick Douglass's works, his complex narrative "The Heroic Slave" (1853) deals with a major slave mutiny at sea and related scenes from the life of its inspiring leader, Madison Washington. The feat of this African American version of the acclaimed freedom fighter George Washington flashed like lightning across the skies of the United States, the Caribbean, and England for a brief moment in December of 1841. Then, just as suddenly, this heroic figure disappeared into the uncharted life of black Nassau, a slavery-free British protectorate in the Bahamas. Bowing to contemporary newspaper accounts, historians have referred to the event as the *Creole* mutiny.[1] The only official documents we have of this successful uprising off the coast of Abaco (in the Bahamas) are the depositions of the white sailors who were on the *Creole* when nineteen slaves led by Madison Washington rose up and took command of the ship. But we also know from several of Douglass's speeches that he drew upon oral history sources for the biographical parts of "The Heroic Slave." We also have transcripts of the court cases involving the insurance companies and the owners of the 135 slaves who wanted to recover their losses after the British governor in Nassau refused to return the "mutineers and murderers" to the United States, a plethora of newspaper accounts from across the United States and abroad, and documents and correspondence dealing with the diplomatic tensions between the United States and England.

Due largely to the rising influence of Atlantic studies in the academy, a once marginal and totally neglected text of United States literary history has now become an important Atlantic-world *exemplum*. But it is owing to the efforts of Atlantic historians that the *Creole* mutiny and other circumatlantic slave revolts have taken on a new relevance.[2] In my reading of "The Heroic Slave" I will discuss the ways in which Douglass used the *Creole* mutiny to reinstate both Madison Washington and the figure of the heroic slave in mainstream US culture and history. The first task was biographical; the second, typological. In my opinion, his narrative is not so much a fictional novella tout court as something more manifold: a hybrid act of the historical imagination. Although a rebuttal to Stowe's *Uncle Tom's Cabin*, "The Heroic Slave" was written with a larger goal in mind—namely, to help create a black historical tradition. In order to appreciate better the Atlantic affinities between the so-called *Creole* affair and Douglass's narrative, I will also discuss the conditions of the text's composition, its exuberant narrative hybridity, and the unaddressed problem of what documents belong to a virtual *Creole* archive with circumatlantic import.

In the final part IV of "The Heroic Slave," Tom Grant—Douglass's *nom à clef* for Zephaniah Gifford, the *Creole's* first mate—stoutly asserts to a skeptical Jack Williams at a marine coffee house in Richmond, Virginia: "[S]ir, I deny that the negro is, naturally, a coward, or that your theory of managing slaves will stand the test of *salt* water. . . . It is . . . quite another thing to quell an insurrection on the lonely billows of the Atlantic, where every breeze speaks of courage and liberty."[3] It was common opinion among whites in both the North and the South that blacks were inferior beings. On the other hand, it was ideologically and psychologically necessary for whites in the South to portray black men as feckless, easily intimidated, and unmanly. But even then, slaveholders lived in constant fear of their bonded laborers, unable to forget the deeds of Denmark Vesey, Nat Turner, and General Dessalines's wholesale killing of whites in nearby Haiti.[4] A bit later in this same scene, Grant reports the following words directly from the mouth of Madison Washington: "Mr. mate, you cannot write the bloody laws of slavery on those restless billows. The ocean, if not the land, is free" (50).

The narrator of "The Heroic Slave" acts as a vicarious witness who testifies in behalf of Madison Washington on the basis of second-order archival evidence: "Glimpses of this great character are all that can now be presented. . . . Speaking of marks, traces, possibles, and probabilities, we come before our readers" (4–5). Undoubtedly, Douglass relied upon newspaper accounts, Senate documents, and diplomatic correspondence (all reported by the abolitionist press) when writing his account of the *Creole* mutiny. But more importantly, he also drew upon oral sources when delineating the biographical dimensions of his heroic slave—secondhand accounts from acquaintances, conversations with informants who met and conversed with the historical Madison Washington. In 1841 Douglass, a fugitive slave, had just begun his active involvement in the abolitionist cause as a speaker for William Lloyd Garrison's Massachusetts Anti-Slavery Society and, we learn from his speeches, was keenly inspired by Madison Washington and the *Creole* uprising. In the January 1842 report of the society, which Douglass would have read, we already have a full account of the event, including extensive newspaper coverage.[5] It is in the light of these and still other sources that his narrative stands as a close analogue of microhistory, a pointedly reconstructed case study tasked with the problems of marshaling documentary evidence controlled largely by a white supremacist culture. As both a historian and a literary scholar have recently noted, Douglass's narrative also became an archival source for further retellings by other writers, including William Wells Brown, Lydia Maria Child, and Pauline E. Hopkins.[6]

While these writers basically told the same story about Madison Washington, they labeled their efforts differently—as history, biography, and fiction, respectively. Though many scholars (in an outpouring of over twenty articles) have acknowledged the vexed status of Douglass's text, they do not fuss over calling it a novella or a historical fiction.[7] But this consensus is a gross simplification. Above all, because it fails to deal seriously with the historical and ideological context of the *Creole* mutiny, which for Douglass was a constitutive feature of "The Heroic Slave"—not just atmospheric context as the genre of historical fiction would suggest but immediate and competing cotext.[8] Perhaps the reason that scholars have not more steadfastly probed this dynamic relation is because they have miscalculated the powers and possibilities of the historical imagination at mid-nineteenth century. More complex than a novella or a historical fiction, Douglass's narrative shares with the case study an openness to different situations, circumstances, and experiences.[9]

One of its framing purposes, therefore, was to deal at the authorial level with the problem of historiographical evidence and white antebellum history writing. As Douglass understood all too well, the sailors' version of the "*Creole* affair" (as news coverage referred to their collective deposition given in New Orleans) could hardly serve as rock-bottom truth. This prejudicial mise en abyme of the uprising and Madison Washington's role in it has certainly contributed to the hybrid nature of Douglass's narrative approach to it. This and its challenging tangle of geocultural scales reaching from Virginia to Canada, back to Virginia, and then out into the Atlantic make "The Heroic Slave" an appealing document for historians and literary scholars alike. According to the historian Krzysztof Pomian, when a historical event such as the *Creole* mutiny and Douglass's important revisitation of it come together, thereby forming a highly condensed cultural site, then we have what he calls a *semiophor*.[10] In 1841, the *Creole* mutiny caused so many political, cultural, economic, judiciary, and historical issues to come crashing together in one flashpoint that a semiophor was formed. And that is what Madison Washington's heroic uprising became for Frederick Douglass in 1852.

The heroic slave's elusive whereabouts are many. Above all, there are his strictly biographical moves: he escapes to Canada from the slave state of Virginia, returns there to fetch his wife, is recaptured, and is then loaded onto a slave ship heading to New Orleans and the auction block. In a further move, he and eighteen others overpower the ship in international waters and have it brought to slave-free Nassau in the British Bahamas, where the slaves are set free and Washington disappears from public view. Another thread of Douglass's narrative traces an ideological and humanitarian theme involving the Atlantic-wide debate over the suppression of slavery and the slave trade. There is also a diplomatic thread (a series of sharp exchanges between England, Nassau, and the United States, followed by Lord Ashburton's hastily appointed ambassadorial mission to Washington, DC) and of foremost importance, a historiographical thread embroiling not only Douglass's narrator but Douglass and US historians as a class. Gathering up all these threads, the *Creole* slave ship itself becomes a highly condensed figure and historical semiophor. In short, it is this skein of entangled themes that makes it necessary to confide in multiple discursive genres when gauging the full effects of Douglass's narrative. Indeed what characterizes the case-study approach is that it foregrounds the embroiled nature of intersecting scales, one of the abiding conditions of atlanticist research practice.

Where, semiophorically speaking, do the various intersecting trajectories of Douglass's "The Heroic Slave" end? And in the case of the *Creole* mutiny, do they end in New Orleans? In Nassau? In London? In abolitionist Boston? In Washington, DC? Such complexities also inform Douglass's text, where competing values and forces are assigned four differently framed scenes of inquiry and testimony. In order to embrace them competently, we must re-sort to an even more contested concept, the as yet unformed *Creole* archive. In spite of the generic elusiveness of "The Heroic Slave," each documentary thread or thematic determination leads us to the contested oceanic order of the Atlantic world. Here again, the issue is not even about scale per se but about jumping from one scale to another: the biographical, the judiciary, the ideological, the political, the historiographical. All of these together create a web of intersecting regional, national, international, and circumatlantic scales. The way we assess this interplay will also affect not only our understanding of the conditions of the heroic slave's narrative representation but also his historical and cultural status. As for Douglass's own intentions in "The Heroic Slave," were they really just literary? Or, more purposefully, might he not have sought to embrace the embryonic black historical tradition as that was pitted against an official historiography grounded in notions of white supremacy? The hybrid nature of the narrative itself suggests even more possibilities, as we shall see below. Such are the hypotheses of this case study.

For several turbulent months from early December 1841 through June of 1842, Madison Washington became a household name in the United States, a mur-derer and mutineer to southern slaveholders and a hero to abolitionists in the North. The *Creole* mutiny took place on the Virginia slaver *Creole* off the coast of Abaco in the Bahamas on November 9, 1841. In the official Senate documents and newspaper accounts, Washington was portrayed as leader of the nineteen slaves who rose up and took control of the brig. As soon as he and the other 134 slaves were set free by the British authorities in Nassau, Washington quickly disappeared from the public record. Perhaps he went to Jamaica or may even have stayed on in Nassau. In spite of calls to learn more about this anonymous hero, Washington the man remained wrapped in mystery. In the latter half of 1852, conceivably spurred on by the success of Harriet Beecher Stowe's *Uncle Tom's Cabin,* an increasingly radicalized Frederick Douglass began writing a long narrative about Washington titled "The Heroic Slave." It was published in early January 1853, first in the gift book *Autographs for Freedom* (edited by Julia Griffiths) and then, after some further editing, in four installments in *Frederick Douglass' Paper*.[11]

Over the years, Douglass apparently kept Washington in the back of his mind, for he cited his example in at least eight speeches extending back to the mid-1840s. This protracted interest has led some Douglass scholars to read "The Heroic Slave" in light of the author's life. Accordingly, Douglass sought to mirror himself in Washington in an effort to celebrate his own conversion to righteous violence, the tradition of black radical abolitionism, and political abolitionism that he had previously shunned.[12] Here I would like to move beyond this prevailing autobiographical emphasis and discuss the relatively unsettled status of Douglass's narrative as an experimental mix of history, rhetoric, fictional reconstruction, and practical abolitionism.[13] Furthermore, its mix of contemporary documentary sources raises the larger, more elusive problem of Douglass's investment in the *Creole* mutiny as a bigoted archival formation.

After the Compromise of 1850 and the implementation of the Fugitive Slave Law by federal officers in the North, radical abolitionists began to raise the specter of slave insurrection and the figure of a black Spartacus.[14] Douglass found one in Madison Washington, whose once haunting presence he was determined to resuscitate.[15] On April 23, 1849, in a speech delivered at the Shiloh Presbyterian Church in New York, Douglass exclaimed to a mostly black audience: "Sir, I want to alarm the slaveholders, and not to alarm them by mere declamation or by mere bold assertions, but to show them that there is really danger in persisting in the crime of continuing Slavery in this land. I want them to know that there are some Madison Washingtons in this country . . . [and] the time may not be distant when the whole South will present again a scene something similar to the deck of the *Creole*."[16] But Douglass's own intentions for his narrative were complex and the challenges facing him many. Starting from this scene of writing means situating our reading of "The Heroic Slave" within the broader formation of a *Creole* archive with Atlantic-world inclusiveness. It is in this still ill-defined cross-disciplinary context that Douglass's narrative can be read as an important historical document in its own right—a document that throws new light on the racist deletions of antebellum historiography, the rising political tensions of the early 1850s, and the campaign to end slavery promoted by Britain and US abolitionists.

While it is accepted that Madison Washington is a historical figure, scrutiny of Douglass's own use of the historical record and his experimental revisitation of the *Creole* affair remain negligible. Given the secretive nature of some of Douglass's conversations with a handful of people who had met and helped Washington on his way to and from Canada, we can only guess at what the author might have known.[17] Once a fugitive himself, Douglass understood how important it was not to give away any information that might help the enemy.[18] This oral history dimension, however covert in the shaping of his prose experiment, certainly qualified his narrative strategy. But to what extent? As he settled down to writing "The Heroic Slave," Douglass—a renowned orator, newspaper editor, and by 1852, political abolitionist—became deeply immersed in the cultural politics of historical knowledge: what John Ernest has identified as an antebellum tradition of "African American liberation historiography."[19] Given his sustained interest in Washington as a black Spartacus, Douglass undoubtedly gathered additional biographical information about his hero's life before the *Creole* mutiny and beyond what appeared in the newspapers and other documents of the early 1840s.[20] There are many clues and tactics in "The Heroic Slave" itself to suggest he was drawing on a rich variety of sources to implement his ambitions for it. The recently published cultural and critical Yale edition of "The Heroic Slave," edited by Robert S. Levine, John Stauffer, and John R. McKivigan, will certainly change the way we approach Douglass's text, as it provides a suggestive constellation of sources that raises new questions about the fluid nature existing among the diverse kinds of documents relevant to Douglass's narrative.[21]

The Creole *Archive*

In the wake of this new edition, readers of what I suggest we call the *Creole* archive will henceforth have to revisit "The Heroic Slave" primarily in terms of the dynamic relation between history and fiction, the mediating role of rhetoric, the text as a form of testimony, and the international compass of its argument. While the Yale edition provides only a token sampling of sources related to the mutiny and Douglass's narrative, it courageously fosters a new archive-based context by enlarging the gambit of relevant documents. In particular, it returns readers to the primary scene of the *Creole* mutiny and the vexed issue of what documents might be said to belong to the *Creole* archive.

Once we set out to formalize this more comprehensive multidisciplinary milieu, we will also have to address the problematic nature of the *Creole* archive itself. For instance, the Yale edition of "The Heroic Slave" includes abridged samples of historical, judiciary, diplomatic, oratorical, journalistic, religious, and literary documents. But it fails to mention an equally important array of others, including correspondence, diplomatic exchanges, Senate debates, court documents from Louisiana, political and religious commentary, black abolitionist commentary, and a considerable number of British responses (depositions, legal briefs, newspaper accounts). Evidently, this edition is more of a casebook than an attempt to take on the larger issue of the *Creole* archive. In their introduction the editors make little effort to clarify the relation between their selections and the documentary pools from which they were lifted. Nevertheless, their casebook inevitably raises the critical issue of the *Creole* archive. In his important new study of Frederick Douglass's autobiographies, Robert Levine, one of the editors of the Yale edition of "The Heroic Slave," alludes to the idea of an archive in relation to his reading of Douglass's narrative, but he does not pursue it.[22]

As one might imagine, worrying over the expansiveness of a distinctly *Creole* archive is closely tied to specific practices of reading primarily associated with historians and literary critics. Scholars across the humanities naturally accumulate an array of sources on whatever topic they are studying, but they do not always explain what they are doing and why. In this case, method is merely the result of the scholarly journey once it is completed. Historians, of course, center their discipline on archival research. While there is a dominant positivist tradition underlying devotion to documents, those relevant to the *Creole* mutiny challenge the very notion of what a historical document is. Since Levine, Stauffer, and McKivigan take for granted that "The Heroic Slave" is a fiction, they include in their edition a number of other so-called fictions of Washington as interesting thematic variations on Douglass's narrative. And yet, as I have noted above, the stories of William Wells Brown, Lydia Maria Child, and Pauline E. Hopkins not only differ in status from each other but can hardly be lumped together simply as fictions.

Besides being considered a strictly literary performance, Douglass's narrative might just as effectively be inserted in an archival series that includes the "Addresses to the Slaves" of Gerrit Smith, William Lloyd Garrison, and Henry Highland Garnet.[23] Undoubtedly, interest in the rhetorical and narrative techniques of "The Heroic Slave" reflects an important reading practice, but too few literary critics have shown equal familiarity with the historical record of the *Creole* mutiny and its Atlantic reverberations.[24] As a whole, neither historians nor literary scholars have felt the need to reflect on the importance of formalizing the miscellaneous nature of the *Creole* archive and the place of Douglass's narrative in it. But it is Douglass himself who raises the archival issue in the opening *mis en cadre* of "The Heroic Slave." At the very outset his narrator-historian presents the scene of writing as a detached cautionary prologue to the discursive challenges he must face in resuscitating Washington's biography.[25]

The historian Carolyn Steedman provides an important caveat regarding archives that is worth mentioning here: "[N]othing starts in the Archive . . . though certain things certainly end up there. You find nothing in the Archive but stories caught half way through: the middle of things; discontinuities."[26] As he sought to revive Madison Washington's story and make him a haunting presence once again, Douglass necessarily became involved in prearchival maneuverings. This involvement, I would suggest, is where we need to start from when assessing his intentions in writing "The Heroic Slave." As Douglass sought ways to address the archival discontinuities and racist bigotry in the documentation of Washington's life, he came up against overwhelming problems. Today, we can gain a much better overview of the challenges Douglass was facing. But to acquire this view, we must above all return to the immediate historic scene of the *Creole* mutiny and reinsert "The Heroic Slave" among the diverse series of discursive genres composing its archive.

Allow me to insist, this archive should now include Senate and court documents (Louisiana Supreme Court and commercial court decisions); the New Orleans Protest (the *Creole* sailors' collective deposition); competing sets of depositions taken at Nassau (English and American); diplomatic exchanges between the Secretary of State Daniel Webster and the American ambassador in London Edward Everett, between Everett and the British foreign minister, and between Webster and Britain's special minister to the United States, Lord Ashburton; the battle of journalistic reportage between the slave South and the antislavery North; oratory (above all, by Douglass and other abolitionists such as Henry H. Garnet and Gerrit Smith); newspaper reprint culture; letters; biography and autobiography (particularly the second-generation slave narratives); testimony; antislavery society reports; reports from the black convention movement; political and legal articles on maritime treaties and maritime law; natural versus positive law; state versus federal law;

and oral history. As these diverse sources suggest, the *Creole* archive is much larger than either historians or literary scholars have so far acknowledged. But my point in listing such an extensive taxonomy is another: it is only from within the site of the *Creole* archive that Douglass's narrative becomes not only a historical "fiction" with abolitionist *coloritura* but also a crucial historical document belonging to the volatile continuum of sources assigned to an as yet rather inchoate *Creole* formation. Arguably, it is this historico-cultural-judiciary archive that will best accommodate the kind of cross-disciplinary reading of "The Heroic Slave" now encouraged by the new Yale edition.

Symptomatic of the experimental quality of Douglass's narrative is its essentially multigeneric, or generically promiscuous, nature—a fact that some scholars have readily acknowledged.[27] After mentioning the problematic status of the depositions of the white *Creole* sailors and the partisan nature of the newspaper accounts of the mutiny, both pro- and antislavery, Celeste-Marie Bernier discusses the central issues of intentionality and intertextuality in Douglass's narrative. But before doing so, she touches on the text's "historical ambiguities" and "generic instability," both of which help to undercut the very notion of a foundational "history" of the *Creole* mutiny and Madison Washington's role in it.[28] As the historian Walter Johnson has argued, representations of the *Creole* mutiny were controversial from the start—shaped as they were by often biased political, ideological, judiciary, and even literary intentions.[29] Bernier also calls our attention to the speeches in which Douglass cites the example of Washington for a variety of purposes, according to audience and occasion.[30] They help us to chart what Douglass might have known about his heroic slave at a particular time, and this knowledge can be traced back to specific sources. With his various audiences in mind, Douglass also put this information to different rhetorical uses. Such performative instances, it should be said, do not make these shifting perspectives on Washington's life fictional. If studied together, it becomes evident that the speeches and "The Heroic Slave" form a *single discursive continuum*. Nevertheless, both the speeches and the historiographic frame of the narrative do indicate that Douglass regularly used slave experience actively, to pass historical judgment and form new historical concepts.[31] One of these concepts, according to Douglass, was the heroic slave as an important but unacknowledged historical type.

In her discussion of the context of "The Heroic Slave," Cynthia Hamilton identifies a number of likely early influences on Douglass.[32] Focusing on political oratory and public correspondence, she singles out what she calls two important "pre-texts": Henry Highland Garnet's "An Address to the Slaves of the United States of America" (given at the National Convention of Colored People in Buffalo, New York, in August of 1843 and later published along with David Walker's *Appeal* in 1848) and John Quincy Adams's open letter to the people of Bangor, Maine, which was published first as Tract no. 5 in *Liberty Incomplete* (Boston, 1843) and then in several abolitionist sheets such as the *Liberator* (August 18, 1843). Garnet was often Douglass's sparring partner when it came to developing a more aggressive stance against slavery. Some of the language used in Garnet's "Address" also appears in "The Heroic Slave," but there is a larger ideological stream of American and Atlantic revolutionary rhetoric from which both Garnet and Douglass drew when texturing their respective rhetorical aims. As for Adams's letter in the *Liberator*, it reminds us that in order to establish what Douglass's knowledge of the *Creole* mutiny and Madison Washington might have been, we need to be aware of the fact that in the early 1840s Douglass was a fervid reader of Garrison's the *Liberator*. As he himself tells it at the close of his autobiographical narrative of 1845: "I . . . finally became a subscriber to it. The paper came, and I read it from week to week. . . . The paper became my meat and my drink. My soul was set all on fire."[33] In the early forties Douglass was growing intellectually by leaps and bounds, so it is likely that he began reading not only other abolitionist sheets but also a few of the major northeastern dailies.[34] And once he became editor of his own newspaper, combing other papers for articles that might be reprinted became a regular national and transatlantic occupation.

By August of 1841, Douglass began working as an agent for the Massachusetts Anti-Slavery Society and came to know and admire the *Liberator*'s famous editor, William Lloyd Garrison.[35] Garrisonians were moral suasionists, which meant they were against the use of violence and allergic to party politics. Douglass followed Garrisonian protocol up until 1851, when he publicly converted to political abolitionism and drew nearer in thought and word to a black radical abolitionism that included in its pantheon figures such as Toussaint Louverture, Denmark Vesey, Nathaniel Turner, Joseph Cinqué, and Madison Washington. In accord with other scholars before her, Cynthia Hamilton acknowledges the "quasi-historical" depiction of Douglass's Washington, but she also admits that the narrative as a whole is "curious" and "quirky."[36] Hamilton is apparently alluding to the futility of assigning Douglass's narrative to a single discursive genre and the problems of reading that arise as a result. I would suggest, however, that the quirkiness of "The

Heroic Slave" is more immediately attributable to Douglass's hastened search for an appropriate narrative mode and accompanying techniques capable of representing not only the public deeds of a meteoric insurrectionist but also the existential intimacies of a fugitive slave as he decides to seek freedom.

The Scene of Writing: Toward a Counterhistory

The structural segmenting of "The Heroic Slave" implies that Douglass sought to capture the specific moments and motivations behind the transformative process of Washington's fugitive trajectory from social death to communal freedom and from mutiny to revolution. Readers of "The Heroic Slave" have often noted the use of heightened rhetoric in parts I (Washington's soliloquy) and IV (Washington's pronouncements to the white sailor Tom Grant), which guarantees the narrative's added value as abolitionist propaganda and a pragmatic call to immediate action. Fictional scenes, if indeed Douglass actually considered them as such, would have to be thoroughly transformed by an act of the historical imagination. The intention behind such a transformative act, if we reason backward from the completed text, would have been to pass off the narrative's mimetic strategies as a rival form of historiography based above all on the combined acts of witnessing and oral testimony. If there seems to be a gray zone between "fiction" and "history" in the narrative, it would have to be the convergent use of narrative technique to represent scene and character. Perhaps this gray zone finds its rightful place in those speeches where Douglass made use of Madison Washington's heroic example.

In the context of the scene of writing, "The Heroic Slave" would also seek to deploy a specifically oratorical flourish: namely, a stridently pitched call to practical abolitionism, a performative intent seemingly incompatible with the self-referential decorum of fiction.[37] But Douglass did not come to his task empty headed. He had already written up his own early life under slavery, with its memorable moments of rebellion and sublime rhetorical apostrophe. This widely read narrative (published in 1845) helped to spark the rise of a whole new genre, the abolitionist slave narrative. As Geneviève Fabre and Robert O'Meally have pointed out, "[T]he first black American historians may have been the authors of slave narratives, those whose testimonies comprised not only eye-witness accounts of remembered experience but also a set of world views with interpretations, analyses, and historical judgments."[38]

They also cite Werner Sollors's comment that slave memories function as a form of counterhistory set against the claims found in exclusionary history.[39] Douglass's interest in the *Creole* mutiny added another, more public dimension to the slave-narrative analogue of Madison Washington's biography. As Robert Levine has noted, Douglass's experiences as a bondman offered him an insider's understanding of the same abusive system that Washington too must have endured,[40] but the task of representing an already recorded slave rebellion involved larger, historiographical challenges.

In the May 6, 1852, issue of the *National Era*, for example, we find the following query regarding the missing chapters on slavery in the latest volume of George Bancroft's best-selling *History of the United States:*

> [I]t is said, and I partly believe it, that several passages in the first volume, if not in subsequent volumes, relating to human bondage, have been in later editions stricken out! . . .Mr. Bancroft, on the publication of his first volume, published before his political aspirations were known to the public or perhaps to himself, commended to me a chapter on Slavery, which he thought would be very gratifying to an "abolitionist." They say this chapter is not found in the late editions, and that passages in other volumes, referring to American slavery, are "non est inventus."[41]

In 1852, George Bancroft was arguably the nation's premier, if not most popular, historian. His willingness to remove any account of slavery from his history as a blot on the country's claim to being the world's champion of liberty was part of a larger cultural blackout. In this same year, when the Hungarian liberator Lajos Kossuth made his triumphal tour of the United States, he purposefully avoided any mention of the existence of southern slavery, choosing instead to praise America as the land of the free.[42] A year later, in 1853, the country's black leaders urgently met in Rochester, New York, and in their choral "Address of the Colored National Convention to the People of the United States" they gave voice to the following lament: "[T]here have been services performed, hardships endured, courage displayed by our fathers, which modern American historians forget to record—a knowledge of which is essential to an intelligent judgment of the merits of our people." And again: "Our white fellow-countrymen do not know us. They are strangers to our character, ignorant of our capacity, oblivious of our history and progress, and are misinformed as to the principles and ideas that control and guide us as a people."[43] One of the five authors of this "Address" was Frederick Douglass, fresh from having written "The Heroic Slave."

According to the Rochester "Address," figures like Madison Washington went unsung and unrecognized in accounts of the nation's history, although in 1841–42 the northern press as a whole pronounced the *Creole* insurrection "justifiable and heroic."[44] And yet, when the *Creole* mutiny was recounted in depositions, newspapers, Senate debates, and diplomatic exchanges, it was by no means clear what actually happened during the revolt and later, when the ship tied up in the harbor of British Nassau. None of the 135 freed slaves (three of these decided to stay on board the *Creole*) left any written form of testimony or comment, for the simple reason that the word of black people had no legal purchase in judiciary forums. Douglass certainly struggled with the fact that the jaundiced sources available to him made it impossible to write a straight story. Composing "The Heroic Slave" would necessarily have to take the form of a counterhistory, however experimental it would have to be. In the end, Douglass's narrative of Washington turned out to be "more a history of *mode* than of *matter*,"[45] with rhetoric rather than fiction playing the dominant role. This distinction is central to our understanding of the boldness of Douglass's historical imagination and his use of narrative techniques deployed indiscriminately by both novelists and romantic historians. In his experiment, he chose to speak the language of history, but on his own terms and with a buoyant variety of narrative tools. As a result, "The Heroic Slave" became a story not only about Madison Washington but also about the challenges of writing black history in a white supremacist nation. It is at this dual level of reception that his narrative presents itself as an important historical document among others belonging to the *Creole* archive.

In truth, when we consider all the pressures and duties Douglass was saddled with in 1852, it is hard to believe that he cared to worry over the genre boundaries between history, rhetoric, testimony, and fiction when he composed "The Heroic Slave." In a letter to Gerrit Smith dated April 15, 1852, Douglass refers back to the early 1840s and "the whirl and excitement of a lecturing life," but this observation is even more applicable to his life during the year he wrote his case study of Washington.[46] As he stole a few hours here and there from his travels and editorial duties in order to work on his narrative, uppermost in his mind must have been the more general problem of how to narrate the process by which the seed of rebellion hidden in an anonymous slave's breast eventually blossomed into a major political-diplomatic event featuring a full-blown Atlantic-world hero.[47] In other words, how could Douglass justify the *Creole* mutiny in such a way that it would take on the legitimacy and authority of history as it might be written, say, by a John Lothrop Motley, a Washington Irving (whose works he possessed), or a George Bancroft. As his personal library indicates, Douglass's readings in history and biography were extensive.

In effect, the choice of frame—or *mis en cadre*—for "The Heroic Slave" comes as no surprise: it was both brilliant and obvious. He decided to begin from the end, with the *Creole* mutiny as an accomplished fact and his subject an unsung hero deserving to take his place in the same ranks as a Thomas Jefferson, a Patrick Henry, and a George Washington. As the narrator of "The Heroic Slave" notes, "Let those account for it who can, but there stands the fact, that a man who loved liberty as well as did Patrick Henry,—who deserved it as much as Thomas Jefferson,—and who fought for it with a valor as high, an arm as strong, and against odds as great, as he who led all the armies of the American colonies through the great war for freedom and independence, lives now only in the chattel records of his native State" (4). From his distinctly African American point of view, Douglass knew that he was making a bold, but hardly preposterous, claim. Unfortunately, in the available documents, his hero did not have the personal aura of Joseph Cinqué of *Amistad* fame.[48] Among other forms of celebration, Cinqué was the central figure of Amasa Hewins's popular 135-foot panorama of the rebellion that so impressed audiences in Connecticut and the Northeast as early as 1839. Impressed by this work, Benjamin Griswold, who taught the *Amistad* captives while they were awaiting trial in the New Haven jail, wrote to the abolitionist Lewis Tappan that Hewins "compares the act of Cinque in liberating himself & companions to the efforts of the man who led the armies of the U.S. in her struggle for independence, & thinks that he has shown as much of the hero, considering the sphere in which he acted."[49]

One wonders if Douglass had the chance to see Hewins's popular work. If he had, he certainly would have recalled it when composing "The Heroic Slave" and his narrator-historian's prologue. In 1852 Madison Washington's name, if remembered, evoked an event more than a person, although that event marked the most successful slave rebellion in US history. Undoubtedly, his name, like Nat Turner's or Toussaint Louverture's, stoked the already inflamed fears of southern slaveholders who could never be sure their smiling house servant was not also nurturing thoughts of murder.[50] By the beginning of the 1850s, use of this fear was becoming an increasingly attractive weapon for black radical abolitionists active in the public sphere. But in 1852 as in 1841, Madison Washington's name remained without a face or a backstory. Already in a short article titled "Madison Washington: Another Chapter in His History," published in the *Liberator* (June 10, 1842), the question was raised, "Will not some British abolitionists obtain for us the story from Madison's own lips?"

As this question implies, Douglass's narrative frame, its function as a comprehensive ordering principle, could not be easily sustained by starting with the historic event and then moving on to the private, even intimate, life of his personage. What got upended in working backward and down, into the very soul of his subject, was precisely the notion of historical "fact." In the incipit of "The Heroic Slave" the abolitionist narrator-historian notes, "Glimpses of this great character are all that can now be presented. He is brought to view only by a few transient incidents, and these afford but partial satisfaction" (4). In his struggle to bring Madison Washington to life at a critical moment in the abolitionist war against the Slave Power, Douglass must have taken to heart the romantic historian's definition of history as the raising of the dead.[51] In "The Heroic Slave" Douglass tried to turn a living phantasm into a vivid presence both for the antislavery cause and for black radical and national historiography.[52] The story's narrator says, "Like a guiding star on a stormy night, he [Madison Washington] is seen through the parted clouds and the howling tempests; . . . he is seen by the quivering flash of angry lightning, and he again disappears covered with mystery" (4). And he adds: "Speaking of marks, traces, possibles, and probabilities, we come before our readers" (5). As these words indicate, Douglass had to use complex narrative strategies in his effort to bring Washington back to life. Part of the challenge was to introduce a new historical type into the public record: not just Washington, but also the general figure of the heroic slave that haunted him through the years and that erupted every now and then into a specific name: Toussaint Louverture from Haiti; Denmark Vesey from Charleston, South Carolina; Nat Turner from Southampton County, Virginia; and Joseph Cinqué, the African hero from the *Amistad*.

The year 1852, when Douglass wrote "The Heroic Slave," was momentous for him. He had recently broken with Garrison over his conversion to political abolitionism, which was conspicuously reflected in the activist views of his all-new *Frederick Douglass' Paper* (with its Liberty Party backing). Editorial duties aside, he was constantly on the move as he attended one political or antislavery meeting after another. On July 7, he wrote to his friend and patron Gerrit Smith, "I have been engaged in writing a speech for the 4th July, which has taken up much of my extra time for the last two or three weeks."[53] On August 22, he addressed an audience of Friends in Salem, Ohio, using this occasion to espouse black violence as the only way to defeat slavery. On this memorable evening Sojourner Truth, who was present in the audience, challenged Douglass with the question, "Is God gone?"[54] Appeal to God was her alternative to violent resistance. At home Douglass was increasingly called upon to provide safe passage for the flow of fugitive slaves passing through Rochester on their way to Canada West.[55] On the literary front, Stowe's *Uncle Tom's Cabin* reminded him of the powerful role the abolitionist press played in the battle to win over public sentiment. With this scenario in mind, study of Douglass's symbolically rich narrative and the *Creole* mutiny takes on even greater resonance. In 1852, ten years after the comet of Madison Washington flashed across the political landscape of a sectionally divided country, the many contexts available to Douglass and the challenges he was then facing as a newspaper editor and a major spokesman of his people were manifold.[56]

Strapped as he was with little time and wanting to implicate a number of different ideas along with their appropriate representational modes, his overall conception of "The Heroic Slave" gave way to improbable coincidences, abrupt narrative divisions, shifting stylistic registers, and multiscaled characters and scenes—not unlike Amasa Hewins's panorama. All of these strategic effects, I would argue, were the result of Douglass's quickened desire to come to terms with both the historical record and the life of an anonymous fugitive slave not that different from himself. Both the record and the life were equally important. For Douglass, Madison Washington was not a fugitive slave so much as a freedom seeker; not an infamous murderer but an acclaimed hero; not a Virginia mutineer but an Atlantic revolutionary. At least this is how Washington was seen among the slaves in the South and the country's free black communities. To remind his readers of the haunting presence that Washington once commanded, Douglass used a variety of discursive and rhetorical techniques and all of his antislavery fervor. But more importantly, he relied on his historical imagination, an imagination tethered to, as well as shaped by, three evidential domains: his limited knowledge of the *Creole* affair, the inside information he gathered orally from those who met Washington as a fugitive, and his own experiences under slavery. Together, these three contributory wellsprings help to make "The Heroic Slave" a valuable historical document within the *Creole* archive, whether we read it as fiction, historical fiction, an exercise in black historiography, a form of testimony, or a call to action through its abolitionist fervor. Faced with a scarcity of sources, themselves flagrantly tainted with prejudice, Douglass relied on his own ingenuity, the way other black historians of his generation would also do. On the other hand, in the antebellum period there was no absolute divide between the historical novels of a Sir Walter Scott and the historical writing of Romantic historians such as Jules Michelet and George Bancroft. Novelists like Charles Dickens and Honoré de Balzac were writing social history well before academic historians.[57]

Immersed in the same fierce abolitionist climate as Douglass, Harriet Beecher Stowe and William Wells Brown made it a point to ground their "fictions" in historical and autobiographical experience, declaring that the authority of *their* narratives depended strictly on prior external events and not on the accounts themselves. In short, they were not making things up, they were simply referencing across worlds. Stowe's *A Key to Uncle Tom's Cabin* is subtitled *Presenting the Original Facts and Documents* (1853), while Brown concluded *Clotel* with an excursus on the value of testimony: "Are the various incidents and scenes related found in truth? I answer, Yes. I have personally participated in many of those scenes."[58] To be sure, one person's science is another's ideology—or should we say, fiction. But both Stowe and Brown insisted that what they had produced were "work[s] of fact."[59] They certainly took for granted that the line between history and fiction, if there was one at midcentury, was drawn in sand, not in stone. Stowe insisted on defining *Uncle Tom's Cabin* in her own terms, and her views are worth considering not only for a clearer understanding of her international best seller but also for the light they might shed on Douglass's own narrative intentions: "This work [*Uncle Tom's Cabin*], more, perhaps, than any other work of fiction that ever was written, has been a collection and arrangement of real incidents,—of actions really performed, of words and expressions really uttered,—grouped together with reference to a general result, in the same manner that the mosaic artist groups his fragments of various stones into one general picture. His is a mosaic of gems,—this is a mosaic of facts."[60] We sometimes forget that historians, too, must depend on their knowledge of the world in order to be able to recount it. In writing history, they also tell a story. History and narration go hand in hand; historical causality is little more than the sequence of events the historian as narrator chooses to recount. Commenting on history writing in Douglass's day, Hayden White has observed, "The conflict between the Romantic novelist and the historian arose most crucially at precisely the point where imagination was forced to take over from the chronicle, at the point where it was necessary to ask: 'What do the facts given in the chronicle *mean?*'"[61] In the case of Madison Washington, the facts were few, the interstices many, and the meaning always imposed. Douglass would acknowledge the consequences and move on from there.

Douglass's knowledge of the world of slavery was firsthand. He did not need to *read* about it in order to denounce its tyranny or recount its inner workings. He only needed to recall incidents from his own life when referencing similar critical moments in Madison Washington's life under slavery. Like the Romantic historians of his day, he applied his historical imagination to reconstruct the "facts" of the heroic slave's story. These facts included not only the bondman's actions but also his thoughts. In this specific case, the interstitial gap separating Madison Washington's biography from that of the fugitive slave in general is equivalent to that between a singularity and a type. In "The Heroic Slave" Douglass was considering both, and both belong to the same historical continuum. When Douglas Egerton wrote his book *Gabriel's Rebellion: The Virginia Slave Conspiracies of 1800 and 1802,* he found it helpful to rely on both traditional archival sources and other more subjective ones: "When possible, I have supplemented the trial sources with material drawn from turn-of-the-century African American autobiographies and the Virginia slave narratives."[62] As we shall see, both conjecture and analogy serve as fundamental resources for Douglass's historian-narrator, who will put them to good use in his study of the heroic slave.

As I noted above, Douglass's historical method was as much a question of mode as it was of matter. In recounting what happened, historians do not explain; they represent. And in representing, they share the same narrative tools that are used by the historical novelist. The historian's argument is coextensive with the plotline he or she constructs. In Douglass's case, we are obliged to account for an important documentary deficit that severely limited his access to the circumstances and possibilities of Madison Washington's story. As Carlo Ginzburg reminds us, "[I]n any society the conditions of access to the production of documentation are tied to a situation of power and thus create an inherent imbalance."[63] This kind of insurmountable imbalance led Douglass's narrator to state in the blocked-off prologue of "The Heroic

Slave" that he would have to work with "possibles, and probabilities" (5). The contemporary historian Natalie Zemon Davis explored the "the realm of historically determined possibilities"[64] to overcome lack of evidence about the obscure life of Martin Guerre. As Edward Gibbon, one of the first modern historians, wrote of his own practice, "I owe it to myself and to historic truth to declare, that some *circumstances* in this paragraph are founded only on conjecture and analogy."[65]

In the spirit of Liberty Party political abolitionism, Douglass certainly intended "The Heroic Slave" to count for one big historical fact: the successful rebellion of nineteen black bondmen led by Madison Washington aboard the *Creole* in early November of 1841. But since his intention was to portray another black Spartacus, Douglass added a number of important tributary facts about the heroic slave's life before the uprising. These additional biographical moments are polythetic in nature—in the sense that they are presented as aesthetic, anthropological, and social truth—and are the inevitable cause of the narrative's willful hybridity. Douglass relied upon publicly available information about his heroic slave, but he also understood that if he wanted to recount the trials of a bondman under slavery and evoke his innate thirst for freedom, he would have to expand conventional historiographical experience. In truth, this enlarged realm of black oppression and yearning was already mined in an outpouring of slave narratives promoted by the abolitionist press. These narratives were a mix of life writing and abolitionist pedagogy. Could they also be considered history?[66] Thanks to references in several of Douglass's published speeches, we know that he gleaned important secondhand information about Washington—who passed through Rochester when returning to Virginia—from the abolitionist and the African American grapevine. Douglass moved to Rochester in 1848, and his home became an important stop on the Underground Railroad.

In speeches delivered previous to "The Heroic Slave," Douglass used the example of Washington in a variety of ways—depending on the occasion, the place, and the audience—but always with the single-minded purpose of stirring people to join the fight against slavery. Even after publishing "The Heroic Slave" he continued to cite the example of Madison Washington in speeches such as "West India Emancipation" (New York, May 1857) and "A Black Hero" (August 1861). We also know that he read about the diplomatic exchanges between Daniel Webster (the American secretary of state), Edward Everett (the American ambassador in London), and the British foreign office that were reported in the newspapers and debated in Congress.[67] Faced with hypocrisy at the highest levels of government, Douglass had to feel enraged.

The whole issue of the *Creole* slaves' agency as freedom fighters was handily upstaged by the relentless political maneuverings of the southern states, whose representatives immediately puffed up a sectional matter into a nationwide storm over yet another act of British tyranny. Indeed, several southern senators called for war and made patriotism the issue. Debate in the Senate quickly formed around the intolerable theft of chattel property and the inviolability of the domestic slave trade rather than focusing on the critical issue of slavery and human rights for enslaved laborers. The heroic actions of the *Creole* rebels were quickly hushed up, as yet another international crisis between the two nations loomed. This strident patriotic campaign finally bore fruit in 1853 as the Anglo-American Claims Commission awarded the *Creole* slave traders $110,330 for their lost (human) cargo.[68] The fact that Douglass wrote and published "The Heroic Slave" in the same year that the reparations were announced helps to align his narrative intentions with the North's rising protest against the belligerent politics of the slave states and their control of the federal government. For all practical purposes, in 1852 the nation was hopelessly divided. Due to the Fugitive Slave Act of 1850, slavery had become national.[69]

The historians George and Willene Hendrick went to some lengths to reconstruct Madison Washington's contacts as he fled to Canada and then back to Virginia about a year later. Thus we know he had help from Lindley Murray Moore, Henry Highland Garnet, John Gurney, and Robert Purvis, all people whom Douglass either knew well or met on several occasions.[70] Through the accounts of these informants it is likely that Douglass had gathered intelligence about Washington that few others possessed.[71] This information, coming as it did from those who had risked assisting a fugitive slave, necessarily had to be encoded in the narrative. But the mere fact that Douglass was the author of "The Heroic Slave" added an aura of authority to it that only he could have bestowed. Of course his hybrid narrative served multiple purposes. In addition to its shrouded veridicality, Douglass also intended "The Heroic Slave" to have an immediate illocutory effect as a rhetorical weapon in the ideological war over recognition of black humanity and the right to revolution based on the principles of 1776, the French Revolution's Declaration of the Rights of Man, and the Haitian Revolution's cry of "Liberty or Death."[72] For this reason Douglass published his case study in two different venues: in the 1853 gift book *Autographs For Freedom,* edited by Julia Griffiths and distributed at antislavery meetings to help finance Douglass's abolitionist sheet and serially, on the front page of *Frederick Douglass' Paper.*[73] Like his many speeches, his narrative was a drawn sword in the abolitionist cause. When he sat down to write "The Heroic Slave" he patently leveraged his well-honed oratorical skills to portray Madison Washington as a black historical icon. He was not only signifying; he was also testifying.

Narrative and Discursive Strategies

As we read "The Heroic Slave," it is crucial that we heed who says what to whom, and with what effects, as if we were attending a play. In Douglass's narrative such effects are intentionally coded to be eventful and are poised to culminate in an overall Madison Washington effect. We first observe the effect of the heroic slave on "a northern traveller," Listwell (part I, 5), then on the *Creole*'s first mate Tom Grant (part IV), and finally, through retrospection, on the historian-narrator's own discursive investments. All the major characters in Douglass's narrative—Madison Washington, Listwell, and Tom Grant—"resolve" to act; Washington "resolves" to choose liberty, while Listwell and Grant "resolve" to turn against slavery because of Madison Washington's effect on them.[74] But most important of all is Washington's effect on the reader, whom the abolitionist narrator addresses again and again in the text. The reader is also treated to a rousing final scene in which Nassau's vigilant black citizens offer Washington and the others a choral hosanna as they disembark from the *Creole*. In addition, the narrator reinforces the Madison Washington effect by having his name appear in capital letters four times. (The last two words of the narrative, given in direct discourse, are "MADISON WASHINGTON.") If "The Heroic Slave" were merely a historical fiction,[75] we would be dealing with the parameters of the past and not of the present.[76] But Douglass patently ends his narrative with a rousing convocation—and the reader feels summoned to join the abolitionist cause. The role of rhetoric is of the utmost importance here.

In part IV, the final legendary frame of "The Heroic Slave," Douglass adds a further dimension to the notion of what constitutes a legitimate form of historical reference, but in order to fully grasp this dimension, we must not forget the torrid historical context of 1841–52. In this closing part of his narrative Douglass sought fiercely to integrate his many themes: combat the white supremacist propaganda of his day, advocate the southern slaves' latent insurrectionary desires, and trumpet Madison Washington's life as yet another circumatlantic revolutionary example. The stage Douglass chose for his climactic ending is "the Marine Coffee-house at Richmond . . . [j]ust two months after the sailing of the Virginia slave brig" (42). A privileged site for casual social encounters and exchange of information, the coffeehouse in antebellum Virginia was also an ideal place for reading proslavery newspapers such as the *Richmond Enquirer* and *Richmond Compiler,* both of which covered the breaking news of the *Creole* affair.[77]

But before the historian-narrator reports "the following conversation, which throws some light on the subsequent history, not only of Madison Washington, but of the hundred and thirty human beings with whom we last saw him chained" (42),[78] he provides an acerbic moral critique of "the smooth and gliding phrase, AMERICAN SLAVE TRADE" as it is countenanced by "our" much vaunted "MODEL REPUBLIC": "The inconsistency is so flagrant and glaring, that it would seem to cast a doubt on the doctrine of the innate moral sense of mankind" (41–42). What Roland Barthes writes of official, state-sponsored forms of writing also captures the polemical spirit of this critique: "[P]ower . . . always ends in creating an axiological writing, in which the distance which usually separates fact from value disappears within the very space of the word, which is given at once as description and as judgment."[79]

Douglass deploys the coffeehouse sociodrama that follows to separate fact from value, as Tom Grant (modeled after Zephaniah Gifford, the *Creole*'s first mate) is forced to defend himself and his crew against charges of cowardice during the *Creole* revolt. An accusatory Jack Williams boasts in a speech that with a whip alone he could have put down the revolt. But Tom Grant contests his understanding of "negro character" and makes a fundamental distinction: "It is quite easy to talk of flogging niggers here on land, where you have the sympathy of the community, and the whole physical force of the government, State and national, at your command; . . . but, sir, I deny that the negro is, naturally, a coward, or that your theory of managing slaves will stand the test of *salt* water." Here Grant contrasts disciplinary conditions on a Virginia plantation with those "on the lonely billows of the Atlantic, where every breeze speaks of courage and liberty" (43–44), and it is this contrast that drives a wedge between description and value in "the very space of the word." As Judah Benjamin would argue in his case before the Louisiana Supreme

Court, it is true that in Virginia waters local proslavery law prevails, but in the open sea it is the law of nature and of nations that rules.[80]

While Williams concedes the point about varying conditions, he persists in arguing about the slave's lack of manliness, "occasionally casting an imploring glance at the company for applause . . . and sympathy for his contempt of negro courage" (44). Grant seems to be backing away from further argument when he says, "I have resolved never to set my foot on the deck of a slave ship, either as officer, or common sailor again; . . . this whole slave-trading business is a disgrace and scandal to Old Virginia." Sensing victory, Williams calls him "as good an abolitionist as Garrison" (44); but he has gone too far, for Grant now takes personal offense, forcing Williams to moderate his tongue. Williams, however, persists in demanding an explanation "about the *case* in hand" (45; my emphasis), and it is now that Douglass introduces a new discursive mode as Williams, in a calmer spirit, says, "I have desired to see you ever since you got home, and to learn from you a full statement of *the facts in the case*" (46; my emphasis).

Through frequent references to the word "case," the last scene of "The Heroic Slave" is codified as a spectacle of confrontation in the form of a judiciary case or mock trial, if you will.[81] In effect, Grant is surrounded by a "tumultuous" company of excited onlookers who unanimously side with Williams. In this unfavorable situation Grant is compelled to defend himself: "I see how you regard this case, and how difficult it will be for me to render our ship's company blameless in your eyes. Nevertheless, I will state the facts precisely as they came under my own observation." The discursive mode adopted here is meant to provide testimony from a privileged eyewitness of the *Creole* uprising. But there is a further turn of the screw in that Grant's account centers above all on "[t]he leader of the mutiny" whose name, "(ominous of greatness,) was MADISON WASHINGTON" (47). Spelled in capital letters as if the leader of the revolt himself were about to be called to testify, the name functions rhetorically. It invokes the actual historical person in absentia while also providing an analogue, a common name (the heroic slave of the title) evoking a class of persons. As the historian Martin Rueff further explains, "Knowledge by case is a knowledge of the proper name."[82] In effect, it is the very name of Madison Washington that stands as the referential anchor of the scene. Even more importantly, the heroic slave makes his presence felt by way of the effect he has on Tom Grant.

Before recounting the revolt itself, Grant begins with a physical description (prosopography) of Madison Washington that includes observations on "[h]is manner and bearing," his physical makeup ("a powerful, good-disposed negro"), his excellent pronunciation, and his intelligence and ability (47). Verification of character is essential in establishing credibility in the forensic context. As the revolt unfolds and Grant comes directly up against Madison Washington—"You murderous villain" (48)—he is stunned into reconsidering the quality of the man standing before him. For Washington could easily have killed him several times but restrains from doing so, thereby suggesting a superior and more judicious character than the first mate had imagined. At this point, Grant deploys the rhetoric of character by quoting Madison Washington's words directly: "You call me a *black murderer.* I am not a murderer. God is my witness that LIBERTY, not *malice,* is the motive for this night's work" (48). Washington continues: "We have struck for our freedom, and if a true man's heart be in you, you will honor us for the deed. We have done that which you applaud your fathers for doing, and if we are murderers, *so were they!"* (48). These haunting words and Washington's physical presence completely disarm Grant, who explains the black insurgent's effect on him as follows: "I forgot his blackness in the dignity of his manner, and the eloquence of his speech. It seemed as if the souls of both the great dead (whose names he bore) had entered him" (49).

When asked to speak about his role in "Gabriel's rebellion," which inflamed the city of Richmond, Virginia, in 1800, one black insurgent is reported to have said, "I have nothing more to offer than what General Washington would have had to offer, had he been taken by the British and put to trial. I have adventured my life in endeavouring to obtain the liberty of my countrymen, and am a willing sacrifice in their cause."[83] As Gabriel marched into Richmond, he planned to carry a flag bearing the words "death or Liberty."[84] In his recent biography of Toussaint Louverture, Philippe Girard recalls that the slaves of Haiti fought under this very banner, "Liberty or death."[85] The intimate moment of the soliloquy that Douglass staged in part I of "The Heroic Slave" had already identified the root cause for his later actions: the desire to be free.

In this closing scene private soliloquy now gives way to a transindividual moment of ideological import. For Madison Washington's political clarifications indicate a rhetorical vanishing point in the history of the American and Haitian Revolutions. Note, however, that Madison's declamatory remarks should not be understood as a mimetic act of traditional documentary history but as history itself. Seized by an equally intense revolutionary spirit, Douglass's historian-narrator recovers a famous historiographic locus from an earlier period.[86] In having Madison Washington echo the principles of 1776, he is giving maximal extension to the heroic slave's proper but also common name. Working with unreliable depositions, legend, and secondhand reports, Douglass could not reproduce the actual sequence of events. Instead, he chose to *produce* the revolutionary spirit animating Madison Washington's rebellion. By doing so, "The Heroic Slave" became a rival document in the *Creole* archive.

Besides pointing to the actual historical person who led the *Creole* revolt, the proper but also common name "Madison Washington" references a general heroic-slave subject position in the *Creole* mutiny narrative. From the perspective of antebellum historiography, this may seem a trivial rhetorical feat. After all, what's in a name? But as common name, "Madison Washington" represents much more: a composite portrait that embraces George Washington (leader of the colonies' Continental army), the insurgent from Gabriel's rebellion who acted according to the principles of 1776, and Frederick Douglass himself, who cited Patrick Henry's (and the Haitian Revolution's) motto "Liberty or Death" in all three of his autobiographies. By strategically jumping representational scales in order to accommodate an absence of archival documentation, the author of "The Heroic Slave" relied upon a typical microhistorical expedient. Madison Washington's words to Tom Grant in the final frame represent an inspirational model based on a deep moral truth first expounded in the opening soliloquy. Now, speaking fervidly and dramatically in the present tense, Madison Washington enacts the *Creole* revolt with stunning illocutionary force.

By resorting to performative speech acts, Douglass gives us much more than historical information on the revolt; he enunciates the central mandate of the revolutionary impulse. In the words of Michel Foucault, "The present becomes the fullest moment, the moment of the greatest intensity, the solemn moment when the universal makes its entry into the real. . . . The present is no longer the moment of forgetfulness . . . it is the moment when the truth comes out."[87] Douglass sought to capture "the present moment" of revolutionary liberation, which the sailors' depositions muted. Thus, in an utterly solemn moment on board the *Creole*, Washington lets the truth come out, thereby turning a scene of historiographic forgetfulness into an ideological epiphany. In classical history, martial heroes and statesmen regularly gave edifying speeches in direct discourse before their troops or political assemblies.[88]

There was a positive tension between the rhetoric of *evidentia* and historical evidence as historians consider it today. For the author of "The Heroic Slave," the inner tension between these two referential modes is further sanctioned by his own motives as author, abolitionist orator, second-degree witness, and journalist.

An Atlantic-World Hero

As a chastened Tom Grant complies with Washington's orders and steers the brig toward British Nassau, where the *Creole* slaves will eventually go free, a storm blows up and the ship risks going under. Throughout this crisis, however, Washington "stood firmly at the helm." When the sea finally calms down again, he turns to Tom Grant and says, "Mr. mate, you cannot write the bloody laws of slavery on those restless billows. The ocean, if not the land, is free." At this point the deck of the *Creole* momentarily becomes a space of consociation, as Madison's effect on Grant is sealed. "I confess, gentlemen, I felt myself in the presence of a superior man," Grant tells the circle of listeners (50). But immediately after, he confesses, "It was not that his principles were wrong in the abstract; for they are the principles of 1776. But I could not bring myself to recognize their application to one whom I deemed my inferior" (51). The momentary understanding between Washington and Grant derives from the freedman's dignified demeanor and elocutionary powers as well as on the principles of the American, French, and Haitian Revolutions. Altogether, these factors combine to turn Washington into an iconic heroic slave, an Atlantic-world black Spartacus. The final moments in the harbor at Nassau are sheer political theater, for the "multitude of sympathizing spectators" on land cheer as the slaves on board the *Creole* parade to the shore "under the triumphant leadership of their heroic chief and deliverer, MADISON WASHINGTON" (51).

Black abolitionist orators often stirred their audiences by ticking off the names of those heroes who had instilled a perpetual fear in the slaveholders' breast. In his famous 1843 "Address to the Slaves of the United States of America" and in the presence of a still impressionable Frederick Douglass, Henry Highland Garnet declaimed, "Many a brave hero fell, but History, faithful to her high trust, will transcribe his name on the same monument with Moses, Hampden, Tell, Bruce, and Wallace, Toussaint Louverture, Lafayette and Washington."[89] Garnet mentioned this broad range of noteworthy valiants from different historical periods because he wanted above all to celebrate a general type, the "brave hero." There were still other names on the roll call that were even dearer to the hearts of his audience, and Garnet did not fail to declaim them as well: Nathaniel Turner, Joseph Cinqué, and Madison Washington—all household names. Rehearsing a popular litany of heroic slaves known to black audiences became one of the standard devices orators like Douglass and Garnet used to create a "history of internalized remembrance" specific to their communities.[90] In 1845, when touring the British Isles on behalf of the antislavery cause, Douglass often resorted to this rhetorical hailing when recalling the deeds of Madison Washington in front of abolitionist audiences. He would continue to do so upon his return to the United States in 1847.[91]

The final scene of "The Heroic Slave" has obvious internal connections and contrastive symmetries with the first scene reporting Madison Washington's soliloquy.[92] In the soliloquy Washington is caught in an existential crisis as he ponders over whether he should escape or not. The soliloquy is staged as a radically personal drama and provides the underlying subjective ontology for the scene of revolt. The final scenario in part IV of Douglass's narrative takes the form of a mock trial pitting Tom Grant (the defendant) against Jack Williams (the plaintiff) as they disagree over the nature of black character. But the scene's central core features Madison Washington's broad political restatement of the moral value of liberty and the right to revolution in the circumatlantic world. Douglass derived his two scenes (his two discursive modes) from his own experience as a slave and the trial format, respectively. These popular generic forms (the slave narrative and the judiciary case so prominent in the post-1850 rendition cases of fugitive slaves) allowed Douglass to switch representational levels at strategic moments in his narrative, so that the problem of the *Creole* archive could be addressed constructively.

It is in this ostensive, dramatic sense that "The Heroic Slave" must be considered a primary archival document in its own right. Rekeying his own apostrophe to liberty in his autobiography of 1845 (but now by closely shadowing Hamlet's famous soliloquy "To be nor not to be") and introducing Madison Washington from the perspective of an eyewitness (namely, the northern traveler Listwell), Douglass presents his heroic slave in multiple ways: as an imaginal truth, a hypothetical figure of black historiography, a composite portrait of the fugitive slave having immediate abolitionist value. By means of this hybrid effort, his narrative becomes an archival resource in itself. Along with other competing *Creole* documents, we can value it by studying the way Douglass ingeniously circumvents a set of historiographical difficulties informing his narrative's very fabric. As the historian-narrator makes quite evident in the prologue, "The Heroic Slave" was explicitly written to foreground the problem of a still virtual *Creole* archive in a very prescient way.

I noted above that in Douglass's day the *Creole* affair was considered an exceptional event, indeed an anomaly. In effect, in the South one could not state in public that a southern slave had the wits to organize a ship revolt at sea.[93] In choosing to bring Madison Washington back to life in the politically critical year of 1852, Douglass argued that the *Creole* affair was actually an example of what the historian Edoardo Grendi called the "exceptional normal."[94] In other words, Madison Washington was *not* a fortuitous accident. There were many boiling African American volcanoes like him, Douglass noted during a famous speech to a Boston antislavery audience in 1848. Accordingly, "The Heroic Slave" must ultimately be considered a documentary event in its own right—an analogue of political action in both a retrospective and a prospective sense. As Douglass's hybrid narrative further demonstrates, the *Creole* slaves' emancipation in Nassau suggests not that they were freed from bonds but that they were well attached—both to a highly efficient southern slave grapevine and to a revolutionary black Atlantic network extending from the Caribbean archipelago to England and the west coast of Africa. Written to challenge white supremacist ideology and historiography, "The Heroic Slave" is political with a vengeance. Douglass's case study culminates in a moment of political recognition as the *Creole*'s blacks are welcomed and integrated into the Nassau community. According to the newspapers, Madison Washington and the others had disappeared from sight, but in fact they had become part of "the people." The final scene clarifies their new political status in the larger Atlantic world. It was no fiction.

III

THE CARTOGRAPHIC CHALLENGE

6

From *Mundus Novus* to Atlantic World
Three Early Modern World Maps

In this chapter I will begin with a haunted question that remains central to a critique of the genealogical beginnings of Atlantic studies: What did navigators like Christopher Columbus, Amerigo Vespucci, and other Portuguese and Spanish explorers at the close of the fifteenth and the start of the sixteenth century mean when they spoke of the *Mundus Novus* (Vespucci's "New World")? Within this dawning imperial framework, I would also like to suggest a comparison (a bridge) between the resourceful ways in which this ideologically charged "New World" was envisioned and the skills that will help us to identify a number of disciplinary signposts and practices germane to the rise of the new Atlantic studies sensibility. I will explore this early modern *Mundus Novus* as both a historical construct and an absolute metaphor—namely, as something that cannot be reduced to or explained away by a concept, something that is native to the imagination itself.[1] Beginning with the transatlantic crossings of navigators such as Christopher Columbus, Juan de La Cosa, Amerigo Vespucci, Pedro Álvares Cabral, the Corte Real brothers, and Giovanni and Sebastiano Caboto, maps in particular were charged with displaying European explorers' imperial engagement with this "New World."[2] Letters and reports by these navigators were usually accompanied by maps, which were needed to vindicate the explorers' claims of having discovered and taken possession of new lands on behalf of their European monarchs. No other kind of document could do this so convincingly, and with the same evidential authority, as maps. Since their discursive function was central to empire building and colonization across the Atlantic, we simply cannot ignore them when dealing genealogically with the formation of a new, anti-imperial and postcolonial Atlantic studies. In the following complementary chapter, I will seek to throw light on the power invested in European cartographic practices as these have helped to codify the hemispheric territories of the Americas.

In the process of European exploration and settlement, maps helped first the Portuguese and the Spanish and then the Dutch, the French, the English, and other European powers to locate and think of themselves as Europeans—a distinct group of peoples speaking different languages but nonetheless living side by side and, above all, sharing a common Christian civilization bound together by an emerging *jus publicum europaeum*. Once I have characterized the prominent role of cartography in early modern European cultures, a role that is undoubtedly familiar to map scholars, I will then move on to reclaim some of the original luster and drama that Renaissance charts of various kinds once had. This task is even more pertinent now that atlanticists from across the disciplines have expressed growing appreciation of cartographic effects in designating the Atlantic world as a new but also historically burdened research area.[3] Perhaps the simplest way of suggesting what is at stake in talking about a new world of any kind is to recount a little story that the Canadian scholar Northrop Frye told me years ago when we spent a wonderful day walking around the city of Venice, Italy. We were talking about that huge northern territory of Canada and how important space is in defining Canadian identity. For Canadians, it is not a question of "Who am I?" but "Where am I?" Frye was saying, and then to illustrate his point he told this little anecdote about a Canadian doctor traveling across the Arctic tundra with an Eskimo as his guide: "A blizzard blew up, and they had to bivouac for the night. What with the cold, the storm, and the loneliness, the doctor panicked and began shouting, 'We are lost! We are lost!' The Eskimo looked at him thoughtfully and said, 'We are not lost. We are here.'" For the urbane and university-trained doctor, the Inuit's "here" was probably not much of a consolation, certainly not as much as the name of a village might have been, however distant. The doctor considered himself lost because he had no immediate idea of where he was, and even with a map in hand the blizzard would have made it quite useless. As for the Inuit's *here*, it is nothing more than a pointing gesture, a deictic reference to nature and the natural order that surrounded them. Evidently, he felt at home in it and his *here* would have alluded to a kind of informal, local knowledge that he probably grew up with. It is unlikely that a regional map of the tundra would have added much to his sense of place. For the doctor, of course, the opposite was true. To make my point, Frye's anecdote provides us with the two representational extremes of cartographic activity, and to span them we must proceed by analogy.

By contrasting a specific topographical point on the land with a larger cartographic picture, we end up with two opposing positions that represent quite different ways of conceiving how we orient ourselves in space. Louis XIV of France could get a comprehensive idea of his colonial possessions in North America by studying the beautiful terrestrial globe Vincenzo Coronelli made for him in the early 1680s. But explorers like Columbus and Vespucci, who were steeped in classical, medieval, and Mediterranean cartography, usually took local native guides with them once they had a foothold in the Western Hemisphere. They relied upon the indigenous people for their local knowledge, which went well beyond the science of cartography as embodied in European portolan or route maps focused on coastal knowledge and port cities. As we will see below, a full appreciation of mapping practices reveals that the two kinds of geographical expertise are wholly complementary. In effect, they are actually part of a single continuum. There are many different types of maps, and if we look at the range of functions and purposes they had in Columbus's day, we will be in a better position to appreciate how expansive our definition of cartography must be to include all of them. That is why it will be necessary to speak of specific signifying functions (what elsewhere I have called cartographic semiosis)[4] if we hope to assess the influence and strategies of European maps in representing the *Mundus Novus*.

A good deal of the power of maps derives from their ability to visually represent the world in all its complexity, and this brings us back to our opening question: What did the first European explorers mean by *Mundus Novus* and what, after all, is a new world? In 1492 Columbus was seeking a western route to the Indies in order to help the king and queen of Aragon and Castile get a competitive hold on the Southeast Asian spice trade. While Portuguese sailors were making progress in discovering the western coast of Africa, there were no official reports that someone had ventured successfully out into the Atlantic on a feasible route to China and the Indian Ocean, although by the 1480s one could extrapolate from current cosmological and cartographic theory and conclude that the distance across the Atlantic was by no means insurmountable. Whatever his shortcomings, Columbus was universally known as an accomplished sailor and cartographer and an exceptionally determined man.[5]

When the king and queen of Aragon and Castile granted Columbus his patent, they were still heady with having driven the Moors from the city of Grenada and expelled all Jews from their kingdoms who refused to convert to Christianity. Obviously affected by this triumphant moment of the arch-defenders of the Catholic faith, Columbus declares at the beginning of his *Journal of the First Voyage:*

> Your Highnesses . . . resolved to send me, Christopher Columbus, to the said
> regions of India to see the said princes and the peoples and lands and determine
> the nature of them and of all other things, and the measures to be taken to con-
> vert them to our holy faith; and you ordered that I should not go by land to the
> East . . . but by way of the West, a route which to this day we cannot be certain
> has been taken by anyone else: . . . And in consideration you granted me great fa-
> vours and honoured me thenceforth with the title "Don" and the rank of Admiral
> of the Ocean Sea and Viceroy and Governor in perpetuity of all the islands and
> mainland that I should discover and take possession of.[6]

When a well-backed and title-rich Columbus finally touched land on the Caribbean island of Guanahani on Friday morning, October 12, 1492, he evidently believed that his firmly held convictions were finally born out. Here is how the *Journal,* edited by Bartolomé de Las Casas, recounts that now well-known primal scene of Atlantic studies:

> [T]he Admiral went ashore in the armed boat with Martin Alonso Pinzon and
> Vicente Yanez, his brother, who was captain of the Nina. The Admiral brought
> out the royal standard, and the captains unfurled two banners of the green cross,
> which the Admiral flew as his standard on all the ships, with an F and a Y, and
> a crown over each letter. . . . The Admiral called the two captains and the others
> who landed, and Rodrigo de Escobedo, secretary of the expedition, and Rodrigo
> Sanchez de Segovia, and made them bear witness and testimony that he, in their
> presence, took possession, as in fact he did take possession, of the said island in
> the names of the King and Queen, his Sovereigns, making the requisite declara-
> tions, as is more fully recorded in the statutory instruments which were set down
> in writing.[7]

What he actually saw on that first landing—the seminaked, brown-skinned people, the tropical flora, the multicolored birds—was surely new to him, although not unexpected. On the basis of his calculations, he was sure he was in the vicinity of the Orient. As the natives gathered around him, he distributed gifts and made friends with these supposedly southeast Asian denizens. As he formed his first impressions, he immediately thought how easy it would be to bring these meek, apparently unsophisticated, and utterly good-natured people to the Christian faith. They would also provide a willing workforce if there were any gold or silver mines on the island, as the body ornaments on some of the natives suggested there might be. In spite of the ferocity and cruelty that would soon be unleashed with the arrival of the first settlers in 1493, this first contact took place under the sign of friendship diplomacy. Communication between them was based on the exchange of gifts and for the most part a language of gentle gestures. During further explorations in the months that followed, this scene would be repeated again and again, but not one of them brought Columbus any closer to the Indian Ocean's spice trade.

With the last two of his four voyages, Columbus had finally touched upon the North American mainland of modern-day Honduras, Costa Rica, and Panama. But it was his letter of 1493, written in Latin and read throughout Europe, that created a stir, for in it he announced that one could sail westward across the Ocean Sea—of which he was now the "Admiral"—to the Orient. But the Bahamas were not the Indies. After the *Victoria,* the only surviving ship from Magellan's expedition, returned from having circled the globe in 1522, European navigators finally had a full cartographic picture of the western route to the Indian peninsula and of the earth's sphere. Realizing the importance of the *Victoria's* achievement, King Emanuel I of Portugal had a small tract published to commemorate the expedition's success. Already by 1544 the Genoese cartographer Battista Agnese dedicated a beautifully decorated world map depicting Magellan's route around the world, which he included in his *Portolan atlas.*[8]

As to Columbus's formal claim to a number of Caribbean islands, his "*otro mundo*" is more of a concept than a real place.[9] Indeed, he did not think it worth using the phrase until he began sailing in the fresh waters from the Orinoco, off the coast of Venezuela, in early August of 1498. If the voyage seemed to justify his title of "Admiral of the Ocean Sea," his geographical concept of a new world inevitably became critical as he continued to look for confirmation of his nearness to the coast of *Cipangu* (Japan) and *Catai* (China). Briefed by the outpouring of postcolonial commentary on this dawning moment of the Spanish presence in the Caribbean, we have become sensitive to the differences between Columbus's role as participant observer and our own critical task of participant objectification.[10]

When he first set out in 1492, the "Admiral" had a great deal to prove, and the stated objectives, although general, were very clear. However, we should keep in mind that he was a foreigner with a largely Spanish crew, had a limited command of the Castilian tongue, and had to keep a constant eye on the strong-minded, often insubordinate Martin Alonso Pinzon, the captain of the *Pinta*. These constraining factors help to explain the pervasive anxiety that seeps through the prose of his letters and journal of the first voyage. Although he returned to Spain with epoch-making news, some gold ornaments, and an exotic cargo that included a few captive Arawaks and some brightly colored parrots, Columbus had failed to deliver the king's letters to the great khan. On November 2, 1492, we read from Columbus's journal as follows:

> The Admiral decided to send out two Spaniards, one . . . certain Luis de Torres who . . . had been a Jew and, he says, knew Hebrew and Chaldean and some Arabic, and with them two Indians, one from among those he had brought from Guanahanì. . . . He gave them instructions on how they should ask for the king of that land and what they should tell him on behalf of the Monarchs of Castile and how they had sent the Admiral on their behalf to present him with letters and a gift and to find out about his state and to establish friendship with him and assist him in whatever he should require of them.[11]

No such desired encounter took place. He met cacique after cacique, each bearing signs of their royal status, but none of them were the great khan. The famous letter of the first voyage, one of the most pivotal civilizational documents of early modern European intentions, basically restates the original agenda set down in the *Journal* and outlines the many excellent reasons for Spanish colonization, the primary ones being the abundant signs of gold on the newly claimed Spanish islands and the meekness of the inhabitants. He was on the right track, he thought, and he also had a map to show where he had been and what he had seen. As he ambitiously promised at the outset of his *Journal*, "I propose to make a new navigational chart, on which I shall note all the sea and land in the Ocean Sea in their proper places with their bearings."[12] With map in hand, the route could be repeated, a seaway established. In his own first letter to Lorenzo di Pierfrancesco de' Medici—sent out on July 18, 1500, from Cadiz—Amerigo Vespucci writes, "I have resolved, Magnificent Lorenzo, that, just as I have given you an account by letter of what happened to me, I shall send you two depictions of the world, made and ordered by my own hand and knowledge: one chart will be a flat rendering and the other a map of the world in spherical form."[13]

Both Columbus and Vespucci were well-traveled observers. What they saw was new to them, and so they often drew on analogy to explain things: the climate was like Andalusia's, the fish were like those of Castile, the meadows were almost comparable to those of Castile, the city was built on water like Venice. Essentially, it was as seamen, explorers, chroniclers, and cartographers that Columbus, Vespucci, and others introduced their European audience to the new worlds and peoples and habitats they met up with in first person. Ultimately, the revolutionary and cultural sense of a "new world" came from below, from those who dared take ship out into the new oceanic road, either out of curiosity or simply because they had no economic future at home. As amateur explorers indiscriminately willing to record almost any scrap of information that passed before their eyes, both Columbus and Vespucci were not so distant in spirit and practice from the early Greek historians and geographers.[14] When at quite different moments in their explorations both Columbus and Vespucci declared in a state of wonder that they were in the presence of a new world, they did so on the basis of personal experience. As Vespucci wrote in the letter to Lorenzo de' Medici quoted above, "It appears to me, then, Magnificent Lorenzo, that by this voyage of mine most philosophers who maintain that one cannot live within the Torrid Zone because of its heat are confuted; . . . which is most certain proof that practice is of greater worth than theory."[15] Columbus had come to this same conclusion even earlier, although in truth he was much slower to abandon his initial calculations.

In trying to explain what is involved in the historical experience of discovering a *Mundus Novus,* whether it be that of Columbus or even the heavily inscribed one of today's Atlantic studies scholar, we inevitably fall back upon the elementary categories of space and time. While the word *new* refers above all to a temporal perception, the word *mundus* (or world) refers to a spatial realm. In his book *Futures Past,* an extended meditation on the semantics of historical time, Reinhart Koselleck gives the two categories of space and time a more recognizable form by reconceptualizing them as the space of experience and the horizon of expectation.[16] As these two categories work against each other and in tandem, they provide us with a general anthropological framework underpinning all possible histories. What Koselleck has tried to do in exploring the cognitive potential of his two categories is sketch the very face of the historical process.

Experience includes memory but goes deeper, while expectation comprehends more than hope and helps to draw the historical process forward. Together they provide the formal determinants that reveal how history works. According to Koselleck, experience is "present past, whose events have been incorporated and can be remembered." On the other hand, expectation is "the future made present" and aims at the not yet.[17] It is by understanding the tension between the space of experience and the horizon of expectation that we can best reconstruct the cultural and existential challenges that beset Columbus, Vespucci, Magellan, Giovanni Caboto, and others who participated in those first transatlantic voyages. As we try to describe an epochal shift, these categories, and more importantly the tension between them, must be kept in the foreground of the historical imagination. We are dealing here with hopes and fears, wishes and desires, cares, receptivity, curiosity, character, preparation, and imperial orders. These sentiments and faculties are both personal and cultural and are determining factors in intercivilizational encounters.

Since we are dealing specifically with the intercivilizational problem of how to approach European rulers', merchants', and navigators' dawning sense of a geocultural *novum* associated with the so-called fourth part of the world, the different levels of receptivity and observation that Columbus expresses in his *Journal* must also be tackled as a difficulty of levels. In other words, we must identify not only an empirical inventory of his different experiences but also foreground the levels themselves *as* different levels of knowledge contained within his well-known cartographic and political vision. How, for example, does one reconcile an exclusively exploitative, utilitarian view of the Caribbean islands with this mythologizing perception of them from Columbus's *Journal:*

> It was marvellous to sail along it with the fresh green woods and the clear water and the birds and the beautiful surroundings and he says that he felt that he did not want to leave. He told his men in his company that a thousand tongues would not suffice to give the monarchs an account of what they had seen, and his hand could not write it for he seemed to be enchanted. He wished that many other cautious and trustworthy people could see it all, and he says that he is certain that they would not praise these things less than he did.[18]

Evidently, there is a shifting set of values at work in this narrative of imperial exploration, and these, in turn, should stir us to explore more attentively
the process of narration. This is the turn of the screw that the emergence of
an epochal shift occasions. The levels of Columbus's *Journal* range from the
political, the religious, and the promotional to the ethnographic, the cartographic, the geographic, and the aesthetic, to name the most prominent. It is
important that we acknowledge and rank these before observing which levels
are at work in what circumstances.

Most importantly of all, however, there is the macrosociological perspective of intercivilizational analysis that students of the Atlantic world cannot
afford to ignore. For the manifestation of a *Mundus Novus* is as much about
encounters between different peoples as it is about appreciating new geographies. Without this macrosociological perspective we risk reducing all such
civilizational encounters to, in Bernard Bailyn's words, "a world in which the
normal rules of civility, native American or European, were suspended, and
human relations were reduced to atavistic conflicts." Bailyn explains further,
"For much of a century . . . everything in the areas of contact and settlement
in the Western Hemisphere was fluid, indeterminate, without stable structures or identities."[19] He refers to this space of experience as a "marchland"
and applies it to describe what amounts to a totally Hobbesian world: "In its
first, original phase Atlantic history in the broadest sense is the story of the
creation of a vast marchland of European civilization, an ill-defined, irregular
outer borderland, thrust into the world of indigenous peoples in the Western
Hemisphere and in the outer reaches of the British archipelago."[20]

As convenient as the notion of a "marchland of European civilization"
is, this emphasis on the "broadest sense" fosters the correlative danger of
ignoring the multiple levels involved in any total history of the first phase
of the rise of an "Atlantic world." Bailyn's "broadest sense" seems implicitly
aimed at confirming his own narrative view of history, a view (as we have
seen in chapter 1) that argues for the notion of the Atlantic world as a "cohesive communication system."[21] But things are much more complicated,
incidental, and discontinuous than a historiography geared to describing this
so-called coherent system is capable of narrating. Both Vespucci's letters and
Columbus's *Journal*, for example, demonstrate quite clearly that the Arawaks,
Caribs, Tupis, and other peoples of the Caribbean islands and the northeastern coast of South America largely structured their encounters with the
Spanish and Portuguese in terms of a politics of alliances, incorporation, and

gift diplomacy. They regularly ordered relations between different peoples by confederating and by gift exchange, or by ritual warfare.

This is especially true of Columbus's own dealings with the Taino peoples during his first journey. Perhaps the high point of this gift politics took place on December 30, when Columbus participated in a very sophisticated ceremony of political friendship. The passage is worth quoting in full:

> The Admiral went ashore to eat and arrived just as five kings, who were subjects of this one called Guacanagarí, had arrived, all with their crowns indicating their high rank, and the Admiral tells the Monarchs that Their Highnesses would have been very pleased at their bearing. On reaching shore, the king came to meet the Admiral and took him by the arm to the same house as yesterday where he had a dais and chairs on which the Admiral sat and then he took off his crown and put it on the Admiral's head, and the Admiral took off a collar of good bloodstones and very beautiful beads of very fine colours which looked good in every way, and put it around the king's neck, and took off a cloak of fine scarlet cloth which he had worn that day, and put it on him, and sent for some coloured boots which he made him put on, and placed on his finger a large silver ring, because they said that they saw a sailor with a silver jewel and he had tried hard to obtain it. He was very happy and content and two of the kings who were with him came to where the Admiral was beside him and brought the Admiral two large plates of gold, one each.[22]

It is important to acknowledge this formal ritual of political friendship based on gift exchange and ceremonial diplomacy since it persisted as a defining structure of intercivilizational encounters well into the nineteenth century and, perhaps even more importantly, remains a major alternative to the Hobbesian view of the world that Bailyn recounts above. What is more, political friendship, the diplomacy of alliances, has strong philosophical roots in Aristotle's *Nicomachean Ethics* and *Eudemian Ethics* and represents a major alternative strain of European political thought rooted in the notions of justice and concordia.[23] In short, a properly worlding historiography sensitive to the full implications of early modern intercivilizational contacts goes well beyond a simplifying Hobbesian division of friend versus enemy.

Returning to what has often been called the primal scene of 1492, Juan Gil and Consuelo Varela note that we have about one hundred documents either directly or indirectly from Columbus's hand, and taken together they give us a very complex portrait of his sense of the new hemisphere.[24] The debate over whether his vision of the world was medieval or modern is ultimately unproductive, since he not only straddled the two but mentally went back and forth between them right to the end. Again, it is a question of levels and their discursively local application. As Koselleck notes in discussing the asymmetrical relationship between experience and expectation, "Experience based on the past is spatial since it is assembled into a totality, within which many layers of earlier times are simultaneously present, without, however, providing any indication of the before and after." And he concludes, "Chronologically, all experience leaps over time; experience does not create continuity in the sense of an additive preparation of the past."[25]

Both cartographer and shipmaster, Columbus significantly helped to draw the horizon of Europeans' understanding of the Humanist *Mundus Novus,* which for Portuguese, Spanish, and Italian navigators, merchants, friars, and colonists, meant a new space of experience and its attractive suggestion of new possibilities yawning behind unexplored cartographic coordinates. As the shock of discovery that marked Columbus's first letter to the king and queen of Castile and Aragon reached the courts and university circles of Europe, a new sense of the world's vastness and variety gradually took hold. This beckoning space was none other than that represented by a formidable *Mare Occidentalis* (Atlantic Ocean), a world beyond Ptolemaic geography and beyond all previous cosmologies. Indeed, theology and cosmology now began to go their separate ways. The *dispersio apostolorum* (Psalms 18:5) of the early Christian church proved not to have embraced any of the peoples, languages, religions, and customs that were missing on medieval and ancient maps. All of a sudden, another land between Europe and Asia loomed, and segment by segment its coasts were rapidly inscribed on the maps that Europe's transoceanic explorers drew up to verify their feats of discovery. Above all it was they, the cartographers, who introduced to court circles a new image of the earth, and to celebrate this role their portraits were often prominently placed on the upper borders of maps and their names mentioned in legends near their discoveries. Those familiar with the all-embracing figure of Jesus Christ on medieval *mappaemundi* could not help being startled by this abrupt shift in authority.

In his important essay "The Age of the World Picture," Martin Heidegger characterized the modern world as that in which the Renaissance explorers successfully converted the world into an image, a *Weltbild,* with the idea of reducing it to a measurable object.[26] This process of reduction went hand in hand with the conquering of it; and the conquered world was subtly exchanged with its iconic reproduction, before which modern scholars and princes then could actively position and orient themselves. This anthropocentric turn self-consciously informed the making of the new European *imago mundi,* which allowed moderns to posture as the sole protagonists of their own destiny.

Heidegger did not include early modern maps in his discussion since he was only interested in elaborating a general philosophical concept, and yet early modern European maps provide convincing evidence in support of his argument.[27] The cartographic notion of projection and, following the revival of Ptolemaic geography in the early fifteenth century, the reintroduction of scale on maps during the so-called heroic period of European exploration (1440s–1550s) help to illustrate the point Heidegger was trying to make. On early maps depicting the Portuguese explorations down and around the west coast of Africa, the various groups of islands in the western Atlantic, and above all the early Spanish and Portuguese transoceanic voyages, the world is placed before us with such skill and accuracy that we as spectators are made to feel part of the new techno-scientific entitlement. Importantly, the "we" in question is now not only princes and kings but also, due to the print revolution, scholars, merchants, clerics, soldiers, and colonists.

In 1507 Martin Waldseemüller (and his main collaborator, Matthias Ringmann) published Vespucci's letters as *Quattuor navigationes* in his famous atlas *Cosmographiae Introductio* and thereby broadcast the news that eventually led to the naming of the Western Hemisphere: "et alia pars per Americum Vesputium . . . inventa est."[28] The new image of the world, Waldseemüller declares, was discovered (literally "invented") by Amerigo Vespucci. When Vespucci sent Lorenzo de' Medici his two American maps in 1500, the Italian word he used for them was *figura.* In short, the existence of the *Mundus Novus* became familiar to European viewers primarily through such *figurae,* or pictures. Thanks to this visual figuralism, these New World maps can justly be considered absolute metaphors of the modern age. No other document could rival them. The map's central function was, and remains, that of making the viewer *see.*

This new confidence in visual cognition and visual projection had its price; for as the philosopher Jean-Luc Nancy observes, "A world that is seen, a world that is represented, is a world suspended by the gaze of a subject-of-the-world."[29] In Nancy's view, this modern "subject-of-the-world" should not be confused with a subject *in* the world to the extent that he or she is part of an exclusively visual pact in which sight and knowledge are considered interchangeable. As a result of this pact, the "world" (as a totality of sense) is subordinated or flattened to a "vision of the world," a process already described by Heidegger in "The Age of the World Picture." In his essay the German philosopher also makes a useful distinction between the medieval and the modern image of the world. The former, the medieval image, is described as an "ens creatum," the fruit of a personal creative act of God understood as first and supreme cause. In no way was the medieval *imago mundi* thought to be the object of man's will or subject to his plans.[30] This would have been blasphemous.

Once again, if we turn to cartography to illustrate the differences between the two images of the world under discussion, Heidegger's point is immediately evident. For as the Italian geographer Franco Farinelli reminds us, maps are also tools of thought.[31] Even more importantly, it is as thinking documents (*imagines agentes*) that they quietly draw attention to their premier role of scenario visualization, by which they give us back the "world." What especially characterizes European medieval maps is their T-O form.[32] The "T" represents the three major bodies of water (the Mediterranean, the Black Sea, and the Aegean) that separate the three known land masses of Asia (the land of Shem), Europe (Japeth), and Africa (Ham), while the "O" indicates the surrounding belt of the ocean beyond which lay darkness and the chaos of the elements. T-O maps are oriented to the east, where Paradise is alleged to be, and the Garden of Eden, with its four rivers, appears at the very top. Europe is to the lower left and Africa the lower right. In addition, the Holy Land is given pride of place, and the city of Jerusalem occupies the center of the map (and by analogy the earth), as Rome once did during the Roman Empire, and Rhodes when the Greek civilization flourished.[33]

These T-O maps, which are meant primarily for religious and doctrinal contemplation and not this-worldly travel, rely heavily on images and scenes from the Old Testament. As Mary Carruthers reminds us in *The Craft of Thought,* the colors and arrangement of the images and the overall symbolic order of these cartographic *picturae,* as they were sometimes called, all contribute to facilitate the process of meditation.[34] It is not mimetic realism that counts in these maps but the instructive iconography of the Christian faith. In keeping with the explicit intentions of this visual order, the only journey that counts in life is one's spiritual progress toward heaven and not one's haphazard and vainglorious travels here on earth. In the famous Ebstorf map of the thirteenth century, biblical history and nature were fused in the *corpus mysticum* (the mystical body) of the resurrected Christ, whose head, hands, and feet extend beyond the map's inhabited surface. Both nature and culture, the map suggests, are redeemed by the Savior's death on the cross.[35] This brief discussion of medieval maps should help us better appreciate the epochal shift brought about by late fifteenth-century European navigators and immediately recorded on early modern maps of the Atlantic world.

I will now examine three of the most stunning maps dealing directly with the geographical articulation of *Mundus Novus* and the radical shift in cartographic intentions they reveal. While T-O maps, which mainly consist of a storm of well-known biblical images and Old Testament geography, seem to claim excellence as colorful works of religious art, modern late fifteenth-century and early sixteenth-century maps tend to base their authority largely, though not exclusively, on their scientific acumen and ideological bravado. This acumen, it should be said, derives mostly from the recovery of Ptolemy's *Geography* by Renaissance Humanists. In keeping with the anthropocentrism of Heidegger's modern world picture, the new Atlantic charts I will discuss below are unabashedly this-worldly. If early modern European maps celebrate anything, it is above all the mundane power of their sovereign prince and the signature expertise of the cartographer. For on their world maps Renaissance chart makers effectively transformed the world from a mystery of creation to a measurable, wholly colonizable object. As Jean-Luc Nancy has pointed out with regard to the effects of this objectifying process, the West may have succeeded in conquering the world, but along the way the world lost its capacity to be the world.[36] A commanding difference between T-O and modern maps is that while the former sought to aid the viewer's memory and lead her or him to meditate on spiritual themes, modern maps of the *Mundus Novus* were meant to stir desire and spur the viewer to worldly action, such as conquest and colonization. With these differences in mind, let us now turn to our three "New World" imperial maps.

Juan de La Cosa's Mappamundi, circa 1500

Juan de La Cosa's portolan world chart (figure 1) is now considered the first extant map to depict the results of Columbus's early voyages and is conventionally dated 1500, two years earlier than the Cantino planisphere I will discuss below.[37] Juan de La Cosa, an important Basque cartographer, was owner of the *Santa Maria* and sailed with Columbus on his first and second voyages. Strikingly, the land mass of the Old World covers three-quarters of the map. Europe, along with Africa, occupies the center and is heavily peppered with place-names. The huge continent of Africa is given significantly more prominence than Europe and is filled with three levels of eye-catching images of cities, buildings, royal personages, and animals. The new islands discovered by Columbus (most notably Hispaniola and Cuba) are on the extreme left of the map, bristle like pincushions with place-names, and bear the king of Aragon and Castile's standard.

Above and below these islands are the dark, green-colored eastern coasts of North and South America, and already they too have a thin, intermittent string of place-names along them and flags from competing European nations. The names on the northeast coast of South America derive from subsequent voyages by La Cosa, and those (a good twenty) on the continent of North America reflect the cartographic achievement of Giovanni Caboto's expeditions of 1497 and 1498. Caboto's names, however, did not stick. La Cosa's is the earliest European map in existence to depict a segment of the North American continent and the only one recording Caboto's explorations, which are marked by the presence of five English flags. In contrast, there are a total of eleven Spanish flags clustered around the Caribbean islands and along the upper coast of South America. Flags and place-names represent microstrategies for declaring possession by the rival European monarchs. Along the western and eastern coasts of Africa the Portuguese explorers established the practice of planting stone columns called *padrões* to mark their territorial claims, and the use of boundary markers eventually became a consolidated practice among all European nations.

La Cosa's marine chart draws heavily on images and the use of bright colors to enhance the pilot-cartographer's many skills, but its space of representation is also controlled by what looks like a double circle of compass roses—and from each compass rose radiates a number of rhumb or loxodromatic lines that cast a navigational web over the map's surface. Shipmasters

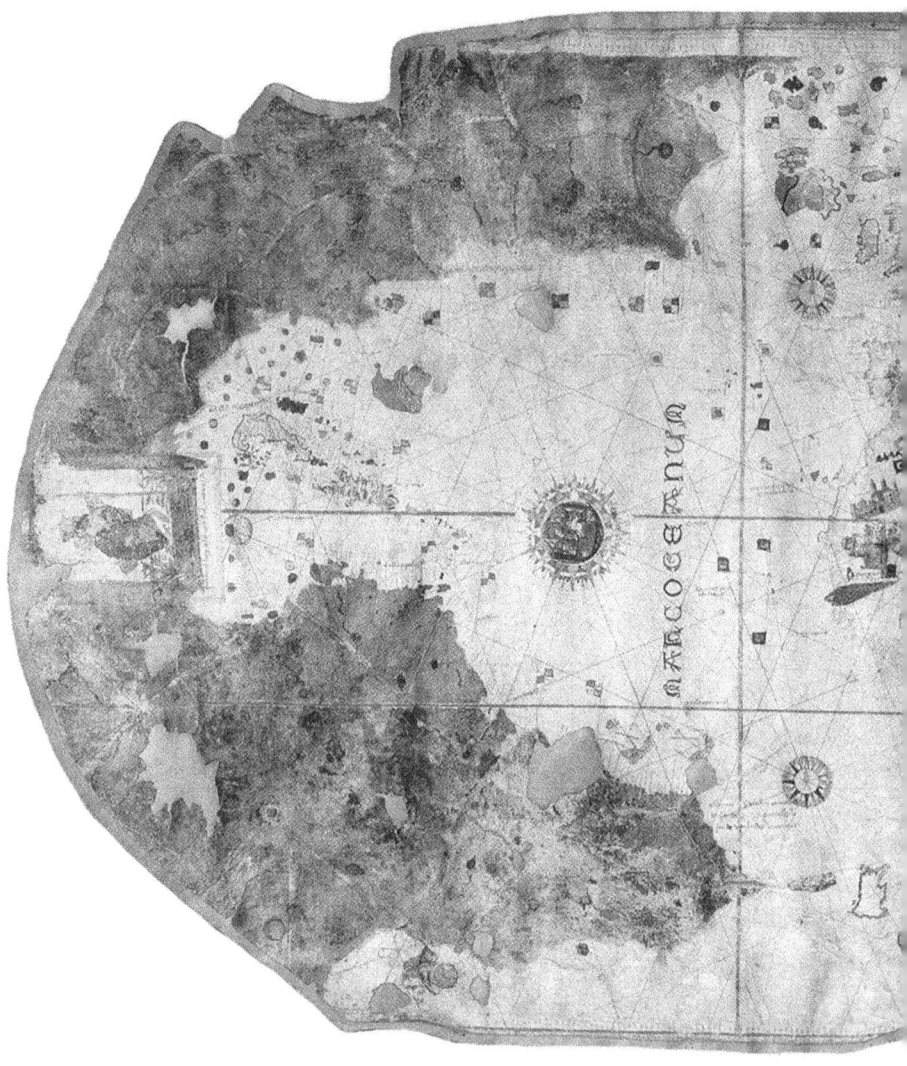

used these lines to orient themselves at sea and, in the Mediterranean at least, each of the lines represented the stable direction of one of the sixteen winds. In effect, La Cosa wants it both ways: on his *mappamundi* he promiscuously uses both the marine chart navigational system of rhumb lines found on Mediterranean *portolani* and the "modern" Ptolemaic system of mathematical coordinates and zones. As for distances, while relying on a single overall

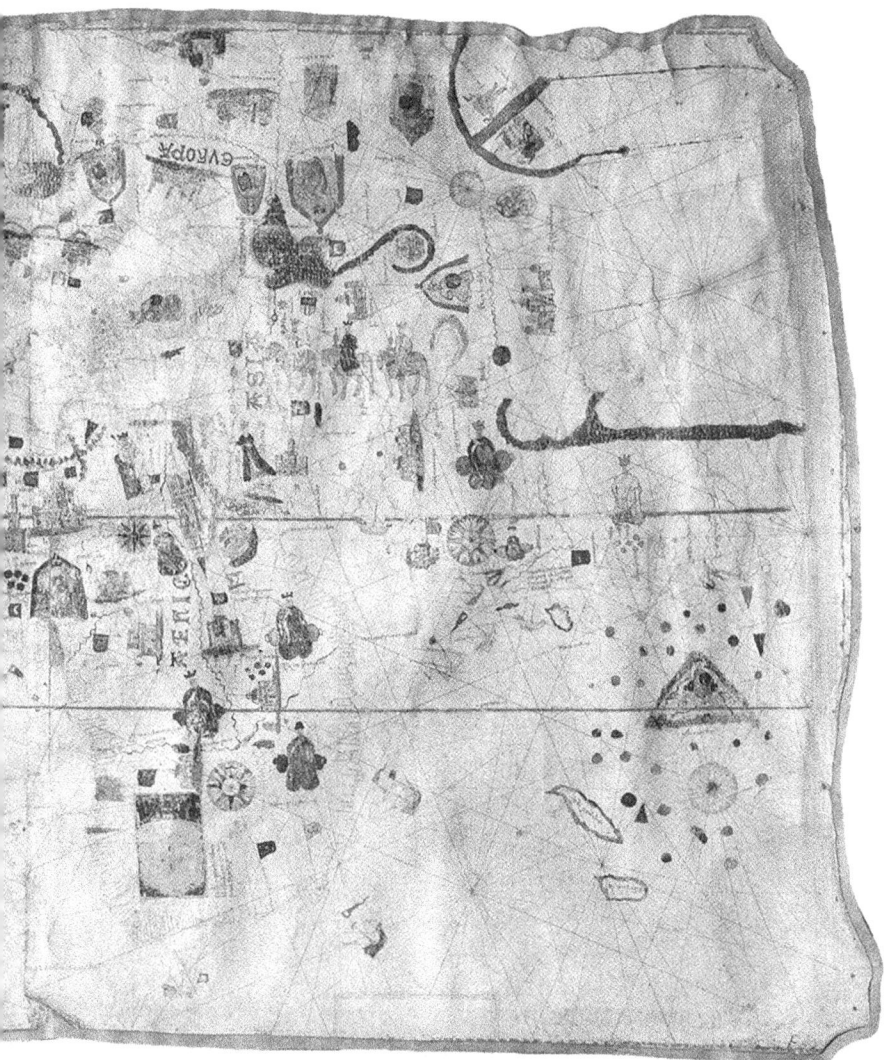

Fig. 1. Juan de La Cosa's world map, 1500.

scale, the chart juxtaposes two different geographical realities—a reduced representation of the Old World (the depiction of which relies heavily on the medieval circular vision and contents of the ecumene) and a pictorial blowup for the *Mundus Novus* (with its startling revelations of previously unknown islands and verdant land masses). As La Cosa knew, Columbus's and Caboto's discoveries obviously represented a cartographic scoop.

To sum up, La Cosa uses the rhetoric of size and color to draw the viewer's attention to the new geography. Even though it is informed by a Spanish perspective, his chart also celebrates an updated delineation of the coasts of Africa, based on a succession of sensational Portuguese voyages by Diogo Cão, Bartolomeu Dias, and Vasco da Gama, and the North Atlantic discoveries of Giovanni Caboto and the Corte Real brothers. It is indicative of the moment that even while triumphantly heralding a picture of the new geography based on the latest triumphs of Atlantic exploration, La Cosa still insists on clinging to cartographic myths, legends, and place-names that date back to medieval cartography. For example, we can still find the perennially elusive island of "*ylla trapobana*" in the Indian Ocean; in the east, images of the three mounted magi riding toward Bethlehem; and in the extreme northeast, a Blemmya (a headless man with eyes in his chest). In northern Africa, instead of Cairo we find the name "*Babilonia*," accompanied by the biblical tower representing man's vanity. Such legends have their source in the Bible and in the universally popular works of the Venetian merchant Marco Polo and the English crusader Sir John Mandeville. In addition, Europe, Asia, and India are littered with icons of rulers and cities and shrines, while the *Mundus Novus* seems conveniently to be nothing but geography devoid of inhabitants—as if La Cosa was intentionally using the zoom-in and the dark-green land mass to promote a scenario of infinite opportunity. In European law, such vacant territory could be possessed and colonized. Undoubtedly, both cartographer and viewers were equally charmed by this scene of seduction.

A word should be said about the origin and function of portolan charts, the kind of map which La Cosa's is modeled upon. The portolan tradition goes back to ancient Greek geography when works were titled *liménes* (portolani), *periploi* (peripli), and *periodoi ges* (trips around the inhabited parts of the earth).[38] *Portolano,* an Italian word, originally referred to the person whose job it was to conduct ships into port. Later, it came to designate the instruction manuals navigators consulted in order to pilot their ships from place to place. The word also referred to a sea chart of the Mediterranean coasts used for the same purpose. Thus, portolans show harbors, the mouths of rivers, shallows, potential obstacles offshore, and other coastal features a pilot needs to know while navigating in and out of port cities. These charts tended to ignore the interior features of countries or inland routes because they were strictly for use at sea. As Schwartz and Ehrenberg point out, portolans were "made by seamen for the use of seamen."[39]

The abundance of compass roses and rhumb lines on La Cosa's map are strong identifying features of its portolan status, and there is an important rhetorical enlargement of the compass rose nearest to the islands of Hispaniola and Cuba, apparently for decorative purposes but also to draw the uninitiated eye to the green swards of the Western Hemisphere. Certainly the most interesting feature of this world chart is the dramatic presentation of St. Christopher (perhaps representing Columbus) bearing the infant Christ (and the Christian faith) to the recently colonized islands across the Western Sea—or perhaps he is on his way to *Cipangu* (Japan) and *Catai* (China). His presence is given special iconographic status by being framed in a sort of illuminated niche, but his feet seem more humbly bathed in the waters of the Ocean Sea, with tropical New World flora around them. The viewer may wonder if La Cosa intended this Christ-bearer to be taken for the New World's patron saint. At any rate, as an early missionary, St. Christopher is the only indication that the "New World" might be inhabited. Again, insofar as it is left bare of people, the rich green of the interior also suggests that it is ripe for colonization. On his second voyage of 1493 Columbus founded the city of Isabela on Hispaniola (in today's Dominican Republic).

Familiar with the stated purposes of Columbus's first voyage, we cannot ignore the suggestion that the two Christophers have become one person and have thus joined secular and spiritual forces in an evangelization project that will quickly lead to the chain of frontier missions run so ruthlessly well by the Franciscan and Jesuit orders.[40] Both St. Christopher and Christopher Columbus also stand for two of the defining faces of Christian Europe. In this capacity the icon announces the spectacular presence of one of the world's great axial civilizations in the initial throes of transforming itself on a macro-societal scale into the Kingdom of God on earth.[41] The Western Hemisphere in particular will become the stage for this pitiless civilizational takeover. As Shmuel Eisenstadt has convincingly argued, modernity itself, which has its roots firmly set in Christian Europe, is a distinct type of civilization[42] and La Cosa's map, insofar as it celebrates the geographical voyages that brought the *Mundus Novus* into focus, is a visual emblem of this dawning moment.

As if to certify the grain of anxiety that helped to worry this anthropocentric, modern civilization into being, La Cosa has placed St. Christopher on the very spot where Columbus and others still believed there was a passage to India. The image, in other words, acts as a kind of Band-Aid to patch over the very zone where Spanish hopes were most thickly congregated. In short, the zone was a sort of geocultural soft spot or, what amounts to its cartographic equivalent, a corridor of *terra incognita*. Columbus's fourth voyage took him to that very zone, and when he left it, La Cosa's icon still expressed an unsolved cartographic mystery.

If we consider the St. Christopher icon primarily as a boost to Columbus's cartographic vision, then what the map has done is place him on the very frontier where he risks everything. For that matter, the very notion of frontier implies a space where everything is always at risk. As the French philosopher Étienne Balibar has recently observed, the drawing of a frontier (or boundary) is the very condition of every definition, whether it be of a territory or a person's identity.[43] Ultimately, the establishment of a frontier, the formulation of a definition, and the configuration of the world have similar aims and follow similar procedures. If the passage to India actually exists, La Cosa's map implies, then Columbus's already embattled life will have ended in triumph. If it does not exist, he will end up the viceroy of a handful of apparently primitive islands and polities and a still totally vague "otro mundo." In other words, he will have failed.

In his novel *The Harp and the Shadow*, first published in 1979 and then translated into English with an eye to the quincentennial anniversary of the discovery of America, Alejo Carpentier has Columbus candidly recapitulate his memorable voyages in the form of a confessional monologue delivered on his deathbed. In the novel we are given an account of each of his four explorations, with Columbus always on the move, never able to find what he was looking for. Resorting to a clever ruse, the various island caciques were quick to send these overly dressed and zealous gold seekers always one or two islands farther, on what proved to be a fruitless chase after a fictitious place where gold could be found in abundance, like a form of New World manna. In the admiral's rendering: "And now those shit-assed Indians . . . the ones from Hispaniola, perhaps to get me off the track of their gold mines, kept telling me to keep going—it's up ahead, farther but not too far, 'you're getting warmer, warmer, warmer,' as if we were playing find-the-button, you're nearly there—urging me to keep on sailing."[44]

Hoping to hit the jackpot through blind perseverance, the same that got him across the great Western Ocean, Columbus continues the chase, only to reflect in quiet bitterness, "Islands, islands, islands. . . . More than five thousand islands, the Venetian chronicles tell us, surround the great kingdom of Cipango. So I must be approaching that great kingdom."[45] Of course, neither

Cuba nor Santo Domingo had the trappings of Japan. Nor did they surrender anything more than small, taunting pieces of gold jewelry to stir him onward to yet another island. In the end a defeated and discredited Columbus could justly lament, "You went into a world that played tricks on you when you thought that you had conquered it and which, in reality, threw you off your course, leaving you with neither *here nor there*."[46]

Every frontier has its own history, and history is at its most intense along frontiers.[47] The one represented as an open secret on La Cosa's map is no exception. In 1500 it basically summed up Columbus's failed hopes. But as I have argued above, beside taking in the wide range of observations in Columbus's writings, particularly in the *Journal of the First Voyage,* we must also focus on the levels of attention and the way they are put into play. These levels come into view when dealing with frontiers. The one on La Cosa's map is not only an external but also an internal frontier. And both have multiple meanings. What the *Journal*—and with a little imaginative leap, also the La Cosa map— so movingly demonstrates is that Columbus himself is the frontier. If we keep this in mind, then we will have absorbed one of the main promptings about identity provided by early modern "New World" cartography. As the admiral and viceroy of the *Santa Maria* moved among the islands and peoples on the *other* side of the Ocean Sea and assiduously wrote up "New World" reality as he went along, he himself became a crossroad—a critical point—of encounter and contraction. And it is the unspooling of this ecological dependency between raconteur and site that Columbus's trajectory becomes an appropriate starting point for contemporary scholarly ventures into the Atlantic world. For those preparing to go down to ship under the atlanticist banner, frontier and intercivilizational analysis function like tiller and sail.

The Cantino World Map, circa 1502

The Cantino planisphere (figure 2), the second of our three maps under examination, is one of the earliest visual documents we have of the Vespuccian *Mundus Novus* and also one of the most beautiful in the history of European cartography. It is conventionally dated 1502 for a couple of reasons. Above the island of Newfoundland there is an inscription about the fate of Gaspar Corte Real, who was lost at sea. Since two of his ships made it back to Lisbon in October of 1501 with the news, the map must have been made after this

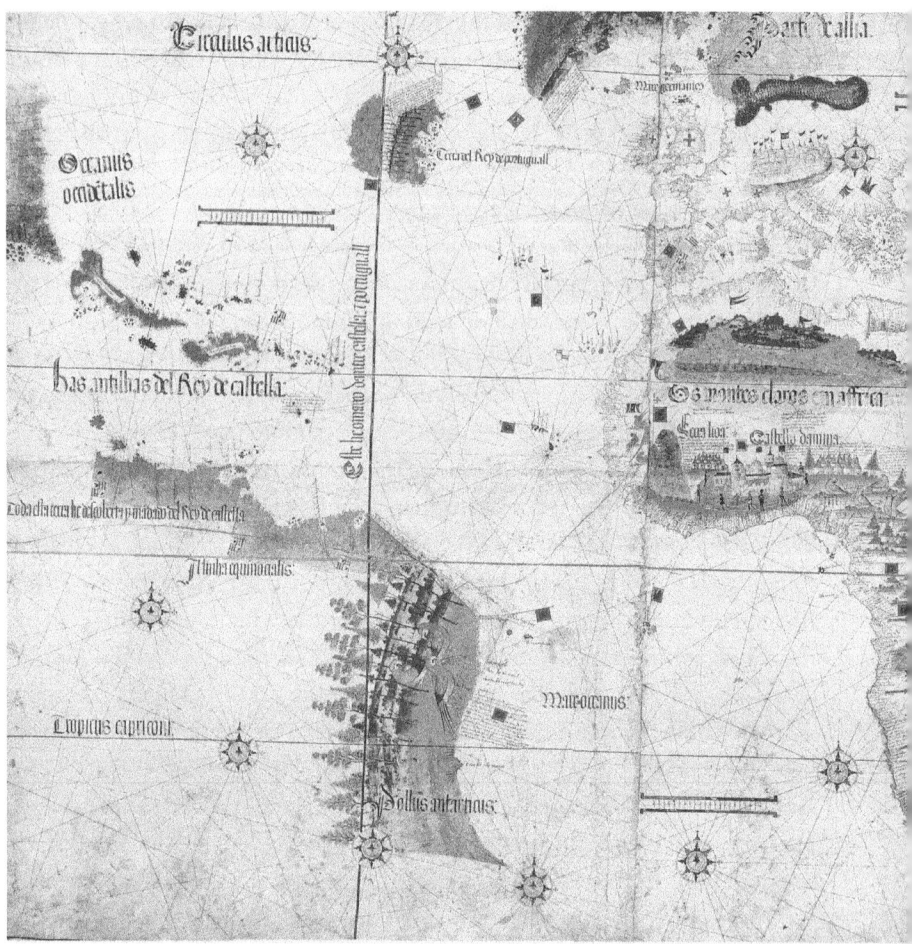

date. We also know that Alberto Cantino, the Duke of Este's envoy at the Portuguese court, covertly sent a copy of the original planisphere to the duke of Ferrara in November of 1502. That leaves us with a margin of little over a year for assigning a date.[48]

The Cantino (2200 × 1050 mm) is much bigger than Juan de La Cosa's chart (1930 × 960 mm) and also less cluttered and better designed. Its depiction of the Indian Ocean and the coasts of India and China are also more advanced. But its general arrangement of the land masses—with Europe and Africa holding the map's center and Africa, covered with an orderly effusion

Fig. 2. Cantino planisphere, 1502.

of beautiful images, visually dominating—still follows the practice of crowd-
ing the *Mundus Novus* off to the left, at the map's very edge. This is not true
of South America, however, which now has become the stage for celebrating
the newly established Portuguese presence. One of the ways the Cantino
map achieves structural clarity is by introducing two symmetrical circles of
compass roses. These are much smaller and more uniform than their counterparts on La Cosa's portolan chart, and the circles have the effect of dividing
cartographic space into two separate centers of focus. Interestingly, the circle
on the left is centered largely on watery space, while the other covers mostly

land. By the mid-sixteenth century, European activity across and around the Atlantic Ocean will have created a new oceanic order.

Perhaps because we are looking at a Portuguese map, there is some real confusion in the handling of the Spanish discoveries. For some reason Cuba is named *Isabella,* and what seems like a representation of the Florida peninsula, which was officially discovered only in 1513, may be either a partially explored Cuba or even an attempt to include the Asian mainland. Both conjectures have a basis in the extant reports. Florida was explored by Vespucci during the first of his voyages financed by the Portuguese king. Most likely, the unknown cartographer was more interested in accurately proclaiming Portuguese interests than in getting the Spanish claims down right. There are very few flags marking the latter, while Portuguese flags—in part also because of their darker color— seem to be everywhere. By everywhere, I mean in that part of the world where papal and other treaties with the king of Castile have permitted them to be.

The dark sea line running vertically through the *Mare oceanus* and cutting the northwestern part of the little-known South American continent in two is the most significant information on the map and information that is quintessentially cartographic at that. But before discussing it, we should first notice the impressive efforts the mapmaker has made to locate and celebrate recent Portuguese discoveries. That Portuguese sailors were considered among the very best in Europe seems to be confirmed by the map's rhetoric of exploration. I am alluding not only to the strategy of compass roses and the vast spiderweb of rhumb lines but also to the appearance of six scales placed strategically in all different parts of the globe.

Four of the scales are distributed among what the map seems to be considering "Portuguese" seas, while the one in Africa provides a sense of coastal distances between the various Portuguese outposts. The overall presence of these scales suggests that Portuguese ships have already taken the measure of a great deal of the earth's surface, in particular that of the various seas and oceans, all of which are named in beautiful red calligraphy. Besides the now fervid civilizational impetus to tame the globe to a domestic object, there is another, older one that helps to explain some of the fury unleashed in "New World" intercivilizational encounters. I am speaking of the Cantino planisphere's decision to celebrate two highly symbolic cities, Venice and Jerusalem. Venice was born as a place of resistance to the invading nomadic peoples from the north, while Jerusalem, which is identified with a place-name, represented the central city of Christendom then under Islamic rule.

The map also contains a good thirty-five inscriptions that provide tele-graphic announcements of events relating mostly to recent Portuguese and Spanish explorations. For example, under the legend and slightly to the right of *Las Antillias del Rey de castella* (the Antilles of the king of Castile) we read: "These are the Western Indies of the king of Castile, discovered by Columbus . . . Admiral of these islands . . . at the command of the powerful and valorous King Don Fernando." These islands are to the left of the vertical black line, which bears a vertical script referring to the Treaty of Tordesillas between Castile and Portugal. To the right of this line and in the north we find the island of Greenland, now bearing the Portuguese flag, and that of Newfoundland, which has been moved eastward so that the Portuguese could claim it as theirs without violating the treaty.

Certainly the most competitive ploy the Cantino map uses to interrupt the unbroken sequence of Spanish triumphs in the new hemisphere is that of using a visually stunning scene to announce the Portuguese presence on the new continent. But the scene brings off an even more sensational coup if we pause to consider that its iconographic arrangement may have been chosen specifically to usurp the utopian pretensions Columbus had already invested in the island of Hispaniola, the Spanish gateway to the newly discovered lands.[49] By positioning what amounts to a Virgilian *locus amoenus* in Portu-guese Brazil rather than in Spanish territory, the map is playing the game of one-upmanship to the hilt. Those who may have thought that the aesthetic value of cartographic images on early modern European world maps were merely ornamental may be persuaded differently by this seductive, archetypal emblem on the Cantino planisphere.

On that very first voyage to the Caribbean in 1492, Columbus expressed his fascination with the bright-colored birds of those islands and associated them with features from the biblical Garden of Eden. The first people he met on the island of Guanahani brought parrots, balls of cotton thread, and other objects as gifts, and as he wrote in his journal on October 11, the day of their landfall, "I have seen no animals of any kind on this island, except parrots."[50] Ten days later, after visiting another island, he notes, "Here and in all the is-land everything is green and the vegetation is like April in Andalusia. And the singing of the birds is such that it would seem that a man would never wish to leave here. And the flocks of parrots that darken the sun, and birds of so many kinds so different from our own that it is a marvel!"[51] Before recrossing the Ocean Sea with his good news, he made sure to take some of these birds back with him. Shortly, early modern maps like Martin Waldseemüller's marine chart of 1516 will refer to Brazil as the Land of Parrots (*Terra Papagalli*).

By the time the Italian painter Tiepolo painted the frescoes in Villa Pisani outside of Venice, the parrot had become one of the most recognizable icons of the Americas. The maker of the Cantino planisphere must also have been acquainted with impressions like this one from Vespucci's first letter about his voyage to "the isles of India," as he called them:

> What I and my men saw there was an infinite number of birds of various forms and colors, and so many parrots, of such diverse kinds, that it was a marvel: some red like cochineal, others green and red and lemon-yellow, still others solid green or black and flesh-colored; and the song of the other birds in the trees was so fair, and so melodious, that many times we halted, seized by their sweetness. The trees there are so beautiful and fragrant, that we thought perhaps we had entered the Earthly Paradise; and not one of those trees, nor their fruits, were like our own.[52]

When in Shakespeare's play *The Tempest* Caliban hears the autochthonous strains of music on the now colonized island he once thought his own, he not only marvels but lets it carry him off to sleep. And then, "when I waked / I cried to dream again."[53] Himself skilled at describing the island's many qualities, he learns during the Duke of Milan's stay what it means to live "stied" in its barren part.[54] The difference between dreaming and being awake, he learns, is colonial history. Few of the indigenous peoples outlived the early rigors of the Spanish *encomienda* system. As Paolo Taviani notes, "In 1517, Charles V authorized La Bresa, a Fleming, to furnish 4,000 slaves a year to Hispaniola, Cuba, Jamaica, and Puerto Rico."[55]

In his *Outlines of a Philosophy of Right*, Hegel famously wrote that America, removed from Europe by a great sea, is outside of history.[56] Apparently, on the other side of the Atlantic, there was only nature. What the Cantino map gives us is a landscape painting made into a map.[57] In its depiction of the Western Hemisphere there is indeed only nature—or so the map would have us believe. As we let ourselves be drawn to the outsized wedge of Portuguese South America and begin to fix our attention on the details of the map's visual intrigue, we can delight in Columbus's and Vespucci's multicolored parrots in a green wood. The Cantino map provided the Italian and Portuguese viewers with a beautiful invitation, a wish image that was already being transformed into a colonial New World history.

The image itself is made up of a sequence of receding planes that give the scene an enticing depth. The parrots themselves are staggered so as to draw us gradually into the landscape. Behind the second parrot, we have rank upon rank of well-spaced and gracefully varied kinds of trees and shrubbery that invite us deep into the heart of the country. If we look around the map, however, we realize how besieged and transitory this oneiric scene is. The *Mundus Novus* is already a screen of polarities where nature and history shed their conceptual clarity as they blend in the very real turf of European colonization.[58] Already in 1502, the year of the map's making, this dazzling scenography must have been a fetish for the powerful Italian Duke Ercole d'Este, to whom we will return below.

Perhaps the most disturbing factor threatening this "New World" peaceable kingdom is the slashing black line that seriously scars the top of the image with its juridical priorities. This emphatic cartographic statement represents the enactment of an international treaty whereby the newly discovered lands were to be divided up between Spain and Portugal, the only two European countries in 1494 with strong Atlantic interests. The line had a global character, as the map indicates, and its structural function was to divide the Ocean Sea in two. Without this treaty line the new hemisphere risked becoming a battleground between the two kingdoms. But as Carl Schmitt explains in his monumental study of international law and political philosophy, *The Nomos of the Earth*, the concept of such "amity lines" is much more consequential.[59]

In effect, the line of 1494 divided Europe from the rest of the world. In her essay "Empire and State" Elizabeth Mancke further notes, "As a result of the regularization of diplomatic relations in the Atlantic basin, French and Spanish diplomats developed the concept of lines of amity; to the north and east of them lay Europe, to the south and west lay the extra-European world."[60] Beyond such amity lines there was a free zone governed by the law of the strongest. The creation of this extra-European zone served to limit and rationalize European war. There was a burgeoning system of European law to regulate relations between European states, but beyond the amity line European monarchs in the process of building their empires had a free hand.

Europe—as a family of nations and a single civilization—positioned itself on one side of the amity line and on the other side lay the "New World." In the early years of colonization the Spanish and Portuguese rulers considered their American possessions an extension of their own kingdoms, but as time went on, Mancke notes, "The French, English, and Dutch challenged the Iberians by redefining extra-European space as initially 'foreign' to all Europeans."[61] As a result, the amity line also came to represent a civilizational divide. One could argue that this is already true of Columbus's second voyage in 1494, when the Spanish began colonizing Hispaniola. Shortly after March 25, 1495, the day an army of several thousand Tainos was ruthlessly defeated on the Vega Real plain, the island was completely subjugated and the people forced to pay tribute in gold and cotton thread.

In keeping with this new state of affairs, Bartolomeo Columbus sent back three hundred Taino "prisoners" to the Spanish peninsula, his order marking the first European deportation of Indian slaves in the Americas. Due to conditions at sea, however, the ships never arrived.[62] In 1979, in a volume of poetry titled *The Star-Apple Kingdom*, the St. Lucian poet Derek Walcott framed such disasters in terms of the Middle Passage in his poem "The Sea Is History."[63] As various European intellectuals such as Juan Ginés Sepúlveda and Francis Bacon reasoned, the indigenous peoples—and later enslaved Africans—were to be considered outside humanity and thus without rights. Beyond the amity line, there were only cannibals and sodomites, and these were banished from nature.[64] By implication, the Cantino planisphere raises these juridical and civilizational issues by giving visible prominence to the treaty line. But there is an even more sweeping consequence that this map introduces: as of now the Ocean Sea itself has become a central place and a defining order.

Martin Waldseemüller's World Map of 1507

While the Juan de La Cosa and Cantino maps are discussed above in terms of the effects of their images, their use of color, and the techno-scientific importance of rhumb lines and treaty lines, the next map has become famous above all for its placement of a single word. Martin Waldseemüller's 1507, twelve-sheet wall map (2480 × 1365 mm, figure 3) is considered the first one to apply the name *America* to what is now Brazil.[65] The choronym derives from Vespucci's first name and honors the fact that he was the first to not only explore but also write about much of the eastern coastline of South America in his voyage of 1499. Waldseemüller also celebrates Vespucci at the top of the map and puts a small inset figure of the new hemisphere alongside him on his right. The other portrait sharing the same high honor is of the ancient Greek cosmographer Claudius Ptolemy, acknowledged to be the father of modern cartography. As if this were not enough, in the lower left-hand corner of the map Waldseemüller added a legend saying that the representation of the New World is based on Vespucci's epistolary account of his four voyages, published as *Mundus Novus.*

As the inset maps at the top indicate, we now have a world drawn completely in man's image. The two cosmographers are shown displaying the tools of their trade for our benefit: Ptolemy exhibits a quadrant and Vespucci a compass. These tools accompanied the first explorers on their transatlantic voyages and helped them not only to find their way but also to represent it cartographically. We have come a long way from the theocentric mentality of the medieval T-O map. The only recognition Waldseemüller gives Columbus is doled out in a legend set in the top left-hand corner as well as in an internal legend acknowledging his exploration of Trinidad and the surrounding islands that he carried out during his third voyage in 1498. By muting Columbus's achievement and exalting instead the colorfully recounted but dubious voyages of Vespucci, Waldseemüller chose news and narrative over the actual discoveries.

After all, it was Vespucci who, in a letter to Lorenzo de' Medici, famously declared:

> In the past I have written to you in rather ample detail about my return from those new regions which we searched for and discovered with the fleet, at the expense and orders of His Most Serene Highness the King of Portugal, and which can be called a new world, since our ancestors had no knowledge of them and they are entirely new matter to those who hear about them. . . . I have discovered a continent in those southern regions that is inhabited by more numerous peoples and animals than in our Europe, or Asia or Africa, and in addition I found a more temperate and pleasant climate than in any other region known to us.[66]

Published by Vespucci as *Mundus Novus* in 1504, this letter then appeared in the influential collection of travels *Paesi novamente retrovati e Novo Mondo da Alberico Vespuzio florentino intitulato,* edited by Fracanzio da Montalboddo. It is the Latin translation of the latter that Waldseemüller included in his *Cosmographiae Introductio* of 1507 and inspired him to place the name *America* on the as yet unlabeled reality of present-day South America. Waldseemüller's

cartographic masterpiece was remarkably influential in the subsequent history of cartography. For example, it helped to shape the New World cartographic vision of Sebastian Münster and Peter Apian, both important sixteenth-century mapmakers. As Rodney Shirley says, "Almost every successive mapmaker of note for the next twenty-five years . . . relied almost exclusively on Waldseemüller's great work."[67]

Fig. 3. Martin Waldseemüller's world map of 1507. From *Universalis cosmographia secundum Ptholomaei traditionem et Americi Vespucii aliorumque lustrationes* (Strasbourg, 1507). Library of Congress, Geography and Map Division, 2003626426.

The heavy use of inscriptions and legends on Waldseemüller's map demonstrates the intervening power of language in domesticating cartographic space. Having closely followed Henricus Martellus's world map of 1489 in this,[68] Waldseemüller then continued the practice in handling the largely unmarked hemisphere soon to be called in its totality *America*. Another important achievement of his map is its portrayal of America as a distinct continent separated from China by a sea. Perhaps this is largely due to the confused state of geographical knowledge in 1507. Thus, on both the north and south continents of the new hemisphere we have the words *terra ultra incognita* (the land beyond is unknown). Both language and cartographic line are used to indicate the limited knowledge of the Portuguese, Spanish, and Italian explorers.

We can only imagine with what impatience and curiosity new and updated maps—many consciously proclaiming themselves *Nova* and *Accuratissima*—were received among Europe's monarchs, merchants, navigators, scholars, and clerics. By now maps were becoming increasingly indispensable as cultural and political documents of burgeoning transatlantic empires, and this centrality went hand in hand with their newsworthiness. Typical of this new breathlessness, Paulo Forlani in 1565 produced a "Mappamondo" with these wholly conventional words written at the top of it: "Universale Descrittione Di Tutta La Terra Conosciuta Fin Qui" (Universal description of the entire earth known so far).[69] By mid-sixteenth century such qualifications were part of normal cartographic competitiveness.

In recognition of the Spanish claims, the Waldseemüller world map has a ribbon-shaped legend running along the entire upper land mass of America that reads "Tota ista provincia inventa est per mandatum regis castelle" (All of this province has been discovered by mandate of the king of Castile). This and other inscriptions take precedence over the array of banners and flags of various nationalities because the map prizes the kind of narrative information that abstract symbols cannot by themselves provide. The narrative ribbon also covers, and thus claims, more territory than a flag could. But there is another practical reason for the proliferation of writing, which has to do with the increased space of the Waldseemüller world map. As Denis Cosgrove explains, "In the late 1480s Henricus Martellus extended Ptolemy's 180-degree ecumene by nearly 100 degrees of longitude; in his *Cosmographia* Martin Waldseemüller pushed it to 360 degrees."[70]

In 1508, a year after the Waldseemüller map, the Italian cartographer Francesco Roselli produced a copperplate world map using for the first time an oval projection.[71] This map, which extends to both poles, is based on a "whole-earth" projection so that, as David Woodward notes, "every point on earth could be theoretically plotted and . . . every potential route for exploration could be shown."[72] But even more importantly from an Atlantic studies perspective, that same year Roselli also drew a small world map "of a navigator's chart within a rectangular frame."[73] What interests us here is that for the first time in the history of European cartography we have a major redistribution of the known land masses, with the two hemispheres now assigned equal cartographic space. We also have a central compass rose positioned in the Atlantic with rhumb lines radiating outward to a surrounding circle of sixteen compass roses. The visual effect is as stunning as it is revolutionary.

However distractedly, this overall process of cartographic recentering represents a significant epochal shift in how the world is pictured and where the source of tension lies between an ever-expanding space of experience and a horizon of expectation beset by an emerging intercivilizational face-off. Apparently not aware of cartographic history, Carl Schmitt has suggested that around the end of the sixteenth century a new spatial order came about, which he calls the Oceanic order—to distinguish it from the Thalassic order of the coastal Mediterranean world.[74] Had he thought to include cartography in his discussion, he certainly would have adjusted his chronology, for the rise of this Oceanic order is already recorded on quite a few European maps of the early sixteenth century. Better than any other cultural or political documents of the time, maps like Roselli's and Giacomo Gastaldi's *Carta Marina Nova Tabula* of 1548 show how rapidly the Atlantic, ocean-centered world began to take center stage in the European sensibility.[75] And as it did so, this oceanic order provided a totally modern world image harboring new energies, new spaces, and a new historical existence. Ships and not horses or castles became the vectors of this new life condition, and their characteristic milieu was the politically and physically untamable one of the high seas. These seas belonged to no nation and were considered free. Land could be divided and conquered but not the ocean. While a host of European nations tried to dominate the Atlantic and claim it for themselves, Schmitt argues that Protestant countries like the Netherlands and Britain eventually proved to be most at home in it.

Every major change in our image of the world and in the structure of our concept of space, according to Schmitt, is connected to geopolitical changes and a new division of the earth.[76] Great historical changes, affecting the political, economic, and cultural spheres, always bring about a new world image. As the world maps of Juan de La Cosa, Cantino, and Martin Waldseemüller bear out, the process of European exploration and colonization led to the tentative sketching of a new hemisphere. In quick order, subsequent European maps restructured the representation of the globe around the Atlantic Ocean, thereby presenting the new planetary revolution as an accomplished fact. To explain this shift from a Thalassic to an Oceanic order, Schmitt uses a striking example to capture the change in perspective: "[F]rom a purely maritime point of view, the mainland is simply a coast, a beach with a hinterland. Seen from the high seas and from a maritime existence, an entire country can even seem but a mere wreck and detritus of the sea."[77]

Columbus's geographically conceived "other world" began to appear on maps as "new lands" (see, for example, Waldseemüller's *Tabula Terra Nova*, 1513). As for Vespucci's *Mundus Novus*, it appeared as a convenient continental label shortly after Waldseemüller's world map of 1507. For example, this label appeared in bold capital letters on the South American continent of Diogo Ribeiro's *Mappemonde* of 1529 and later, on Sebastian Münster's *Novae Insulae, XVII Nova Tabula* and Battista Agnese's *World Map* of 1543–44.[78] But by the 1550s this general choronym disappeared and in its place could be found more specific regional names like Tierra Francisca, Nova Francia, Regio del Peru, Regio de Brasil, Hispania Nova, La Virgenia Pars, and so on. As these regional place-names began to appear, the coasts of the two continents also filled up with the names of Native American villages and towns and the towns and fortified outposts of the various European settlers. In the hinterland or along the western edges of these continents there appeared more frequently the words *Terra Incognita*. What these rapidly evolving naming strategies suggest is that cartography was as much about mapping practices as about actual maps. For that matter, there was much at stake. In the following chapter such practices will receive our full attention.

John Pickles points out that recent scholars in the history of cartography have tried to embrace a larger definition of "map" and "cartography" in order "to include a wide variety of representational and symbolic forms under the rubric of 'the history of cartography.'"[79] The early maps of the new hemisphere I have discussed above point to some of the new expository strategies that were developed to meet the challenges of Europe's dawning Oceanic order. In various ways, sea captains and settlers relied on indigenous expertise for local knowledge of all kinds. European pilots depended upon native guides as they sought to orient themselves in the Caribbean archipelago and along the coastlines of the Americas. The countless indigenous place-names on early modern maps suggest that colonial peoples not only lived alongside but also depended on their Native American neighbors in order to survive in their new surroundings. Native peoples also created their own cartographic traditions well before the period of European conquest and settlement.

Although it is beyond my scope and expertise to address pre-Columbian Mesoamerican and native North American maps here, it should be said that there is a vast and varied spectrum of preconquest map types and conventions that offers quite different world views and often scenario visualizations and testimony of anticolonial import. Many of these types can be found in the rare codices now housed in various European and American research libraries (for example, the Codex Mendoza, the Codex Nutall, the Codex Xolotl, and the Codex Boturini). These types range from Maya and Mixtec boundary maps, property and city plans, cartographic histories, and gestural maps to Aztec cosmographical and celestial maps. Pictorial maps (*pinturas*) were often appended to the *relaciones geograficás* compiled by Spanish officials in the late sixteenth century, and these maps reveal indigenous cartographic techniques. Native North American maps were often drawn on birchbark and animal skins and required an array of traditional skills. Scholars Barbara E. Mundy and G. Malcolm Lewis offer a comprehensive overview of these rich and often anticolonial traditions in their highly illustrated contributions to *The History of Cartography* published by the University of Chicago Press.[80]

The first to filter and represent the breaking news coming from beyond the Ocean Sea, pilot-cartographers like Columbus, Juan de La Cosa, and Amerigo Vespucci were among the most important European savants of their day. This is for a very simple reason: as shipmasters, cosmographers, geographers, and chroniclers all rolled into one, they served their king in various critical capacities. Columbus and Vespucci are fitting examples of a common Humanist type in the vanguard of European imperialist expansion. Although Columbus was not a particularly educated man, he was steeped in cosmological theory and in ancient geography and history. He knew Latin and spoke Portuguese, Italian, and, albeit roughly, the Castilian tongue. In addition, he was a resolute and practical man who knew how to depict the world on a map and learn what he could from the indigenous peoples. In 1493, upon returning to Hispaniola to found a colony and put the Taino people to work mining for gold, he commissioned Fray Ramón Pané—who learned the native peoples' tongue—to study their customs and beliefs. Edward Gaylord Bourne calls Pané's written report "our most authentic record of the religion and folklore of the long since extinct Tainos, the aboriginal inhabitants of Hayti."[81] Paradoxically, such haunting encounters—apparently so full of promise and possibility—were quickly followed by dire scenes of intercivilizational conflict and extermination. Steering a ship, drawing an island, and picking up local knowledge are all processes of wayfinding. As the three maps discussed above suggest, ship and map worked in tandem in Europe's epoch-making age of exploration and imperial expansion.[82]

On many of these early Atlantic world maps, we also have a rich visual archive of ethnographic images that I will discuss in the following chapter. Here again, we find scenes of encounter as well as scenes of conflict. As such, these maps can also serve as important intercivilizational documents once we begin more purposefully to gather them in a common site for comprehensive study. Their visual effects seem to speak for themselves, but the maps hosting them are full of political and cultural cunning that go well beyond my discussion of them here and in the next chapter. Once assembled, this archive of cartographic images and strategies will undoubtedly help to cast new light on the cultural role of cartographic semiosis in intercivilizational encounters and conflicts. Visualization scenarios and conventions also play a pervasive role in the rich pre- and post-Columbian Native American mapping practices from various cultural regions of the Americas and the Caribbean. Little has yet been done to bring these still relatively cloistered archival sites into a sustained and fruitful dialogue. The cross-disciplinary and multilingual framework of Atlantic studies should help to foster this much-needed confrontation.

7

Mapping Practices
Word, Line, Image

Several scholars have noted that the European discovery of the new hemisphere was not so much an event as it was a gradual process. Eviatar Zerubavel, for example, argues that it took a good three hundred years and involved "a long mental voyage."[1] In this chapter I will take a closer look at what early modern *cartographic practices* have to tell us about this preeminently cognitive voyage, and once we have a firmer hold on how such maps work as a set of strategies, we can then make use of this expertise as an aid toward delineating the geohistorical *novum* of the new Atlantic studies. The circumatlantic world is above all a space and a critical space at that. It is critical because, like the human face, it is situational—never still or easy to interpret. In short, it is a face with a history, even if much of it is watery surface. As the caption under the depiction of "Geographie" (figure 4) reads in le Sieur de La Croix's *Nouvele metode pour aprendre la geographie universele,* "Vous pouve's par cet Art posseder tout le Monde et savoir La grandeur de la Terre et de L'onde" (By this art you can possess the whole world and know the grandeur of the earth and the sea).[2] The figure of "Geographie" in the print indicates that it is above all cartographic knowledge that leads to mastery and possession.

Without a few tools, though, such knowledge is hard to come by. Ernst Gombrich tells about a group of students who were on a sketching expedition. When their teacher brought them before one of Peking's old city gates and told them to sketch it, they were baffled and didn't know how to begin. Finally, one of the students asked if they could at least be given a picture postcard of the site so that they would have something to copy.[3] The point of the anecdote is that it takes a certain amount of preliminary

Fig. 4. "Geographie," frontispiece, Sieur de La Croix, *Nouvelle metode pour aprendre la geographie universele* (Lyon: Leonard Plaignard, 1717).

training to understand or represent the world. Sieur La Croix explains the *Carte Geographique* (geographic map) by listing four different kinds: general, chorographic, topographical, and geometrical.[4] If we arrange these vertically, one on top of the other, they can be said to cover the same space. But they do so in radically different ways, with each kind of map turning the world into a different object.

A general map depicts the whole world or synthesizes a collection of smaller maps of kingdoms and states, while a chorographic map gives us a closer representation of a region or a city. Topographical and geometrical maps depict specific places and many of the local features in them: fields, woods, hills, roads, rivers, property lines, and so on. By geometrical maps La Croix probably means cadastral maps used originally as a basis for taxation. In the opening drawing of La Croix's book, one of the muses of Geography is looking through a telescope, suggesting that things can be seen at a great distance or close up. Scale is the cartographer's first preoccupation.

Cartographic mimesis, therefore, is always based on an initial decision regarding focus and the level of detail. As we saw in both the La Cosa and Cantino world maps, with respect to the Old World the new islands and continental coasts were considerably enlarged in order to enhance their novelty and attractiveness. Literally, they were made to appear bigger than they were with respect to the land masses of the Old World. In effect, all maps are basically projections and depend on analogy no matter what degree of detail they employ. It is scale and cartographic kind that encourage us to define any map as a set of arbitrary relations and forms. Thus, while we study the representation of space on them, we should be equally aware of the way they maneuver representational space. The two regimes are interdependent as La Croix's different kinds of maps with their different functions indicate. Henri Lefebvre nicely captures this critical relation between maps and the world when he asks, "How many maps, in the descriptive or geographical sense, might be needed to deal exhaustively with a given space, to code and decode all its meanings and contents?"[5] The question is cleverly Faustian, for the answer is "a sort of instant infinity." But Lefebvre would be the first to say that in practice there are only as many maps as there are mapmakers and their specific sets of needs.

In pointing out the new role cartography has currently assumed in the human and social sciences, John Pickles notes that "maps provide the very conditions of possibility for the worlds we inhabit and the subjects we become."[6] This claim is even more true in the early modern period, during the golden age of European cartography. As Spanish, Portuguese, French, English, and Dutch explorers and cartographers gained access to the Western Hemisphere in the first years of the sixteenth century, they also began converting it into a world that suited them, and this imperial process of conversion—acted out on a vast intercivilizational stage involving a host of native peoples and cultures—led equally to their own remaking. Putting up a cross, claiming possession of already inhabited lands, locating mineral-rich territories, setting up a fortified outpost, enforcing the *encomienda* system on the native populations—all these actions are aimed at making the world over into a recognizable European image or scheme. They are also related to cartographic practices in the service of conquest and settlement.

Cartographers not only transmit information; they also produce it. These activities involve procedures such as reduction, synthesis, and translation. Maps miniaturize the world, and in doing so, they convert it into a specifically cartographic idiom. This idiom is extremely rich, and once it is understood, we can better appreciate early modern maps not only as fundamental civilizational documents but also as a set of practices inscribed in the very way the world was understood and transformed. In the spirit of the age, if whole "new worlds" could be discovered, then it seemed that anything was possible. European man had no limits. The inventors of empire in the new hemisphere were driven by their cartographic imagination. In the heyday of discovery and conquest, maps themselves embodied the new secular spirit of utopia as well as its failure, spectacularized by the frequent phenomenon of shipwreck. Sponsored by these two impulses, early modern European maps invented a cartographic semiosphere that went well beyond their own material surfaces. In the sixteenth and seventeenth centuries in particular, the world that counted was very often the one on the map. And the spirit behind the making of them was the same that drove shipmasters to discover the world.

The perennially composite nature of maps is already evident in the variety of names indicating their many functions as well as their versatility: *pinax, pictura, tabula picta, tabula, mappa, itinerarium pictum,* chart, portolano, planisphere, mappemonde, and so on. As William Stahl writes, "You will know them by their maps."[7] As several of these terms indicate, the identity of maps is played out between art and science, and between routes and territory. Maps that resemble pictures (*pictura, tabula picta, itinerarium pictum*) are appreciated especially for their artistic value, while maps that rely above all on tech-

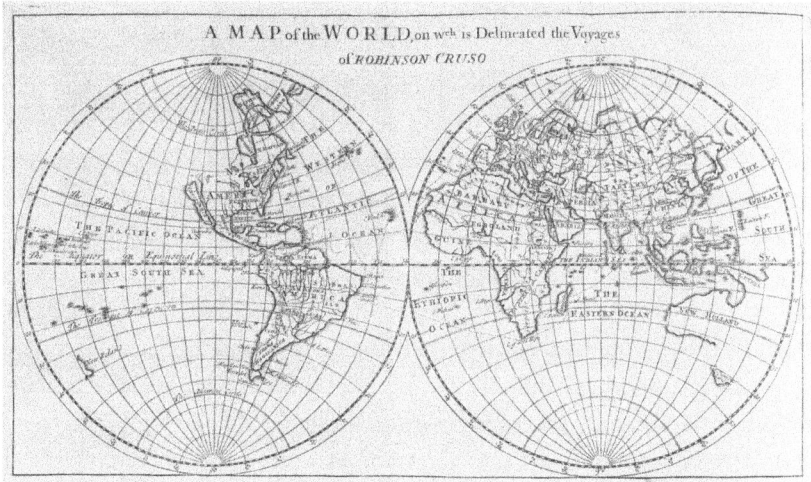

Fig. 5. *A Map of the World on w[hi]ch is Delineated the Voyages of Robinson Cruso[e]*, 1719, from Daniel Defoe, *The Life and Strange Surprizing Adventures of Robinson Crusoe* . . . , Beinecke Rare Book & Manuscript Library, Yale University, Object ID 2034440.

nical and mathematical criteria (the portolano and the planisphere) display a superior scientific knowledge. Sailors used portolan charts to navigate along coasts, while a planisphere is the result of transforming the spherical globe onto a flat surface. This process is called projection.

But maps also invest in a range of representational strategies that go from humble description to high drama, from mirroring nature to staging cultural conflict or circumnavigating the globe. When the great Dutch mapmakers began producing their atlases in the early seventeenth century, they significantly called them either *speculum mundi* or *theatrum mundi* (mirror of the world or theater of the world),[8] thus identifying the two cartographic alternatives of description and dramatization. There are maps made specifically to show the oceanic routes taken by Magellan, Drake, and Cook in their globe-spanning travels, while novels like Defoe's *Robinson Crusoe* begin with a world map to show where their heroes met up with shipwreck (figure 5). In the days of the Roman empire, *itineraria picta* maps (literally, painted itineraries) were used the way we use road maps today, only they were organized around different kinds of sites that were beautifully illustrated. In the early fourteenth century there was a Mediterranean map that was called a *compasso*—from the

Arab word for map, *kunbas*—and it served as a sea chart used specifically for navigation.[9]

As we have seen in the previous chapter, Columbus, Vespucci, Caboto, and other early explorers relied on and made maps to represent the two most important aspects of their enterprise: the route they took and the lands they visited and claimed for their monarch. The term for the first was *periplus*, taken from ancient geography and meaning circumnavigation or an account of a circumnavigation. The term for representing the lands they explored was either *chorographia* or *topographia*, depending on the degree of detail sought. Both of these terms also refer to traditional rhetorical figures used to describe a scene or bring before the reader's eyes something that is absent. This technical terminology suggests a close relation, if not a homology, between cartographic representation and narration. Narration, too, is fundamentally made up of action and exposition. In the first centuries of European exploration and colonial expansion, there was also a close working relation between navigation and narration, and this symbiosis provides further evidence of the new oceanic order emerging with the circumatlantic world. Both cartographic practice and various kinds of narrative reports (including the early novel) achieved mastery in their own right by attending to routes and describing the exotic sites to which they led.

The more we study early modern European cartography for what it can tell us about the rise of the capitalist world system, the more we realize that these maps made use of an extremely broad palette of knowledges and practices that include geometry, arithmetic, astronomy, cosmology, geography, history, aesthetics, art, political science, civilizational analysis, rhetoric, botany, zoology, travel, and by no means least, other maps. It is the uninhibited use of such a wide range of disciplines that makes early Atlantic imperialist maps not only astonishing and indispensable cultural documents but also the absolute metaphor of the age they helped bring into being. When explaining the difficulties he was having in compiling his encyclopedia, d'Alembert famously wrote in his *Preliminary Discourse to the Encyclopedia:* "It is a kind of mappemonde that must show the principal countries, their position and reciprocal dependence, the path that goes in a straight line from one to the other. This is often inhibited by a thousand obstacles which the inhabitants or explorers in each country cannot know, and which could not be shown except in many distinct maps, rich in details. These distinct maps will be the various articles of the Encyclopedia, and the tree or figurative system will be its mappemonde."[10]

D'Alembert's use of cartography to explain how the encyclopedia was organized reminds us of how influential mapping practices had become outside the workshop of mapmakers. Indeed, what is at work here is less a comparison between two forms of knowledge than a way of thinking about reality. Even more importantly, this way of cartographic thinking has a semiotics—a signifying system—of its own. In another famous example of the applicability of the cartographic sign to the nature of language, we read in *La logique de Port-Royal:*

> [W]hen one only looks at a given object as a representation of another, the idea one has of it is an idea of sign and this first object is called a sign. This is the way one ordinarily looks at maps. . . . Because the visible relation existing between these kinds of signs and things clearly indicates that when one claims for the sign the thing signified, one does not mean that this sign is really this thing but that it signifies it and is a figure of it. Thus one will say spontaneously . . . of a map of Italy that it is Italy.[11]

Without the world the map would be a mere ornament, a figment of the cartographer's imagination. But it is equally true that the map is not the world. As the above passage affirms, it is a figure of it. In fact, one of the conventional early modern names for maps was the Latin *figura.*

Thomas More titled his map of Utopia *Utopiae insulae figura,* and later Captain John Mason provided a *figura* of the Indian village of Mystic to illustrate how during the Pequot War the Indians—men, women, and children—were shot down or run through with a sword as they tried to escape (figure 6). The idea of the map itself as a figure and as employing the modal figures of chorography and topography to describe the world at close range, indicates that this term may serve both as a local and a totalizing sign. The term *figure* also points to an implicit passage between map and narration, since narratives, too, are composed of a fabric or syntax of figures. For the purposes of building a broad multidisciplinary approach to the circumatlantic world, I will deal with both map and narration under the rubric of *cartographic semiosis*—meaning the production of signs peculiar to mapping practices but shared by those human sciences that rely on narrative to validate their atlanticist research claims.

Cartographic semiosis (signification) largely depends on an elaboration of the notion of figure as both an all-embracing source of representation—for example, the configuration of the globe—and a local descriptive strategy

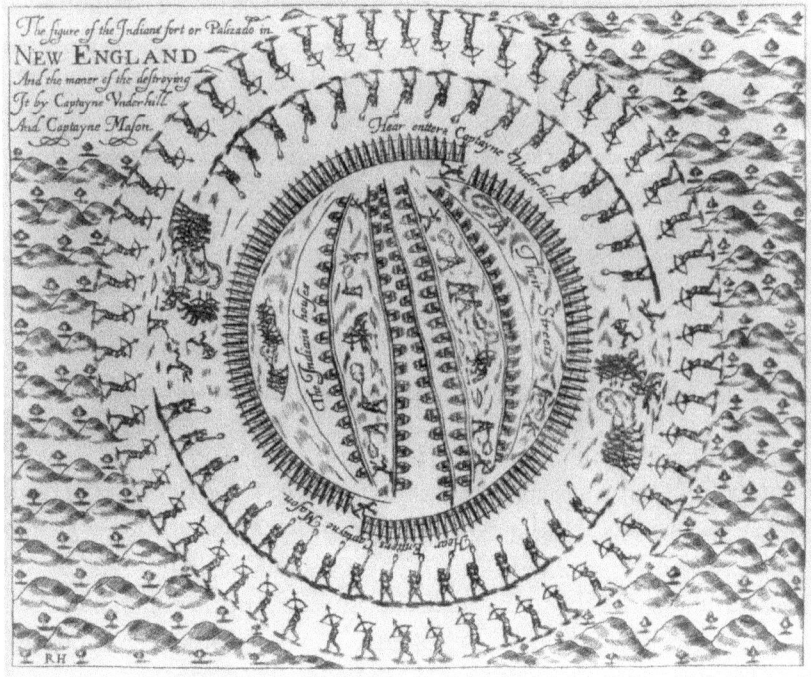

Fig. 6. "The figure of the Indians' fort or Palizado in New England and the manner of the destroying It by Captayne Underhill and Captayne Mason," from John Underhill, *Newes from America* (London: Printed by J.D. for Peter Cole, 1683). Library of Congress, Rare Book and Special Collections Division, LC-USZ62-32055.

involving the use of images of various kinds. The kinship between map and narration that the figurative activity of maps oversees can be diagrammed as follows:

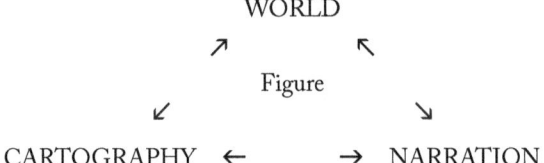

The figure's ability to participate in more than one kind of representation without changing its signifying function provides a structural link between the descriptive work of both maps and narratives. The activity of writing up the world and drawing it are equally figurative, although they use different media. What is important here is that in both cases the scope is to make us *see* the world. In truth, maps configure the world through the use of not only visual imagery but also language. Let us, therefore, take a closer look at the various representational systems they use in substituting a figure of the world for the world itself.

A sophisticated vehicle of communication, the map brings together three different sign systems, which I have elsewhere called *line, word,* and *image* in order to distinguish each of them as separate and often competing semiotic activities.[12] Each system produces its own kind of cartographic information, and maps generally rely on all three, although unequally. As they compete with each other for representational space on the map's surface, these systems create a field of tension that generates the map's semiosphere.[13] It is this higher order of convergence that I am referring to when speaking of cartographic semiosis. When we say that maps are not only about the world but also about maps, we are implicitly calling attention to the representational dynamics of their semiosphere. By appreciating the ways in which images, inscriptions (including titles and place-names), and lines interact on any given map, we are also concerned with its higher order. For while the three activities may seem to form a continuum on the map's surface, they are actually arranged hierarchically, according to the cartographer's coded priorities.[14] In other words, maps are never innocent.

The representational space of maps has a territorial character, and it is this primary fact that the cartographer must deal with when plotting his or her intentions. These intentions are expressed through the use of lines, language (inscriptions, naming practices, titles), and images. Cartographic space comes to life by means of these three systems, and each of them represents a specific kind of expertise. Their combination produces a certain world in a certain rhetorical light and not the world in itself. At the edges of early modern maps of the Western Hemisphere, for example, the cartographic imagination was always running up against its own limits. To deal with these limits, mapmakers have used various strategies to cope with unexplored and unknown terrain. As we have seen, images like St. Christopher could be used to suggest future action and allude to geographical theory rather than expose the mapmaker's own factual shortcomings. Some cartographers chose to extend the words *Terra Incognita* in various type sizes across the blank spaces, as Martin Waldseemüller did on the western edges of *America*. This solution was accompanied by the firm delineation of the continent's western coast even though this line was a total fiction. Other cartographers used the line system in a different way, choosing to blur borders or, if the line in question was the contour of a colored image, thinning or fading the color along the limits in question. It is in critical zones such as the western shores of the new hemisphere that the advantages and limitations of each cartographic system come to light.

Since it is scale that establishes a map's dominant frame of reference, the choosing of it will always have consequences for the systemic alliances among word, line, and image. Furthermore, even when a specific scale is chosen, most maps remain fully aware of other levels of referential space that have been excluded. Thus what was meant to be an internally stable cartographic surface often ends up being troubled and elusive. This absent presence of other levels implies that there is no normative hierarchy among the various possible cartographic scales. This is so because of the nature of the world and the mapmaker's specific aims. No single cartographic scale can exhaust the world's plenitude. Early sixteenth-century maps of the Atlantic world may have superbly captured the first heady voyages of exploration, and discovery, but they came up short when tasked with representing the often destructive effects of settlement and colonization.

While maps must work within the limits they set for themselves, what they include in this space is always framed by what they exclude. On the other hand, each of the three cartographic systems works both with and against the other two, confirms or challenges what the others produce, and is often charged with semioticizing what remains below or above the signifying threshold of the other two. As a result, the map's surface can be a very lively place. To sum up, this liveliness is produced by the map's semiosphere, which referees the tension between the three systems:

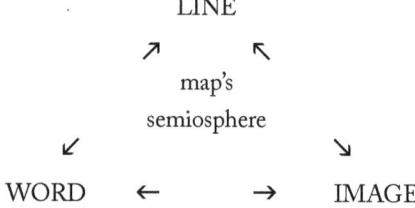

Since maps communicate through lines, words, and images and owe their characteristic astuteness to the seemingly infinite combinations of these three functions, I will now examine how each of these systems produces carto-graphic information, starting with the line.

The Semiosphere's Line System

In his journal of the first voyage, Columbus is always busy charting the route and describing what he sees from the deck of the *Santa Maria*. When he goes ashore, it is to replenish his supplies, repair the ship, or meet some of the native peoples to gather information. But mostly he recounts his route and the particulars of sailing. Thus, in the November 21, 1492, entry we read:

> At sunrise he steered E with a S wind. . . . Then the wind changed to the E and he went S by E and by sunset he had made 12 miles. At this point the Admiral found himself 42 degrees N of the equinoctial line, as at Puerto de Mares. . . . He says that seeing the North Star as high as in Castile led him to believe that the quadrant was accurate. . . . But in that case where were these islands which he had close at hand?[15]

The passage, which has a clipped nautical rigor to it, shows Columbus at his very best but also his most vulnerable. An extremely skilled sailor, we see him logging his route, consulting his quadrant and the North Star, and doing all that is necessary to map his voyage of exploration in its every detail. He had planned this westward route for years and was acquainted with the latest cosmological and cartographic evidence before setting sail.

The map he had with him expressed both his actual knowledge of the earth's expanse and the personal hunch that led him out into the uncharted Ocean Sea. Seven days earlier, his journal—edited by Las Casas—reads, "And he [Columbus] says that he believes that these are the innumerable islands which appear on world maps at the eastern edge (in the waters of the China Sea). He says that he thought that there were great riches and precious stones and spices on them, and that they extend a long way to the S and spread out in every direction."[16] The world maps he is referring to are very likely Ptole-my's, Paolo Toscanelli's, and perhaps Henricus Martellus's (1489–90) or ones very similar to them. The aim of his voyage was steadfastly to produce a west-ern route to China, so that now, when examining the local spices and minerals of the Caribbean islands, he construes them as products of the Orient's fabled trade (mastic, aloes, pepper, and so on). By November 21, 1492, however, the shadow of a doubt crossed his mind and worried his cartographic confidence, leading him to wonder, "But in that case where were these islands which he had close at hand?"

There is a critical lapse that runs through all four of Columbus's voyages, and it is due to the failed correspondence between his cartographic conception of where he was and his actual physical position. Evidently, the map he was relying on had its own powerful logic and presented the world according to his priorities. He had staked everything on it. In crossing the Ocean Sea he sailed along its rhumb lines as much as on salt water. Rhumb lines are abstract and Euclidean, analytical and superficial. They defined his route and gave it a needed clarity. Such lines are the perfect metaphor for the scientific paradigm Columbus put his faith in. The rhumb line that led him to the Caribbean archipelago was utopian in its logic. The picture of the world could be perfected, but it was the picture and not the world that was at issue. In 1516 the logic of the cartographic line helped to model More's *Utopia*.

The problem with Columbus's map is that it had nothing to do with the Caribbean. It got him where he was but not where he wanted to be. To put things right, he simply corrected the geography before him by making it conform to his map. In this case, the most neglected object of the geometric line, whether as scale or rhumb line, was reality. Working within the continuity of the cartographic line's network, the first thing that Columbus sacrificed was the world. What was left of it after he checked it against his map, as he wrote in his journal on November 21, was "these islands which he had close at hand." Columbus claimed possession of a number of Caribbean islands for the king and queen of Castile and Aragon, but on that first voyage he found and forgot them in a single gesture. The early maps representing his voyages all confirm his presence in the seas off China.

The perplexities of Columbus's first voyage help us to distinguish between two kinds of cartographic line, and these indicate the extremes of the line system's representational work as a whole. The first is the geometrical line, which includes above all rhumb lines, lines of latitude and longitude, and scale and administrative lines based on abstract calculation. Scale, for instance, allows us to measure distances; it turns landscape into a smooth surface of standard spatial units. Rhumb lines convert the ocean's surface into a conventional roadway. At the other extreme we have the geographical line, which is descriptive, figurative, and situated more convincingly in the world. In passing

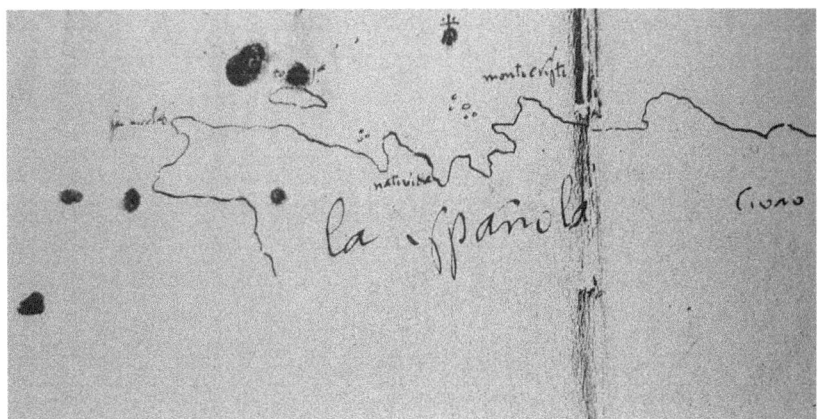

Fig. 7. Columbus's freehand drawing of the coast of Hispaniola. Facsimile reproduction, collection of the author.

from geometrical to geographical line we switch from science to art, so to speak. When Columbus did a freehand drawing of the coast of Hispaniola, he was drawing a geographical line (figure 7).

The closer the geometrical line comes to the real conditions of the world, the more it resembles the concrete, binding work of the cartographic image. The line system contributes to the map's semiosphere in various ways. It establishes scale and casts a web of rhumb lines over the map's surface, but it also traces coastlines, rivers, and the shape of islands and continents. Still, the line's most characteristic activity is geometrical and mathematical, perhaps because it is in this capacity that it provides modern maps with their peculiar rational order and aura. When we want to draw a route or measure the distance between two towns, we must rely on calculation to do so, and these activities belong to the line system.

When, after the American Revolution, surveyors divided up federal land into townships and counties according to the Land Ordinance of 1785, maps of the Northwest Territory displayed a landscape turned into an orthogonal grid. This grid, which eventually covered three-quarters of the nation's territory, is already visible on the continental map Jedidiah Morse included in his *The American Geography; or, A View of the Present Situation of the United States of America,* published in 1792.[17] When the line system completely takes over the map's semiosphere, it can look like Nicolas de Fer's world map of 1705, *Mappe-Monde ou Carte Generale de la Terre.*[18] De Fer has covered the entire globe—the continents, the seas, the islands—with an analytic grid. Underneath the grid lies the world, now seemingly tamed and measured. Besides being a map of the world, this *Carte Generale* also gives us an autopsy of the mapmaker. Images have been eliminated as superfluous, and place-names are reduced to an absolute minimum. Instead, the grid reigns supreme. Reason has triumphed, along with a kind of calm mathematical perfection. The geographer Gunnar Olsson once asked, "What is geography if it is not the drawing and interpreting of a line?"[19]

The Semiosphere's Word System

Beyond the line, of course, is the world, and for cartographic semiosis, language and images. While the line system characteristically produces geometric space, the word system generates semantic space and the image, figurative space. When the line system outlines a continent or an island, it converges with the image system, although its purpose remains exquisitely mathematical. The word system is above all tasked with placing names on things of various sizes such as continents, regions, states, islands, cities, towns, rivers, mountains, and lakes, but it also accounts for inscriptions of all kinds, from a map's title to legends and other short bits of narrative prose and poetry. Pursuing a different emphasis than Gunnar Olsson, Giorgio Mangani argues, "Geography, in reality, is a problem of names, of geographical etymologies, of relations between names and places."[20] Today, perhaps even more than the pages Columbus dedicated to crossing the Atlantic and sailing among the Bahamas and the Greater Antilles in the Caribbean archipelago, we are especially struck by his practice of naming the islands he came upon, as if they were uninhabited and unclaimed.

One of the illustrations that accompanied the Latin edition of Columbus's letter of 1493 shows a Spanish ship in full sail and behind it the islands that he discovered on his first voyage. Each of the islands bears a name in Spanish. As we learn from the letter, they were named in the following order: San Salvador, Santa Maria de Concepcion, Ferrandina, Ysabella, Juana, and Spañola.[21] This picture of the newly named Spanish islands tells us more than any theory could. Had we not been told the sequence in which they were discovered, we could have reconstructed it all the same by studying the obligatory hierarchy of names. Columbus was both a man of faith and a loyal servant of his monarchs. King Ferdinand and Queen Isabella, too, were very devout Catholics, so the first name Columbus gave to an island the Arawaks called Guanahani makes perfect sense: *San Salvador.* Having been saved from the twin perils of turbulent sea and rebellious crew, he must have felt plucked from failure by the Savior himself. Thus the name was also an act of thanksgiving. Then comes the name of the ever merciful mediatrix, *Santa Maria de Concepcion,* and after that the names of members of the royal family.

The last name, *Spañola,* announces the future unity of the Spanish peninsula under the expanding influence of the king of Aragon and the queen of Castile and its first piece of transatlantic empire. Hispaniola would shortly become the Spanish gateway to the Caribbean and would host the first European colony in the Western Hemisphere. As we have already seen, Columbus's first official act when landing on the island of Guanahani was to take possession of it. But to do so a name was necessary. The act of naming and that of claiming possession went hand in hand. By naming the island, Columbus got an initial grip on the Western Hemisphere and turned it into a Spanish place. As he went along, *San Salvador* became part of a chain of Castilian islands, and on the map they appeared as a chain of place-names. This toponymic sequence exhibited a new but totally familiar symbolic order on the western side of the Ocean Sea. All the names he gave refer to other names and have their own genealogies. But his are tied to places and must be read and understood in space. It is this ecological perspective that cartographic semiosis takes for granted. Without such a geohistorical awareness, it is impossible to understand the process of building European empires in the Atlantic world.

On the map's semiosphere we see the place-names for what they are—names in place—and this turns them into hieroglyphs of a sort. As signs of inhabited spaces, they represent an administrative system and evoke a European urban order overlaying an already present indigenous order. The visibility and position of names on these early imperial maps always form part of a cultural narrative in space. In the case of Columbus and those who came after him, place-names on early modern Atlantic maps document patterns of civilizational dissemination, confrontation, and annihilation, depending on the removal and addition of names. When studied on a sequence of maps—all dealing with the same island, region, or continent—this toponymic dissemination has inestimable archival value. Christian Jacob has referred suggestively to such early maps as offering "a cemetery of names."[22] Place-names also map first intentions, primal scenes of cultural presence, geographical penetration, and patterns of settlement and withdrawal.

Such first language proclaims and creates a world while canceling another. *San Salvador* alone stood for the beginning of a new presence, as well as a radical discontinuity. Names alluding to the Holy Savior and the Holy Mother Mary mark the taking place of a Christian ethos and Castilian diplomacy. They signified not only an act of possession but also the staging of a cultural perspective. In his journal of the first voyage it did not take Columbus long to begin referring to himself and his fellow Castilians as Christians and to the natives as poor, naked, preposterously generous, and perhaps most importantly, godless. It was a papal bull that gave Columbus the right to evangelize non-Christian peoples and obliged him to look after their spiritual welfare. Taking possession of the land was thus legitimated by canon law. Once the natives began to resist, then the law of war came into effect and colonial scruples disappeared. But these two forms of law were often circumvented, since the natives, in their generosity, freely gave their land away. Or so Columbus observed in his journal.[23]

There are different hierarchies of toponyms and different kinds of toponymic activity. The early use of *Mundus Novus,* for example, announces the dawning of the utopian mentality of Europe's distinctly modern civilization. That a new world could be said to actually exist in space was an implicitly stunning claim. The name itself was floated in large capital type in various places on maps by different European cartographers. It was usually illuminated by a backdrop of blank space, in keeping with modernity's claim that before it there was only prehistory and after, only more of modernity. Thus the words *Mundus Novus* negated temporality and implied in a sense the end or culmination of history. The name was also accompanied by a new order of absolute liberty, especially in its most literal form of the free movement of large groups of European peoples—Hobbes's multitudes.

When the place-name *Mundus Novus* began to be substituted by other vaguely attached national place-names, the epistemic moment of a supposedly halcyon "New World" was rapidly transformed into geopolitical competition for colonies among the European nations. These national names were basically choronyms; that is, they represented a large regional space the boundaries of which were generally unknown. Such choronyms—like Sir Francis Drake's *New Albion* in Northern California, or *Terra Florida* or *Peru* or *Nova Gallia* or *Virginia* or *Nova Spagna*—were written large and made to stretch far so that national claims could be publicized well ahead of actual settlement. In this sense cartographic testimony often preceded colonial practice. The European choronyms often represented projects in unknown lands before they became realities. The word "Nova" or "New" preceding a specific European nation's toponymic claims continued the utopian outlook first introduced with *Mundus Novus*.

Smaller-sized, and thus less important choronyms, as on John Smith's mother map of Virginia of 1612, indicated the substantial presence of native peoples. This kind of cartographic information is now often the only evidence we have of their original whereabouts and their language. Archaeologists have used such maps to locate the sites of lost towns and lost peoples. As time passed and settlement became a priority, topographical maps like Smith's *Virginia* and Jacques Le Moyne de Morgues' *Floridae descriptio* (circa 1556) were needed, and these present a much more detailed picture of the intercivilizational theater of the colonial period. Facing each other across a river like the James in Virginia, the names of native and European villages stood for ethnonyms—that is, places representing different peoples, customs, languages, and beliefs. Sometimes colonial maps will provide two place-names for the same town, the original indigenous and the new colonial one. As we have seen, this cultural balancing act is one of the interesting features of the introductory map to Cotton Mather's *Magnalia Christi Americana*, first published in 1702.[24] Although the map was meant to celebrate the triumphal expansion of the congregational churches in New England, it is on the western frontier that the process remained critical.

Like the cartographic line, the word system also has a representational range that goes from the abstract to the concrete. Inscriptions and names in the Americas often celebrate European common places or, at the other extreme, seek to capture something notable in the place they represent. If the latter, they are descriptive; but if they seek to commemorate, say, a European prince or monarch, as the name of the Virginia colony was chosen to honor Queen Elizabeth, then we immediately have an abrupt split between word and place. Native American place-names are usually descriptive and provide us with local knowledge of the landscape. In the colonial and national periods, new European place-names were frequently linked to specific political occasions and reflected the cultural agenda of their day. Although place-names are spread over the land like a blanket and seem all uncannily current on the map, they obviously represent a variety of historical strata and myriads of linked and truncated histories, myths, and legends. Each place-name represents a scene, an act; and many, a founding. Thanks to these names on early modern European maps, we can read the Americas as an inexhaustible memory theater and a graffiti board of almost endless opinions about the world. Attached to specific sites, these names are not like ordinary language. Quite literally, cartographic words stand for places and territories and thus have a special witnessing function. Perhaps for this very reason, towns cannot cast off the shadow of their name: *stat nominis umbra* (the name's shadow remains). Often, through the course of history, that foundational name becomes greater than the town itself.

The Semiosphere's Image System

On maps, place-names and titles and inscriptions must compete or cooperate with the two other cartographic activities of line and image. The word system, particularly through the agency of titles and place-names, can help to conceptualize and locate abstract projects, such as nation building, or they can point to local singularities embedded in a specific place. In the latter case, they help to evoke a scenography, which is proper to the image system. In what is perhaps the most important cartographic *figura* accompanying Columbus's first letter (figure 8), we see a European galley in the foreground and in the middle distance a smaller boat with two well-dressed ambassadors near a handsome island marked *Insula hyspana*. In Columbus's journal the entry for December 9, 1492, reads, "Opposite there are some meadows, the most beautiful in the world and almost comparable with the lands of Castile, although these have the advantage, for which reason he gave the island the name Isla Espanola."[25] One of these ambassadors is offering a cup to a group of naked natives, the first of whom is also extending a gift of some sort to the two Spaniards in the boat. Another set of natives, also naked, is uniformly turned away in fear.

This drawing represents what is certainly one of the most important intercivilizational scenes we have of the early period of exploration and colonization in the Western Hemisphere. I have found few others like it.[26] That the gift economy framed all such diplomatic encounters between native peoples and European explorers and colonizers seems finally to have won some attention among historians and cultural studies scholars, although its importance as a competing interpretive paradigm for the circumatlantic world remains

Fig. 8. *Insula hyspana*, from Columbus's first letter, *De Insulis nuper in mari Indico repertis* (Basel, 1494). Facsimile reproduction, collection of the author.

undertheorized.[27] As I mentioned in the previous chapter, the historian Bernard Bailyn coined the term "marchland" to conceptualize the "atavistic conflicts" along the frontier line of intercivilizational contact and European settlement in the Western Hemisphere, but he completely passes over the equally important paradigm of gift diplomacy.[28] Columbus's journal is very much about gift exchange and setting up alliances with the peoples he meets. That modern Europeans also operated on the basis of hospitality and political friendship is evident in the gifts the admiral brought with him to give to the great khan and in the gift-giving ceremony that sealed his alliance with the head cacique of Hispaniola.

As more and more European colonies were planted in the various coastal regions and islands of the Western Hemisphere, synthetic representations of the Atlantic world began to be supplemented by more detailed topographical maps laden with images of ethnographic and iconographic scenes. These images recorded the local peoples, their everyday habits and dress, their tools and weapons, the products of the earth, the habitat, and, crucially, scenes of intercivilizational encounters governed by cooperation and outright conflict. Through this frequent investment in visual images, maps became a dominant and precious means of information and are now of enormous archival value for Atlantic studies scholars. As we have seen, the place-name *Isla Espanola* substituted the island's indigenous name and immediately polarized things, the way a magnet would a scattering of iron shavings. The island now became simultaneously a place of alliance and antithesis and a place of gift exchange and fear.

As the images (*figurae*) accompanying Columbus's first letter spread throughout Europe, Hispaniola was exposed to view. The name itself became a European byword, and the ethnographic scene glossed the name. Images on maps, whether topographical or not, were generally used to fill in what cartographers called the blank spaces, but their function was often more than decorative. From these blank spaces—and later on, from the outside borders of the highly embellished Dutch maps of the sixteenth century—their job was to visualize what was happening or what could be found in the inhabited places of the Americas. Continuing the rhetorical tradition of *laus urbis* based on classical celebrations of the city of Athens, they also provided triumphant views of the new European towns. Such images undoubtedly helped to promote colonization and performed a task only they could fulfill: namely, seduce the viewer by pulling him or her below the order of the line and the word and into the territory as a well-ordered and familiar place.

Stunning images invited not only contemplation but also action. These early maps often persuaded through images, and occasionally images became the dominant means of persuasion within the map's semiosphere. When the image system dominates, we have a picture map or chorographic map. Cartographic images are either scenographic or iconic. Just as a map can be reduced to the geometrical machinations of a Euclidean system of lines, so can it be enlarged to represent a single image such as that of the Mundus Novus. Both systems, line and image, are theoretically total systems. On early modern maps the latter system was employed above all to narrate moments of discovery and intercivilizational encounters and contractions. By studying such cartographic scenographies systematically, across the mapmaking traditions of the different European countries as well as the visual documents from the various indigenous civilizations, we can trace a unique version of the rise of Western civilization and the concomitant destruction of native civilizations on the very stage where these processes took place. On one hand, we have quasi-mythic images of a New World Eden—in his third voyage Columbus actually believed on good geographical evidence that he had located the biblical Paradise. And on the other, we have scenes of savagery beyond the bounds of humanity. Let us first take a look at Paradise and then at the vexed issue of cannibalism.

As Giovanni Battista Ramusio's pace-setting, three-volume compendium *Navigationi et Viaggi* of 1550–59 bears out, the most typical early images of Native American life were those of canoes, hammocks, weapons, and domesticated agricultural plants such as maize, pumpkins, and tobacco. There are also other kinds of images on sixteenth- and seventeenth-century maps, and these are often clustered into narrative scenes of different aspects of Mesoamerican or Native North American village life.[29] Such images and scenes are often the first visual signs of early "American" civilizations available to us from a European perspective. Already in March of 1494, when Castilians began to colonize Hispaniola, Columbus commanded a simple priest, one Brother Ramón Pané, to live among the people of the island, learn their language and collect data on their religious beliefs. Brother Pané lived a year in the region of Macoris, in the land of the cacique Guanaoconel, and then for two years in the territory of the cacique Guarionex. As Las Casas writes in his *Apologetica*, this simple priest was the only one to learn the language of the island.[30] The result of his fieldwork was published in *Historie Del S.D. Fernando Colombo* in Venice in 1571 as "Scrittura di fra Roman delle antichità de gl'Indiani, le quali egli con diligenza, come huomo che sa la lor lingua, ha raccolte per commandamento dello Ammiraglio."[31] This authoritative study is now considered the first "pre-Columbian" ethnographic report we have of the religion of the Taino peoples of Hispaniola.[32]

This important document, until recently seldom discussed by scholars of the period, captures some of the civilizational prejudices and curiosity the Spanish colonists must have had when faced for the first time with a new and unknown humanity—peoples who threatened the belief that the human race sprang wholly from Adam. We should remember, too, that the Castilian colonists on the island of Hispaniola had a simple agenda: extract gold and silver and convert the natives. This latter task quickly took the brutal form of the *requerimiento* and the *encomienda* system, the first authorized by the papacy and the second by the king of Aragon and Castile. But there was also much debate over what legal and moral principles should be applied in dealing with these apparently unsophisticated peoples. This was one of the controversial issues of the early sixteenth century. According to an attractive philosophical thread woven into the unfolding civilizational narrative of the rapidly modernizing European societies, the peoples of the New World were living in a state of nature, the way the ancient Mediterranean peoples once did in the Golden Age. The Americans were born free, went about naked, stood tall, and lived without the corruption and decadence of war-torn Europe. The oneiric picture Vespucci painted of them in his 1502 letter to Lorenzo de' Medici echoes through the work of Montaigne, Shakespeare, and Rousseau:

> We found the entire land inhabited by people completely naked, men as well as women, without at all covering their shame. . . . They have no law or religious faith, they live as nature dictates, they do not know of the immortality of the soul. They have no private property among them, for they share everything. They have no borders of kingdoms or province; neither have they a king or anyone they obey: each is his own master. They do not administer justice, which is not necessary for them, since greed does not prevail among them. They live together and the houses are made like very big huts, and, for people who have no iron or any other metal, these huts or rather houses can well be called miraculous.[33]

Again and again, maps like Juan Vespucci's world chart of 1526 and Johannes Janssonius's regional map of Brazil (circa 1640, detail in figure 9) display images of huts to symbolize the idealized order set forth in the above passage. The hut assumed special iconic status on maps of the Americas because of

Fig. 9. Image of indigenous longhouse (bottom left), from *Accuratissima Brasiliae Tabula,* by Johannes Janssonius, published in Amsterdam, circa 1640.

ethnographic curiosity and also because of the mythically charged perception of native life in the New World. In 1516 Thomas More, although thinking back to Plato and Lucian, set his ideal city of Utopia somewhere in the hemisphere of the New World. What is more, his internal narrator, a Portuguese-born sailor named Raphael Hythloday, "joined himself in company with Amerigo Vespucci, and in the three last voyages of those four that be now in print and abroad in every man's hands, he continued still in his company, saving that in the last voyage he came not home again with him."[34] Although spatially distant, utopia was internally near. Somewhere in the Caribbean archipelago or along the northern coast of Brazil lay More's island of Utopia. We are given a map of it, but not directions on how to get there.

In 1492, the very year Columbus sailed westward across the Ocean Sea, Duke Ercole I had the architect Biagio Rossetti begin work on enlarging the medieval city of Ferrara. Rossetti's audaciously open plan, which became the model of the Renaissance city, was based on two "corsi" or orthogonal axes that cut through and defined the modern part of the city. Where they intersected, Ercole I built his famous Diamanti Palace. The Renaissance addition was a huge urbanistic composition in which every detail (church, piazza, and palace) counted in itself but was also an integral part of the whole. Taking note of this new conception of urban space, the historian Jacob Burckhardt called Ferrara Europe's first modern city.[35] The utopian spirit of secular perfectibility inhabited not only Rossetti's modern urban plan of Ferrara but also informed the early Atlantic voyages, modern European maps of the Atlantic world, and of course More's *Utopia*. All of them invested deeply in different forms of rational order: the straight and true rhumb line, Rossetti's orthogonal grid, and the totally planned space of the island of *Utopia*. At this point we should also recall that Carl Schmitt's definition of the new Atlantic world as an Oceanic order was unwittingly cartographic. The perfect emblem of modern European expansionism, cartographic semiosis during this period enabled the Europeans to turn the Atlantic—and then the Western Hemisphere—into their own backyard. Needless to say, the consequences for the indigenous American peoples were catastrophic.

That a burgeoning modern civilization based on a techno-scientific vision of the world became enchanted with the simple huts of so-called primitive peoples in Vespucci's New World should come as no surprise. As the philosopher Robert Redeker has observed, utopia is the result of a blending of dream and reason, the oneiric and the rational. It is a "dream that finds itself inscribed and immediately hidden in the account book of reason."[36] In like fashion, the cartographic line, with its rational and mathematical sense of the world, and the cartographic image, with its addiction to the world's circumstantial plenitude, can be seen to compete with and complement each other on early modern Atlantic maps. The spirit of the line, too, has oneiric ambitions; it would dream away the world's imperfections through a process of detachment, delocalization, and deterritorialization.

More's cartographically framed *Utopia* is a land recently discovered. An offspring of 1492, the modern version of this genre sprung from Vespucci's *Mundus Novus*. The gradually dawning presence of a new hemisphere allowed Europeans to observe themselves from the outside, to project on faraway Hispaniola a number of inner questions about their increasingly restless and conquering soul.[37] That Columbus's account of Hispaniola and More's island of Utopia share similar beginnings is a fact suggested by More himself: "But King Utopus, whose name as conqueror the island beareth (for before his time it was called Abraxa), . . . brought the rude and wild people to that excellent perfection in all good fashions, humanity, and civil gentleness, wherein they now go beyond all the people of the world."[38] In a spirit reminiscent of Ferrara's Biagio Rossetti, Utopus cut and dug up some fifteen miles of ground in order to have the sea surround the land. In this way Utopia became an island. Columbus,

Vespucci, Rossetti, and Utopus all embody the exuberance of this new civilizational mentality.

The image of the hut immediately became a standard cartographic locus on sixteenth- and seventeenth-century maps. As such, it condensed and stiffened into iconic form all that the New World and its native peoples came to represent for European observers. Apart from this archetypal value, the hut and related scenes worked in complex ways. As part of a topica of New World icons meant to induce footloose European adventurers to start life over, the hut invited viewers to appropriate this charming reality for colonial purposes. But it also stood for a state or a concept that functioned critically. For instance, in the seventeenth century the primitive hut evoked the noble savage and a pristine relation with elementary nature, a nature uncontaminated by modern civilization. What may have seemed theory in Giambattista Vico's *Scienza nuova* became simple fact in the Americas. Earlier than Vico, in the first architectural tracts of the early modern period, the hut represented the origins of the constructive principle, an immediate truth or natural model of the originary act of architecture itself.[39]

Such cartographic loci as the hut or scenographies of native village life on early maps of the Americas not only stirred the reader's dawning ethnographic curiosity but also set up the conditions for speculation and criticism. Like loci in rhetoric, they opened up a space of analogy and confrontation as their iconic status rubbed against the other signifying systems of the map's semiosphere as well as the indexical circumstances of their placement. The locus of the hut was quickly offset by the rival archetypal image of the native as cannibal (figure 10), and for a time these two images worked side by side in the same way as the opposing political categories of gift exchange and marchland. Also in the narratives of Columbus and Vespucci we find these contrasting descriptions and political paradigms, and cartographers were quick to depict such tensions as part of their cultural mission. In fact, these two scenes—of Edenic dwelling and abominable cannibalism—represent the extremes of intercivilizational encounter and contraction. More's King Utopus is described as bringing refinement, civility, and humanity to the island of Abraxa, and we are told he did so through conquest. Like Prospero's dealings with Caliban in Shakespeare's play *The Tempest,* so Utopus's refashioning of the Abraxans has a long and often muted foreground. Nevertheless, in Hawthorne's romance *The Scarlet Letter* the "American" Hester Prynne refuses to bow her head in that exemplary city on a hill.

Fig. 10. Image of cannibals, from Janssonius's map of Brazil.

Sebastian Münster's map of 1546, *Novae Insulae,* is a deceptively simple embodiment of many of the signifying machinations I have discussed above.[40] Strikingly, all of its information is communicated by means of the two systems of image and word, and this gives it a pictorial clarity and geographical eloquence it otherwise would not have. In keeping with the decision to give top priority to the Western Hemisphere's completed profile, the line system has been reduced to providing a clear geographical configuration of the continents. This configuring work is theoretically interesting above all for its depiction of the borders of the north and south land masses. Münster was the first to do so in an earlier map of 1540. The 1546 map also introduces the presence of Giovanni da Verrazzano's inner sea (visible above *Terra Florida* and believed to be an open corridor to Cathay), the extreme placement of *Francisca* to the east, and the proximity of *Zipangu* (Japan) and other islands in the China Sea.

The word system is used sparingly and for this very reason to great effect. It is not allowed to distract from the map's principal scope of configuring New World geography. The most spectacular writing is in the form of the place-name Die Nüw Welt (in Münster's attention-getting Gothic script) which is further accompanied by a Latin inscription explaining that this hemispheric island is also called America and Brasilia. There is no cluttering effect of names of towns or colonies, only a few regional names, all of which are rendered in universal Latin rather than the modern colonial vulgates. These spare choronyms are set off by a color-block system used to segment the lands politically, although there are no flags or other national icons to suggest political face-offs or mar the simple pastel washes of color. The overall effect of this hard-won semiospheric simplicity is that of a peaceable world. Adding to this visually soft use of color are stylized groupings of trees distributed rhythmically and sparingly among the various lands, thereby greening the New World in promise.

There are, however, two images that significantly adjust the map's oneiricism. The first, the colossal image of a ship, is meant to celebrate Magellan's circumnavigation of the globe, a feat that signaled the triumph of an energetic civilization with world-historical pretensions. Magellan's voyage radically affected cartographic thinking and led to the "scoop" represented by Münster's map. The ship was named *Victoria* and also appeared on other maps of the period.[41] The second image is that of a bush-like structure from which is dangling the truncated leg of a human being and the head of either a cannibal or his victim. The bush seems made up of cut-off branches and may also represent a primitive, makeshift hut. If this is the case, then it contradicts the conventional archetypal image of the hut as an emblem of paradise. There is also an accompanying inscription, *Canibali,* that leaves no doubt about the meaning of the scene. After Münster's map, Brasilia became the chosen site for the placement of scenes of cannibalism, and it was used repeatedly as a civilizational marker, as on Johannes Janssonius's *Accuratissima Brasiliae Tabula* of the early seventeenth century.

Like the hut image, that of the cannibal can be called a *figurant,* to emphasize the extraordinary effect it had on European viewers. The term *figurant* stands for the ongoing signifying energy of the figure rather than the figure understood in its already signified sense. As rhetorical loci, images of the hut and the cannibal could also be called *imagines agentes* (literally, active images), but what is important here is to stress their iconic forcefulness. This signifying energy is due to their ability to condense major intercivilizational issues. As privileged civilizational documents, early modern maps of the Western Hemisphere recorded and dramatized the encounters and conflicts of different peoples and societies. The major way they did this was through a highly focused repertoire of iconographic images and scenes that became increasingly polarized as the process of colonization began in earnest. While such icons as the parrot, the hut, and the hammock were coveted symbols of a new and originary civilizational order, scenes of cannibalism represented the deepest fears and anxieties of the European colonizers, if not the absolute negation of civilization itself. While King Ferdinand of Castile fully approved of the intermarriage of Indians and Spaniards, by the 1550s the rights and privileges of mestizos began to be curtailed.[42] As narratives like those of Álvar Núñez Cabeza de Vaca's *Naufragios* testified, the most civilized Spaniard from the peninsula could easily regress to cannibalism if he were stripped of cultural restraints and starving.[43] Maps of the Americas visually captured the colonial settler's "predicamental vision"[44] and externalized their innermost fears.

In his recent book *L'aperto*, the philosopher Giorgio Agamben discusses "the anthropological machine" that each culture regularly and obsessively uses to define what is human and what inhuman, what belongs to the category of humanity (*humanitas*) and what to that of animality (*animalitas*).[45] This is done over and over again simply because *Homo sapiens* is constitutively both human and animal. What is always at stake here is the production of the human first by opposing man and animal, the human and the inhuman, and then by excluding features of the second term. Agamben writes, "Exactly because the human is, in fact, every time already presupposed, the machine actually produces a sort of state of exception, a zone of indeterminacy in which the outside is only the exclusion of an inside and the inside, in its turn, only the inclusion of an outside."[46] Returning to the civilizational images discussed above, the map's semiosphere uses the image of the cannibal to produce an outside that then becomes a way of exorcizing a set of inner fears and anxieties. Again, by including a radically negative image of inhumanity and savagery within its representational space, the map also seeks to exclude those brutish inclinations hidden in the breast of the European colonizer.

These repeated acts of cartographic exclusion attempted to forestall the colonizer's inner urge to "go native" by including outrageous scenes of beastliness and treachery on the map's surface. These acts also helped to legitimate the even more outrageous deeds of inhumanity famously narrated by Hernán Cortés, Francisco Pizarro, and other conquistadors. In effect, the process of conquering, converting, and enslaving native populations, stigmatized by the blighting effects of human sacrifice and cannibalism, suggests that the gears of Agamben's anthropological machine never stopped turning during the building of Nova Spagna. Nor would they stop in the building of the Virginia and New England colonies. While some native peoples did eat the adult male flesh of their enemy in a ritualized context, what early modern maps such as

Münster's suggest is that all of the inhabitants of *Die Nüw Welt* were cannibals and ate human flesh as a normal everyday practice.[47]

On Sebastiano Caboto's handsome world map of 1544, all three cartographic systems make equally spectacular contributions to a representation
of the circumatlantic world that is as much *speculum* (mirror) as it is *theatrum*
(theater). I would like to draw our attention to the map's dramatic battle scene
between the Spanish conquistadors and what is probably the army of the
Inca cacique Atahualpa. The battle scene, as the map indicates, is set in *Peru*
provincia and alludes to the conquest of the cities of Cajamarca and the royal
capital Cusco in the years 1532 and 1534 by Francisco Pizarro, Hernán de Soto,
and a small contingent of a little over two hundred men. What is interesting
is that these men were not professional soldiers but artisans, notaries, and
traders; yet they were willing to face thousands of Inca warriors for the sole
purpose of getting rich.[48] And rich they became. As Henry Kamen writes:

> The amassing of the Inca's treasure was one of the most emblematic acts in the
> history of all empires. It displayed to perfection the obsession of Europeans with
> the wealth associated with precious metals. Above all it displayed their complete
> indifference to the destruction of the cultures with which they came into contact.
> As the ornaments were rounded up by the Incas' messengers from the four corners
> of his [Atahualpa's] part of the empire—plates, cups, jewelry, tiles from temples,
> artifacts—they were systematically melted down under Spanish supervision, and
> reduced to ingots.[49]

Within a few months much of the artistic heritage of the Inca civilization was destroyed, that is, reduced to a fabulous 13,420 pounds of gold and
26,000 pounds of silver. The native peopless that appear on early modern
maps are rarely clothed the way the warriors are in the battle scene mentioned above. Usually they are presented within the binary vise of naked
primitives or bestial cannibals, the latter having a defensive function implying
a coded form of intercivilizational censure. These scenes are often located in
a specific geographical area, like Brazil, but their real setting is civilizational
rather than geographical. Thus, while there may be a metonymic relation
between a scene of cannibalism and a particular region, the scene also has
implications for whole societies and communities in the Americas. Read as
total social facts, cartographic images of cannibalism can be seen as helping
to cue the kind of ruthless action for which Pizarro and Cortés have become

famous. This intimate relationship between the symbolic activity of maps and the events of colonial history in the circumatlantic world have yet to be studied systematically and with the added appreciation of cartographic sign production. Perhaps with the renewed interest in civilizational analysis and the multidisciplinary needs of a burgeoning Atlantic studies matrix, early modern maps and their dynamic mix of different kinds of knowledges will lead to a reevaluation of cartographic archives and their full integration into the developments described in chapters 1 and 2.

In Pierre Desceliers's slightly later world map of 1550, we have an even more elaborate intercivilizational staging, thanks primarily to the runaway effects of the map's image system.[50] There are several scenographic flashpoints on the southern continent that add a further gloss to cartographic uses of the cannibal icon. In the northwest part we have two groups of native peoples at war with each other, with those to the right apparently associated with a peaceful setting composed of huts, hammocks, and parrots. In the northwest part of the continent, in the area indicated by the regional name *Le Peru* we have another battle scene, this time between the Spaniards and the Incas. The Spaniards, who are grouped next to a wooden fortification, are armed with modern weapons and cannons, while the Inca warriors, who are clothed in tunics of sorts, are armed with bows and arrows.

Above the fort is the legend *La conqueste du perou faicte par Les espaignoles* (The conquest of Peru by the Spaniards) and above the group of Indian warriors we read in slightly larger letters *canibales*. In the immediate vicinity are also a number of icons of castles and towns, in particular one indicating the royal Inca city of Cusco. But what is especially important is the transfer of the cannibal label onto the Incas as a whole. In *La relazione del viaggio che fece il capitano Fernando Pizarro per ordine del governatore suo fratello . . .* by Francesco de Xerez, we find this confirmation: "[T]hey came with a great captain called Luminabe . . . who was to come during the night into the lodges of the Spaniards, and the first to die was to be the governor, and they were going to free Atahualpa their lord from prison. And he said that of the people of Quito 200,000 warriors were coming and 30,000 Caribs, who eat human flesh."[51] Were we to create an inventory of all of the images and scenes on Desceliers's map, we would have a fairly representative thesaurus of the icons of Spanish conquest at mid-sixteenth century.

It is seldom recognized, however, that this century also gave birth to two major literary *figurae*, both of which owe their structuring horizons to cartographic sign production. The first, utopia, needs no introduction, given its recognized status as a literary and political text. Like the cartographic line, it seeks to dominate space, to impose a rational order on messy reality. Its narrative priority is chorographic, its perspective governed by a scientific or philosophical eye. Like early modern maps, utopias strive to create an *imago mundi* (image of the world) or, to borrow from Derek Gregory, "an orderly projection of the world made available for inspection by the mind."[52] It is this ultimately extreme ambition that makes it hyperbolic and doomed to failure. The second figure, *naufragium* (shipwreck), has gone largely unexamined as a codified cultural site.[53]

Many of our most significant Atlantic narratives invest in or are defined by the chronotope of shipwreck, from Columbus's first letter of 1493, Antonio Pigafetta's *Primo viaggio intorno al globo terracqueo,* and Álvar Núñez Cabeza de Vaca's *Naufragios* to Antonio de Guevara's *Libro de los inventares del arte del marear,* the first sixteenth-century compilations of sea voyages by Ramusio, the Hakluyts, William Strachey's "True Reportory of the Wrack," the narratives of John Smith, Sir Walter Raleigh, and a significant part of the literature of the middle passage, to name a few. We should not forget that ships were the vehicles that made the European oceanic order possible.[54] Sensitive to the special relation between new cartographic information and ships, early modern cartographers scattered them freely around the watery surface of their maps, visually suggesting that Europe's colonial ambitions were truly global. Nevertheless, ships were foundering or disappearing or losing their cargo all the time—to the point that shipwreck, too, came to epitomize the oceanic experience, only now not its utopian moment but utopia's impossibility. In the Atlantic world shipwreck became a commonplace. Utopia and *naufragium* together represent the two extremes of the same geopolitical and geohistorical experience.

Here I would like to make a few preliminary observations about *naufragium*'s cartographic affinities. Once the cartographic line system cast a web of rhumb lines over the Atlantic world—as in the Gastaldi map mentioned in chapter 6—it seemed as if that world had been tamed and that sea voyaging had now become an increasingly routine event. Taken to its extreme *ratio,* this network of lines not only allowed for routed travel but also represented a world reduced to a picture, as if surging seas and wild weather were now under human control. More's Utopus was a very busy and successful town planner, and in the opening pitch to the reader in Francis Bacon's *New At-*

lantis, we read: "This fable my Lord devised, to the end that he might exhibit therein a model or description of a college instituted for the interpreting of nature and the producing of great and marvellous works for the benefit of men, under the name of Salomon's House."[55]

Bacon's fable, another utopia, begins with a happy shipwreck. Adrift and starving in the open seas on their way from Peru to China, Bacon's Spanish-speaking sailors happen upon the island called New Atlantis. There, on a very special occasion, one of the fathers of the House of Salomon informs the narrator, "The End of our Foundation is the knowledge of Causes, and secret motions of things; and the enlarging of the bounds of Human Empire, to the effecting of all things possible."[56] Here geographical expansionism has committed its tropes to scientific progress. Now empire is seen above all in terms of knowledge. On early modern maps, images of ships were charged with expanding the modern utopian spirit, but almost invariably these ships had to share oceanic space with the "secret motions of things" in the ocean's depths.

On Gastaldi's world map of circa 1560 the seas are haunted by monsters that rival the ships' supremacy both visually and philosophically.[57] While ships represent the techno-scientific progress of modernity as a civilization in its own right, sea monsters stand for the ocean's—and nature's—nonconceptuability.[58] Sea monsters were to the ocean what cannibals were to Brazil and Peru. And we might add, utopia is to the land what shipwreck is to the ocean, keeping in mind that here land is positively connoted, while the ocean is not. The dialectical wrestling match between land and sea helped to define the emerging oceanic order. During the period of exploration, discovery, and colonization, *navigatio* (navigation) and *narrare* (narration) worked side by side and merged in cartographic sign production. That is why in the sixteenth and seventeenth centuries, a good map was worth one's life. The decision by cartographers to gradually eliminate sea monsters from the map's surface suggests a process of disenchantment parallel to Bacon's "the enlarging of the bounds of Human Empire." And yet this removal of sea monsters was a form of whistling in the dark. Most early modern cartographers preferred to exploit their presence as a literary holdover from the classical and biblical periods, as a subtle way of measuring cartographic control of the new seas.

But as Nicola van Sype's world map (circa 1585) *La herdike enterprinse faict par le signeur Draeck d'avoir circuit toute la terre* suggests, the feat of circumnavigating the globe had its price. This is alluded to in the representation of Drake's shipwreck in the lower right-hand insert.[59] The map also claims

Fig. 11. *Captain John Smith's Adventures among the Turks and Tarters*, engraving by Martin Droeshout, in *The True Travels, Adventures, and Observations of Captain John Smith in Europe, Asia, Africa, and America* (1630). A detail from *The Travels of Captaine John Smith* (New York: Macmillan, 1907), 2:160.

that Drake himself saw and corrected the information on it ("Carte veuee et corige par le dict Signeur Drack"). The *figura* of John Smith's shipwreck off the coast of southern France is equally eloquent (figure 11). If one survived to tell about it, shipwreck could be touted as a way to glory. Other great explorers had maps dedicated to their voyages but did not live to see or correct the information on them. For instance, Gaspar Corte Real, Giovanni Caboto, and later Miguel Corte Real, Gaspar's brother, all sailed away into the blue without ever coming back.

Christopher Columbus experienced shipwreck off the coast of Portugal when he was young and recounted his providential survival in one Atlantic storm after another. Although Magellan began his voyage around the world with five ships, only one made it back to Portugal, and that without Magellan. Pedro Álvares Cabral started out for India with a fleet of thirteen ships but quickly lost six in the Atlantic. In short, there is truly no end to the ocean's punchy mutability. Cartographers charted both the achievements and the limits of these missing shipmasters in map after map of the emerging oceanic order and engaged the figures of utopia and *naufragium* to elaborate their signifying spectacles. On the Cantino chart, above the island of Newfoundland, there is an inscription that reads: "This land was discovered by order of the very high and excellent prince, king of Portugal, D. Manuel, and the man who discovered it was Gaspar de Corte Real, gentleman of the court of said king; he who discovered it sent a ship with men and women who belonged to that land, and he went off with the other ship and never returned but was lost."[60]

On December 27, 1492, Columbus wrote a long philosophical meditation in which he expressed his situation in chiaroscuro: "It is certain, Sovereign Princes, that where there are such lands there must be innumerable things of value, but I am not delaying in any harbour because I would like to see as many lands as possible in order to give Your Highnesses an account of them. Furthermore, I do not know the language and the people of these lands do not understand me, nor do I nor anyone I have with me understand them."[61] Apart from the immediate sense of this passage, the broader dilemma Columbus expresses here could easily be construed as that of today's Atlantic studies scholar. The desire to move from island to island in order to get a sense of the whole and the rival need to stop and learn a people's language, culture, and history represent a typically circumatlantic dialectic that early modern maps accounted for through their own developing practices. As we have seen, Atlantic maps employ the two representational extremes of line and image, and these produce two opposing critical procedures, which reflect two equally different approaches to the American world, namely surface travel and deep travel.

Columbus's "I would like to see as many lands as possible" is equivalent to the signifying activity of the line system, which charts routes and is concerned with direction, connectivity, and a whole system of potentially exploitable positions. On the other hand, when he talks about "innumerable things of value," "the people of these lands," and their language, he is no longer on the quarterdeck of his ship. Now he is on land and trying to understand what the native peoples are saying and what the cultural sense of his encounter is. This form of deep travel is captured best by the image system on maps and often concerns local knowledge and a participatory being-there. As for the word system, it mediates between the two and tacks back and forth between local description and the promotion of an abstract colonial project.

In the fifteenth and sixteenth centuries, what was initially seen as an object of discovery, a brave New World, quickly became something much more complex, if not deeply problematic. Caught between land and sea, a set of mercantile and cultural expectations and actual experience, colonial projects and the overwhelming presence of other peoples, languages, and civilizations, the early explorers and settlers did little more than touch upon the things they saw. And in the circumatlantic world this eminently spatial pattern of encounter and conflict produced a defining form of contingent history, in which two or more narratives literally shared a common perimeter and little more. It is this contingent history that characterizes the rhythmic movement of Columbus's journal and, at a much more significant level, the great travel compilations of Giovanni Battista Ramusio, Richard Hakluyt, and Samuel Purchas.

This same contingent (literally, *cum* + *tangere*) format can be found in the great atlases of the seventeenth century, where sheets and sheets of different maps, inevitably representing different scales, are placed alongside each other with the same compositional intent as d'Alembert's encyclopedia. Once we realize that intercivilizational encounters and contractions are most intense exactly along that cultural frontier where two peoples—and two histories— touch each other in a radically haphazard way, then we have fully grasped the homology between cartographic sign production as I have outlined it above and an Atlantic studies sensibility with cross-disciplinary possibilities. The contingent, peculiarly modern, histories we find in the great Renaissance collections of voyages are in reality vast narrative archipelagoes defined by a touch-and-go fluidity that we also find in, say, Benedetto Bordone's *Libro . . . de Tutte L'Isole del Mondo* (1528) or the great Dutch atlases of the seventeenth century.[62] Understood as archival sites, they are indicative of the critical status of modernity and the burgeoning capitalist world system and reflect an exquisitely cartographic state of mind.

The abstract space governed by the line system on Atlantic maps is not really homogeneous; it simply has homogeneity as its goal. Different scales represent entirely different spaces of reference, and each scale is defined by its borders. Atlantic studies scholars must learn to move spatially from map to map and scale to scale, the way Atlantic narratives do. Usually, circumatlantic lives must be charted on many maps. Olaudah Equiano's, for example, was a system of differently scaled places that he moved across in looped trajectories. Having revolutionized the writing of history by breaking it up into three different kinds of time-spaces, Fernand Braudel once confessed, "In effect, in the language of history as I imagine it, there can be no perfect synchrony: a sudden freezing that suspends all the different durations is in itself absurd."[63]

Indeed, Braudel was more interested in the thresholds themselves than in the strata they created. That is why, almost ten years after having written his masterpiece on the Mediterranean world, he could joyously write, "Occasionally I have compared [historical] models to ships: for me, once the ship is built, the interesting thing is to put it in water to see if it floats, then make it rise or descend the waters of time at will. Shipwreck is always the most significant moment."[64] For Braudel the model is both object and problem, in much the same way as the figures of utopia and shipwreck inform cartographic and discursive practice in the early sixteenth century. In commenting on the method of his *Arcades Project,* Walter Benjamin wrote in a note, "The method of this work: literary montage. I have nothing to say. Only to show. I will subtract nothing that is precious and I will not make use of any clever expression. Instead, flotsam and jetsam, not to make an inventory of it, but to do it justice in the only way possible: by using it."[65] And if in the process of showing what we have found in our research trips around the Atlantic, we actually began to use the maps we consulted to navigate this world? This is the cartographic challenge of the new Atlantic studies matrix.

Conclusion
Atlantic Studies and Global Currents

One of the central instructions that Atlantic studies scholars have shared with late twentieth-century Atlantic historians was the call to go beyond the confining narrows of national history and culture. The perspective of a specifically circumatlantic scale, disciplined by a transnational and transcultural frame, became decisive to scholars committed to investigating such fugitive themes as diaspora, migration, intercivilizational encounters, slaving and slave smuggling, the Middle Passage, slave insurrections, Creole hybridity, pidgin languages, piracy and privateering, wartime mercantile trade, Atlantic news, the circulation of revolutionary ideas, the rise of public opinion, the spread of diseases and cultigens, weather zones, and a host of phenomena dealing with life inside and beyond European amity lines. It is this predominantly oceanic order that demands a polycentric, multilingual, and contextual understanding of peoples inhabiting the maritime and coastal zones around and beyond the Atlantic, where worlds often meet without there being a meeting of worlds. At issue here is not just the creolization of understanding but also moments of cultural incommensurability.[1]

We wonder endlessly about what actually happened in those famous first meetings between peoples from different shores. The Atlantic world in the early modern period abounds with remarkable intercivilizational encounters where problems of translation and communication were paramount. One thinks of those engagements between Cortés and Moctezuma in 1522, between Pizarro and Atahualpa a few years later, between Samuel de Champlain and the Huron chief Ochasteguin in 1609, or between the sailors of European and American cruisers and slavers and the fierce-looking, tattooed members of the Kru tribe whose service on ships along the African coast was indispensable.[2] It is with such scenarios in mind that the historian Sanjay Subrahmanyam proposed what he calls "connected histories" across imperial spaces.[3] Indebted to the Italian school of *microstoria* (microhistory), Subrahmanyam coined his historiographic brand in 1997, a year after Joseph Roach published his inspiring book of "connected histories," *Cities of the Dead: Circum-Atlantic Performance.* Given its relevance as a bridge between Atlantic history and Atlantic studies as well as a viable approach to world history founded on linked biographical, local, regional, and imperial contexts, I will return to the concept of "connected histories" below.

In promoting his three-dimensional approach to the Atlantic world, David Armitage claimed that it "is the only oceanic history to possess these three conceptual dimensions [cisatlantic, transatlantic, circumatlantic]," and "it may be the only one that can be construed as at once transnational, international, and national in scope." Having said this, he also expresses a predilection for cisatlantic history, which "is the history of any particular place—a nation, a state, a region, even a specific institution—in relation to the wider Atlantic world."[4] He cites D. W. Meinig's study *Atlantic America, 1492–1800* as an example of this approach, and we might also mention two more recent cisatlantic exemplars: Armitage's book *The Declaration of Independence: A Global History,* in which he traces the implications of American independence "for the emerging international order of the late eighteenth-century Atlantic world,"[5] and Jonathan Israel's *The Expanding Blaze: How the American Revolution Ignited the World, 1775–1848.*[6] Indeed, Israel argues that the American and French Revolutions can be examined as variants of "a single Atlantic Revolution."[7] While Armitage's book is an exercise in the history of ideas, tracing a single document's "international origins and global afterlives,"[8] Meinig integrates geography, culture, history, and politics to explore the rise of the North American republic in the context of the Atlantic Ocean as a dynamic space of connectedness. At the cisatlantic scale, the ocean provides Meinig with the necessary, though ancillary, syntax for connecting the birth and burgeoning of the nation with larger horizons: "The Atlantic world was the scene of a vast interaction rather than merely the transfer of Europeans onto American shores."[9]

Challenged anew by a method featuring the conjunction or even juxtaposition of multiple scales, scholars following in the wake of Meinig and Armitage have sought to explain the processes of ethnogenesis and nation building by going beyond the category of nation proper. In effect, as Michael Zeuske notes, the Atlantic was an important "transcultural space of exchange ('Creole space') from the onset of European expansion," and only the construction of national perspectives led to its marginalization.[10] Noticing that even the cisatlantic focus tends to blur as one pursues its tributary threads, Armitage concluded his discussion of it with an upending shrug: How far in space are we justified in extending the Atlantic zone? It remains a good, but exquisitely circumstantial, question. Were we to follow New England ships around Cape Horn and into the Pacific in the early decades of the nineteenth century, we would be confronted immediately with the grasping effects of the West's rush to exploit new resources (seal skins, whale oil, hides off the coast of California, sandalwood from the Fiji Islands, guano from Peru) in the name of progress and civilization.[11] As the *Pequod* from Nantucket approached the narrow Sunda Strait in Southeast Asia, even Ishmael, the elusive narrator of Melville's whaling novel *Moby-Dick,* took a swipe at "the all-grasping western world."[12] Several decades later, New England's Ishmaels might have hailed a bark captained by the Anglophile writer Joseph Conrad. As the historian Maya Jasanoff has recently reminded us, "About half of everything Conrad ever published took place in Southeast Asia: six novels, more than a dozen short stories and novellas, chunks of memoirs."[13]

What Armitage wrote of Atlantic history over fifteen years ago still holds true for atlanticists today: "[T]he field is fluid, in motion, and potentially boundless, depending on how it is defined."[14] Not surprisingly, attempts to define it have never been pacific. With the recent groundswell of interest in world history and global history, even Fernand Braudel's and Immanuel Wallerstein's versions of the Atlantization of Western Europe and the endogenous rise of an Atlantic modern world system have come to seem like "ideology dressed up as history"[15]—more assertion than demonstration. In an observation that encourages focus on the Atlantic world as a legitimate area of study, Braudel asked, "Is not America . . . perhaps the truest explanation of Europe's greatness?"[16] Willy-nilly, the various European imperial histories seem to have taken this as dogma. Needless to say, "greatness" was based on the African slave trade, colonial conquest and settlement, and the plantation production of such luxury commodities as sugar, tobacco, cocoa, coffee, rum, and indigo as well as cotton, meat, lumber, peltry, and other raw materials.

Today, claims that the capitalist world system began with and in Western Europe are highly contested and Braudel's observation cited above is only true as far as it goes. For huge amounts of Spanish American bullion ended up in China and Asia, where every explorer from Columbus and the Cabotos to Champlain and Verrazzano hoped to arrive via an always elusive ocean route or nonexistent northwest passage. As the dozens of ships sailing across the Indian Ocean and into southeast Asia on Fra Mauro's famous world map of 1450 suggest, "[S]hips were capitalist enterprises virtually from the start."[17] In effect, according to Albert Bergesen and other macrosociologists, in the early modern period Asia, not Western Europe, was the hegemonic power in world history.[18] As for Braudel's and Wallerstein's several world systems, Andre Gunder Frank would have us think in terms of a single "Afroeurasian world economy . . . with a continual cyclical development."[19] In a reassessment of his pathbreaking book *The Rise of the West,* published in 1963, William H. Mc-Neill admitted that he had overlooked the emergence of a transcivilizational process and concluded, "I missed the centrality of China and Chinese civilization in these centuries."[20] The point is, Western Europe's world economy did not invent capitalism by itself, as historians of European exceptionalism once argued. Albert Bergesen put it in even stronger terms when he declared, "The rise of the West is now a hegemonic blip in world history."[21]

Three years before Paul Gilroy published his explosive Atlantic studies exemplar *The Black Atlantic,* the World History Association—founded in 1980—came out with the first issue of its house organ the *Journal of World History.* In his foreword, "A New Forum for Global History," Jerry H. Bentley stated that many historical processes—such as mass migrations, economic cycles, issues of weather and climate, the spread of infectious diseases, the expansive ambitions of empires, oceanic trade, the spread of ideas and beliefs, and the rise of supranational institutions—simply do not fit into national or even cultural boundaries. In order to study these processes, scholars have had to adopt "a global point of view," meaning "historical analysis undertaken not from the viewpoint of national states, but rather from that of the global community."[22] It is easy to imagine why historians of British imperial history were quick to rally around the flag of global history, given the aforementioned emphasis on adopting a worldwide field of vision. Undoubtedly, processes of globalization in the last quarter of the twentieth century sent everybody scrambling after larger theoretical frameworks, but nagging tensions between a top-down and a bottom-up approach to transnational forces and exchanges refuse to go away. Opting for history from below, Simon J. Potter and Jonathan Saha write, "Connected histories of empire might offer accounts that accord more agency to individuals, and recognise the crucial importance of choice, contingency and chance."[23]

In effect, imperial historians have traditionally focused on public history—governing bodies, administrative structures, diplomacy, policing, and war—and have tended to view the world from a centralizing metropolitan core. Belonging to a cadre of historians working to revise the way empires are studied, Potter and Saha have embraced Sanjay Subrahmanyam's "connected history" to foreground processes of circulation, exchange, and cultural interaction among people involved in linking distant places. Their advocacy of this historiographic approach (with its accompanying methodological and epistemological implications) allows them to capture the myriad ways in which peripheries have learned to talk back to, circumvent, and influence the ruling elites in the metropole. Scholars of "connected history" prefer to study "the 'connectors' that provided concrete links between different places and peoples, 'the actual ways and means that characterise the encounter of their historical trajectories.'"[24] By doing so, exponents of "connected history" are less concerned with formal borders. They do not consider the construct "empire" (or the spaces between empires) a given or even a discrete entity. This predilection for microanalysis, biographical trajectories, and intercultural encounters across oceans and continents actually reveals a well-organized strategy for decentering the narrative of empire (and of colonies perceived as separate units). Equally important, such situated history also renders the interpretation of global interdependency more accountable and tangible. Thus a merchant or missionary who traveled, say, from Lisbon to "Calicut" necessarily had to cope with a variety of challenges, situations, institutions, and officials on many different scales of encounter. The current embrace of "connected history" (and microhistory, as we shall see) has helped further to break down the already vulnerable methodological and disciplinary barriers between the sister fields of history, geography, and cultural and literary studies.

A parallel process of field overhauling worth mentioning here is the horizon shift currently gripping the discipline of comparative literature. Besieged by the rise of postcolonial literatures and challenged by theories of globalization and world history, scholars of comparative literature have begun to consider how cultural globalization affects their own methodologies and choice of themes. David Palumbo-Liu, Bruce Robbins, and Nirvana Tanoukhi, for example, have discussed the relevance of Wallerstein's world-systems analysis for comparative analysis, while Gayatri Chakravorty Spivak and Franco

Moretti have introduced the notions of planetary consciousness and "world texts," respectively. The need to embrace shifting geographical scales, a constitutive element of Atlantic studies perspectivism, has become a central issue for Nirvana Tanoukhi, while still other scholars (Pascale Casanova, Christopher Prendergast, and Emily Apter) have elected to address the paradigmatic issue of world literature and its corollary, translatability.[25] Perhaps the most ambitious attempt to outline "a literary history of globalization" and world consciousness as the new theoretical norm is that of the German comparatist Ottmar Ette, whose recent books *TransArea* and *Writing-Between-Worlds* represent a qualitative refocusing on the recent proliferation of "literatures-without-a-fixed-abode."[26] His discussion of the languages, religions, and peoples of the island of Mauritius awakens us to the increasingly routine migration of peoples around the world. Nobody more than the coolies epitomize this phenomenon of globalization from below.

Toward the last decade of the twentieth century, as processes of integration on a global scale began to affect scholarship across the disciplines, Atlantic historians and Atlantic studies scholars realized they needed to redate the historical process of globalization back beyond the early modern period and Europe's heroic Age of Exploration.[27] Those using "connected history" to study circulation and exchange across distant cultural zones have not only contributed to reorder previous periodizations of world systems but have also been led to reexamine the narrowly defined concept of modernity—above all by disconnecting it from the linear temporality informing Western discussions of it. More generally, one of the major effects of writing world history from below has been to challenge established Western narratives of non-Western centers. As a result, we now have a thriving historiography of the Indian Ocean and equally burgeoning Pacific and Pacific Rim studies, both of which have contributed to deprovincialize Western accounts of these areas.[28] This debunking (or recalibrating) of a largely European view of the world marks a major shift in the way scholars are now studying the Atlantic zone within a world-history framework. We should not forget that during the Cold War, Atlantic history stood for "an early form of global history, centered on the Atlantic world."[29] But when we consider current Atlantic scholarship, those years now seem long ago.

There are any number of signs of the global shift affecting the human sciences that could be mentioned here.[30] For example, in 2004, the year in which the journal *Atlantic Studies* was launched, the Leiden-based English-language journal *Itinerario*, established in 1977 by the university's Institute for the History of European Expansion, decided to change its subtitle from *European Journal of Overseas History* to *International Journal on the History of European Expansion and Global Interaction*. As Caroline Douki and Philippe Minard note, though the change seemed to concede that the rise of European capitalism was basically a complementary process of global trade, the journal's approach has remained remarkably Eurocentric.[31] In 2014, after a decade of publishing articles and special issues aimed at mapping Atlantic studies as a new cross-disciplinary paradigm, the editors of the journal *Atlantic Studies*, headed by Dorothea Fischer-Hornung, decided to adjust its horizon to a "progressively globalized world."

After featuring articles on such interdisciplinary topics as Creole architecture, the Atlantic slave trade, diasporic theater, whiteness as a transatlantic experience, circumatlantic jazz, Francophone literature, the Irish coffin ships to North America, and cities as sites of slave memorialization, the editors decided to embrace the new historical awareness of global interdependency by retitling the journal *Atlantic Studies: Global Currents*. With the idea of expanding the journal's horizon to make it even more inclusive, the editors now reenvisioned "the Atlantic as constitutive of wider oceanic, historical, political, and cultural networks beyond the margins of its own physical geography."[32] Having identified and hosted many circumatlantic themes in its first decade, the journal's new editorial policy now seeks to chart "the necessary association of the Atlantic space and time with wider oceanic configurations, including the Pacific and Pacific Rim, and the Indian Ocean." Thus, the subtitle *Global Currents* is meant specifically to capture the "continuous onward movement and circulation" of those agents active not only across but also intersecting with the Atlantic world from beyond it. In an apparent nod to current interest in microhistorical and "connected history" methodologies, the editors call for articles "examining entangled histories," possibly reflecting on such entrenched thematics as imperialism, postcoloniality, diaspora studies, cosmopolitanism, hemispheric, and oceanic studies.[33]

Predictably, world and global history's arrival on the scene was bound to stir an antiphonal call to decenter the geography of Atlantic studies and contextualize it in Andre Gunder Frank's single world economy. In effect, the Atlantic world is finally being appreciated for what it always was: a participating member in a much larger world. It comes as no surprise that the new editorial team of *Atlantic Studies: Global Currents* was eager to shake off any vestiges of parochialism imputable to its first working decade. Thus the editorial informs us: "The focus is on movement rather than stasis; on circulation rather than linearity; on exchange rather than on production; on mutual transformations rather than on ordinary configurations."[34] These methodological inflections epitomize the two fronts on which Atlantic studies scholars are now called to contend. On the one hand, they must unlearn the ideological scripting of swaths of previous histories and cultural narratives divided up into empires, nations, and colonies long considered natural units of analysis; on the other, they must not only school themselves in new sites of knowledge but also assemble corresponding interdisciplinary approaches to them. As Sanjay Subrahmanyam argued in his foundational essay on "connected history," "Contrary to what 'area studies' implicitly presumes, a good part of the dynamic in early modern history was provided by the interface between the local and the regional (which we may call the 'micro'-level), and the supra-regional, at times even global (what we may term the 'macro'-level)."[35] Subrahmanyam's scalar "dynamic" of the early modern period seems to correspond perfectly with what Atlantic studies perspectivism has always put forward: local sites are intersections of many tributary forces, some of them transatlantic, some circumatlantic, and others global.

It appears that one of the most successful ways of tracing such seams and sutures across local, regional, and even "global" spaces is to tag along after the intercultural and intercivilizational itineraries of seagoing merchants, ambassadors, sailors, missionaries, and scribes. This microhistorical approach is what Marcus Rediker pursued in his recent biography of the English-born Benjamin Lay, *The Fearless Benjamin Lay: The Quaker Dwarf Who Became the First Revolutionary Abolitionist*. It did not hurt that among Lay's several vocations (glove maker, sheep herder, shoemaker, producer of honey, maker of his own clothes) was that of sailor, a wretched occupation that took him to the slave-rich island of Barbados, where he became a militant abolitionist before settling with his wife in Philadelphia. Commenting on Lay's death on February 3, 1759, Rediker writes, "Thus ended forty-one years of 'zealous testimony against African slavery.'"[36] The complexity of Lay's biography demanded of Rediker a resilient form of "connected history," inasmuch as Lay's theatrical imagination led him to protest Quaker spirituality and Quaker involvement in slavery in frequently shocking public acts. An autodidact who was often openly ridiculed as a madman, this forefather of abolitionism collected a large library in his later years, which he abundantly used to pen a baggy and eclectic abolitionist tract titled *All Slave-Keepers That Keep the Innocent in Bondage, Apostates,* published by Benjamin Franklin in 1738. Rediker follows Lay around in his oceanic travels and frequent journeys on foot and patiently foregrounds the historical context of his beliefs and actions. He spends considerable time as an exegete tracing down the antinomian ideas and religious and philosophical masters that inspired him to write. After we have turned the last page of Rediker's "connected history," we, along with the author in his introduction, cannot help wonder why this important Quaker has escaped the attention of historians for so long.

But let us return to questions of method. Subrahmanyam's influential historiography comes in the wake of the Italian school of *microstoria* (microhistory), which first introduced the complexities of multiscalar analysis in the 1970s.[37] As Jean-Paul Zuniga has noted, "Thanks to the microhistorical approach, the study of extremely narrow objects has made it possible for a single researcher to analyze multiple dimensions of one reality, by breaking through the fences that had been raised between social, cultural, economic, and political history."[38] In a sympathetic quip, Jacques Revel once summed up the microhistorian's approach by having him say, "Why make things simple when we can make them complex[?]"[39] Perhaps Revel is referring to the often hypothetical nature of microhistorical investigation, in which scarcity of documentation forces the historian to work with an often dazzling variety of clues, traces, and probabilities. In the end, the question that was originally posed may prove more important than the tentative answer.

The microhistorian Giovanni Levi provided a helpful description of his method in his contribution to Peter Burke's survey of contemporary historiography: "Microhistory tries not to sacrifice knowledge of individual elements to wider generalization, and in fact it accentuates individual lives and events. But, at the same time, it tries not to reject all forms of abstraction since minimal facts and individual cases can serve to reveal more general phenomena."[40] Zuniga likens the aims of global history to those of microhistory in that both seek to transcend previously entrenched geographical and cultural borders as well as time-worn academic disciplinary restrictions. The key word here, according to Levi, is "*circulation* in space of men, objects, concepts or categories, which could not be accommodated by the narrow perspectives of the nation-state, the most common horizon, nor could it be as a frame of reflection, of historical studies."[41] No wonder, therefore, that biography has become a privileged vehicle for assessing the various kinds of constraints and possibilities affecting an individual as she or he moves from one contextualizing milieu to another. As individuals travel across borders, oceans, and continents, their entanglements can offer keen personal insight into the worlds around them. In her important essay on the feasibility of "global microhistory" Francesca Trivellato notes that macrohistory by itself tends to simplify historical reality "in the interest of generalizability."[42] From the point of view of microhistory Giovanni Levi states that "historians should not generalize their answers; the real definition of history is that of a discipline that generalizes its questions, that is, a discipline that poses questions which have a general significance and yet recognizes that infinite answers are possible, depending on the local context."[43] Local context and situated narration are essential to microhistory, but by no means do they represent the historian's goal. Francesca Trivellato cites Carlo Ginzburg when noting that while the microhistorian may favor a case-study approach, she or he does so in order "to provide the basis for an extensive comparison."[44] In this way narrative and a social scientific (or synchronic) focus work in tandem to yoke abstraction and detail in what can be called global microhistory.

Also worth mentioning here are the recent efforts of Vera Kutzinski and Ottmar Ette to identify in the prodigious oeuvre of Alexander von Humboldt a remarkably prescient approach to pursuing world-connecting patterns in, say, the Mexican hieroglyphs, Peruvian quipus (or talking knots), or ancient calendric systems. Now that the University of Chicago Press has published Humboldt's massive *Views of the Cordilleras and Monuments of the Indigenous Peoples of the Americas* and several other newly edited and translated works, we can verify for ourselves the pathbreaking aesthetic and cognitive implications of what Kutzinski and Ette refer to as this polymath's method of epitome, his steadfast ability to see in a single text, object, or site a suggestive range of intercivilizational resonances.[45] According to Kutzinski, what distinguishes Humboldt's perspective approach is "his insistently holistic vision (of nature primarily but by no means exclusively) and his abiding interest in movement, change, and exchange, that is, in the dynamic forces behind distributions, interactions, and migrations, not just on a hemispheric but on a global scale."[46] In the mid-nineteenth century, in order to express his influence on them, writers, intellectuals, and scientists in the Americas often spoke of the Age of Humboldt. This is so because of his openness to the world, his constant scouring for parallels, similarities, and interrelationships among cultures. The publication of his *Views* will undoubtedly stir scholars to explore his equally vast *Cosmos: A Sketch of a Physical Description of the Universe, 1844–1858* and the daunting network of correspondents that he created during his lifetime.

The Atlantic Ocean remains a vested site for studying processes of circulation and multiple forms of modernity and temporality across different imperial and interstate orders. As I have tried to suggest here, Atlantic studies scholars can do world history, connected history, comparative history, and microhistory while remaining focused on exchanges in the Atlantic world. Contrary to older national and imperial histories, Atlantic studies has abandoned the attempt to create grand narrative syntheses for more apprehensive narratives made up of multifaceted connections, long-distance trajectories, cases, influences, and chance encounters, which frequently require the scholar to jump nimbly from one scale to another while marking the gap in between. In this primarily oceanic context, emphasis is no longer placed on the presumed unity of the Atlantic world so much as on the often provisional networks that traverse and tissue it. As Sanjay Subrahmanyam concluded back at the turn of the century, "[W]e cannot attempt a 'macro-history' of the problem [in this case, millenarianism] without muddying our boots in the bogs of 'micro-history.'"[47]

In recent years, no area of Atlantic-world scholarship has focused more intensely on the human body than slavery studies—of the captive body of the Middle Passage, of countless slave ship insurrections, of the commodified enslaved worker on the plantation economies of Brazil, Cuba, the Caribbean islands, and the US South, and of the slave body turned into value as a "world currency."[48] Although so much has already been written about the slave trade and slavery in all of its world-historical aspects, this new focus on the slave body has courageously—and even redemptively—chosen to go where once it was thought the language of history and cultural studies could not follow.[49] For the existential trials and physical sufferings of the slave and the scenes of cruelty and torture that took place onboard ships and within the tyrannical confines of the plantation were until recently left to the imaginative powers of the novelist, the poet, and the once-neglected authors of the slave narrative. In his research on the period of "second slavery"—from 1808, when the slave trade was legally terminated across the Atlantic, up into the 1880s when slaving was ended in Cuba and Brazil—the German historian Michael Zeuske has identified what he rightly calls "the Hidden Atlantic." In fact, during this period of rising abolitionism there was a massive boom in slave smuggling and "accumulation of capital based on human bodies." Behind the establishment of this Atlantic network was a host of *negreros* (Cuban slave traders) and *mongos* (business people, a Mande term for "big man") who trafficked in what the author calls a form of legally illegal "corporeal capitalism."[50] Only now, thanks to the work of historians such as Walter Johnson, Marcus Rediker, Edward Baptist, Daina Ramey Berry, and Sowande' M. Mustakeem have we begun to fathom what "corporeal capitalism" means in terms of human suffering and trauma.

What further characterizes the period of "second slavery" is the fact that now men from the Americas, and not from Europe, dominated the so-called hidden Atlantic. Zeuske followed up his book on the Amistad case with a "Slave Traders Project" based primarily on a microhistorical approach to the role that slave captains (he estimates there were over thirty-five thousand of them) played in this dark side of the hidden Atlantic.[51] In effect, when Zeuske speaks of the "structure" of "second slavery," he means an entirely tangible account of its composite features: the material instruments of terror (chains, neck and foot shackles, ropes, wooden yokes, whips), the slave catchers and caravans, the barracoons, the slave courts along the Slave Coast, factors, captains and pilots, slave traders, forts, trading posts, water containers, canoes, rowers, oceangoing ships, their multinational crews, surgeons, cooks, healers, medicines, interpreters, ports, plantations with security equipment, commercial establishments, large-scale speculators, branch offices, the political elites, and so forth.[52] Above all, Zeuske's project focuses on the life histories of ship captains entering and leaving the ports of the United States, Cuba, Brazil, and other places in the Caribbean. It deals with rich, enterprising men like the *Amistad*'s Ramón Ferrer, Pedro Blanco ("the Rothschild of the slave trade"),[53] Théophile Conneau, and the German Daniel Botefeur. A microhistorical approach to ship captains brings together all of the "structural" features of "slavery modernity" (the ships and ports, the crews and the tools of the trade) in a single life.[54] By vocation, Zeuske the microhistorian seeks to interweave the globalization of capital generated by the hidden Atlantic with what took place in the holds of the slavers and in the hearts and minds of those who chose to rebel against impossible odds.

Not so long ago, narratives of slave ship terror and plantation cruelty were considered either negligible or beyond the pale of history. In the nineteenth century, history from the perspective of the nation-state, egregiously theorized by Hegel in his *Lectures on the Philosophy of World History*, favored the public sphere and recounted a hierarchical world governed by the genie of Progress.

According to Hegel, the Spirit of World History expressed itself through the state. This led to the remarkable corollary "No state, no history"—a view that conveniently relocated the lives of colonized peoples from India, Africa, and the archipelago of the Caribbean to the basement of prehistory. Hegel believed that Africa had no history and that its people lived in a state of savagery, without any awareness of the concept of freedom.[55] It was commonly thought among slavocrats that they were doing their African captives a favor by exposing them to the superior civilization of plantation slavery. Postcolonial historians were among the first to unravel the logic behind "how World-history tells its stories."[56]

Before the rise of postcolonial and Atlantic studies, accounts of those who crossed the Atlantic in the holds of ships (whether Africans, Irish-famine emigrants, or prisoners destined to an Australian penal colony) were regularly excluded from histories of the Atlantic as a capitalist world system, as if historians were explicitly encouraged to recount only the "virtuous" exploits of the winners. As Ranajit Guha, the founder of subaltern history in India, states, "The noise of World-history and its statist concerns has made historiography insensitive to the sighs and whispers of everyday life."[57] Guha's point is well taken. Historians of world and global history need not think only in terms of extension, for the common or universal dimensions of human experience can also be recounted through vertical or intensive research—for example, the kind of inquiry that focuses on the gendered slave body, the dying Irish emigrants in the coffin ships of 1846–47, and countless immigrants to the Americas who crossed in steerage with little but hope as their baggage. It is true that "when the existential tangles with the epistemological, words tend to slide out of their habitual semantic grooves."[58] Undoubtedly, this is in part why Atlantic historians for well over one hundred years have chosen not to consider the everyday life and sufferings of its marginalized peoples.

According to Guha, we must question Hegel further when he states that the prose of history emerges out of the prose of the world. That is, we should do nothing less than overturn the traditional relation between "historicality" (the everyday life of the colonized and the enslaved) and historiography as it has been developed in the West. We can begin by retrieving those portions of experience that Hegel and many an imperial and national historian after him consigned to the contemptible realm of "prehistory,"[59] a metaphoric black hole containing the everyday temporalities of many a "historyless" people. In his critique of Hegel, Guha further states that in order for colonized peoples to reengage with their own historicality, there must be "a shift from a particular paradigm of storytelling to another."[60] Although he does not cite him, Guha easily could have mentioned Sanjay Subrahmanyam, whose advocacy of "connected history" as an inclusive historiographic poetics seeks to bring together the extensive horizon of world history with the intensive delving of microhistory.

In concluding, it is worth recalling that the Italian school of microhistory became influential exactly by exploring the lost historicality of minor figures who were previously deemed insignificant by both church and state. Carlo Ginzburg's classical study of Menochio, a miller from sixteenth-century Friuli condemned to death for heresy, and his morphological work on the witches' sabbath are two prominent examples of this historical method. There are many other contemporary works that correspond with Guha's call for a paradigmatic shift in how history is written. I have already mentioned the work of a handful of Atlantic historians and cultural studies scholars on different aspects of the gendered slave body and Zeuske's microhistorical project on ship captains during the period of "second slavery." Both of these historiographies have availed themselves of the multiscalar perspectivism as well as the disciplinary tools of cultural and discourse analysis pioneered by several of the Atlantic studies scholars mentioned in the first two chapters of this book. Following the paradigm shift from traditional Atlantic history to Atlantic studies, scholars of the Atlantic world began to recover portions of everyday experience that were previously excluded from the historical record. Evidently, research on the slave trade and the Middle Passage led or forced scholars to plumb the deep structures of historicality that such investigations were bound to uncover. At the microhistorical level, many stories of the Atlantic world—stories of misery and solidarity and mere everyday living—remain to be told. And while many of these originate in or cross through the Atlantic, they are likely to be entangled further in trajectories having global connections.

Notes

Introduction

1. See Antonio Gramsci, *Selections from the Prison Notebooks,* trans. Geoffrey Nowell-Smith (London: Lawrence and Wishart, 1971); and Gramsci, *Selections from Cultural Writings,* trans. William Boelhower (London: Lawrence and Wishart, 1985).

2. Gayatri Chakravorty Spivak, "Can the Subaltern Speak? Speculations of Widow Sacrifice," *Wedge* 7.8 (Winter–Spring 1985): 120–30.

3. See in particular Edward Said, *Culture and Imperialism* (London: Vintage, 1994), 56–59; and Said, "History, Literature, and Geography," in *Reflections on Exile and Other Essays* (Cambridge, MA: Harvard University Press, 2000), 453–73.

4. Said, *Culture and Imperialism,* 235.

5. For a recent attempt to define colonialism, see Jürgen Osterhammel, *Colonialism: A Theoretical Overview,* trans. Shelley Frisch (Princeton, NJ: Marcus Wiener Publishers, 2005): "Colonialism is a relationship of domination between an indigenous (or forcibly imported) majority and a minority of foreign invaders. The fundamental decisions affecting the lives of the colonized people are made and implemented by the colonial rulers in pursuit of interests that are often defined in a distant metropolis. Rejecting cultural compromises with the colonized population, the colonizers are convinced of their own superiority and of their ordained mandate to rule" (16–17).

6. See Michael Zeuske, *Amistad: A Hidden Network of Slavers and Merchants,* trans. Steven Rendall (Princeton, NJ: Markus Wiener, 2015), 12.

7. Edward Said, *Orientalism: Western Conceptions of the Orient* (1978; London: Penguin, 1995), 25. In his study, Said was deeply influenced by Gramsci's concept of hegemony. See pp. 6–7.

8. Homi K. Bhabha, *The Location of Culture* (London: Routledge, 1994), mimicry 85–92, hybridity 207–9, Other (othering) 66–84, difference 66–84, doubling 136–38, stereotype 75–84, race 236–256, metonymy 54–57.

9. Gayatri Chakravorty Spivak, *The Postcolonial Critic: Interviews, Strategies, Dialogues,* ed. Sarah Harasym (London: Routledge, 1990); and Spivak, *A Critique of Postcolonial Reason: Toward a History of the Vanishing Present* (Cambridge, MA: Harvard University Press, 1999).

10. See Aimé Césaire, *Discourse on Colonialism*, trans. John Pinkham (New York: Monthly Review Press, 1972); Albert Memmi, *The Colonizer and the Colonized* (New York: Orion, 1965); Frantz Fanon, *The Wretched of the Earth*, trans. Constance Farrington (New York: Grove, 1963);Fanon, *Black Skin, White Masks*, trans. Charles Lam Markmann (New York: Grove Weidenfeld, 1967); Ngũgĩ wa Thiong'o, *Decolonising the Mind: The Politics of Language in African Literature* (London: Currey, 1986); Édouard Glissant, *Poétique de la relation* (Paris: Gallimard, 1990); Kamau Brathwaite, *Roots* (Ann Arbor: University of Michigan Press, 1993); and Wilson Harris, *Selected Essays: The Unfinished Genesis of the Imagination*, ed. Andrew Bundy (London: Routledge, 1999).

11. For a further distinction between these two groups of critics, see Jan C. Jansen and Jürgen Osterhammel, *Decolonization: A Short History*, trans. Jeremiah Riemer (Princeton, NJ: Princeton University Press, 2017), 169–70.

12. I am thinking in particular of the work of the historians Peter Linebaugh and Marcus Rediker, whose work I will discuss in the first two chapters. See also William Boelhower, "'I'll Teach You How to Flow': On figuring Out Atlantic Studies," *Atlantic Studies* 1.1 (April 2004): 28–48.

13. Adrienne Rich, "Notes Toward a Politics of Location," in *Blood, Bread, and Poetry: Selected Prose* (New York: Norton, 1994), 212.

14. Quoted in Seymour I. Schwartz and Ralph E. Ehrenberg, *The Mapping of America* (New York: Harry N. Abrams, 1980), 84.

15. Sanjay Subrahmanyam, "Connected Histories: Notes Towards a Reconfiguration of Early Modern Eurasia," *Modern Asian Studies* 31.3 (1997): 735–62.

16. Quoted in Gilles Deleuze and Felix Guattari, *A Thousand Plateaus: Capitalism and Schizophrenia*, trans. Brian Massumi (Minneapolis: University of Minnesota Press, 1987), 21.

17. Ibid.

18. See Peter Linebaugh and Marcus Rediker, *The Many-Headed Hydra: The Hidden History of the Revolutionary Atlantic* (London: Verso, 2000); Marcus Rediker, *Between the Devil and the Deep Blue Sea: Merchant Seamen, Pirates, and the Anglo-American Maritime World, 1700–1750* (Cambridge: Cambridge University Press, 1987); Siân Rees, *Sweet Water and Bitter: The Ships That Stopped the Slave Trade* (Durham: University of New Hampshire Press, 2011).

19. Walter Benjamin, *The Arcades Project*, trans. Howard Eiland and Kevin McLaughlin (Cambridge, MA: Belknap Press of Harvard University Press, 1999), [N1a, 8].

20. Walter Johnson, *Soul by Soul: Life inside the Antebellum Slave Market* (Cambridge, MA: Harvard University Press, 1999); Marcus Rediker, *The Slave Ship: A Human History* (New York: Viking, 2007); Edward E. Baptist, *The Half Has Never Been Told: Slavery and the Making of American Capitalism* (New York: Basic Books, 2014); Sowande' M. Mustakeem, *Slavery at Sea: Terror, Sex, and Sickness in the Middle Passage* (Urbana: University of Illinois Press, 2016); Daina Ramey Berry, *The Price for Their Pound of Flesh: The Value of the Enslaved, from Womb to Grave, in the Building of a Nation* (Boston: Beacon, 2017); Kay Wright Lewis, *A Curse upon the Nation: Race, Freedom, and Extermination in America and the Atlantic World* (Athens: University of Georgia Press, 2017).

21. Baptist, *The Half Has Never Been Told*, 428n1.

22. Robert Ralston Cawley, "Shakespeare's Use of the Voyagers in The Tempest," *PMLA* 41 (1926): 688–726; George Lamming, *Water with Berries* (London: Longman, 1971); Aimé Césaire, *A Tempest*, trans. Richard Miller (New York: Ubu Repertory Theater Publications, 1986).

23. See William Boelhower, "Three Early Modern Genres: A Microhistorical Approach to World Literature," *Atlantic Studies: Global Currents* 16.2 (2019): 170–87.

24. William Boelhower, "Framing a New Ocean Genealogy: The Case of Venetian Cartography in the Early Modern Period," *Atlantic Studies: Global Currents* 15.2 (June 2018): 279–97.

1. Atlantic Studies Prospects: Complexities and Singularities, Flows and Places

1. Milan Kundera, *Il Sipario,* trans. Massimo Rizzante (Milan: Adelphi, 2005), 86.

2. Fernand Braudel, "En guise de conclusion," *Review (Fernand Braudel Center)* 1.3/4 (1978): 243–61.

3. Quoted in Ruggiero Romano, *Braudel e noi* (Rome: Donzelli, 1995), 16.

4. See Bernard Bailyn, *Atlantic History: Concept and Contours* (Cambridge, MA: Harvard University Press, 2005), 3–4; Donna Gabaccia, "A Long Atlantic in a Wider World," *Atlantic Studies* 1.1 (2004): 4; Nicholas Canny, "Writing Atlantic History; or, Reconfiguring the History of Colonial British America," *Journal of American History* 86 (1999): 1093–1114.

5. "Editorial," *Atlantic Studies: History, Literary, Cultural and Historical Perspectives,* 1.1 (April 2004).

6. D. W. Meinig, *Atlantic America, 1492–1800* (New Haven, CT: Yale University Press, 1986); David Armitage and Michael J. Braddick, eds., *The British Atlantic World, 1500–1800* (New York: Palgrave Macmillan, 2002); Barbara L. Solow, ed., *Slavery and the Rise of the Atlantic System* (New York: Cambridge University Press, 1993); Bailyn, *Atlantic History.*

7. Meinig, *Atlantic America,* xvi.

8. See Sollors's map in Olaudah Equiano, *The Interesting Narrative of the Life of Olaudah Equiano, or Gustavus Vassa, the African, Written by Himself,* ed. Werner Sollors (New York: Norton, 2001), 2–4.

9. Jacques-Loup Rivière, "Yoknapatawpha," in *Cartes et figures de la terre,* ed. Giulio Macchi (Paris: Centre Georges Pompidou, 1980), 214.

10. See Pierre Bourdieu and Loïc J. D. Wacquant, *An Invitation to Reflexive Sociology* (Chicago: University of Chicago Press, 1992), 208.

11. See Sollors, introduction to Equiano, *The Interesting Narrative,* xxiv.

12. Bailyn, *Atlantic History,* 4.

13. Ibid., 38, 23, 43–44; Marco Mariano, "Remapping America: Continentalism, Globalism, and the Rise of the Atlantic Community, 1939–1949," in *Defining the Atlantic Community,* ed. Marco Mariano (New York: Routledge, 2010), 71–90.

14. W. Jeffrey Bolster, *Black Jacks: African American Seamen in the Age of Sail* (Cambridge, MA: Harvard University Press, 1997), 7–43; Peter Linebaugh and Marcus Rediker, *The Many-Headed Hydra: The Hidden History of the Revolutionary Atlantic* (London: Verso, 2000), 243–47.

15. Bailyn, *Atlantic History,* 86.

16. Victor Enthoven, "Dutch Crossings: Migration between the Netherlands and the New World, 1600–1800," *Atlantic Studies* 2.2 (2004): 160.

17. For a larger estimate, see John Hope Franklin, *From Slavery to Freedom: A History of American Negroes,* rev. ed. (New York: Knopf, 1956), 57–58.

18. Solow, *Slavery and the Rise of the Atlantic System,* 1.

19. Bailyn, *Atlantic History,* 83.

20. See Horst Pietschmann, ed., *Atlantic History: History of the Atlantic System, 1580–1830* (Gottingen: Vandenhoeck and Ruprecht, 2002), 35–43; David Armitage, "Three Concepts of Atlantic History," in *The British Atlantic World, 1500–1800,* ed. David Armitage and Michael J. Braddick (New York: Palgrave Macmillan, 2002), 18.

21. Armitage, "Three Concepts of Atlantic History," 16.

22. Jürgen Osterhammel, *The Transformation of the World: A Global History of the Nineteenth Century* (Princeton, NJ: Princeton University Press, 2014), 277–82.

23. Guy Chet, *The Ocean Is a Wilderness: Atlantic Piracy and the Limits of State Authority, 1688–1856* (Amherst: University of Massachusetts Press, 2014), 7.

24. David Armitage and Michael Braddick, *The British Atlantic World,* 3.

25. Ibid., 1.

26. John Elliott, "Afterword: Atlantic History, a Circumnavigation," in Armitage and Braddick, *The British Atlantic World,* 237.

27. For the concept of "absolute metaphor," see Hans Blumenberg, *Paradigms for a Metaphorology,* trans. Robert Savage (Ithaca, NY: Cornell University Press, 2016), chapter 2.

28. Stephen Mennell, *Norbert Elias: An Introduction* (Dublin: University College Dublin Press, 1992), 253.

29. Ibid., 72.

30. Ibid., 252.

31. Armitage, "Three Concepts of Atlantic History," 15–25.

32. Bailyn, preface to *The British Atlantic World,* xiv.

33. See Lucien Febvre, "Civilization: Evolution of a Word and Group of Ideas," in *A New Kind of History. From the Writings of Lucien Febvre,* ed. Peter Burke, trans. K. Folca (New York: Harper and Row, 1973), 219–57; Jean Starobinski, "Le mot Civilisation," in *Le temps de la réflexion* N. IV (October 1983): 13–22; Shmuel N. Eisenstadt, "The Civilizational Dimension of Modernity," in *Rethinking Civilizational Analysis,* ed. Said Amir Arjomand and Edward A. Tiryakian (London: Sage, 2004), 48–66.

34. William O'Reilly, "Genealogies of Atlantic History," *Atlantic Studies* 1.1 (April 2004): 66–84.

35. See Armitage, "Three Concepts of Atlantic History," 13–14; Elliott, "Afterword," 233; Gabaccia, "A Long Atlantic in a Wider World," 5–6, 14–16.

36. See Said Amir Arjomand and Edward A. Tiryakian, eds., *Rethinking Civilizational Analysis* (London: Sage, 2004), 2, 207–10, 21–29.

37. Armitage, "Three Concepts of Atlantic History," 12. See also Bailyn, *Atlantic History;* O'Reilly, "Genealogies of Atlantic History," 66–84.

38. Arjomand and Tiryakian, *Rethinking Civilizational Analysis,* 4.

39. Obviously, this new oceanic order—so named by Franz Rosenzweig and Carl Schmitt—was as expansive as the capitalist world system of Immanuel Wallerstein and extended into the East Indies and the China Sea as well. See Franz Rosenzweig, *Globus: Per una teoria storico-universale dello spazio,* trans. Stefania Carretti (Genoa: Marietti, 2007); Carl Schmitt, *Land and Sea: A World-Historical Meditation,* trans. Samuel Garrett Zeitlin (Candor NY: Telos Press Pub-

lishing, 2015); Immanuel Wallerstein, *The Modern World-System,* vol. 1, *Capitalist Agriculture and the Origins of the European World-Economy in the Sixteenth Century* (New York: Academic, 1974).

40. Paul Gilroy, *The Black Atlantic: Modernity and Double Consciousness* (Cambridge, MA: Harvard University Press, 1993), 15.

41. Bailyn, *Atlantic History,* 4.

42. Bernard Bailyn, *On the Teaching and Writing of History: Responses to a Series of Questions,* ed. Edward C. Lathem (Hanover, NH: University Press of New England, 1994), 36. This painterly poetics, I would suggest, is exquisitely Braudelian.

43. Bailyn, *Atlantic History,* 60.

44. Ibid., 61.

45. Ibid., 61.

46. Ibid., 62.

47. Quoted in Meinig, *Atlantic America,* 77.

48. Ibid., xv.

49. Ibid., 76.

50. See Romano, *Braudel e noi,* 53.

51. J. M. Blaut, *The Colonizer's Model of the World: Geographical Diffusionism and Eurocentric History* (New York: Guilford, 1993), 1–42.

52. Ibid., 12, 18.

53. Gurminder K. Bhambra, *Rethinking Modernity: Postcolonialism and the Sociological Imagination* (New York: Palgrave Macmillan, 2007), 1–14, 34–55, 83–123.

54. George Blaustein, *Nightmare Envy and Other Stories: American Culture and European Reconstruction* (New York: Oxford University Press, 2018).

55. See Krzysztof Pomian, *L'ordine del tempo* (Turin: Einaudi, 1992), 89–94; Romano, *Braudel e noi,* 17–54.

56. See Paul Ricoeur, *Temps et récit* (Paris: Seuil, 1983), 1:146–52.

57. Solomon Northup, *Twelve Years a Slave,* ed. David Wilson (Auburn, NY: Derby and Miller, 1853).

58. See William Boelhower, "'I'll Teach You How to Flow': On Figuring Out Atlantic Studies," *Atlantic Studies* 1.1 (April 2004): 28–48; and Boelhower, "New Orleans in the Atlantic World," *Atlantic Studies* 5.2 (2010): 1–11.

59. Osterhammel, *The Transformation of the World,* 77–113.

60. Armitage, "Three Concepts of Atlantic History," 13.

61. Alison Games, "Atlantic History: Definitions, Challenges, and Opportunities," *American Historical Review* 111.3 (2006): 749.

62. Édouard Glissant, *Poétique de la relation* (Paris: Gallimard, 1990).

63. Quoted in Michael J. Dash, *Édouard Glissant* (Cambridge: Cambridge University Press, 1995), 175.

64. Bailyn, *Atlantic History,* 30, 61.

65. Manuel Castells, *The Castells Reader on Cities and Social Theory,* ed. Ida Susser (Oxford: Blackwell, 2002), 315–49.

66. See Pierre Nora, and Charles-Robert Ageron, *Les lieux de mémoire (Paris: Gallimard, 1997).*

67. François Hartog, *Évidence de l'histoire: Ce que voient les historiens* (Paris: EHESS, 2005), 193; Carlo Ginzburg, *The Judge and the Historian: Marginal Notes on a Late-Twentieth-Century Miscarriage of Justice,* trans. Antony Shugaar (London: Verso, 2002).

68. Walter Johnson, *Soul by Soul: Life inside the Antebellum Slave Market* (Cambridge, MA: Harvard University Press, 1999); Mark Reinhardt, *Who Speaks for Margaret Garner?* (Minneapolis: University of Minnesota Press, 2010).

69. Arjomand and Tiryakian, *Rethinking Civilizational Analysis,* 122, 123, 125, 135.

70. Elliott, "Afterword," 249.

71. Gabaccia, "A Long Atlantic in a Wider World," 18.

72. Armitage, "Three Concepts of Atlantic History," 26–27.

73. Enzo Melandri, *La linea e il circolo: Studio logico-filosofico sull'analogia* (Macerata: Quodlibet, 2004), 12.

74. Armitage, "Three Concepts of Atlantic History," 26.

75. Armitage and Braddick, *The British Atlantic World,* 4.

2. A Brief Genealogy: From Atlantic History to Atlantic Studies

1. Thomas Kuhn, *The Structure of Scientific Revolutions* (Chicago: University of Chicago Press, 1962).

2. Immanuel Wallerstein, *The Modern World-System,* vol. 1, *Capitalist Agriculture and the Origins of the European World-Economy in the Sixteenth Century* (New York: Academic, 1974).

3. Eric Williams, *Capitalism and Slavery* (Chapel Hill: University of North Carolina Press, 1944); Philip D. Curtin, ed., *Africa Remembered: Narratives by West Africans from the Era of the Slave Trade* (Madison: University of Wisconsin Press, 1967); Curtin, *The Atlantic Slave Trade: A Census* (Madison: University of Wisconsin Press, 1969); David Brion Davis, *The Problem of Slavery in Western Culture* (Ithaca, NY: Cornell University Press, 1966); Davis, *The Problem of Slavery in the Age of Revolution, 1770–1823* (Ithaca, NY: Cornell University Press, 1975); Eugene D. Genovese, *From Rebellion to Revolution: Afro-American Slave Revolts in the Making of the Modern World* (Baton Rouge: Louisiana State University Press, 1979); Orlando Patterson, *Slavery and Social Death: A Comparative Study* (Cambridge, MA: Harvard University Press, 1982); Sidney Mintz, *Sweetness and Power: The Place of Sugar in Modern History* (New York: Viking, 1985); Robin Blackburn, *The Making of New World Slavery: From the Baroque to the Modern, 1492–1800* (London: Verso, 1997); David Eltis, *The Rise of African Slavery in the Americas* (Cambridge: Cambridge University Press, 2000); David Eltis, Stephen D. Behrendt, and Herbert S. Klein, eds., *The Transatlantic Slave Trade: A Database on CD-ROM* (Cambridge, U.K.: Cambridge University Press, 1999).

4. Arna Bontemps, *Great Slave Narratives* (Boston: Beacon, 1969); Henry Louis Gates Jr. and William L. Andrews, eds., *Pioneers of the Black Atlantic: Five Slave Narratives from the Enlightenment, 1772–1815* (Washington, DC: Civitas Counterpoint, 1998). Once an almost unique exemplar, the influence of Equiano's autobiography has led scholars to discover a whole new text type, namely black Atlantic memoirs. See, for example, Vincent Carretta's collection *Unchained Voices: An Anthology of Black Authors in the English-Speaking World of the Eighteenth Century*

(Lexington: University Press of Kentucky, 1996); Vincent Caretta and Philip Gould, eds., *Genius in Bondage: Literature of the Early Black Atlantic* (Lexington: University Press of Kentucky, 2001); Lisa A. Lindsay and John Wood Sweet, eds. *Biography and the Black Atlantic* (Philadelphia: University of Pennsylvania Press, 2013).

5. Patterson, *Slavery and Social Death*, 17–101.

6. See Donna Gabaccia, "A Long Atlantic in a Wider World," *Atlantic Studies* 1.1 (April 2004): 1–27; Alison Games, "Atlantic History: Definitions, Challenges, and Opportunities," *American Historical Review* 111.3 (June 2006): 743; Jack P. Greene and Philip D. Morgan, "Introduction: The Present State of Atlantic History," in *Atlantic History: A Critical Appraisal*, ed. Jack P. Greene and Philip D. Morgan (New York: Oxford University Press, 2008), 6.

7. Gabaccia, "A Long Atlantic in a Wider World," 18.

8. Paul Gilroy, *The Black Atlantic: Modernity and Double Consciousness* (Cambridge, MA: Harvard University Press, 1993), 1–40.

9. Gabaccia, "A Long Atlantic in a Wider World," 5. It is worth noting that all but one of the articles in the first issue of *Atlantic Studies* cite the importance of Gilroy's book.

10. Joseph Roach, *Cities of the Dead: Circum-Atlantic Performance* (New York: Columbia University Press, 1996).

11. David Armitage, "Three Concepts of Atlantic History," in *The British Atlantic World, 1500–1800*, ed. David Armitage and Michael J. Braddick (New York: Palgrave Macmillan, 2002), 16.

12. Ibid., 17.

13. Marcus Rediker, *Between the Devil and the Deep Blue Sea: Merchant Seamen, Pirates, and the Anglo-American Maritime World* (Cambridge: Cambridge University Press, 1987), 11.

14. Peter Linebaugh and Marcus Rediker, *The Many-Headed Hydra: The Hidden History of the Revolutionary Atlantic* (London: Verso, 2000).

15. Marcus Rediker, *The Slave Ship: A Human History* (New York: Viking, 2007). For a discussion of this book, see Dennis Moore, William Boelhower, Sean X. Goudie, Karen N. Salt, Emma Christopher, Ned Blackhawk, and Marcus Rediker, "Colloquy with Marcus Rediker on *The Slave Ship: A Human History*," *Atlantic Studies* 7.1 (March 2010): 5–45.

16. Gilroy, *The Black Atlantic*, 4.

17. Peter Linebaugh and Marcus Rediker, "The Many-Headed Hydra," *Journal of Historical Sociology* 3.3 (September 1990): 225–53.

18. Werner Sollors, introduction to *The Interesting Narrative of the Life of Olaudah Equiano, or Gustavus Vassa, the African, Written by Himself*, ed. Sollors (New York: Norton, 2001), xv.

19. Michel Foucault, *Le corps utopique, les hétérotopies* (Paris: Nouvelles Éditions Lignes, 2010), 35–36; my translation. Full translation, "Of Other Spaces: Utopias and Heterotopias," translated by Jay Miskowiec, available at web.mit.edu/allanmc/www/foucault1.pdf.

20. Moore et al., "Colloquy with Marcus Rediker," 40.

21. Marcus Rediker, *The Fearless Benjamin Lay: The Quaker Dwarf Who Became the First Revolutionary Abolitionist* (Boston: Beacon, 2017).

22. David Armitage, "The Red Atlantic," *Reviews in American History* 29.4 (December 2001): 480.

23. Ibid., 482.

24. Ibid., 485.

25. Ibid., 486.

26. Armitage, "Three Concepts of Atlantic History," 16.

27. Eliga H. Gould, "Atlantic History and the Literary Turn," *William and Mary Quarterly* 55.1 (January 2008): 175–80. Gould is replying to Eric Slauter's article "History, Literature, and the Atlantic World," *William and Mary Quarterly* 64.2 (April 2007): 251–54.

28. Gould, "Atlantic History and the Literary Turn," 175.

29. Roach, *Cities of the Dead*, 5.

30. Felicity A. Nussbaum, "The Theatre of Empire: Racial Counterfeit, Racial Realism," in *A New Imperial History: Culture, Identity, and Modernity in Britain and the Empire, 1660–1840*, ed. Kathleen Wilson (Cambridge: Cambridge University Press, 2004), 71. This inside-out focus became a conventional critical perspective of postcolonial critics interested in documenting ways in which the empire writes back. A highly rewarding transatlantic development of this practice is Paul Giles's sweeping *Atlantic Republic: The American Tradition in English Literature* (Oxford: Oxford University Press, 2006). Here the author provides an impressive sequence of illuminating readings of a host of English authors responsive to the republican experiment begun by the American Revolution.

31. See Laura Doyle, "Reconstructing Race and Freedom in Atlantic Modernity: Daniel Defoe's *Robinson Crusoe* and Olaudah Equiano's *Interesting Narrative*," *Atlantic Studies* 4.2 (October 2007): 195–224.

32. See, for example, Lindsay and Sweet, *Biography and the Black Atlantic*; Mary Louise Pratt, *Imperial Eyes: Travel Writing and Transculturation* (New York: Routledge, 1992); Christopher Mulvey, *Transatlantic Manners: Social Patterns in Nineteenth-Century Anglo-American Travel Literature* (Cambridge: Cambridge University Press, 2008); Helen Thomas, *Romanticism and Slave Narratives: Transatlantic Testimonies* (Cambridge: Cambridge University Press, 2004); Ralph Bauer, *The Cultural Geography of Colonial American Literatures: Empire, Travel, Modernity* (Cambridge: Cambridge University Press, 2003); Beth L. Lueck, Brigitte Bailey, and Lucinda L. Damon-Bach, eds., *Transatlantic Women: Nineteenth-Century American Women Writers and Great Britain* (Durham: University of New Hampshire Press, 2012); Susan Manning, *Poetics of Character: Transatlantic Encounters, 1700–1900* (Cambridge: Cambridge University Press, 2013); and James D. Lilley, *Common Things: Romance and the Aesthetics of Belonging in Atlantic Modernity* (New York: Fordham University Press, 2014).

33. Laura Doyle, *Freedom's Empire: Race and the Rise of the Novel in Atlantic Modernity, 1640–1940* (Durham, NC: Duke University Press, 2008), 99.

34. Armitage, "Three Concepts of Atlantic History," 15.

35. Ibid., 22. Recently, scholars also have sought to remake hemispheric studies, although they do not consciously cultivate the rich perspective challenges offered by Atlantic studies. See, for example, Caroline F. Levander and Robert S. Levine, *Hemispheric American Studies* (New Brunswick, NJ: Rutgers University Press, 2008); and Caroline F. Levander, "The Times of Transnational Studies," *American Literary History* 26.3 (Fall 2014): 559–68.

36. Pierre Bourdieu and Loïc J. D. Wacquant, *An Invitation to Reflexive Sociology* (Chicago: University of Chicago Press, 1992), 74n14.

37. Armitage, "Three Concepts of Atlantic History," 26.

38. See Paul Giles, "Narrative Reversals and Power Exchanges: Frederick Douglass and British Culture," *American Literature* 73.4 (December 2001): 779–810. Later, Giles incorporated this essay in a much larger canvas of sophisticated transatlantic readings titled *Virtual Americas: Transnational Fictions and the Transatlantic Imaginary* (Durham, NC: Duke University Press, 2002).

39. Giles, "Narrative Reversals and Power Exchanges," 787.

40. See William Boelhower, "The Rise of the New Atlantic Studies Matrix," *American Literary History* 20.1–2 (Spring–Summer 2008): 96–97.

41. See, for example, J. H. Elliot's summa, *Empires of the Atlantic World: Britain and Spain in America, 1492–1830* (New Haven, CT: Yale University Press, 2006); Jack P. Greene, *Peripheries and Center: Constitutional Development in the Extended Polities of the British Empire and the United States, 1607–1788* (New York: Norton, 1990); Bernard Bailyn, *Voyagers to the West: A Passage in the Peopling of America on the Eve of the Revolution* (New York: Vintage, 1988).

42. The Harvard International Seminar on the History of the Atlantic World was dominated by British Atlantic scholarship. Many other institutes now offer regular seminars and lectures on Atlantic cultures, such as the Harriet Tubman Research Centre on the African Diaspora at York University (http://www.tubmaninstitute.ca/the_harriet_tubman_series_on_the_african_diaspora) and the Institute for Black Atlantic Research at the University of Central Lancaster (ibaruclan.com).

43. Games, "Atlantic History," 754. One of the most blatant examples of this blindness is R. R. Palmer's classic study *The Age of the Democratic Revolution: A Political History of Europe and America, 1760–1800* (Princeton, NJ: Princeton University Press, 2014), in which he failed to discuss the Haitian Revolution.

44. For a recent discussion of the various means used by indigenous peoples and European colonialists to communicate with each other in the early modern Americas, see Matt Cohen and Jeffrey Glover, eds., *Colonial Mediascapes: Sensory Worlds of the Early Americas* (Lincoln: University of Nebraska Press, 2014); for an example of recent scholarship on patterns of transatlantic affiliation constructed by antebellum southerners and northerners, see Christopher Hanlon, *America's England: Antebellum Literature and Atlantic Sectionalism* (Oxford: Oxford University Press, 2013); for the exchange of plants and animals, see Alfred W. Crosby, *The Columbian Exchange: Biological and Cultural Consequences of 1492* (Westport, CT: Praeger, 1972). Another exemplary text for incorporating Latin American history into the transatlantic dialogue is Jorge Cañizares-Esguerra's award-winning study *How to Write the History of the New World: Histories, Epistemologies, and Identities in the Eighteenth-Century Atlantic World* (Stanford, CA: Stanford University Press, 2001).

45. Paul Giles, *The Global Remapping of American Literature* (Princeton, NJ: Princeton University Press, 2011); D. W. Meinig, *Atlantic America, 1492–1800* (New Haven, CT: Yale University Press, 1986.), xvi.

46. Meinig, *Atlantic America,* xv.

47. Giles, *The Global Remapping of American Literature,* 2–3, 74, 77–78.

48. See Matthew Pratt Guterl, *American Mediterranean: Southern Slaveholders in the Age of Emancipation* (Cambridge, MA: Harvard University Press, 2008); and Walter Johnson, *River*

of Dark Dreams: Slavery and Empire in the Cotton Kingdom (Cambridge, MA: Belknap Press of Harvard University Press, 2013).

49. Paul Giles, *Transatlantic Insurrections: British Culture and the Formation of American Literature, 1730–1860* (Philadelphia: University of Pennsylvania Press, 2001), 78. For a discussion of Rowlandson's literary influence in England and print capitalism, see Nancy Armstrong and Leonard Tennenhouse, *The Imaginary Puritan: Literature, Intellectual Labor, and the Origins of Personal Life* (Berkeley: University of California Press, 1992), 202–12.

50. For the theme of imperialism in the early national period, see David Kazanjian, *The Colonizing Trick: National Culture and Imperial Citizenship in Early America* (Minneapolis: University of Minnesota Press, 2003); for an exploration of Latino culture in a hemispheric context, see Kirsten Silva Gruesz, *Ambassadors of Culture: The Transamerican Origins of Latino Writing* (Princeton, NJ: Princeton University Press, 2002).

51. Anna Brickhouse, *Transamerican Literary Relations and the Nineteenth-Century Public Sphere* (Cambridge: Cambridge University Press, 2004), 2.

52. Ibid., 2–3.

53. Ibid., 30.

54. Brickhouse's multilingual project hails back to the important work of Werner Sollors and his edited volume *Multilingual America: Transnationalism, Ethnicity, and the Languages of American Literature* (New York: New York University Press, 1998).

55. Sibylle Fischer, *Modernity Disavowed: Haiti and the Cultures of Slavery in the Age of Revolution* (Durham, NC: Duke University Press, 2004).

56. Ibid., 37.

57. Ibid., 2–3.

58. Ibid., 16–17.

59. See Kathryn Kish Sklar and James Brewer Stewart, eds., *Women's Rights and Transatlantic Antislavery in the Era of Emancipation* (New Haven, CT: Yale University Press, 2007); Lueck, Bailey, and Damon-Bac, *Transatlantic Women.*

60. Sean X. Goudie, *Creole America: The West Indies and the Formation of Literature and Culture in the New Republic* (Philadelphia: University of Pennsylvania Press, 2006).

61. Ibid., 66.

62. See Charles Stewart, ed., *Creolization: History, Ethnography, Theory* (Walnut Creek, CA: Left Coast, 2007).

63. Rien Fertel, *Imagining the Creole City: The Rise of Literary Culture in Nineteenth-Century New Orleans* (Baton Rouge: Louisiana State University Press, 2014); Catharine Savage Brosman, *Louisiana Creole Literature: A Historical Study* (Jackson: University Press of Mississippi, 2013); William Boelhower, ed., *New Orleans in the Atlantic World: Between Land and Sea* (New York: Routledge, 2010); Ottmar Ette and Gesine Müller, eds., *New Orleans and the Global South: Caribbean, Creolization, Carnival* (Hildesheim: Georg Olms Verlag, 2017).

64. Ira Berlin, "From Creole to African: Atlantic Creoles and the Origins of African-American Society in Mainland America," *William and Mary Quarterly* 53.2 (April 1996): 251–88.

65. See C. A. Bayly, *The Birth of the Modern World 1780–1914: Global Connections and Comparisons* (Oxford: Blackwell, 2004); Sven Beckert, *Empire of Cotton: A Global History* (New York:

Knopf, 2014); Jürgen Osterhammel, *The Transformation of the World: A Global History of the Nineteenth Century,* trans. Patrick Camiller (Princeton, NJ: Princeton University Press, 2014); Sven Beckert and Dominic Sachsenmaier, ed., *Global History, Globally: Research and Practice around the World* (London: Bloomsbury, 2018).

66. Sorcha Gunn and Neil Lazarus edited a special issue on "World Literature" for *Atlantic Studies* 16.2, published in the spring of 2019, while Nicole Poppenhagen and Jens Temmen edited a special issue on the connections between Atlantic and transpacific studies for the same journal: 1.2 (June 2018).

3. Caliban's Scamels: From Shakespearean Romance to Ethnographic Site

1. Leo Marx, *The Machine in the Garden: Technology and the Pastoral Ideal in America* (New York: Oxford University Press, 1964), 34–72.

2. Houston Baker, "Caliban's Triple Play," *Critical Inquiry* 13 (Autumn 1986): 182–96.

3. Max Dorsinville, *Caliban without Prospero: Quebec and Black Literature* (Erin, ON: Press Porcepic, 1974), quoted in Elaine Showalter, *Sister's Choice: Tradition and Change in American Women's Writing* (Oxford: Clarendon, 1991), 26.

4. Showalter, *Sister's Choice,* 22–41.

5. Sylvia Wynter, "Beyond Miranda's Meanings: Un/Silencing the 'Demonic Ground' of Caliban's Women," in *Out of the Kumbla: Caribbean Women and Literature,* ed. C. Boyce Davies and E. I. S. Fido (Trenton, NJ: Africa World, 1990), 358–66; for a further development of Wynter's thesis, see Katherine McKittrick, *Demon Grounds: Black Women and the Cartographies of Struggle* (Minneapolis: University of Minnesota Press, 2006), 121–42.

6. Gloria Naylor, *Mama Day* (New York: Vintage, 1989).

7. Michelle Cliff, *No Telephone to Heaven* (1987; New York: Vintage, 1989); Marina Warner, *Indigo; or Mapping the Waters* (London: Vintage, 1993).

8. Naylor, *Mama Day,* 206.

9. Ibid., 207.

10. Ibid., 79.

11. Derek Walcott, *The Antilles: Fragments of Epic Memory* (New York: Farrar, Strauss and Giroux, 1993).

12. See William Boelhower, "Owning the Weather: Reading *The Tempest* after Hurricane Katrina," *Borrowers and Lenders: The Journal of Shakespeare and Appropriation* 5.2 (Fall–Winter, 2010); Gwilym Jones, *Shakespeare's Storms* (Manchester: Manchester University Press, 2015), 125–50.

13. William Strachey, "A True Reportory of the Wracke . . . ," in Samuel Purchas, *Hakluytus Posthumus or Purchas His Pilgrimes* (New York: AMS Press Inc., 1965), 19:5–72.

14. William Shakespeare, *The Tempest,* ed. Arthur Quiller-Couch and John Dover Wilson (Cambridge: Cambridge University Press, 1971). Subsequent in-text citations are to this edition.

15. Cristoforo Columbo, *Cinque lettere autografe sulla scoperta dell'America,* ed. Sergio Musitelli (Turin: Messaggerie Pontremolesi, 1873), 79.

16. Frank Kermode, ed., *The Tempest,* by William Shakespeare (London: Routledge, 1988), 31n340.

17. Strachey, "A True Reportory of the Wracke," 19:29.

18. Antonio Gramsci, *Quaderni del Carcere,* ed. Valentino Gerratana, vol 1, *Quaderno 1–5* (Turin: Einaudi, 1973), 333 (my translation).

19. Walcott, *The Antilles,* n.p.

20. Toni Morrison, "The Site of Memory," in *Inventing the Truth: The Art and Craft of Memoir,* ed. William Zinsser (Boston: Houghton Mifflin, 1987), 119.

21. Ruth Ronen, *Possible Worlds in Literary Theory* (Cambridge: Cambridge University Press, 1994), 136.

22. Antonio Pigafetta, *Il primo viaggio intorno al mondo* (Rome: Edizioni Associate, 1989), 151n166.

23. Kermode, *The Tempest,* 68n172.

24. Henry David Thoreau, *A Week on the Concord and Merrimack Rivers, Walden, The Maine Woods, Cape Cod* (New York: Library of America, 1985), 908.

25. William Strachey, "A True Reportory of the Wracke," 22–23.

26. Adrienne Rich, "Diving into the Wreck," in *Diving into the Wreck* (New York: Norton, 1973), 23.

27. Siegfried Kracauer, *History: The Last Things before the Last,* edited by Paul Oskar Kristeller (New York: Oxford University Press, 1969), 168.

28. Ibid., 130.

29. Orlando Patterson, *An Absence of Ruins* (London: Hutchinson, 1967), 104–5.

30. George Lamming, "In the Beginning," in *The Pleasures of Exile* (London: Allison and Busby, 1984), 14.

31. See Clifford Geertz, *Local Knowledge: Further Essays in Interpretive Anthropology* (New York: Basic Books, 1983), 259.

32. Lamming, "In the Beginning," 16.

33. Ibid.

34. Christian Jacob, "Carte greche," in *Geografia e geografi nel mondo antico,* ed. Francesco Prontera (Bari: Laterza, 1983), 53, 62.

35. Geertz, *Local Knowledge,* 185.

4. Apple of Peru, Hester Prynne, and Colonial Boston

1. Viewable online from the New York Public Library: https://digitalcollections.nypl.org/items/510d47da-f086-a3d9-e040-e00a18064a99.

2. See Cotton Mather, *Magnalia Christi Americana; or, The Ecclesiastical History of New England from Its First Planting in 1620, until the Year of Our Lord 1698,* book 1 (London, 1702), 30.

3. Ibid.

4. Michel Serres, *Rome: The Book of Foundations,* trans. Felicia McCarren (Stanford, CA: Stanford University Press, 1991), 3.

5. Mather, *Magnalia Christi Americana,* book 1, 30.

6. Ibid., book 2, 1.

7. See Ernst Robert Curtius, *European Literature and the Latin Middle Ages*, trans. Willard R. Trask (Princeton, NJ: Princeton University Press, 1990), 128–30.

8. By semiotope, I mean a highly condensed cartographic site having insuppressible signifying powers. (The term is mine.)

9. See William Boelhower, "Inventing America: Towards a Model of Cartographic Semiosis," *Word & Image* 4.2 (April 1988): 475–97.

10. John C. Huden, *Indian Place Names of New England* (New York: Museum of the American Indian, Heye Foundation, 1962).

11. Serres, *Rome*, 23.

12. Cotton Mather, *Theopolis Americana: An Essay on the Golden Street of the Holy City (Address to the General Assembly of the Massachusetts Province in New England)* (Boston, 1709), 42.

13. Ibid., 7.

14. Ibid., 1.

15. Ibid., 24.

16. Nathaniel Hawthorne, *The Scarlet Letter* (New York: Norton, 1962), 174, 173. Subsequent in-text citations are to this edition.

17. Herman Melville, *Moby-Dick* (New York: Norton, 1967), 292.

18. See the suggestive discussion of the concept "nomos" by Carl Schmitt, *Nomos of the Earth in the International Law of the* Jus Publicum Europaeum, translated by G. L. Ulmen (New York: Telos, 2006).

19. See Andrew F. Smith, *The Tomato in America: Early History, Culture, and Cookery* (Urbana: University of Illinois Press, 2001), 13–15.

20. See "Nicandra physalodes" at http://gobotany.newenglandwild.org species/nicandra /physalodes/; see also Estelle Levetin and Karen McMahon, *Plants and Society* (New York: McGraw-Hill, 1999), 91–93; and Michael Pollan, *The Botany of Desire: A Plant's-Eye View of the World* (New York: Random House, 2002).

21. Marcel Mauss, *The Gift: The Form and Reason for Exchange in Archaic Societies,* trans. W. D. Halls (London: Routledge, 1990), 78.

22. Ibid., 3.

23. Marshal Sahlins, "The Spirit of the Gift," in *The Logic of the Gift: Toward an Ethic of Generosity,* ed. Alan Schrift (London: Routledge, 1997), 84.

24. Mauss, *The Gift,* 5–6.

25. Ibid., 4.

26. Ibid., 13.

27. Jacques T. Godbout, *Le don, la dette, et l'identité* (Montreal: La Découverte, 2000), 16.

28. Mauss, *The Gift,* 3.

29. Julia Kristeva, *Desire in Language: A Semiotic Approach to Literature and Art,* ed. Leon S. Roudiez (New York: Columbia University Press 1980), 237–70.

30. Ibid., 238.

31. See Giorgio Agamben, *Homo Sacer: Sovereign Power and Bare Life,* trans. Daniel Heller-Roazen (Stanford, CA: Stanford University Press, 1998), 81–86.

32. See Margaret R. Miles, "The Virgin's One Bare Breast: Female Nudity and Religious Meaning in Tuscan Early Renaissance Culture," in *The Female Body in Western Culture*, ed. Susan Robin Suleiman (Cambridge, MA: Harvard University Press, 1986), 201.

33. Ibid.

34. Agamben, *Homo Sacer*, 84.

35. Ibid., 86.

36. See Cristiano Grottanelli, *Il sacrificio* (Bari: Laterza, 1999), 16–27.

37. Alain Caillé, *Il terzo paradigma: antropologia filosofica del dono*, trans. Ada Cinato (Turin: Bollati Boringhieri, 1998), 55–56.

38. See Françoise Meltzer, *For Fear of the Fire: Joan of Arc and the Limits of Subjectivity* (Chicago: University of Chicago Press, 2001), 38.

39. Michel de Certeau, *The Writing of History*, trans. Tom Conley (New York: Columbia University Press, 1988), 277.

40. Alison Ainley, "The Ethics of Sexual Difference," in *Abjection, Melancholia and Love: The Work of Julia Kristeva*, ed. John Fletcher and Andrew Benjamin (London: Routledge, 1990), 58.

41. John Caputo and Michael Scanlon, eds., *God, the Gift, and Postmodernism* (Bloomington: Indiana University Press, 1999), 8.

42. Ibid., 200.

43. Certeau, *The Writing of History*, 281.

44. Ibid., 282.

45. Ibid., 272.

46. Rocco Ronchi, *Il pensiero bastardo: Figurazione dell'invisibile e communicazione indiretta* (Milan: Christian Marinotti Edizioni, 2001), 305.

47. Marc Fumaroli, preface to *L'art de la conversation*, ed. J. Hellgouarch (Paris: Garnier, 1997), xii.

48. Ronchi, *Il pensiero bastardo*, 307.

49. Mauss, *The Gift*, 29.

50. Bonnie Honig, *Democracy and the Foreigner* (Princeton, NJ: Princeton University Press, 2001), 34.

51. Michelle Boulous Walker, *Philosophy and the Maternal Body: Reading Silence* (London: Routledge, 1998), 107–13.

52. Ludwig Wittgenstein, *Tractatus Logico-Philosophicus*, trans. C. K. Ogden (London: Routledge and Kegan Paul, 1974), sec. 6.522.

53. See Jurij M Lotman and Boris A. Uspenskij, *Semiotica e cultura*, trans. Donatella Ferrari-Bravo (Milan: Riccardo Ricciardi Editore, 1975), 59–95.

5. "A Refugee from History": Douglass's Heroic Slave in the Atlantic World

1. See, for example, George Hendrick and Willene Hendrick, *The Creole Mutiny: A Tale of Revolt aboard a Slave Ship* (Chicago: Ivan R. Dee, 2003); Walter Johnson, "White Lies: Human Property and Domestic Slavery aboard the Slave Ship Creole," *Atlantic Studies* 5.2 (2008): 237–63.

2. See Doris L. Garraway, ed., *Tree of Liberty: Cultural Legacies of the Haitian Revolution in the Atlantic World* (Charlottesville: University of Virginia Press, 2008); Howard Jones, *Mutiny on the* Amistad: *The Saga of a Slave Revolt and Its Impact on American Abolition, Law, and Diplomacy* (New York: Oxford University Press, 1987); Marcus Rediker, *The* Amistad *Rebellion: An Atlantic Odyssey of Slavery and Freedom* (New York: Penguin Books, 2013); Eric Robert Taylor, *If We Must Die: Shipboard Insurrections in the Era of the Atlantic Slave Trade* (Baton Rouge: Louisiana State University Press, 2006); Sowande' M. Mustakeem, *Slavery at Sea: Terror, Sex, and Sickness in the Middle Passage* (Urbana: University of Illinois Press, 2016).

3. Frederick Douglass, *The Heroic Slave: A Cultural and Critical Edition*, ed. Robert S. Levine, John Stauffer, and John R. McKivigan (New Haven, CT: Yale University Press, 2015), 43. Subsequent in-text citations are to this edition.

4. See Philippe Girard, *Toussaint Louverture: A Revolutionary Life* (New York: Basic Books, 2016), 187–88, 239, 255.

5. *Tenth Annual Report of the Board of Managers of the Mass. Anti-Slavery Society* (Boston: Dow and Jackson's, 1842), 89–99.

6. Hendrick and Hendrick, *The* Creole *Mutiny,* 123–52; Ivy G. Wilson, "On Native Ground: Transnationalism, Frederick Douglass, and 'The Heroic Slave,'" *PMLA* 121.2 (2006): 453–68.

7. See Robert B. Stepto, "Storytelling in Early Afro-American Fiction: Frederick Douglass's 'The Heroic Slave,'" *Georgia Review* 36 (Summer 1982): 355–68; William L. Andrews, "The Novelization of Voice in Early African American Narrative," *PMLA* 105.1 (January 1990): 23–34; Eric J. Sundquist, *To Wake the Nations: Race in the Making of American Literature* (Cambridge, MA: Harvard University Press, 1993); Shelly Fishkin Fisher and Carla Peterson, "'We Hold These Truths to Be Self-Evident': The Rhetoric of Frederick Douglass's Journalism," in *Frederick Douglass: New Literary and Historical Essays,* ed. Eric J. Sundquist (New York: Cambridge University Press, 1990), 189–204; Richard Yarborough, "Race, Violence, and Manhood: The Masculine Ideal in Frederick Douglass's 'The Heroic Slave,'" in *Frederick Douglass: New Literary and Historical Essays,* ed. Sundquist, 166–88; Maggie Montesinos Sale, *The Slumbering Volcano: American Slave Ship Revolts and the Production of Rebellious Masculinity* (Durham, NC: Duke University Press), 1997; Russ Castronovo, *Fathering the Nation: American Genealogies of Slavery and Freedom* (Berkeley: University of California Press, 1995); Stanley Harrold, "Romanticizing Slave Revolt: Madison Washington, the *Creole* Mutiny, and Abolitionist Celebration of Violent Means," in *Antislavery Violence: Sectional, Racial, and Cultural Conflict in Antebellum America,* ed. John R. McKivigan and Harrold (Knoxville: University of Tennessee Press, 1999), 89–107; William Boelhower, "The Dramaturgy of Witnessing: Hamlet, Douglass, and 'The Heroic Slave,'" in *Making America: The Cultural Work of Literature,* ed. Susanne Rohr, Peter Schneck, and Sabine Sielke (Heidelberg: Universität C. Winter, 2000), 171–84; Roy E. Finkenbine, "The Symbolism of Slave Mutiny: Black Abolitionist Responses to the *Amistad* and *Creole* Incidents," in *Rebellion Repression Reinvention: Mutiny in Comparative Perspective,* ed. Jane Hathaway (Westport, CT: Praeger, 2001), 233–52; Philip Troutman, "Grapevine in the Slave Market: African American Geopolitical Literacy and the 1841 *Creole* Revolt," in *The Chattel Principle: Internal Slave Trade in the Americas,* ed. Walter Johnson (New Haven, CT: Yale University Press, 2004); Celeste-Marie Bernier, "From Fugitive Slave to Fugitive Abolitionist: The Oratory of Frederick Douglass and

the Emerging Heroic Slave Tradition," *Atlantic Studies* 3.2 (October 2006): 201–24; Hendrick and Hendrick, *The* Creole *Mutiny;* Ivy G. Wilson, *Specters of Democracy: Blackness and the Aesthetics of Politics in the Antebellum U.S.* (New York: Oxford University Press, 2011). The latest scholar, a historian, to call "The Heroic Slave" a fictional narrative pure and simple, is David W. Blight, *Frederick Douglass: Prophet of Freedom* (New York: Simon and Schuster, 2018), 248–51.

8. For a definition of cotext (vs context), see Umberto Eco, *The Role of the Reader: Explorations in the Semiotics of Texts* (Bloomington: Indiana University Press, 1979), chapter 1, "Text and Encyclopaedia." According to Eco, when one of a number of possible contexts (defined as type-scenes making up the author's and reader's cultural encyclopedia) becomes activated by the narrative at hand, it becomes a cotext.

9. See Jean-Claude Passeron and Jacques Revel, "Penser par cas: Raisonner à partir de singularités," in *Penser par cas*, ed. Passeron and Revel (Paris: École des Hautes Études en Sciences Sociales, 2005), 9–44.

10. Krzysztof Pomian, *Che cos'è la storia* (Milan: Mondadori, 2001), 113–14, 129–45.

11. Frederick Douglass, "The Heroic Slave," in *Autographs for Freedom,* ed. Julia Griffiths (Boston: John P. Jewett, 1853); Douglass, "The Heroic Slave," *Frederick Douglass' Paper,* March 4, 11, 18, 25, 1853. Although *Autographs* was dated 1853, it was ready for press in late 1852. (See, for example, "Superb Gift Books: Books in Press," *National Era,* December 16, 1852, 5.

12. See Stepto, "Storytelling in Early Afro-American Fiction,'" 359; Sundquist, *To Wake the Nations,* 115; Wilson, "On Native Ground,'" 463. William McFeely says "The Heroic Slave" is Douglass's "fantasy of his own heroism." See McFeely, *Frederick Douglass* (New York: Norton, 1991), 175. Douglass voted against the publication of Henry Highland Garnet's "Address to the Slaves" given at the national black convention in Buffalo in 1843. See Manisha Sinha, *The Slave's Cause: A History of Abolition* (New Haven, CT: Yale University Press, 2016), 418–19.

13. Several scholars have called Douglass's narrative a historical fiction. But while there have been any number of appreciations of "The Heroic Slave" as a work of fiction, there has been little effort to pin down the narrative's historical dimension, especially as this is related to the conventions of Romantic historiography and other discursive genres forming part of the Douglass archive. In addition, we need to know more about Douglass's readings in the genre of history.

14. Frederick Douglass, "The Prospect in the Future," in *Selected Speeches and Writings,* ed. Philip S. Foner, abridged Yuval Taylor, 398–401 (Chicago: Lawrence Hill Books, 1999), 400.

15. The idea of bringing the dead back to life was a convention of Romantic historians, beginning with Jules Michelet. In early 1842 the *New-York Colored American* urged a similar call: "Let the spirit of a Hancock, a Leonidas, and of a Toussaint Louverture prevail; let a Spartan band be found, who'll stick by the ship . . . and determine to die upon the soil" (*Tenth Annual Report,* 20–21).

16. Frederick Douglass, "Slavery, the Slumbering Volcano," in *The Frederick Douglass Papers,* Series One, *Speeches, Debates, and Interviews,* vol. 2, *1847–1854,* 148–58 (New Haven, CT: Yale University Press, 1982), 153, 156.

17. Hendrick and Hendrick, *The* Creole *Mutiny,* 13–37.

18. In his 1845 autobiography, he states: "I deem it proper to make known my intention not to state all the facts connected with the transaction [his escape]." Frederick Douglass, *Autobiographies* (New York: Library of America, 1994), 84.

19. John Ernest, *Liberation Historiography: African American Writers and the Challenge of History, 1794–1861* (Chapel Hill: University of North Carolina Press, 2004), 138.

20. In a note in the *New-York Daily Tribune* (February 25, 1852, 5) titled "Brooklyn Items," we read: "We learn that Fred. Douglass, the Anti-Slavery lecturer, and Rev. Saml. H. Cox, D. D., of Brooklyn, will sail to day or to-morrow for Nassau, New-Providence. The former goes on an Anti-Slavery mission and the latter for the benefit of his health." There was also a "Letter from Wm. C. Nell," that appeared in *Frederick Douglass' Paper* (March 18, 1852), indicating that in 1852 Madison Washington was alive and living in Nassau (Cynthia S. Hamilton, "Models of Agency: Frederick Douglass and 'The Heroic Slave,'" *Proceedings of the American Antiquarian Society* 114.1 [2005]: 97.) See Robert S. Levine, John Stauffer, and John R. McKivigan, introduction to *The Heroic Slave: A Cultural and Critical Edition,* by Frederick Douglass, ed Levine, Stauffer, and McKivigan (New Haven, CT: Yale University Press, 2015), xxiv.

21. Douglass, *The Heroic Slave: A Cultural and Critical Edition.*

22. Robert S. Levine, *The Lives of Frederick Douglass* (Cambridge, MA: Harvard University Press, 2016), 147.

23. See Harrold, "Romanticizing Slave Revolt." Harrold also foregrounds the scene in which the "Addresses" were delivered (37–52). Douglass was present when Smith, Garrison, and Garnet delivered their famous speeches. All three are immediately relevant to the writing of "The Heroic Slave."

24. The major exception is Sale, *The Slumbering Volcano*, 120–45, 173–97.

25. In the book version of "The Heroic Slave" the historian-narrator's prologue is literally set off from the rest of the narrative by an intervening blank space. See Frederick Douglass, "The Heroic Slave," in *Autographs for Freedom* (Boston: John Jewett, 1853), 176. When Douglass began serial publication of "The Heroic Slave" in *Frederick Douglass' Paper*, he used a line to separate the framing prologue from the rest of the narrative. See Douglass, "The Heroic Slave," part I, in *Frederick Douglass' Paper,* March 4, 1853, col. 6.

26. Carolyn Steedman, *Dust: The Archive and Cultural History* (Manchester: Manchester University Press, 2001), 45.

27. See Melba P. Jensen, "Frederick Douglass's *The Heroic Slave:* Text, Context, and Interpretation" (PhD diss., Univ. of Massachusetts Amherst, 2005), 128–33; Levine, Stauffer, and McKivigan, introduction to *The Heroic Slave: A Cultural and Critical Edition,* xi–xxxvi; Levine, *The Lives of Frederick Douglass,* 123–24, 132, 151.

28. Celeste-Marie Bernier, "'Dusky Powder Magazines': The *Creole* Revolt (1841) in Nineteenth Century American Literature (Dissertation, University of Nottingham, 2002), 2–3.

29. See Johnson, "White Lies," 237–63; and on the historical documents, Howard Jones, "The Peculiar Institution and National Honor: The Case of the *Creole* Slave Revolt," *Civil War History* 21 (March 1975): 28–50; Edward D. Jervey and C. Harold Huber, "The *Creole* Affair," *Journal of Negro History* 65.3 (Summer 1980): 196–211.

30. Bernier, "From Fugitive Slave to Fugitive Abolitionist," 201–42.

31. Reinhart Koselleck, *L'expérience de l'histoire,* trans. Alexandre Escudier (Paris: Gallimard Le Seuil, 1997), 201–3.

32. Hamilton, "Models of Agency," 87–136.

33. Douglass, *Autobiographies,* 96.

34. See the article from the abolitionist newspaper *Friend of Man* reprinted as "Madison Washington: Another Chapter in His History," *Liberator,* June 10, 1842, 11; Frederick Douglass, "Slavery, the Slumbering Volcano," delivered at New York, April 1849, and printed in *North Star,* May 11, 1849, and the *Liberator,* May 11, 1849, in *Frederick Douglass Papers,* Series One, *Speeches, Debates, and Interviews,* vol. 2, *1847–1854,* 154–58; see also the excellent chapter "Madison Washington before the Mutiny" in Hendrick and Hendrick, *The* Creole *Mutiny,* 13–37. "The Heroic Slave" appeared both in *Autographs for Freedom,* edited by Julia Griffiths (Boston: John P. Jewett 1853), 174–239, and in *Frederick Douglass' Paper* March 4, 11, 18, 25, 1853.

35. See Levine, *The Lives of Frederick Douglass,* 31–118.

36. Hamilton, "Models of Agency," 113–15, 89–90. Hamilton is not alone in noting the awkwardnesses of Douglass's narrative. See Stepto, "Storytelling in Early Afro-American Fiction." Levine mentions Douglass's use of a startling variety of both sources and narrative techniques and modes, including dialogue, soliloquies, melodrama, coincidence, and oratorical set pieces. See Levine, *The Lives of Frederick Douglass,* 146.

37. Already in one of Douglass's earliest surviving speeches, we hear him rhythmically calling his audience to action: "Do it—and they who are ready to perish shall bless you! Do it! And all good men will cheer you onward! Do it! And God will reward you for the deed." "Great Meeting in Faneuil Hall," in *Tenth Annual Report,* appendix, 18.

38. Geneviève Fabre and Robert O'Meally, introduction to *History and Memory in African-American Culture* (New York: Oxford University Press, 1994), 6.

39. Fabre and O'Meally, introduction, 7–8.

40. Levine, *The Lives of Frederick Douglass,* 123–27.

41. Manhattan, "Letter from New York," *National Era* (Washington, DC), May 6, 1852, 3.

42. Sinha, *The Slave's Cause,* 365–67.

43. "Address of the Colored National Convention, to the People of the United States," in *Proceedings of the Colored National Convention Held in Rochester, July 6th, 7th and 8th, 1853* (Rochester, NY: Printed at the Office of Frederick Douglass' Paper, 1853), 13.

44. Gerrit Smith, "Address of the Anti-Slavery Convention of the State of New York Held in Peterboro, January 19th, 1842, to the Slaves in the U. States of America," in *The Rise of Aggressive Abolitionism. Addresses to the Slaves,* ed. Stanley Harrold (Lexington: University Press of Kentucky, 2004), 155.

45. Ernest, *Liberation Historiography,* 210.

46. In that same letter, he says, "I have a large share of veneration for great *men.*" *The Frederick Douglass Papers,* Series Three, *Correspondence,* vol. 1, *1842–1852* (New Haven, CT: Yale University Press, 2009), 529.

47. Some reports spoke of "the immortal nineteen." "Madison Washington," *Liberator,* June 10, 1842, 1.

48. On Joseph Cinqué, see Rediker, *The Amistad Rebellion,* 160–76.

49. Quoted ibid., 168.

50. We have the famous remark of James McDowell who, during Virginia's debate over the Turner rebellion, challenged proslavery spokesmen by saying, "Was it the fear of Nat Turner . . . which produced such effects? . . . No sir: it was the suspicion that a Nat Turner might be in every

family." See Eugene D. Genovese, *From Rebellion to Revolution: Afro-American Slave Revolts in the Making of the Modern World* (Baton Rouge: Louisiana State University Press, 1979), 116.

51. See Hayden White, *Metahistory: The Historical Imagination in Nineteenth-Century Europe* (Baltimore: Johns Hopkins University Press, 1975), 158, 135–62; Steedman, *Dust:* "[T]he resurrectionist historian creates the past that he purports to restore, in Michelet's case attributing feelings, beliefs and desires that he acknowledged were not actually experienced by those restored to life" (38).

52. His microhistory would seem to fit Arthur A. Schomburg's description of early African American history as "compendiums of exceptional men and women . . . it was apologetics turned into biography." See Schomburg, "The Negro Digs Up His Past," in *The New Negro: An Interpretation,* ed. Alain Locke (New York: Arno, 1968), 231.

53. Douglass, *The Frederick Douglass Papers,* Series Three, *Correspondence,* vol. 1, *1842–1852,* 545. See his famous speech "The Meaning of July Fourth for the Negro," which he delivered at Rochester, his hometown, on July 5, 1852, in: *The Frederick Douglass Papers,* Series One, *Speeches, Debates, and Interviews,* vol. 2, *1847–1854,* 359–88.

54. Oliver Johnson, *Pennsylvania Freeman,* September 4, 1852; Carleton Mabee, *Sojourner Truth: Slave, Prophet, Legend* (New York: New York University Press, 1995), 83–92.

55. See Milton C. Sernett, *North Star Country: Upstate New York and the Crusade for African American Freedom* (Syracuse, NY: Syracuse University Press, 2002).

56. See Kendrick and Kendrick, *The* Creole *Mutiny;* Johnson, "White Lies," 237–63; Sinha, *The Slave's Cause,* 411–16; and Douglass, *The Heroic Slave: A Cultural and Critical Edition.*

57. See Carlo Ginzburg's discussion of the relation between the historical novel and history writing in *Threads and Traces: True, False, Fictive* (Berkley: University of California Press, 2012), 54–71.

58. Harriet Beecher Stowe, *A Key to "Uncle Tom's Cabin": Presenting the Original Facts and Documents* (1853; Bedford, MA: Applewood Books, 2015); William Wells Brown, *Clotel; or, The President's Daughter: A Narrative of Slave Life in the United States.* (1853; Upper Saddle River, NJ: Gregg, 1969), 244.

59. Stowe, *A Key,* iii.

60. Ibid., 5.

61. White, *Metahistory,* 387.

62. Douglass Egerton, *Gabriel's Rebellion: The Virginia Slave Conspiracies of 1800 and 1802* (Chapel Hill: University of North Carolina Press, 1993), xii.

63. Ginzburg, *Threads and Traces,* 202.

64. Ibid., 57.

65. Quoted in Ginzburg, *Threads and Traces,* 67.

66. Today, many a historian has mined the slave narrative for historical evidence. See, for example, Walter Johnson, *Soul by Soul: Life inside the Antebellum Slave Market* (Cambridge, MA: Harvard University Press, 1999).

67. See William Jay, *The* Creole *Case and Mr. Webster's Despatch: With Comments by the N.Y. American* (New York: Office of the New York American, 1842). Douglass famously commented on the British response in his address "Slavery, the Slumbering Volcano," which he delivered

in New York on April 23, 1849 and published in *North Star,* May 11, 1849, in *Frederick Douglass Papers,* Series One, *Speeches, Debates, and Interviews,* vol. 2, *1847–1854,* 148–58.

68. See Jervey and Huber, "The *Creole* Affair"; Jones, "The Peculiar Institution and National Honor"; Johnson, "White Lies."

69. See Andrew Delbanco, *The War before the War: Fugitive Slaves and the Struggle for America's Soul from the Revolution to the Civil War* (New York: Penguin, 2018), 317–49.

70. See the article from *Friend of Man* reprinted as "Madison Washington: Another Chapter in His History," 1; Douglass, "Slavery, the Slumbering Volcano,"; see also the excellent chapter "Madison Washington before the Mutiny" in Hendrick and Hendrick, *The* Creole *Mutiny,* 13–37.

71. We know from an insert in the *New York Times* that he planned a trip to Nassau in the early part of 1852, leading to speculations that he may have wanted to meet Washington or others from the *Creole* uprising.

72. Douglass's use of Madison Washington's example in his speeches and in "The Heroic Slave" are not qualitatively different; they form a continuum in which rhetoric, history, and biography alternate and intersect at various moments. For appreciations of Douglass as orator, see the detailed accounts of Douglass in action by William J. Wilson, "A Leaf from My Scrapbook," *Autographs for Freedom* (Rochester: Wanzer, Beardsley and Co.,1854), 165–73; William Wells Brown, *The Works of William Wells Brown,* ed. Paula Garrett and Hollis Robbins (New York: Oxford University Press, 2006), 342–43, 434–35); and the *National Era*'s reportage in Douglass, *Frederick Douglass Papers* Series One, *Speeches, Debates, and Interviews,* vol. 1, *1842–1846,* 28–29.

73. Douglass, "The Heroic Slave," *Frederick Douglass' Paper,* March 4, 11, 18, 25, 1853; and "The Heroic Slave," in *Autographs for Freedom,* 174–239.

74. Douglass, *A Heroic Slave: A Cultural and Critical Edition,* 6 (Madison: "My resolution"); 9 (Listwell: "I shall go to my home in Ohio resolved to atone"); 45 (Grant: "I have resolved never to set my foot on the deck of a slave ship"; "I'm resolved never to endanger my life again in a cause which my conscience does not approve"). In meeting after meeting of the antislavery societies and black conventions, people drew up "resolutions," voted on them, and "resolved" to carry them out. The word rang in Douglass's ears as he learned to appreciate the deliberative process they taught.

75. See McFeely, *Frederick Douglass,* 174.

76. See Frank Ankersmit, *Meaning, Truth, and Reference in Historical Representation* (Ithaca, NY: Cornell University Press, 2012), 122.

77. See *Richmond Enquirer,* December 16, 1841, 2 (on the first news about *Creole* affair); *Richmond Compiler,* December 17, 1841, qtd. in *Emancipator* January 20, 1842, 4.

78. The figure of 130 slaves indicates that Douglass's narrator was not privy to the contestations Judah Benjamin made to the Supreme Court of Louisiana regarding the ship's being overcrowded, beyond the legal number of human cargo allowed for that ship size.

79. Roland Barthes, *Writing Degree Zero and Elements of Semiology,* trans. Annette Lavers and Colin Smith (Boston: Beacon, 1970), 20.

80. "Slavery is against the law of nature; and although sanctioned by the law of nations, it is so sanctioned as a local or municipal institution, of binding force within the limits of the nation that chooses to establish it, and on the vessels of such nation on the high seas, but as having no force or binding effect beyond the jurisdiction of such nation." Judah Benjamin, in *Thomas*

Mccargo v. the New Orleans Insurance Company, Supreme Court of Louisiana, Eastern District, New Orleans (1845 La. LEXIS 122; 10 Rob. 202, March 1845, Decided, 164).

81. See Terry Baxter, *Frederick Douglass's Curious Audiences: Ethos in the Age of the Consumable Subject* (New York: 2004), 43.

82. Martin Rueff, "L'historien et les noms propres," *Critique* 67.769–70 (June–July 2011): 515.

83. Egerton, *Gabriel's Rebellion,* 102.

84. Ibid., 51.

85. Girard, *Toussaint Louverture,* 115.

86. Douglass gave a special place to this intertextual moment of liberty in all of his autobiographies; thus: "Patrick Henry, to a listening senate, thrilled by his magic eloquence, and ready to stand by him in his boldest flights, could say, 'GIVE ME LIBERTY OR GIVE ME DEATH,' and this saying was a sublime one, even more for a freeman; but, incomparably more sublime, is the same sentiment, when practically asserted by men accustomed to the lash and chain—men whose sensibilities must have become more or less deadened by their bondage." Douglass, *Autobiographies,* 312.

87. Michel Foucault, *Society Must Be Defended: Lectures at the Collège de France, 1975–76,* trans. David Macey (New York: Picador, 2003), 227–28.

88. See Sandra M. Gustafson, *Eloquence Is Power: Oratory and Performance in Early America* (Chapel Hill: University of North Carolina Press, 2001), 7, 201.

89. Garnet, "Address to the Slaves of the United States of America," 187.

90. John Ernest, *Liberation Historiography,* 69.

91. These addresses, given during the period 1845–49 in Ireland, Scotland, London, Boston, and New York, reveal that Douglass must have had "his" heroic slave constantly in mind, a fact that fuels the idea that he himself saw Washington's example as intimately contributing to the political animus of his own abolitionist efforts. See Celeste-Marie Bernier's important essay on these six addresses and their relation to "The Heroic Slave" in "From Fugitive Slave to Fugitive Abolitionist." Note, however, that she does not consider the archival problem these variously modulated addresses raise as they reuse and reshape Madison Washington's history. Before Douglass, black leaders like Richard Allen, Peter Williams, and Henry Highland Garnet delineated a pantheon of black liberators and leaders. See Richard Newman, "'A Chosen Generation': Black Founders and Early America," in *Prophets of Protest,* ed. Timothy Patrick McCarthy and John Stauffer (New York: New Press, 2006), 69.

92. Briefly, part II of Douglass's narrative features a scene of fraternal solidarity between Washington the fugitive and a white abolitionist farmer, Listwell. The setting is domestic, the family home of the Listwells in Ohio. On his way to Canada, Washington stops by chance at their home and is taken in and comforted. In the morning Listwell helps Washington to escape by boat to Canada. In the first scene, having witnessed Washington's soliloquy, Listwell "resolves" to become an abolitionist. In the second scene he becomes a practical abolitionist, by helping the fugitive slave escape. In part III, Listwell again meets up with Washington, who has now been recaptured and is being sent to New Orleans to be sold at auction. Here again, Washington is able to update Listwell on his life, and the latter is able to slip Washington a few iron files as he is being loaded onto the *Creole.* It is probable that Listwell is a code name for one of the people who helped Washington during his flight to Canada. His presence suggests Douglass's advocacy of an interracial front against slavery typical of the many vigilance committees in the north

committed to helping fugitive slaves. In part II, Listwell and Washington become friends, and in part III they become political allies in a rebellion. The progression is important as it proceeds from an act of solidarity to one of violent resistance.

93. The first southern newspaper accounts claimed that a Baptist minister stirred the slaves to revolt—implying that otherwise they would not have done so. See "The Case of the Creole," *Richmond Enquirer,* December 16, 1841, 1; "The Creole Mutiny," *Cleveland Daily Mirror,* December 29, 1841, 3.

94. Quoted in Carlo Ginzburg, "Réflexions sur une hypothèse vingt-cinq ans après," 37–47 in *L'interprétation des indices: Enquête sur le paradigm indiciare avec Carlo Ginzburg,* ed. Denis Thouard (Villeneuve d'Ascq: Presses Universitaires du Septentrion, 2007), 42.

6. From *Mundus Novus* to *Atlantic World: Three Early Modern World Maps*

1. Blumenberg, *Paradigms for a Metaphorology,* trans. Robert Savage (Ithaca, NY: Cornell University Press, 2016).

2. As Fernand Braudel reminds us, "The world was 'discovered' a long time ago, well before the Great Discoveries. . . . Europe's own achievement was to discover the Atlantic and to master its difficult stretches, currents and winds. This late success gained it the doors and routes of the seven seas." Quoted in D. W. Meinig, *Atlantic America, 1492–1800* (New Haven, CT: Yale University Press, 1986), 1.

3. See Denis Cosgrove, *Apollo's Eye: A Cartographic Genealogy of the Earth in the Western Imagination* (Baltimore: John Hopkins University Press, 2001); Ricardo Padrón, *The Spacious Word: Cartography, Literature, and Empire in Early Modern Spain* (Chicago: University of Chicago Press, 2004); G. Malcolm Lewis, ed., *Cartographic Encounters: Perspectives on Native American Mapmaking and Map Use* (Chicago: University of Chicago Press, 1998); and John Pickles, *A History of Spaces: Cartographic Reason, Mapping and the Geo-Coded World* (London: Routledge, 2004).

4. William Boelhower, "Inventing America: Towards a Model of Cartographic Semiosis," *Word & Image* 4.2 (April 1988): 475–97.

5. See the oft-quoted observation by Fernando Colombo: "Dico adunque. Che nella sua picciola età imparò lettere, e studiò in Pavia, che gli bastava per intendere i Cosmografi, alla cui lezione fu molto affezionato: per lo qual rispetto ancora si diede all'Astrologia, e alla Geometria: perciocchè queste scienze sono in tal maniera concatenante, che l'una non può star senza l'altra; e ancora, perché Tolomeo nel principio della sua Cosmografia dice, che niuno può esser buon Cosmografo, se ancora non sarà pittore, participò ancora del disegno, per piantar le terre e formar i corpi cosmografici in piano, e in tondo." Colombo, *Le historie della vita e dei fatti di Cristoforo Colombo,* 2 vols. (Milan: Edizioni Alpes, 1930), 1:23–25.

6. Christopher Columbus, *Journal of the First Voyage,* ed. B. W. Ife (Warminster: Aris and Phillips, 1990), 3.

7. Columbus, *Journal,* 29.

8. Battista Agnese, *Portolan atlas of 9 charts and a world map, etc. Dedicated to Hieronymus Ruffault, Abbot of St. Vaast* (1544), map, 14r-v. The world map depicting Magellan's route around

the world appears on leaf 14 (of 15). The *Portolan atlas* is viewable online at the Library of Congress: https://www.loc.gov/item/98687206/.

9. I am indebted here two Italian Columbus scholars: Paolo Emilio Taviani, *Christopher Columbus*, ed. and trans. Luciano Farina, 3 vols. (Rome: Italian Geographic Society, 2000), 2:151–302; Ilaria Luzzana Caraci, *The Puzzling Hero: Studies on Christopher Columbus and the Culture of His Age,* trans. Mayta Munson (Rome: Carocci, 2002), 183–204. See also Christoforo Columbo, *La lettera della scoperta,* ed. Luciano Formisano (Naples: Liguori, 1992); and Juan Gil, *Miti e utopie della scoperta,* trans. Michela Fornassi Pardo (Milan: Garzanti, 1991).

10. For a discussion of these concepts, see Pierre Bourdieu and Loïc J. D. Wacquant, *An Invitation to Reflexive Sociology* (Chicago: University of Chicago Press, 1992), 253–55.

11. Columbus, *Journal,* 67.

12. Ibid., 5.

13. Amerigo Vespucci, *Letters from a New World,* trans. David Jacobson (New York: Marsilio, 1992), 17.

14. See Christian Jacob, "Geografia," in *Il sapere greco: Dizionario critico,* ed. Jacques Brunschwig and Geoffrey E. R. Lloyd, 2 vols. (Turin: Einaudi, 2005), 1: 395–410.

15. Vespucci, *Letters,* 8.

16. Reinhart Koselleck, *Futures Past: On the Semantics of Historical Time,* trans. Keith Tribe (New York: Columbia University Press, 2004), 255–75.

17. Ibid., 259.

18. Columbus, *Journal,* 100–101.

19. Bailyn, *Atlantic History: Concept and Contours* (Cambridge, MA: Harvard University Press, 2005), 68.

20. Ibid., 62–63.

21. Ibid., 83.

22. Columbus, *Journal,* 171.

23. For a discussion of this major line of political thinking, see Giorgio Carnevali, *Dell'amicizia politica, tra teoria e storia* (Bari: Laterza, 2004), especially 3–50. See also Carl Schmitt, *Le categorie del "politico,"* trans. Pierangelo Schiera (Bologna: Mulino, 1972), 101–210, on the Hobbesian philosophy of friend and enemy.

24. Juan Gil and Consuelo Varela, "Cristoforo Colombo," in *Nuovo mondo: Gli italiani,* ed. Paolo Collo and Pier Luigi Crovetto (Turin: Einaudi, 1991), 5–7; see also Geoffrey Symcos, ed., *Repertorium Columbianum* (Turnhout: Brepols, 1993–). There are now over thirteen volumes containing documents by and about Columbus.

25. Koselleck, *Futures Past,* 260.

26. Martin Heidegger, "The Age of the World Picture," in *The Question Concerning Technology, and Other Essays* (New York: Harper and Row, 1977), 115–54. I have used an Italian translation of this essay that was originally included in *Sentieri interrotti,* trans. Pietro Chiodi (Florence: La Nuova Italia, 1984), 71–102.

27. See Derek Gregory, *Geographical Imaginations* (Oxford: Blackwell, 1998), 34–37; Pickles, *A History of Spaces,* 7, 84; and above all Cosgrove, *Apollo's Eye,* 110–23.

28. Martin Waldseemüller, *Cosmographiae Introductio,* trans. Joseph Fischer and Franz von Wieser (Ann Arbor, MI: University Microfilms, 1966). For a discussion of this map, see Seymour

Schwartz, *Putting "America" on the Map: The Story of the Most Important Graphic Document in the History of the United States* (Amherst, NY: Prometheus, 2007); and Toby Lester, *The Fourth Part of the World: The Race to the Ends of the Earth, and the Epic Story of the Map That Gave America Its Name* (New York: Free Press, 2009), 325–403.

29. Jean-Luc Nancy, *La creazione del mondo o la mondializzazione,* trans. Davide Tarizzo (Turin: Einaudi, 2003), 18.

30. Heidegger, *Sentieri interrotti,* 89.

31. Franco Farinelli, *Geografia: Un'introduzione ai modelli del mondo* (Turin: Einaudi, 2003), 128.

32. See Isidore of Seville's seventh-century T-O map at https://www.loc.gov/exhibits/exploring-the-early-americas/interactives/heavens-and-earth/earth/artifact6-earth.html.

33. On T-O maps, see R. V. Tooley and Charles Bricker, *Landmarks of Mapmaking: An Illustrated Survey of Maps and Mapmakers* (Dorset: Westminster Editions, 1981), 22–25; Rodney W. Shirley, *The Mapping of the World: Early Printed World Maps, 1472–1700* (London: Holland, 1983), xix–xxii; and Marica Milanesi, "Terra Incognita," in *Hic sunt leones,* eds. Omar Calabrese, Renato Giovannoli, and Isabella Pezzini (Milan: Electa, 1983), 11–14.

34. Mary Carruthers, *The Craft of Thought: Meditation, Rhetoric, and the Making of Images, 400–1200* (Cambridge: Cambridge University Press, 1998), 200, 210, 222–23, 236.

35. Ebstorf map viewable at http://www.landschaftsmuseum.de/Seiten/Museen/Ebstorf1.htm.

36. Nancy, *La creazione del mondo,* 6–8.

37. For the La Cosa map see Kenneth Nebenzahl, *Atlante di Colombo e Le Grandi Scoperte,* trans. Miriam Bait, Attilio Trentini, and Stefano Viviani (Milan: SugarCo, 1990), 38–40); Seymour I. Schwartz and Ralph E. Ehrenberg, *The Mapping of America* (New York: Harry N. Abrams, 1980), 18–20. For all of the maps discussed here, I have relied on the scholarly compendium of maps and commentary edited by Osvaldo Baldacci, *Atlante colombiano della grande scoperta* (Rome: Istituto poligrafico e zecca dello stato, Libreria dello stato, 1992).

38. Francesco Prontera, introduction to *Geografia e geografi nel mondo antico* (Rome and Bari: Laterza, 1983), xviii–xix; in this same volume see the essay by Christian Jacob, "Carte greche," 47–68; see also Tooley and Bricker, *Landmarks,* 24–25.

39. Schwartz and Ehrenberg, *The Mapping of America,* 20; for further commentary on portolan charts, see Susanna Biadene, ed., *Carte da navigar: Portolani e carte nautiche del museo corer 1318–1732* (Venice: Marsilio Editore, 1990); Michel Mollat du Jourdin and Monique de la Roncière, *Les Portulans: Cartes marines du XIII au XVII siècle* (Fribourg: Office du Livre, 1984).

40. See Henry Kamen, *Empire: How Spain Became a World Power, 1492–1763* (New York: Perennial, 2004), 264–83; Francesca Cantù, *La Conquista spirituale: Studi sull'evangelizzazione del Nuovo Mondo* (Rome: Viella, 2007).

41. See Shmuel N. Eisenstadt, "The Civilizational Dimension of Modernity," in *Rethinking Civilizational Analysis,* ed. Said Amir Arjomand and Edward A. Tiryakian (London: Sage, 2004), 48–66.

42. Ibid., 48–49.

43. Étienne Balibar, *La crainte des masses: Politique et philosophie avant et après Marx* (Paris: Galilée, 1997), 372.

44. Alejo Carpentier, *The Harp and the Shadow*, trans. Thomas and Carol Christensen (1979; San Francisco: Mercury House, 1990), 93.

45. Ibid., 109.

46. Ibid., 126.

47. On the frontier as a semiotic notion, see Jurij Lotman, *La semiosfera*, trans. Simonetta Salvestroni (Venice: Marsilio, 1985), 58–63.

48. On the Cantino planisphere see Nebenzahl, *Atlante di Colombo e Le Grandi Scoperte*, 42–45; Schwartz and Ehrenberg, *The Mapping of America*, 20–24; and Christian Jacob, *L'empire des cartes* (Paris: Albin Michel, 1992), 212–14, 236–37.

49. Taviani, *Christopher Columbus*, 3:161.

50. Columbus, *Journal*, 31.

51. Ibid., 51.

52. Vespucci, *Letters*, 5.

53. William Shakespeare, *The Tempest*, in *The Complete Works*, ed. Stanley Wells and Gary Taylor (Oxford: Clarendon, 1986), 3.3.145–46.

54. Ibid., 1.2.345.

55. Taviani, *Christopher Columbus*, 3:149.

56. G. W. F. Hegel, *Outlines of a Philosophy of Right*, trans. T. M. Knox (New York: Oxford University Press, 2008), par. 247.

57. Jacob, *L'empire des cartes*, 213.

58. For a further discussion of this "dialectics of seeing," see Susan Buck-Morss, *The Dialectics of Seeing: Walter Benjamin and the Arcades Project* (Cambridge MA: MIT Press, 1989), 52–62; see also Gregory, *Geographical Imaginations*, 235–41.

59. Carl Schmitt, *The Nomos of the Earth*, trans. G. L. Ulmen (New York: Telos Press, 2006), 90–91; for a full discussion, see ibid., 90–100. On the Treaty of Tordesillas, see Taviani, *Christopher Columbus*, 3:162–64. This treaty established the line 270 leagues west of the Cape Verde Islands.

60. Elizabeth Mancke, "Empire and State," in *The British Atlantic World, 1500–1800*, ed. David Armitage and Michael J. Braddick (New York: Palgrave, 2002), 175; for a full discussion see ibid., 175–95.

61. Ibid., 178.

62. Taviani, *Christopher Columbus*, 3:147–52.

63. Derek Walcott, *Collected Poems, 1948–1984* (London: Faber and Faber, 1992), 364.

64. Schmitt, *The Nomos of the Earth*, 93–99.

65. See Shirley, *Mapping of the World*, 28–31.

66. Vespucci, *Letters*, 45. See also Mario Pozzi, introduction to *Il Mondo Nuovo di Amerigo Vespucci: Vespucci autentico e apocrifo*, ed. Pozzi (Milan: Serra e Riva, 1984), 9–27; I have also relied on Ilaria Luzzana Caraci, ed., *Amerigo Vespucci*, 2 vols. (Rome: Istituto poligrafico e zecca dello stato, 1996).

67. Shirley, *Mapping of the World*, 29.

68. See Eviatar Zerubavel, *Terra Cognita: The Mental Discovery of America* (New Brunswick, NJ: Rutgers University Press, 1992), plates 4 and 5. Placed face to face, these two plates of the Martellus and Waldseemüller maps show remarkable similarities in style and vision. See

Henricus Martellus's map of circa 1490 at https://commons.wikimedia.org/wiki/File:Martellus_world_map.jpg.

69. See Pierluigi Portinaro and Franco Knirsch, *The Cartography of North America, 1500–1800* (New York: Bison Book, 1987), 94, plate 41.

70. Cosgrove, *Apollo's Eye*, 114.

71. Francesco Roselli, oval copper plate world map, 1508. Viewable online at National Maritime Museum, Greenwich, London. http://collections.rmg.co.uk/collections/objects/244434.html.

72. David Woodward, "Maps and the Rationalisation of Geographic Space," in *Circa 1492: Art in the Age of Exploration* (New Haven, CT: Yale University Press, 1991), 83–87, qtd. in Cosgrove, *Apollo's Eye*, 114; see also Shirley, *Mapping of the World*, 32–33.

73. Rodney Shirley, *Mapping of the World*, 33.

74. Carl Schmitt, *Land and Sea: A World-Historical Meditation*, translated by Samuel Garrett Zeitlin (Candor NY: Telos, 2015), 25–47. .

75. Giacomo Gastaldi's *Carta marina nova tabula* of 1550 is viewable online at the Library of Congress: https://loc.gov/resource/g3200.ct007014r/.

76. Schmitt, *Land and Sea*, 59–64.

77. Ibid., 79.

78. These maps can be found in Schwartz and Ehrenberg, *The Mapping of America*, 40, 48, 50.

79. Pickles, *A History of Spaces*, 15.

80. Thirty-seven of these *pinturas* are held in the map archives at the University of Texas, Austin. See Karl W. Butzer and Barbara J. Williams, "Addendum: Three Indigenous Maps from New Spain Dated ca. 1580," *Annals of the Association of American Geographers* 82.3 (September 1992): 536–42. Barbara E. Mundy, "Mesoamerican Cartography," and G. Malcolm Lewis, "Maps, Mapmaking, and Map Use by Native North Americans," in David Woodward and G. Malcolm Lewis, eds., *Cartography in the Traditional African, American, Arctic, and Pacific Societies* (Chicago: University of Chicago Press, 1998), 183–256, 51–183. See also G. Malcolm Lewis, *Cartographic Encounters: Perspectives on Native American Mapmaking and Map Use* (Chicago: University of Chicago Press, 1998).

81. Edward Gaylord Bourne, *Columbus, Ramon Pane and the Beginnings of American Anthropology* (Worcester: Reprint, Proceedings of the American Antiquarian Society, 1906), 4; Thomas Benjamin, *The Atlantic World: Europeans, Africans, Indians and Their Shared Society, 1400–1900* (New York: Cambridge University Press, 2009), 282–83.

82. See William Boelhower, "'I'll Teach You How to Flow': On Figuring Out Atlantic Studies," *Atlantic Studies* (April 2004): 33–39; Pickles, *A History of Spaces*, 11–12.

7. Mapping Practices: Word, Line, Image

1. Eviatar Zerubavel, *Terra Cognita: The Mental Discovery of America* (New Brunswick, NJ: Rutgers University Press, 1992), 37–38.

2. Sieur de La Croix, *Nouvele metode pour aprendre la geographie universele* (Lyon: Leonard Plaignard, 1717), frontispiece.

3. E. H. Gombrich, *Art and Illusion: A Study in the Psychology of Pictorial Representation* (Princeton, NJ: Princeton University Press, 1969), 84.

4. La Croix, *Nouvele metode pour aprendre*, 187.

5. Henri Lefebvre, *The Production of Space,* trans. Donald Nicholson-Smith (Oxford: Blackwell, 1994), 85. Lefebvre's book has become required reading for anyone interested in geopolitical and ecosocial issues.

6. Pickles, *A History of Spaces: Cartographic Reason, Mapping and the Geo-Coded World* (London: Routledge, 2004), 5.

7. William H. Stahl, "Li riconoscerai dalle loro carte," in *Geografia e geografi nel mondo antico,* ed. Francesco Prontera (Rome: Laterza, 1983), 17–46; on further names for maps, see P. D. A. Harvey, *The History of Topographical Maps: Symbols, Pictures and Surveys* (London: Thames and Hudson, 1980), 10. Harvey notes that all these different names in different languages "reflect the fact that the map is a relative latecomer to the cultural scene. The name [map] applied to it was that of a closely related object, and this name may or may not have acquired a more specialized, more specific, meaning as the map became fully established as an object in its own right" (10).

8. For a discussion of the metaphor of theater applied to maps and other kinds of documents, see Giorgio Mangani, "I luoghi del sapere," in *Hic sunt leones,* ed. Omar Calabrese, Renato Giovannoli, and Isabella Pezzini (Milan: Electa, 1983), 72–75.

9. Amir D. Aczel, *L'enigma della bussola,* trans. Andrea Antonini (Milan: Raffaello Cortina, 2005), 103.

10. D'Alembert, *Discorso preliminare all'enciclopedia,* trans. Arturo Pasa (Treviso: Libreria Editrice Canova, 1957), 132.

11. This passage from *La logique de Port-Royal* is quoted in Louis Marin, "Les voies de la carte," in *Cartes et figures de la terre (*Paris: Centre Georges Pompidou, 1980), 47.

12. William Boelhower, "Inventing America: Towards a Model of Cartographic Semiosis," *Word & Image* 4.2 (April 1988), 475–97. I have also dealt in a more general way with cartographic practices in Boelhower, *Through a Glass Darkly: Ethnic Semiosis in American Literature* (New York: Oxford, 1992), 41–79.

13. For a discussion of the notion of semiosphere, see Jurij Lotman, *La semiosfera,* trans. Simonetta Salvestroni (Venice: Marsilio, 1985), 51–65. I am adapting Lotman's concept to the specific semiotic activity of cartography.

14. See Christian Jacob, *L'empire des cartes* (Paris: Albin Michel, 1992), 269.

15. Columbus, *Journal of the First Voyage,* ed. B. W. Ife (Warminster: Aris and Phillips, 1990), 89.

16. Ibid., 83.

17. For a discussion of this, see William Boelhower, "Stories of Foundation, Scenes of Origin," *American Literary History* 5.3 (Fall 1993): 391–428; see also Boelhower, *Through a Glass Darkly,* 64–71; Martin Brückner, *The Geographical Revolution in Early America* (Chapel Hill: University of North Carolina Press, 2006), 16-50, 113-20.

18. Nicolas de Fer, *Mappe-monde ou carte générale de la terre* (1705). Viewable at https://www .loc.gov/item/83694567.

19. Gunnar Olsson, quoted in Pickles, *A History of Spaces,* 3.

20. Mangani, "I luoghi del sapere," 73.

21. Cristoforo Colombo, *Lettere autografe di Cristoforo Colombo* (Bologna: Arnaldo Forni Editore, 1974), 72, 74.

22. Jacob, *L'empire des cartes,* 309.

23. Columbus, *Journal,* 65. I will say more about this generosity below.

24. Boelhower, "Stories of Foundation, Scenes of Origin," 391–95.

25. Columbus, *Journal,* 121.

26. There is a gift scene in Jacques Le Moyne de Morgues's topographical work, which has survived in Theodor de Bry's *America,* part II. See *The Work of Jacques Le Moyne de Morgues,* ed. Paul Hulton, vol. 2 (London: British Museum Publications, 1977), plate 94.

27. See, for example, Peter Hulme, *Colonial Encounters: Europe and the Native Caribbean, 1492–1797* (London: Routledge, 1992), 137–52.

28. Bernard Bailyn, *Atlantic History: Concept and Contours* (Cambridge, MA: Harvard University Press, 2005), 68.

29. See, for example, the outstanding scenes in *The Work of Jacques Le Moyne de Morgues,* vol. 2, plates 93–99. There is also an incisive reading of them by Frank Lestringant, "Isolarii," in *Hic sunt leones,* edited by Omar Calabrese, Renato Giovannoli, Isabella Pezzini (Milan: Electa, 1983), 62–71.

30. The relevant text from Las Casas appears in the appendix to Ramón Pané, *Le antichità degli indiani,* ed. Roberta Pieraccioli and Maurizio Rippa Bonati (Turin: Edizioni Paoline: 1992), 216–23.

31. Pané's report first appeared as "Scrittura di fra Roman delle antichità de gl'Indiani, le quali egli con diligenza, come huomo che sàla lor lingua, ha raccolte per commandamento dello Ammiraglio," in *Historie Del S. D. Fernando Colombo* (Venice: Francesco de' Franceschi Sanese, 1571), 124–45.

32. Ramón Pané, *Relación acerca de las antigüedades de los Indios,* ed. José Juan Arrom (Mexico City: Siglo Veintiuno XXI Editores, 1988).

33. Amerigo Vespucci, *Letters from a New World,* trans. David Jacobson (New York: Marsilio, 1992), 31.

34. Thomas More, *Utopia,* trans. Ralph Robinson (London: Dent, 1988), 15.

35. See *L'Italia: Emilia Romagna* (Milan: Touring Editore, 2005), 6:655, 689; see above all the incisive pages on a homology conflating the structure of Tasso's poem "Gerusalemme Liberata" (Europe's first modern poem), Biagio Rossetti's urban plan for Ferrara, and Columbus's voyage by Franco Farinelli, *Geografia: Un'introduzione ai modelli del mondo* (Turin: Einaudi, 2003), 140–49.

36. Robert Redeker, "L'utopia, ovvero rimettere in libertà la potenza di sognare," in *Utopia e modernità,* ed. Marcel Gauchet and Robert Redeker, trans. Paola Baiocco (Troina: Città Aperta Editore, 2005), 76.

37. See the convincing pages on utopia by Marcel Gauchet, "I volti dell'altro: La traiettoria della coscienza utopica," in *Utopia e modernità,* ed. Gauchet and Redeker, 71–93.

38. More, *Utopia,* 5.

39. For a discussion of this icon, see Franco Bernabei, *Percorsi della critica d'arte* (Padua: CLEUP, 1991), 134–41.

40. Sebastian Münster, *Novae Insulae, XVII Nova Tabula,* (Basel: Henrich Petri, 1540). Viewable at http://www.oshermaps.org/map/1640.0001.

41. See, for example, the image of Magellan's ship *Victoria* ibid.

42. Henry Kamen, *Empire: How Spain Became a World Power, 1492–1763* (New York: Perennial, 2004), 353–54.

43. Álvar Núñez Cabeza de Vaca, *Naufragio* (Turin: Einaudi, 1989), 48, 60.

44. I have borrowed this term from Benjamin Nelson, *On the Roads to Modernity: Conscience, Science and Civilizations,* ed. Toby E. Huff (Totowa, NJ: Rowman and Littlefield, 1981), 210, 231.

45. Giorgio Agamben, *Aperto* (Turin: Einaudi, 2002), 30–43.

46. Ibid., 43.

47. See the discussion in Peter Burke, *Eyewitnessing: The Uses of Images as Historical Evidence* (London: Reaktion Books, 2001), 127–28.

48. For a recent summary, see Kamen, *Empire,* 106–12.

49. Ibid., 108–9.

50. World map by Pierre Desceliers, 1550. Viewable from the British Library at http://www.bl.uk/onlinegallery/onlineex/mapsviews/desceliers/large17690.html.

51. Francesco di Xerez, *La relazione del viaggio che fece il capitano Fernando Pizarro per ordine del governatore suo fratello . . .,* in Giovanni Battista Ramusio, *Navigazioni e viaggi,* ed. Marica Milanesi (Turin: Einaudi, 1988), 6:785–86.

52. Derek Gregory, *Geographical Imaginations* (Oxford: Blackwell, 1998), 36.

53. See William Boelhower, "Three Early Modern Genres: A Microhistorical Approach to 'World Literature,'" in special issue on world literature, ed. Sorcha Gunne and Neil Lazarus, *Atlantic Studies: Global Currents* 16.2 (2019): 170–87.

54. For further critical discussion on the relationship between the figure of the ship and rhetoric, see especially Hans Blumenberg, *Shipwreck with Spectator: Paradigm of a Metaphor for Existence,* trans. Steven Rendall (Cambridge, MA: MIT Press, 1997), 7–102; Dolf Sternberger, *Immagini enigmatiche dell'uomo* (Bologna: Il Mulino, 1991), 83–96; Paolo Rossi, *Naufragi senza spettatore* (Bologna: Il Mulino, 1995), 21–44.

55. Francis Bacon, *Nuova Atlantide / Nova Atlantis / New Atlantis* (Milan: Silvio Berlusconi Editore, 1996), 193.

56. Ibid., 260.

57. World map by Giacomo Gastaldi, circa 1560. Viewable at https://www.loc.gov/resource/g3200m.gct00087/?sp=15.

58. For a discussion of this concept, see Blumenberg, *Shipwreck with Spectator,* 81–102.

59. Sir Francis Drake's shipwreck, bottom right, in Nicola van Sype's 1585 world map *La herdike enterprinse faict par le signeur Draeck d'avoir cirquit toute la terre.* Viewable at http://hdl.loc.gov/loc.gmd/g3201s.rb000011.

60. Quoted in Seymour I. Schwartz and Ralph E. Ehrenberg, *The Mapping of America* (New York: Harry N. Abrams, 1980), 22–23.

61. Columbus, *Journal,* 101.

62. Benedetto Bordone, *Libro . . . de Tutte L'Isole del Mondo* (Amsterdam: Theatrum Orbis Terrarum, 1966).

63. Fernand Braudel, *Scritti sulla storia*, trans. Alfredo Salsano (Milan: Mondadori, 1989), 74.

64. Ibid., 82–83.

65. Walter Benjamin, *The Arcades Project*, trans. Howard Eiland and Kevin McLaughlin (Cambridge, MA: Belknap Press of Harvard University Press, 1999), [N1a, 8].

Conclusion: Atlantic Studies and Global Currents

1. See Sanjay Subrahmanyam, "Par-delà l'incommensurabilité: pour une histoire connectée des empires aux temps modernes," *Revue d'histoire moderne et contemporaine* 54.4 (2007): 34–53.

2. For a discussion of the role of the Kru tribe on European ships see Siân Rees, *Sweet Water and Bitter: The Ships That Stopped the Slave Trade* (Durham: University of New Hampshire Press, 2011), 36–37; Emma Christopher, *Slave Ship Sailors and Their Captive Cargoes, 1730–1807* (Cambridge: Cambridge University Press, 2006), 144, 174.

3. See Sanjay Subrahmanyam, "Connected Histories: Notes towards a Reconfiguration of Early Modern Eurasia," *Modern Asian Studies* 31.3 (July 1997): 735–62; Subrahmanyam, *Aux origines de l'histoire globale* (Paris: Collège de France / Fayard, 2014).

4. David Armitage, "Three Concepts of Atlantic History," in *The British Atlantic World, 1500–1800*, ed. David Armitage and Michael J. Braddick (New York: Palgrave Macmillan, 2002), 26, 22.

5. David Armitage, *The Declaration of Independence: A Global History* (Cambridge, MA: Harvard University Press, 2007), 63.

6. Jonathan Israel, *The Expanding Blaze: How the American Revolution Ignited the World, 1775–1848* (Princeton, NJ: Princeton University Press, 2017). According to Israel, the American Revolution "formed part of a wider transatlantic revolutionary sequence, a series of revolutions in France, Italy, Holland, Switzerland, Germany, Ireland, Haiti, Poland, Spain, Greece, and Spanish America." Ibid., 17.

7. Ibid., 4.

8. Armitage, *The Declaration of Independence*, 139.

9. D. W. Meinig, *Atlantic America, 1492–1800* (New Haven, CT: Yale University Press, 1986), 65.

10. Michael Zeuske, "Out of the Americas: Slave Traders and the *Hidden Atlantic* in the Nineteenth Century," trans. Dorothea Fischer-Hornung, *Atlantic Studies: Global Currents* 15.1 (March 2018): 103.

11. See James Kirker, *Adventures to China: Americans in the Southern Oceans, 1792–1812* (New York: Oxford University Press, 1970).

12. Herman Melville, *Moby-Dick* (New York: Norton, 1967), 318.

13. Maya Jasanoff, *The Dawn Watch: Joseph Conrad in a Global World* (London: William Collins, 2017), 133.

14. Armitage, "Three Concepts of Atlantic History," 26.

15. Teshale Tibebu, "On the Question of Feudalism, Absolutism, and the Bourgeois Revolution," *Review* 13.1 (Winter 1990): 83–84.

16. Fernand Braudel, *The Perspective of the World* vol. 3, *Civilization & Capitalism, 15th–18th Century*, trans. Sian Reynolds (New York: Harper and Row, 1984), 387.

17. Andre Gunder Frank, "The Modern World System Revisited: Rereading Braudel and Wallerstein," in *Civilizations and World Systems: Studying World-Historical Change*, ed. Stephen K. Sanderson (Walnut Creek, CA: AltaMira, 1995), 188; on Fra Mauro's world map, see William Boelhower, "Framing a New Ocean Genealogy: The Case of Venetian Cartography in the Early Modern Period," *Atlantic Studies: Global Currents* 15.2 (June 2018): 279–97.

18. Albert Bergesen, "Let's Be Frank about World History," in *Civilizations and World Systems,* ed. Sanderson, 202.

19. Frank, "The Modern World System Revisited," 164–65.

20. William H. McNeill, "*The Rise of the West* After Twenty-Five Years," *Journal of World History* 1.1 (Spring 1990): 5.

21. Bergesen, "Let's Be Frank about World History," 203.

22. Jerry H. Bentley, "A New Forum for Global History," *Journal of World History* 1.1 (1990): iv.

23. Simon J. Potter and Jonathan Saha, "Global History, Imperial History and Connected Histories of Empire," *Journal of Colonialism and Colonial History* 16.1 (2015): 3.

24. Ibid., 4.

25. See David Palumbo-Liu, Bruce Robbins, and Nirvana Tanoukhi, introduction to *Immanuel Wallerstein and the Problem of the World* (Durham, NC: Duke University Press, 2011), 1–23; Gayatri Chakravorty Spivak, "World Systems & the Creole," *Narrative* 14.1 (January 2006), 102–12; Franco Moretti, "World-Systems Analysis, Evolutionary Theory, 'Weltliteratur,'" *Distant Reading* (London: Verso, 2013), 67–77; Nirvana Tanoukhi, "The Scale of World Literature," in *Immanuel Wallerstein and the Problem of the World,* ed. David Palumbo-Liu, Bruce Robbins, and Nirvana Tanoukhi (Durham, NC: Duke University Press, 2011), 78–98; Emily Apter, *Against World Literature: On the Politics of Untranslatability* (London: Verso, 2013); Pascale Casanova, *The World Republic of Letters,* trans. M. B. DeBevoise (Cambridge, MA: Harvard University Press, 2004); Christopher Prendergast, "The World Republic of Letters," in *Debating World Literature,* ed. Prendergast (London: Verso, 2004), 1–25.

26. Ottmar Ette, *TransArea: A Literary History of Globalization,* trans. Mark W. Pearson (Berlin: De Gruyter, 2016); Ette, *Writing-Between-Worlds: TransArea Studies and the Literary-without-a-Friend-Abode,* trans. Vera Kutzinski (Berlin: De Gruyter, 2016).

27. See, for example, Janet Abu-Lughod, *Before European Hegemony: The World System A.D. 1250–1350* (New York: Oxford University Press, 1989).

28. See, for example, Sanjay Subrahmanyam, *Explorations in Connected History: From the Tagus to the Ganges* (Oxford: Oxford University Press, 2005); Subrahmanyam, *Aux origines de l'histoire globale;* Matt K. Matsuda, *Pacific Worlds: A History of Seas, Peoples, and Cultures* (Cambridge: Cambridge University Press, 2012); and David Armitage and Alison Bashford, eds., *Pacific Histories: Ocean, Land, People* (Houndmills: Palgrave Macmillan, 2014).

29. See Caroline Douki and Philippe Minard, "Histoire globale, histoires connectées: Un changement d'échelle historiographique?" *Revue d'histoire moderne et contemporaine* 54.4 (2007): 7–21. English version ("Global Histories, Connected Histories: A Shift of Historiographical Scale?") online at https://www.cairn-int.info/article-E_RHMC_545_0007-global-history-connected-histories, paragraph 13.htm. The authors provide an excellent overview of the current methodologies in history.

30. See, for example, Arjun Appadurai, "Grassroots Globalization and the Research Imagination," in *Globalization,* ed. Appadurai (Durham, NC: Duke University Press, 2001), 1–21.

31. Douki and Minard, "Global History, Connected Histories: A Shift of Historical Scale," online at https://www.cairn-int.info/article-E_RHMC_545_0007-global-history-connected-histories.htm, paragraph 8.

32. Editorial, *Atlantic Studies: Global Currents* 11.1 (2014): 1.

33. Ibid., 2.

34. Ibid.

35. Sanjay Subrahmanyam, "Connected Histories," 745.

36. Marcus Rediker, *The Fearless Benjamin Lay: The Quaker Dwarf Who Became the First Revolutionary Abolitionist* (Boston: Beacon, 2017), 120.

37. See Carlo Ginzburg, "Microhistory: Two or Three Things That I Know about It," in *Threads and Traces, True False Fictive* (Berkeley: University of California Press, 2012), 193–214.

38. Jean-Paul Zuniga, "L'Histoire impériale à l'heure de l'histoire global: Une perspective atlantique," *Revue d'histoire moderne et contemporaine* 54.4 (2007): 55.

39. Jacques Revel, "L'histoire au ras du sol," in *Le pouvoir au village: Histoire d'un exorciste dans le Piémont du XVIIe siècle,* by Giovanni Levi, trans. Monique Aymard (Paris: Gallimard, 1989), xxiv.

40. Giovanni Levi, "On Microhistory," in *New Perspectives on Historical Writing,* ed. Peter Burke (University Park: Pennsylvania State University Press, 1992), 109.

41. Ibid.

42. Francesca Trivellato, "Is There a Future for Italian Microhistory in the Age of Global History?," *California Italian Studies* 2.1 (January 2011), https://escholarship.org/uc/item/0z94n9hq.

43. Giovanni Levi, "Intervista a Giovanni Levi," in *Microstoria: A vent'anni da L'eredità immateriale; saggi in onore di Giovanni Levi,* ed. Paola Lanaro (Milan: Franco Angeli, 2011), 175.

44. Trivellato, "Is There a Future for Italian Microhistory?"

45. See William Boelhower, review of *Views of the Cordilleras and Other Monuments of the Indigenous Peoples of the Americas: A Critical Edition,* by Alexander von Humboldt, and *Alexander von Humboldt and the Americas,* ed. Vera Kutzinski, Ottmar Ette, and Laura Dassow Walls, *AAG Review of Books* 1.4 (2013): 191.

46. Vera Kutzinski, introduction to *Alexander von Humboldt's Transatlantic Personae,* ed. Kutzinski (London: Routledge, 2012), 1–2; see Ottmar Ette, "Everything Is Interrelated, Even the Errors in the System: Alexander von Humboldt and Globalization," in, *Alexander von Humboldt's Transatlantic Personae,* ed. Kutzinski, 15–28.

47. Subrahmanyam, "Connected Histories," 750. For other exemplary exercises in Atlantic-world biography see See Linda Colley, *The Ordeal of Elizabeth Marsh: How a Remarkable Woman Crossed Seas and Empires to Become a Part of World History* (London: Harper, 2007); Emma Rothschild, *The Inner Life of Empires: An Eighteenth-Century History* (Princeton, NJ: Princeton University Press, 2011); Natalie Zemon Davis, *Trickster Travels: A Sixteenth-Century Muslim between Worlds* (New York: Hill and Wang, 2007); Tony Ballantyne and Antoinette M. Burton, "Introduction: Bodies, Empires, and World Histories," in *Bodies in Contact: Rethinking Colonial Encounters in World History,* ed. Ballantyne and Burton (Durham, NC: Duke University Press, 2005), 1–15.

48. Zeuske, "Out of the Americas," 109.

49. See, for example, Eric Robert Taylor, *If We Must Die: Shipboard Insurrections in the Era of the Atlantic Slave Trade* (Baton Rouge: Louisiana State University Press, 2006); Sowande' M. Mustakeem, *Slavery at Sea: Terror, Sex, and Sickness in the Middle Passage* (Urbana: University of Illinois Press, 2016); Kay Wright Lewis, *A Curse upon the Nation: Race, Freedom, and Extermination in America and the Atlantic World* (Athens: University of Georgia Press, 2017); Edward Baptist, *The Half Has Never Been Told: Slavery and the Making of American Capitalism* (New York: Basic Books, 2014); Daina Ramey Berry, *The Price for Their Pound of Flesh: The Value of the Enslaved, from Womb to Grave, in the Building of a Nation* (Boston: Beacon, 2017).

50. Zeuske, "Out of the Americas," 104, 108, 114, 107, 111. See also Dale Tomich and Michael Zeuske, "Introduction, the Second Slavery: Mass Slavery, World-Economy, and Comparative Microhistories," *Review (Fernand Braudel Center)* 31.2 (20008): 91–100. "Second slavery" refers to slave trading after abolition of the slave trade.

51. See Michael Zeuske, *Amistad: A Hidden Network of Slavers and Merchants,* trans. Steven Rendall (Princeton, N J: Marcus Wiener, 2015). Zeuske makes it a point to say that his examination of the *Amistad* case is "an Atlantic story" and much more than a court case, as it is primarily considered in the history of the United States. In fact, Marcus Rediker's book on the *Amistad* takes a decidedly *cisatlantic* approach, circling as it does mainly around the US events. See *i*bid., x, 1.

52. Zeuske, "Out of the Americas," 112, 105, 118; see also Michael Zeuske, "The Hidden Atlantic: Michael Zeuske Reflects on His Recent Research," interview by Dorothea Fischer-Hornung, *Atlantic Studies: Global Currents* 15.1 (March 2018): 136–47.

53. Zeuske, "Out of the Americas," 108.

54. Ibid., 114, 117.

55. G. W. F. Hegel, *Lectures on the Philosophy of World History*, trans. H. B. Nisbet (Cambridge: Cambridge University Press, 1982), 64, 126–27.

56. Ranajit Guha, *History at the Limit of World-History* (New York: Columbia University Press, 2002), 7, 47.

57. Ibid., 73.

58. Ibid., 88.

59. Ibid., 24, 23.

60. Ibid., 54.

Bibliography

Published Sources

Abu-Lughod, Janet. *Before European Hegemony: The World System, A.D. 1250–1350.* New York: Oxford University Press, 1989.

Aczel, Amir. D. *L'enigma della bussola.* Translated by Andrea Antonini. Milan: Raffaello Cortina, 2005.

"Address of the Colored National Convention, to the People of the United States." In *Proceedings of the Colored National Convention Held in Rochester, July 6th, 7th and 8th, 1853,* 7–18. Rochester, NY: Printed at the Office of Frederick Douglass' Paper, 1853.

Agamben, Giorgio. *Homo Sacer: Sovereign Power and Bare Life.* Translated by Daniel Heller-Roazen. Stanford, CA: Stanford University Press, 1998.

———. *L'aperto: L'uomo e l'animale.* Turin: Einaudi, 2002.

Agnese, Battista. *Portolan atlas of 9 charts and a world map, etc. Dedicated to Hieronymus Ruffault, Abbot of St. Vaast.* 1544. https://www.loc.gov/item/98687206/. Accessed December 8, 2018.

Ainley, Alison. "The Ethics of Sexual Difference." In *Abjection, Melancholia and Love: The Work of Julia Kristeva,* edited by John Fletcher and Andrew Benjamin, 53–62. London: Routledge: 1990.

Andrews, William L. "The Novelization of Voice in Early African American Narrative." *PMLA* 105.1 (January 1990): 23–34.

Ankersmit, Frank. *Meaning, Truth, and Reference in Historical Representation.* Ithaca, NY: Cornell University Press, 2012.

Appadurai, Arjun. "Grassroots Globalization and the Research Imagination." In *Globalization,* edited by Appadurai. Durham, NC: Duke University Press, 2001.

Apter, Emily. *Against World Literature: On the Politics of Untranslatability.* London: Verso, 2013.

Arjomand, Said Amir, and Edward A. Tiryakian, eds. *Rethinking Civilizational Analysis.* London: Sage, 2004.

Armitage, David. "The Red Atlantic." *Reviews in American History* 29.4 (December 2001): 479–86.

———. "Three Concepts of Atlantic History." In *The British Atlantic World, 1500–1800,* edited by David Armitage and Michael J. Braddick, 11–27. New York: Palgrave Macmillan, 2002.

———. *The Declaration of Independence: A Global History.* Cambridge MA: Harvard University Press, 2007.

Armitage, David, and Alison Bashford, eds. *Pacific Histories: Ocean, Land, People.* Houndmills: Palgrave Macmillan, 2014.

Armitage, David, and Michael J. Braddick, eds. *The British Atlantic World, 1500–1800.* New York: Palgrave Macmillan, 2002.

Armstrong, Nancy, and Leonard Tennenhouse. *The Imaginary Puritan: Literature, Intellectual Labor, and the Origins of Personal Life.* Berkeley: University of California Press, 1992.

Bacon, Francis. *Nuova Atlantide / Nova Atlantis / New Atlantis.* Milan: Silvio Berlusconi Editore, 1996.

Bailyn, Bernard. *Voyagers to the West: A Passage in the Peopling of America on the Eve of the Revolution.* New York: Vintage, 1988.

———. *On the Teaching and Writing of History: Responses to a Series of Questions.* Edited by Edward C. Lathem. Hanover, NH: University Press of New England, 1994.

———. Preface to *The British Atlantic World, 1500–1800,* edited by David Armitage and Michael J. Braddick, xiv–xx. New York: Palgrave, 2002.

———. *Atlantic History: Concept and Contour.* Cambridge, MA: Harvard University Press, 2005.

Baker, Houston. "Caliban's Triple Play." *Critical Inquiry* 13 (Autumn 1986): 182–96.

Baldacci, Osvaldo, ed. *Atlante colombiano della grande scoperta.* Rome: Istituto poligrafico e zecca dello stato, Libreria dello stato, 1992.

Balibar, Étienne. *La crainte des masses: Politique et philosophie avant et après Marx.* Paris: Galilée, 1997.

Ballantyne, Tony, and Antoinette M. Burton. "Introduction: Bodies, Empires, and World Histories." In *Bodies in Contact: Rethinking Colonial Encounters in World History,* edited by Ballantyne and Burton, 1–15. Durham, NC: Duke University Press, 2005.

Baptist, Edward. *The Half Has Never Been Told: Slavery and the Making of American Capitalism.* New York: Basic Books, 2014.

Barthes, Roland. *Writing Degree Zero and Elements of Semiology.* Translated by Annette Lavers and Colin Smith. Boston: Beacon, 1970.

Bauer, Ralph. *The Cultural Geography of Colonial American Literatures: Empire, Travel, Modernity.* Cambridge: Cambridge University Press, 2003.

Baxter, Terry. *Frederick Douglass's Curious Audiences: Ethos in the Age of the Consumable Subject.* New York: 2004.

Bayly, C. A. *The Birth of the Modern World, 1780–1914: Global Connections and Comparisons.* Oxford: Blackwell, 2004.

Beckert, Sven. *Empire of Cotton: A Global History.* New York: Knopf, 2014.

Beckert, Sven, and Dominic Sachsenmaier, eds. *Global History, Globally: Research and Practice around the World.* London: Bloomsbury, 2018.

Bell, Howard Holman. *A Survey of the Negro Convention Movement, 1830–1861.* New York: Arno, 1969.

Benjamin, Thomas. *The Atlantic World: Europeans, Africans, Indians and Their Shared Society, 1400–1900.* New York: Cambridge University Press, 2009.

Benjamin, Walter. *The Arcades Project.* Translated by Howard Eiland and Kevin Mc-Laughlin. Cambridge, MA: Belknap Press of Harvard University Press, 1999.

Bentley, Jerry H. "A New Forum for Global History." *Journal of World History* 1.1 (1990): iii–v.

Bergesen, Albert. "Let's Be Frank about World History." In *Civilizations and World Systems: Studying World-Historical Change,* edited by Stephen K. Sanderson, 195–205. Walnut Creek, CA: AltaMira, 1995.

Berlin, Ira. "From Creole to African: Atlantic Creoles and the Origins of African-American Society in Mainland America." *William and Mary Quarterly* 53.2 (April 1996): 251–88.

Bernabei, Franco. *Percorsi della critica d'arte.* Padua: CLEUP, 1991.

Bernier, Celeste-Marie. "'Dusky Powder Magazines': The *Creole* Revolt (1841) in Nineteenth Century American Literature." PhD diss., University of Nottingham, 2002.

———. "From Fugitive Slave to Fugitive Abolitionist: The Oratory of Frederick Douglass and the Emerging Heroic Slave Tradition." *Atlantic Studies* 3.2 (2006): 201–24.

Berry, Daina Ramey. *The Price for Their Pound of Flesh: The Value of the Enslaved, from Womb to Grave, in the Building of a Nation.* Boston: Beacon, 2017.

Bhabha, Homi K. *The Location of Culture.* London: Routledge, 1994.

Bhambra, Gurminder K. *Rethinking Modernity: Postcolonialism and the Sociological Imagination.* New York: Palgrave Macmillan, 2007.

Biadene, Susanna, ed. *Carte da navigar: Portolani e carte nautiche del museo corer 1318–1732.* Venice: Marsilio Editore, 1990.

Blackburn, Robin. *The Making of New World Slavery: From the Baroque to the Modern, 1492–1800.* London: Verso, 1997.

Blaustein, George. *Nightmare Envy and Other Stories: American Culture and European Reconstruction.* New York: Oxford University Press, 2018.

Blaut, J. M. *The Colonizer's Model of the World: Geographical Diffusionism and Eurocentric History.* New York: Guilford, 1993.

Blight, David. W. *Frederick Douglass: Prophet of Freedom.* New York: Simon and Schuster, 2018.

Blumenberg, Hans. *Shipwreck with Spectator: Paradigm of a Metaphor for Existence.* Translated by Steven Rendall. Cambridge, MA: MIT Press, 1997.

———. *Paradigms for a Metaphorology.* Translated by Robert Savage. Ithaca, NY: Cornell University Press, 2016.

Boelhower, William. "Inventing America: Towards a Model of Cartographic Semiosis." *Word & Image* 4.2 (April 1988): 475–97.

———. *Through a Glass Darkly: Ethnic Semiosis in American Literature.* 1987; New York: Oxford, 1992.

———. "Stories of Foundation, Scenes of Origin." *American Literary History* 5.3 (Fall 1993): 391–428.

———. "The Dramaturgy of Witnessing: Hamlet, Douglass, and 'The Heroic Slave.'" In *Making America: The Cultural Work of Literature,* edited by Susanne Rohr, Peter Schneck, and Sabine Sielke, 171–84. Heidelberg: Universität C. Winter, 2000.

———. "'I'll Teach You How to Flow': On Figuring Out Atlantic Studies." *Atlantic Studies* 1.1 (April 2004): 28–48.

———. "The Rise of the New Atlantic Studies Matrix." *American Literary History* 20.1–2 (Spring–Summer 2008): 83–101.

———. "New Orleans in the Atlantic World." *Atlantic Studies* 5.2 (2010): 1–11.

———. "Owning the Weather: Reading *The Tempest* after Hurricane Katrina." *Borrowers and Lenders: The Journal of Shakespeare and Appropriation* 5.2 (Fall–Winter, 2010).

———, ed. *New Orleans in the Atlantic World: Between Land and Sea.* New York: Routledge, 2010.

———. Review of *Views of the Cordilleras and Monuments of the Indigenous Peoples of the Americas: A Critical Edition,* by Alexander von Humboldt, and *Alexander von Humboldt and the Americas,* edited by Vera Kutzinski, Ottmar Ette, and Laura Dassow Walls. *AAG Review of Books* 1.4 (2013): 189–93.

———. "Framing a New Ocean Genealogy: The Case of Venetian Cartography in the Early Modern Period." *Atlantic Studies: Global Currents* 15.2 (June 2018): 279–97.

———. "Three Early Modern Genres: A Microhistorical Approach to 'World Literature.'" *Atlantic Studies: Global Currents* 16.2 (2019): 170–87.

Bolster, W. Jeffrey. *Black Jacks: African American Seamen in the Age of Sail.* Cambridge, MA: Harvard University Press, 1997.

Bontemps, Arna. *Great Slave Narratives.* Boston: Beacon, 1969.

Bordone, Benedetto. *Libro . . . de Tutte L'Isole del Mondo.* Amsterdam: Theatrum Orbis Terrarum, 1966.

Bourdieu, Pierre, and Loïc J. D. Wacquant. *An Invitation to Reflexive Sociology.* Chicago: University of Chicago Press, 1992.

Bourne, Edward Gaylord. *Columbus, Ramon Pane and the Beginnings of American Anthropology.* Reprint, Worcester, MA: Proceedings of the American Antiquarian Society, 1906.

Brathwaite, Kamau. *The Development of Creole Society in Jamaica, 1770–1820.* Oxford: Clarendon, 1978.

———. *Roots.* Ann Arbor: University of Michigan Press, 1993.

Braudel, Fernand. *The Mediterranean and the Mediterranean World in the Age of Philip II.* Translated by Sian Reynolds. New York: Harper and Row, 1972–73.

———. "En guise de conclusion." *Review (Fernand Braudel Center)* 1.3/4 (1978): 243–61.

———. *The Perspective of the World.* Vol. 3, *Civilization & Capitalism, 15th–18th Century,* translated by Sian Reynolds. New York: Harper and Row, 1984.

———. *Scritti sulla storia.* Translated by Alfredo Salsano. Milan: Mondadori, 1989.

Brickhouse, Anna. *Transamerican Literary Relations and the Nineteenth-Century Public Sphere.* Cambridge: Cambridge University Press, 2004.

Brosman, Catharine Savage. *Louisiana Creole Literature: A Historical Study.* Jackson: University Press of Mississippi, 2013.

Brown, William Wells. *Clotel; or, The President's Daughter: A Narrative of Slave Life in the United States.* 1853; Upper Saddle River, NJ: Gregg, 1969.

———. *The Works of William Wells Brown.* Edited by Paula Garrett and Hollis Robbins. New York: Oxford University Press, 2006.

Brückner, Martin. *The Geographical Revolution in Early America: Maps, Literacy, and National Identity.* Chapel Hill: University of North Carolina Press, 2006.

Buck-Morss, Susan. *The Dialectics of Seeing: Walter Benjamin and the Arcades Project.* Cambridge, MA: MIT Press, 1989.

Burke, Peter. *Eyewitnessing: The Uses of Images as Historical Evidence.* London: Reaktion Books, 2001.

Butzer, Karl W., and Barbara J. Williams, "Addendum: Three Indigenous Maps from New Spain Dated ca. 1580," *Annals of the Association of American Geographers* 82.3 (September 1992): 536–42.

Caillé, Alain. *Il terzo paradigma: Antropologia filosofica del dono.* Translated by Ada Cinato. Turin: Bollati Boringhieri, 1998.

Cañizares-Esguerra, Jorge. *How to Write the History of the New World: Histories, Epistemologies, and Identities in the Eighteenth-Century Atlantic World.* Stanford, CA: Stanford University Press, 2001.

Canny, Nicholas. "Writing Atlantic History; or, Reconfiguring the History of Colonial British America." *Journal of American History* 86 (1999): 1093–1114.

Cantù, Francesca. *La Conquista spirituale: Studi sull'evangelizzazione del Nuovo Mondo.* Rome: Viella, 2007.

Caputo, John D., and Michael J. Scanlon, eds. *God, the Gift, and Postmodernism.* Bloomington: Indiana University Press, 1999.

Caraci, Ilaria Luzzana, ed. *Amerigo Vespucci.* 2 vols. Rome: Istituto poligrafico e zecca dello stato, 1996.

———. *The Puzzling Hero: Studies on Christopher Columbus and the Culture of His Age.* Translated by Mayta Munson. Rome: Carocci, 2002.

Carnevali, Giorgio. *Dell'amicizia politica: Tra teoria e storia.* Bari: Laterza, 2004.

Carpentier, Alejo. *The Harp and the Shadow.* Translated by Thomas and Carol Christensen. 1979; San Francisco: Mercury House, 1990.

Carretta, Vincent, ed. *Unchained Voices: An Anthology of Black Authors in the English-Speaking World of the Eighteenth Century.* Lexington: University Press of Kentucky, 1996.

Caretta, Vincent, and Philip Gould, eds. *Genius in Bondage: Literature of the Early Black Atlantic.* Lexington: University Press of Kentucky, 2001.

Carruthers, Mary. *The Craft of Thought: Meditation, Rhetoric, and the Making of Images, 400–1200.* Cambridge: Cambridge University Press, 1998.

Casanova, Pascale. *The World Republic of Letters.* Translated by M. B. DeBevoise. Cambridge, MA: Harvard University Press, 2004.

"The Case of the Creole." *Richmond Enquirer,* December 16, 1841, 1.

Castells, Manuel. *The Castells Reader on Cities and Social Theory.* Edited by Ida Susser. Oxford: Blackwell, 2002.

Castronovo, Russ. *Fathering the Nation: American Genealogies of Slavery and Freedom.* Berkeley: University of California Press, 1995.

Cawley, Robert Ralston. "Shakespeare's Use of the Voyagers in The Tempest." *PMLA* 41 (1926): 688–726.

Césaire, Aimé. *Discourse on Colonialism.* Translated by John Pinkham. New York: Monthly Review Press, 1972.

———. *A Tempest.* Translated by Richard Miller. New York: Ubu Repertory Theater Publications, 1986.

Certeau, Michel de. *The Writing of History.* Translated by Tom Conley. New York: Columbia University Press, 1988.

Chet, Guy. *The Ocean Is a Wilderness: Atlantic Piracy and the Limits of State Authority, 1688–1856.* Amherst: University of Massachusetts Press, 2014.

Christopher, Emma. *Slave Ship Sailors and Their Captive Cargoes, 1730–1807.* Cambridge: Cambridge University Press, 2006.

Cliff, Michelle. *No Telephone to Heaven.* 1987; New York: Vintage, 1989.

C. L. M. "American Hypocrisy." *Anti-Slavery Bugle,* April 17, 1852, 1.

Cohen, Matt, and Jeffrey Glover, eds. *Colonial Mediascapes: Sensory Worlds of the Early Americas.* Lincoln: University of Nebraska Press, 2014.

Colley, Linda. *The Ordeal of Elizabeth Marsh: How a Remarkable Woman Crossed Seas and Empires to Become a Part of World History.* London: Harper, 2007.

Colombo, Cristoforo. *Cinque lettere autografe sulla scoperta dell'America.* Edited by Sergio Musitelli. Turin, Messaggerie Pontremolesi,. reprint 1873.

———. *Lettere autografe di Cristoforo Colombo.* Bologna: Arnaldo Forni Editore, 1974.

———. *La lettera della scoperta.* Edited by Luciano Formisano. Naples: Liguori, 1992.

Colombo, Fernando. *Le historie della vita e dei fatti di Cristoforo Colombo.* 2 vols. Milan: Edizioni Alpes, 1930.

Columbus, Christopher. *Journal of the First Voyage.* Edited by B. W. Ife. Warminster: Aris and Phillips, 1990.

Cooper, James Fenimore. *The Last of the Mohicans.* New York: Oxford University Press, 2009.

Cosgrove, Denis. *Apollo's Eye: A Cartographic Genealogy of the Earth in the Western Imagination.* Baltimore: John Hopkins University Press, 2001.

"The Creole Mutiny." *Cleveland Daily Mirror,* December 29, 1841, 3.

Crosby, Alfred W. *The Columbian Exchange: Biological and Cultural Consequences of 1492.* Westport, CT: Praeger, 1972.

Curtin, Philip D. *Africa Remembered: Narratives by West Africans from the Era of the Slave Trade.* Madison: University of Wisconsin Press, 1967.

———. *The Atlantic Slave Trade: A Census.* Madison: University of Wisconsin Press, 1969.

Curtius, Ernst Robert. *European Literature and the Latin Middle Ages.* Translated by Willard R. Trask. Princeton, NJ: Princeton University Press, 1990.

D'Alembert. *Discorso preliminare all'enciclopedia.* Translated by Arturo Pasa. Treviso: Libreria Editrice Canova, 1957.

Dash, J. Michael. *Édouard Glissant.* Cambridge: Cambridge University Press, 1995.

Davis, David Brion. *The Problem of Slavery in Western Culture.* Ithaca, NY: Cornell University Press, 1966.

———. *The Problem of Slavery in the Age of Revolution, 1770–1823.* Ithaca, NY: Cornell University Press, 1975.

Davis, Natalie Zemon. *Trickster Travels: A Sixteenth-Century Muslim between Worlds.* New York: Hill and Wang, 2007.

Debray, Régis. *Transmettre.* Paris: Editions Odile Jacob, 1997.

De La Croix, Sieur. *Nouvele metode pour aprendre la geographie universele.* Lyon: Leonard Plaignard, 1717.

Delbanco, Andrew. *The War before the War: Fugitive Slaves and the Struggle for America's Soul from the Revolution to the Civil War.* New York: Penguin, 2018.

Deleuze, Gilles, and Felix Guattari. *A Thousand Plateaus: Capitalism and Schizophrenia.* Translated by Brian Massumi. Minneapolis: University of Minnesota Press, 1987.

Derrida, Jacques. *Donare il tempo: La moneta falsa.* Translated by Graziella Berto. Milan: Raffaello Cortina Editore, 1996.

Derrida, Jacques, and Jean-Luc Marion. "On the Gift: A Discussion between Jacques Derrida and Jean-Luc Marion, Moderated by Richard Kearney." In *God, the Gift, and Postmodernism,* edited by John D. Caputo and Michael J. Scanlon, 54–78. Bloomington: Indiana University Press, 1999.

De Vaca, Álvar Núñez Cabeza. *Naufragio.* Turin: Einaudi, 1989.

Di Xerez, Francesco. *La relazione del viaggio che fece il capitano Fernando Pizarro per ordine del governatore suo fratello.* . . . In Giovanni Battista Ramusio, *Navigazioni e viaggi,* edited by Marica Milanesi, 6:707–92. Turin: Einaudi, 1988.

Dorsinville, Max. *Caliban without Prospero: Quebec and Black Literature.* Erin, ON: Press Porcepic, 1974.

Douglass, Frederick. "The Heroic Slave." *Frederick Douglass' Paper,* March 4, 11, 18, 25, 1853.

———. "The Heroic Slave." In *Autographs for Freedom,* edited by Julia Griffiths, 174–239. Boston: John P. Jewett, 1853.

———. "The Meaning of July Fourth for the Negro." In *The Frederick Douglass Papers,* Series One, *Speeches, Debates, and Interviews,* vol. 1, *1842–1846,* 359–88. New Haven, CT: Yale University Press, 1979.

———. "Slavery, the Slumbering Volcano." In *The Frederick Douglass Papers.* Series One, *Speeches, Debates, and Interviews,* vol. 2, *1847–1854,* 148–58. New Haven, CT: Yale University Press, 1982.

———. *Autobiographies.* New York: Library of America, 1994.

———. "The Prospect in the Future." In *Selected Speeches and Writings,* edited by Philip S. Foner, abridged by Yuval Taylor, 398–401. Chicago: Lawrence Hill Books, 1999.

———. *The Frederick Douglass Papers.* Series Three, *Correspondence,* vol. 1, *1842–1852.* New Haven, CT: Yale University Press, 2009.

———. *The Heroic Slave: A Cultural and Critical Edition.* Edited by Robert S. Levine, John Stauffer, and John R. McKivigan. New Haven, CT: Yale University Press, 2015.

Douki, Caroline, and Philippe Minard. "Histoire globale, histoires connectées: Un changement d'échelle historiographique?" *Revue d'histoire moderne et contemporaine* 54.4 (2007): 7–21. English version online at https://www.cairn-int.info/article-E _RHMC_545_0007--global-history-connected-histories.htm.

Doyle, Laura. "Reconstructing Race and Freedom in Atlantic Modernity: Daniel Defoe's Robinson Crusoe and Olaudah Equiano's Interesting Narrative." *Atlantic Studies* 4.2 (October 2007): 195–224.

———. *Freedom's Empire: Race and the Rise of the Novel in Atlantic Modernity, 1640–1940.* Durham, NC: Duke University Press, 2008.

Du Jourdin, Michel Mollat, and Monique de la Roncière. *Les Portulans: Cartes marines du XIII au XVII siècle.* Fribourg: Office du Livre, 1984.

Eco, Umberto. *The Role of the Reader: Explorations in the Semiotics of Texts.* Bloomington: Indiana University Press, 1979.

Editorial. *Atlantic Studies: Literary, Cultural and Historical Perspectives* 1.1 (April 2004): n.p.

Editorial. *Atlantic Studies: Global Currents* 11.1 (2014): 1–6.

Edwards, Brent Hayes. *The Practice of Diaspora: Literature, Translation, and the Rise of Black Internationalism.* Cambridge MA: Harvard University Press, 2003.

Edwards, Bryan. *The History, Civil and Commercial, of the British Colonies in the West Indies.* 3 vols. London: John Stockdale, 1801.

Egerton, Douglas R. *Gabriel's Rebellion: The Virginia Slave Conspiracies of 1800 and 1802.* Chapel Hill: University of North Carolina Press, 1993.

Eisenstadt, Shmuel N. "The Civilizational Dimension of Modernity." In *Rethinking Civilizational Analysis,* edited by Said Amir Arjomand and Edward A. Tiryakian, 48–66. London: Sage, 2004.

Elliott, John H. "Afterword: Atlantic History, a Circumnavigation." In *The British Atlantic World, 1500–1800,* edited by David Armitage and Michael J. Braddick, 233–49. New York: Palgrave, 2002.

———. *Empires of the Atlantic World: Britain and Spain in America, 1492–1830.* New Haven, CT: Yale University Press, 2006.

Eltis, David. *The Rise of African Slavery in the Americas.* Cambridge: Cambridge University Press, 2000.

Eltis, David, Stephen D. Behrendt, and Herbert S. Klein, eds. *The Transatlantic Slave Trade: A Database on CD-ROM.* Cambridge: Cambridge University Press, 1999.

Enthoven, Victor. "Dutch Crossings: Migration between the Netherlands and the New World, 1600–1800." *Atlantic Studies* 2.2 (2004): 153–76.

Equiano, Olaudah. *The Interesting Narrative of the Life of Olaudah Equiano, or Gustavus Vassa, the African, Written by Himself.* New York: Norton, 2001.

Ernest, John. *Liberation Historiography: African American Writers and the Challenge of History, 1794–1861.* Chapel Hill: University of North Carolina Press, 2004.

Ette, Ottmar. "Everything Is Interrelated, Even the Errors in the System: Alexander von Humboldt and Globalization." In *Alexander von Humboldt's Transatlantic Personae,* edited by Vera M. Kutzinski, 15–28. London: Routledge, 2012.

———. *Writing-Between-Worlds: TransArea Studies and the Literary-without-a-Friend-Abode.* Translated by Vera Kutzinski. Berlin: De Gruyter, 2016.

———. *TransArea: A Literary History of Globalization.* Berlin: DeGruyter, 2017.

Ette, Ottmar, and Gesine Müller, eds. *New Orleans and the Global South: Caribbean, Creolization, Carnival.* Hildesheim: Georg Olms Verlag, 2017.

Fabre, Geneviève, and Robert O'Meally. Introduction to *History and Memory in African-American Culture*, edited by Fabre and O'Meally, 3–17. New York: Oxford University Press, 1994.

Fanon, Frantz. *The Wretched of the Earth*. Translated by Constance Farrington. New York: Grove, 1963.

———. *Black Skin, White Masks*. Translated by Charles Lam Markmann. New York: Grove Weidenfeld, 1967.

Farinelli, Franco. *Geografia: Un'introduzione ai modelli del mondo*. Turin: Einaudi, 2003.

Faubert, Pierre. *Ogé, ou, Le préjugé de couleur*. Paris: C. Maillet-Schmitz, 1856.

Febvre, Lucien. "Civilization: Evolution of a Word and Group of Ideas." In *A New Kind of History: From the Writings of Lucien Febvre*, edited by Peter Burke, translated by K. Folca, 219–57. New York: Harper and Row, 1973.

———. *A New Kind of History: From the Writings of Lucien Febvre*. Edited by Peter Burke. London: Routledge and Kegan Paul, 1973.

Fertel, Rien. *Imagining the Creole City: The Rise of Literary Culture in Nineteenth-Century New Orleans*. Baton Rouge: Louisiana State University Press, 2014.

Finkenbine, Roy E. "The Symbolism of Slave Mutiny: Black Abolitionist Responses to the *Amistad* and *Creole* Incidents." In *Rebellion Repression Reinvention: Mutiny in Comparative Perspective*, edited by Jane Hathaway, 233–52. Westport, CT: Praeger, 2001.

Fisher, Shelly Fishkin, and Carla Peterson. "'We Hold These Truths to Be Self-Evident': The Rhetoric of Frederick Douglass's Journalism." In *Frederick Douglass: New Literary and Historical Essays*, ed. Eric J. Sundquist, 189–204. New York: Cambridge University Press, 1990.

Fischer, Sibylle. *Modernity Disavowed: Haiti and the Cultures of Slavery in the Age of Revolution*. Durham, NC: Duke University Press, 2004.

Fontanier, Pierre. *Les figures du discours*. Paris: Flamarion, 1968.

Foucault, Michel. *Society Must Be Defended: Lectures at the Collège de France, 1975–76*. Translated by David Macey. New York: Picador, 2003.

———. *Le corps utopique, les hétérotopies*. Paris: Nouvelles Éditions Lignes, 2010

———. "Of Other Spaces: Utopias and Heterotopias." Translated by Jay Miskowiec. web.mit.edu/allanmc/www/foucault1.pdf.

Fox, Claire F. "Commentary: The Transnational Turn and the Hemispheric Return." *American Literary History* 18.3 (Fall 2006): 639–47.

Frank, Andre Gunder. "The Modern World System Revisited: Rereading Braudel and Wallerstein." In *Civilizations and World Systems: Studying World-Historical Change*, edited by Stephen K. Sanderson, 163–94. Walnut Creek, CA: AltaMira, 1995.

Franklin, John Hope. *From Slavery to Freedom: A History of American Negroes*. Rev. ed. New York: Knopf, 1956.

Fumaroli, Marc. Preface to *L'art de la conversation*. Edited by J. Hellgouarch. Paris: Garnier, 1997.

Gabaccia, Donna. "A Long Atlantic in a Wider World." *Atlantic Studies* 1.1 (2004): 1–27.

Games, Alison. "Atlantic History: Definitions, Challenges, and Opportunities." *American Historical Review* 111.3 (2006): 741–57.

Garnet, Henry Highland. "Address to the Slaves of the United States of America." In *The Rise of Aggressive Abolitionism: Addresses to the Slaves*, ed. by Stanley Harold, 179–88. Lexington: University Press of Kentucky, 2004.

Garraway, Doris L., ed., *Tree of Liberty: Cultural Legacies of the Haitian Revolution in the Atlantic World*. Charlottesville: University of Virginia Press, 2008.

Gates, Henry Louis, Jr., and William L. Andrews, eds. *Pioneers of the Black Atlantic: Five Slave Narratives from the Enlightenment, 1772–1815.* Washington, DC: Civitas Counterpoint, 1998.

Gauchet, Marcel. "I volti dell'altro: La traiettoria della coscienza utopica." In *Utopia e modernità*, edited by Marcel Gauchet and Robert Rediker, translated by Paola Baiocco, 71–93. Troina: Città Aperta Editore, 2005.

Gauchet, Marcel, and Robert Redeker, ed. *Utopia e modernità.* Translated by Paola Baiocco. Troina: Città Aperta Editore, 2005.

Geertz, Clifford. *Local Knowledge: Further Essays in Interpretive Anthropology.* New York: Basic Books, 1983.

Genovese, Eugene D. *From Rebellion to Revolution: Afro-American Slave Revolts in the Making of the Modern World.* Baton Rouge: Louisiana State University Press, 1979.

Gil, Juan. *Miti e utopie della scoperta.* Translated by Michela Fornassi Pardo. Milan: Garzanti, 1991.

Gil, Juan, and Consuelo Varela. "Cristoforo Colombo." In *Nuovo mondo: Gli italiani,* edited by Paolo Collo and Pier Luigi Crovetto, 3–94. Turin: Einaudi, 1991.

Giles, Paul. "Narrative Reversals and Power Exchanges: Frederick Douglass and British Culture." *American Literature* 73.4 (December 2001): 779–810.

———. *Transatlantic Insurrections: British Culture and the Formation of American Literature, 1730–1860.* Philadelphia: University of Pennsylvania Press, 2001.

———. *Virtual Americas: Transnational Fictions and the Transatlantic Imaginary.* Durham, NC: Duke University Press, 2002.

———. *Atlantic Republic: The American Tradition in English Literature.* Oxford: Oxford University Press, 2006.

———. *The Global Remapping of American Literature.* Princeton, NJ: Princeton University Press, 2011.

Gilroy, Paul. *The Black Atlantic: Modernity and Double Consciousness.* Cambridge, MA: Harvard University Press, 1993.

Ginzburg, Carlo. *The Judge and the Historian: Marginal Notes on a Late-Twentieth-Century Miscarriage of Justice.* Translated by Antony Shugaar. London: Verso, 2002.

———. "Réflexions sur une hypothèse vingt-cinq ans après." In *L'interprétation des indices: Enquête sur le paradigm indiciare avec Carlo Ginzburg,* edited by Denis Thouard, 37–47. Villeneuve d'Ascq: Presses Universitaires du Septentrion, 2007.

———. *Threads and Traces: True, False, Fictive* Berkeley: University of California Press, 2012.

Girard, Philippe. *Toussaint Louverture: A Revolutionary Life.* New York: Basic Books, 2017.

Glissant, Édouard. *Poétique de la relation.* Paris: Gallimard, 1990.

Godbout, Jacques T. *Le don, la dette, et l'identité.* Montreal: La Découverte, 2000.

Gombrich, E. H. *Art and Illusion: A Study in the Psychology of Pictorial Representation.* Princeton, NJ: Princeton University Press, 1969.

Goudie, Sean X. *Creole America: The West Indies and the Formation of Literature and Culture in the New Republic.* Philadelphia: University of Pennsylvania Press, 2006.

Gould, Eliga H. "Atlantic History and the Literary Turn." *William and Mary Quarterly* 55.1 (January 2008): 175–80.

Gramsci, Antonio. *Selections from the Prison Notebooks.* Translated by Geoffrey Nowell-Smith. London: Lawrence and Wishart, 1971.

———. *Quaderni del Carcere.* Vol 1, *Quaderno 1–5,* edited by Valentino Gerratana. Turin: Einaudi, 1973.

———. *Selections from Cultural Writings.* Translated by William Boelhower. London: Lawrence and Wishart, 1985.

"Great Meeting in Faneuil Hall." In *Tenth Annual Report of the Board of Managers of the Mass. Anti-Slavery Society,* appendix, 9–20. Boston: Dow and Jackson's, 1842.

Greene, Jack P. *Peripheries and Center: Constitutional Development in the Extended Polities of the British Empire and the United States, 1607–1788.* New York: Norton, 1990.

Greene, Jack P., and Philip D. Morgan. "Introduction: The Present State of Atlantic History." In *Atlantic History: A Critical Appraisal,* edited by Greene and Morgan, 3–34. New York: Oxford University Press, 2008.

Gregory, Derek. *Geographical Imaginations.* Oxford: Blackwell, 1998.

Grottanelli, Cristiano. *Il sacrificio.* Bari: Laterza, 1999.

Gruesz, Kirsten Silva. *Ambassadors of Culture: The Transamerican Origins of Latino Writing.* Princeton, NJ: Princeton University Press, 2002.

Guha, Ranajit. *History at the Limit of World-History.* New York: Columbia University Press, 2002.

Gustafson, Sandra M. *Eloquence Is Power: Oratory and Performance in Early America.* Chapel Hill: University of North Carolina Press, 2000.

Guterl, Matthew Pratt. *American Mediterranean: Southern Slaveholders in the Age of Emancipation.* Cambridge, MA: Harvard University Press, 2008.

Hamilton, Cynthia S. "Models of Agency: Frederick Douglass and 'The Heroic Slave.'" *Proceedings of the American Antiquarian Society* 114.1 (2005): 87–136.

Hanlon, Christopher. *America's England: Antebellum Literature and Atlantic Sectionalism.* Oxford: Oxford University Press, 2013.

Harris, Wilson. *Selected Essays: The Unfinished Genesis of the Imagination.* Edited by Andrew Bundy. London: Routledge, 1999.

Harrold, Stanley. "Romanticizing Slave Revolt: Madison Washington, the *Creole* Mutiny, and Abolitionist Celebration of Violent Means." In *Antislavery Violence: Sectional, Racial, and Cultural Conflict in Antebellum America,* edited by John R. McKivigan and Harrold, 89–107. Knoxville: University of Tennessee Press, 1999.

———. *The Rise of Aggressive Abolitionism: Addresses to the Slaves.* Lexington: University Press of Kentucky, 2004.

Hartog, François. *Évidence de l'histoire: Ce que voient les historiens.* Paris: EHESS, 2005.

Harvey, P. D. A. *The History of Topographical Maps: Symbols, Pictures and Surveys.* London: Thames and Hudson, 1980.

Hawthorne, Nathaniel. *The Scarlet Letter.* New York: Norton, 1962.

———. "Rappaccini's Daughter." In *Tales and Sketches,* edited by Roy Pearce, 59–72. New York: Library of America, 1982.

Hegel, G. W. F. *Lectures on the Philosophy of World History.* Translated by H. B. Nisbet. Cambridge: Cambridge University Press, 1982.

———. *Outlines of a Philosophy of Right.* Translated by T. M. Knox. New York: Oxford University Press, 2008.

Heidegger, Martin. "The Age of the World Picture." In *The Question Concerning Technology, and Other Essays,* 115–54. New York: Harper and Row, 1977.

———. *Sentieri interrotti.* Translated by Pietro Chiodi. Florence: La Nuova Italia, 1984.

Hendrick, George, and Willene Hendrick. *The* Creole *Mutiny: A Tale of Revolt aboard a Slave Ship.* Chicago: Ivan R. Dee, 2003.

Honig, Bonnie. *Democracy and the Foreigner.* Princeton, NJ: Princeton University Press, 2001.

Huden, John C. *Indian Place Names of New England.* New York: Museum of the American Indian, Heye Foundation, 1962.

Hulme, Peter. *Colonial Encounters: Europe and the Native Caribbean, 1492–1797.* London: Routledge, 1992.

Humboldt, Alexander von. *Views of the Cordilleras and Monuments of the Indigenous Peoples of the Americas: A Critical Edition.* Edited by Ottmar Ette and Vera Kutzinski, translated by Vera Kutzinski. Chicago: University of Chicago Press, 2015.

Israel, Jonathan. *The Expanding Blaze: How the American Revolution Ignited the World, 1775–1848.* Princeton, NJ: Princeton University Press, 2017.

Jacob, Christian. "Carte greche." In *Geografia e geografi nel mondo antico,* edited by Francesco Prontera, 47–68. Rome: Laterza, 1983.

———. *L'empire des cartes: Approche théorique de la cartographie à travers l'histoire*. Paris: Albin Michel, 1992.

———. "Geografia." In *Il sapere greco: Dizionario critico*, edited by Jacques Brunschwig and Geoffrey E. R. Lloyd, 1:395–410. Turin: Einaudi, 2005.

Jansen, Jan C., and Jürgen Osterhammel. *Decolonization: A Short History*. Translated by Jeremiah Riemer. Princeton, NJ: Princeton University Press, 2017.

Jasanoff, Maya. *The Dawn Watch: Joseph Conrad in a Global Perspective*. London: William Collins, 2017.

Jay, William. *The* Creole *Case and Mr. Webster's Despatch: With Comments by the N.Y. American*. New York: Office of the New York American, 1842.

Jensen, Melba P. "Frederick Douglass's *The Heroic Slave:* Text, Context, and Interpretation." PhD diss., University of Massachusetts Amherst, 2005.

Jervey, Edward D., and C. Harold Huber. "The *Creole* Affair." *Journal of Negro History* 65.3 (Summer 1980): 196–211.

Johnson, Oliver. *Pennsylvania Freeman*, September 4, 1852.

Johnson, Walter. *Soul by Soul: Life inside the Antebellum Slave Market*. Cambridge, MA: Harvard University Press, 1999.

———. "White Lies: Human Property and Domestic Slavery aboard the Slave Ship Creole." *Atlantic Studies* 5.2 (2008): 237–63.

———. *River of Dark Dreams: Slavery and Empire in the Cotton Kingdom*. Cambridge, MA: Belknap Press of Harvard University Press, 2013.

Jones, Gwilym. *Shakespeare's Storms*. Manchester: Manchester University Press, 2015.

Jones, Howard. "The Peculiar Institution and National Honor: The Case of the *Creole* Slave Revolt." *Civil War History* 21 (March 1975): 28–50.

———. *Mutiny on the* Amistad: *The Saga of a Slave Revolt and Its Impact on American Abolition, Law, and Diplomacy*. New York: Oxford University Press, 1987.

Jones, Howard, and Donald A. Rakestraw. *Prologue to Manifest Destiny: Anglo-American Relations in the 1840s*. Wilmington, DE: Scholarly Resources, 1997.

Kamen, Henry. *Empire: How Spain Became a World Power, 1492–1763*. New York: Perennial, 2004.

Kazanjian, David. *The Colonizing Trick: National Culture and Imperial Citizenship in Early America*. Minneapolis: University of Minnesota Press, 2003.

Kennedy, George A. *A New History of Classical Rhetoric*. Princeton, NJ: Princeton University Press, 1994.

Kermode, Frank, ed. *The Tempest*, by William Shakespeare. London: Routledge, 1988.

Kirker, James. *Adventures to China: Americans in the Southern Oceans, 1792–1812*. New York: Oxford University Press, 1970.

Koselleck, Reinhart. *L'expérience de l'histoire*. Translated by Alexandre Escudier. Paris: Gallimard Le Seuil, 1997.

———. *Futures Past: On the Semantics of Historical Time.* Translated by Keith Tribe. New York: Columbia University Press, 2004.

Kracauer, Siegfried. *History: The Last Things before the Last.* Edited by Paul Oskar Kristeller. New York: Oxford University Press, 1969.

Kristeva, Julia. *Desire in Language: A Semiotic Approach to Literature and Art.* Edited by Leon S. Roudiez. New York: Columbia University Press, 1980.

Kuhn, Thomas. *The Structure of Scientific Revolutions.* Chicago: University of Chicago Press, 1962.

Kundera, Milan. *Il sipario.* Translated by Massimo Rizzante. Milan: Adelphi, 2005.

Kutzinski, Vera. Introduction to *Alexander von Humboldt's Transatlantic Personae,* edited by Kutzinski, 1–14. London: Routledge, 2012.

———. *The Worlds of Langston Hughes: Modernism and Translation in the Americas.* Ithaca, NY: Cornell University Press, 2012.

Kutzinski, Vera, Ottmar Ette, and Laura Dassow Walls, eds. *Alexander von Humboldt and the Americas.* Berlin: Edition Tranvia, Verlag Walter Frey, 2012.

Lamming, George. *Water with Berries.* London: Longman, 1971.

———. "In the Beginning." In *The Pleasures of Exile,* 14–24. London: Allison and Busby, 1984.

Lefebvre, Henri. *The Production of Space.* Translated by Donald Nicholson-Smith. Oxford: Blackwell, 1994.

Le Moyne de Morgues, Jacques. *The Work of Jacques Le Moyne de Morgues.* Vol. 2. Edited by Paul Hulton. London: British Museum Publications, 1977.

Lester, Toby. *The Fourth Part of the World: The Race to the Ends of the Earth, and the Epic Story of the Map That Gave America Its Name.* New York: Free Press, 2009.

Lestringant, Frank. "Isolarii." In *Hic sunt leones,* edited by Omar Calabrese, Renato Giovannoli, Isabella Pezzini, 62–71. Milan: Electa, 1983.

Levander, Caroline F. "The Times of Transnational Studies." *American Literary History* 26.3 (Fall 2014): 559–68.

Levander, Caroline F., and Robert S. Levine, eds. *Hemispheric American Studies.* New Brunswick, NJ: Rutgers University Press, 2008.

Levetin, Estelle, and Karen McMahon. *Plants and Society.* New York: McGraw-Hill, 1999.

Levi, Giovanni. "On Microhistory." In *New Perspectives on Historical Writing,* edited by Peter Burke, 93–113. University Park: Pennsylvania State University Press, 1992.

———. "Intervista a Giovanni Levi." In *Microstoria: A vent'anni da L'eredità immateriale; saggi in onore di Giovanni Levi,* edited by Paola Lanaro, 169–77. Milan: Franco Angeli, 2011.

Levine, Robert S. *The Lives of Frederick Douglass.* Cambridge, MA: Harvard University Press, 2016.

Levine, Robert S., John Stauffer, and John R. McKivigan. Introduction to *The Heroic Slave. A Cultural and Critical Edition,* by Frederick Douglass, xi–xxxvi, edited by Levine, Stauffer, and McKivigan. New Haven, CT: Yale University Press, 2015.

Levi-Strauss, Claude. "Introduction to the Work of Marcel Mauss." In *The Logic of the Gift: Toward an Ethic of Generosity,* edited by Alan Schrift, 45–69. London: Routledge, 1997.

Lewis, G. Malcolm. "Maps, Mapmaking, and Map Use by Native North Americans." In *Cartography in the Traditional African, American, Arctic, and Pacific Societies,* edited by David Woodward and G. Malcolm Lewis, 51–183. Chicago: University of Chicago Press, 1998.

——, ed. *Cartographic Encounters: Perspectives on Native American Mapmaking and Map Use.* Chicago: University of Chicago Press, 2004.

Lewis, Kay Wright. *A Curse upon the Nation: Race, Freedom, and Extermination in America and the Atlantic World.* Athens: University of Georgia Press, 2017.

Lilley, James D. *Common Things: Romance and the Aesthetics of Belonging in Atlantic Modernity.* New York: Fordham University Press, 2014.

Lindsay, Lisa A., and John Wood Sweet, eds. *Biography and the Black Atlantic.* Philadelphia: University of Pennsylvania Press, 2013.

Linebaugh, Peter, and Marcus Rediker. "The Many-Headed Hydra." *Journal of Historical Sociology* 3.3 (September 1990): 225–53.

——. *The Many-Headed Hydra: The Hidden History of the Revolutionary Atlantic.* London: Verso, 2000.

L'Italia: Emilia Romagna. Milan: Touring Editore, 2005.

Long, Edward. *The History of Jamaica.* 3 vols. 1774; Cambridge: Cambridge University Press, 2010.

Lotman, Jurij M. *La semiosfera.* Translated by Simonetta Salvestroni. Venice: Marsilio, 1985.

Lotman, Jurij M., and Boris A. Uspenskij. *Semiotica e cultura.* Translated by Donatella Ferrari-Bravo. Milan: Riccardo Ricciardi Editore, 1975.

Lueck, Beth L., Brigitte Bailey, and Lucinda L. Damon-Bach, eds. *Transatlantic Women: Nineteenth-Century American Women Writers and Great Britain.* Durham: University of New Hampshire Press, 2012.

Mabee, Carleton. *Sojourner Truth: Slave, Prophet, Legend.* New York: New York University Press, 1995.

"Madison Washington: Another Chapter in His History." *Liberator,* June 10, 1842, 1.

Mancke, Elizabeth. "Empire and State." In *The British Atlantic World, 1500–1800,* edited by David Armitage and Michael J. Braddick, 175–95. New York: Palgrave, 2002.

Mangani, Giorgio. "I luoghi del sapere." In *Hic sunt leones,* edited by Omar Calabrese, Renato Giovannoli, and Isabella Pezzini, 72–75. Milan: Electa, 1983.

Manhattan. "Letter from New York." *National Era* (Washington, DC), May 6, 1852, 3.

Manning, Susan. *Poetics of Character: Transatlantic Encounters, 1700–1900.* Cambridge: Cambridge University Press, 2013.

Mariano, Marco. "Remapping America: Continentalism, Globalism, and the Rise of the Atlantic Community, 1939–1949." In *Defining the Atlantic Community,* edited by Mariano, 71–90. New York: Routledge, 2010.

Marin, Louis. "Les voies de la carte." In *Cartes et figures de la terre,* 47–54. Paris: Centre Georges Pompidou, 1980.

Marx, Leo. *The Machine in the Garden: Technology and the Pastoral Ideal in America.* New York: Oxford University Press, 1964.

Mather, Cotton. *Magnalia Christi Americana; or, The Ecclesiastical History of New England from Its First Planting in 1620, until the Year of Our Lord 1698.* London, 1702.

———. *Theopolis Americana: An Essay on the Golden Street of the Holy City (Address to the General Assembly of the Massachusetts Province in New England).* Boston, 1709.

Matsuda, Matt K. *Pacific Worlds: A History of Seas, Peoples, and Cultures.* Cambridge: Cambridge University Press, 2012.

Matthiessen, F. O. *The American Renaissance: Art and Expression in the Age of Emerson and Whitman.* New York: Barnes and Noble, 2009.

Mauss, Marcel. *The Gift: The Form and Reason for Exchange in Archaic Societies.* Translated by W. D. Halls. 1925; London: Routledge, 1990.

McFeely, William S. *Frederick Douglass.* New York: Norton, 1991.

McKittrick, Katherine. *Demon Grounds: Black Women and the Cartographies of Struggle.* Minneapolis: University of Minnesota Press, 2006.

McNeill, William H. "*The Rise of the West* after Twenty-Five Years." *Journal of World History* 1.1 (Spring 1990): 1–21.

Meinig, D. W. *Atlantic America, 1492–1800.* New Haven, CT: Yale University Press, 1986.

Melandri, Elio. *La linea e il circolo: Studio logico-filosofico sull'analogia.* 1968; Macerata: Quodlibet, 2004.

Melville, Herman. *Moby-Dick.* New York: Norton, 1967.

Meltzer, Françoise. *For Fear of the Fire: Joan of Arc and the Limits of Subjectivity.* Chicago: University of Chicago Press, 2001.

Memmi, Albert. *The Colonizer and the Colonized.* New York: Orion, 1965.

Mennell, Stephen. *Norbert Elias: An Introduction.* Dublin: University College Dublin Press, 1992.

Milanesi, Marica. "Terra Incognita." In *Hic sunt leones,* edited by Omar Calabrese, Renato Giovannoli, and Isabella Pezzini, 11–14. Milan: Electa, 1983.

Miles, Margaret R. "The Virgin's One Bare Breast: Female Nudity and Religious Meaning in Tuscan Early Renaissance Culture." In *The Female Body in Western Culture,* edited by Susan Robin Suleiman, 193–208. Cambridge, MA: Harvard University Press, 1986.

Mintz, Sidney. *Sweetness and Power: The Place of Sugar in Modern History.* New York: Viking, 1985.

Moore, Dennis, William Boelhower, Sean X. Goudie, Karen N. Salt, Emma Christopher, Ned Blackhawk, and Marcus Rediker. "Colloquy with Marcus Rediker on The Slave Ship: A Human History." *Atlantic Studies* 7.1 (March 2010): 5–45.

More, Thomas. *Utopia.* Translated by Ralph Robinson. London: Dent, 1988.

Moretti, Franco. "World-Systems Analysis, Evolutionary Theory, 'Weltliteratur.'" In *Immanuel Wallerstein and the Problem of the World,* 67–77. Durham, NC: Duke University Press, 2011.

Morrison, Toni. "The Site of Memory." In *Inventing the Truth: The Art and Craft of Memoir,* edited by William Zinsser, 83–102. Boston: Houghton Mifflin, 1987.

Morse, Jedidiah. *The American Geography; or, A View of the Present Situation of the United States of America.* London: John Stockdale, 1792.

Mourt's Relation: A Journal of the Pilgrims at Plymouth. Ed. Dwight B. Heath. Cambridge: Applewood Books, 1986.

Mulvey, Christopher. *Transatlantic Manners: Social Patterns in Nineteenth-Century Anglo-American Travel Literature.* Cambridge: Cambridge University Press, 2008.

Mundy, Barbara E. "Mesoamerican Cartography." In *Cartography in the Traditional African, American, Arctic, and Pacific Societies,* edited by David Woodward and G. Malcolm Lewis, 183–256. Chicago: University of Chicago Press, 1998.

Mustakeem, Sowande' M. *Slavery at Sea: Terror, Sex, and Sickness in the Middle Passage.* Urbana: University of Illinois Press, 2016.

Nancy, Jean-Luc. *La creazione del mondo o la mondializzazione.* Translated by Davide Tarizzo. Turin: Einaudi, 2003.

Naylor, Gloria. *Mama Day.* New York: Vintage, 1989.

Nebenzahl, Kenneth. *Atlas of Columbus and the Great Discoveries.* Chicago: Rand McNally, 1990.

———. *Atlante di Colombo e Le Grandi Scoperte.* Translated by Miriam Bait, Attilio Trentini, and Stefano Viviani. Milan: SugarCo, 1990

Nelson, Benjamin. *On the Roads to Modernity: Conscience, Science and Civilizations.* Edited by Toby E. Huff. Totowa, NJ: Rowman and Littlefield, 1981.

"The New-England [Anti-Slavery] Convention." *Liberator,* June 10, 1842, 2.

"Nicandra physalodes." Go Botany. http://gobotany.newenglandwild.org/species /nicandra/physalodes/. Accessed July 13, 2013.

Nora, Pierre, and Charles-Robert Ageron. *Les lieux de mémoir.* Paris: Gallimard, 1997.

Northup, Solomon. *Twelve Years a Slave.* Edited by David Wilson. Auburn, NY: Derby and Miller, 1853.

Nussbaum, Felicity A. "The Theatre of Empire: Racial Counterfeit, Racial Realism." In *A New Imperial History: Culture, Identity, and Modernity in Britain and the*

Empire, 1660–1840, edited by Kathleen Wilson, 71–90. Cambridge: Cambridge University Press, 2004.

O'Reilly, William. "Genealogies of Atlantic History." *Atlantic Studies* 1.1 (April 2004): 66–84.

Orgel, Stephen. Introduction and notes to *The Tempest.* Oxford: Oxford University Press, 1987.

Osterhammel, Jürgen. *Colonialism: A Theoretical Overview.* Translated by Shelley Frisch. Princeton, NJ: Marcus Wiener Publishers, 2005.

———. *The Transformation of the World: A Global History of the Nineteenth Century.* Translated by Patrick Camiller. Princeton, NJ: Princeton University Press, 2014.

Padrón, Ricardo. *The Spacious Word: Cartography, Literature, and Empire in Early Modern Spain.* Chicago: University of Chicago Press, 2004.

Palmer, R. R. *The Age of the Democratic Revolution: A Political History of Europe and America, 1760–1800.* Princeton, NJ: Princeton University Press, 2014.

Palumbo-Liu, David, Bruce Robbins, and Nirvana Tanoukhi. Introduction to *Immanuel Wallerstein and the Problem of the World.* Edited by Palumbo-Liu, Robbins, and Tanoukhi, 1–23. Durham, NC: Duke University Press, 2011.

Pané, Ramón. "Scrittura di fra Roman delle antichità de gl'Indiani, le quali egli con diligenza, come huomo che sàla lor lingua, ha raccolte per commandamento dello Ammiraglio." In *Historie Del S.D. Fernando Colombo,* 124–145. Venice: Francesco de' Franceschi Sanese, 1571.

———. *Relación acerca de las antigüedades de los Indios.* Edited by José Juan Arrom. Mexico City: Siglo Veintiuno XXI Editores, 1988.

———. *Le antichità degli indiani.* Edited by Roberta Pieraccioli and Maurizio Rippa Bonati. Turin: Edizioni Paoline, 1992.

Passeron, Jean-Claude, and Jacques Revel. "Penser par cas: Raisonner à partir de singularités." In *Penser par cas,* edited by Passeron and Revel, 9–44. Paris: École des Hautes Études en Sciences Sociales, 2005.

Patterson, Orlando H. *An Absence of Ruins.* London: Hutchinson, 1967.

———. *Slavery and Social Death: A Comparative Study.* Cambridge, MA: Harvard University Press, 1982.

Pickles, John. *A History of Spaces: Cartographic Reason, Mapping and the Geo-Coded World.* London: Routledge, 2004.

Pietschmann, Horst, ed. *Atlantic History: History of the Atlantic System, 1580–1830.* Gottingen: Vandenhoeck and Ruprecht, 2002.

Pigafetta, Antonio. *Il primo viaggio intorno al mondo.* Rome: Edizioni Associate, 1989.

Pollan, Michael. *The Botany of Desire: A Plant's-Eye View of the World.* New York: Random House, 2002.

Pomian, Krzysztof. *L'ordine del tempo.* Turin: Einaudi, 1992.

———. *Che cos'è la storia.* Milan: Mondadori, 2001.

Portinaro, Pierluigi, and Franco Knirsch. *The Cartography of North America, 1500–1800.* New York: Bison Book, 1987.

Potter, Simon J., and Jonathan Saha. "Global History, Imperial History and Connected Histories of Empire." *Journal of Colonialism and Colonial History* 16.1 (2015): 1–35.

Pozzi, Mario. Introduction to *Il Mondo Nuovo di Amerigo Vespucci: Vespucci autentico e apocrifo,* edited by Pozzi, 9–27. Milan: Serra e Riva, 1984.

Pratt, Mary Louise. *Imperial Eyes: Travel Writing and Transculturation.* New York: Routledge, 1992.

Prendergast, Christopher. "The World Republic of Letters." In *Debating World Literature,* edited by Prendergast, 1–25. London: Verso, 2004.

Prontera, Francesco. Introduction to *Geografia e geografi nel mondo antico,* ix–xxxii. Rome: Laterza, 1983.

Ramusio, Giovanni Battista. *Navigazioni e Viaggi.* 6 vols. Edited by Marica Milanesi. 1550–1559; Turin: Einaudi, 1988–1997.

Rediker, Marcus. *Between the Devil and the Deep Blue Sea: Merchant Seamen, Pirates, and the Anglo-American Maritime World, 1700–1750.* Cambridge: Cambridge University Press, 1987.

———. *The Slave Ship: A Human History.* New York: Viking, 2007.

———. *The* Amistad *Rebellion: An Atlantic Odyssey of Slavery and Freedom.* New York: Penguin Books, 2013.

———. *The Fearless Benjamin Lay: The Quaker Dwarf Who Became the First Revolutionary Abolitionist.* Boston: Beacon, 2017.

Rediker, Robert. "L'utopia, ovvero rimettere in libertà la potenza di sognare." In *Utopia e modernità,* edited by Marcel Gauchet and Robert Redeker, trans. Paola Baiocco, 29–70. Troina: Città Aperta Editore, 2005.

Rees, Siân. *Sweet Water and Bitter: The Ships That Stopped the Slave Trade.* Durham: University of New Hampshire Press, 2011.

Reinhardt, Mark. *Who Speaks for Margaret Garner?* Minneapolis: University of Minnesota Press, 2010.

Rueff, Martin. "L'historien et les noms propres." *Critique* 67.769–70 (June–July 2011): 515.

Revel, Jacques. "L'histoire au ras du sol." In *Le pouvoir au village: Histoire d'un exorciste dans le Piémont du XVIIe siècle,* by Giovanni Levi, i–xxxiii, translated by Monique Aymard. Paris: Gallimard:1989.

Reynolds, Larry J. *Righteous Violence: Revolution, Slavery, and the American Renaissance.* Athens: University of Georgia Press, 2011.

Rich, Adrienne. "Diving into the Wreck." In *Diving into the Wreck,* 23. New York: Norton, 1973.

———. "Notes Toward a Politics of Location." In *Blood, Bread, and Poetry: Selected Prose,* 210–31. New York: Norton, 1994.

Ricoeur, Paul. *Temps et récit.* 3 vols. Paris: Seuil, 1983.

Rivière, Jacques-Loup. "Yoknapatawpha." In *Cartes et figures de la terre,* edited by Giulio Macchi, 214. Paris: Centre Georges Pompidou, 1980.

Roach, Joseph. *Cities of the Dead: Circum-Atlantic Performance.* New York: Columbia University Press, 1996.

Robinson, J. *The Yorker's Stratagem; or, Banana's Wedding: A Farce in Two Acts.* New York: T. and J. Swords, 1792.

Romano, Ruggiero. *Braudel e noi.* Rome: Donzelli, 1995.

Ronchi, Rocco. *Il pensiero bastardo: Figurazione dell'invisibile e communicazione indiretta.* Milan: Christian Marinotti Edizioni, 2001.

Ronen, Ruth. *Possible Worlds in Literary Theory.* Cambridge: Cambridge University Press, 1994.

Rosenzweig, Franz. *Globus: Per una teoria storico-universale dello spazio.* Translated by Stefania Carretti. Genoa: Marietti, 2007.

Rossi, Paolo. *Naufragi senza spettatore.* Bologna: Il Mulino, 1995.

Rothschild, Emma. *The Inner Life of Empires: An Eighteenth-Century History.* Princeton, NJ: Princeton University Press, 2011.

Sahlins, Marshall. "The Spirit of the Gift." In *The Logic of the Gift: Toward an Ethic of Generosity,* edited by Alan Schrift, 70–99. London: Routledge, 1997.

Said, Edward. *Culture and Imperialism.* London: Vintage, 1994.

———. *Orientalism: Western Conceptions of the Orient.* 1978; London: Penguin, 1995.

———. "History, Literature, and Geography." In *Reflections on Exile and Other Essays,* 453–73. Cambridge, MA: Harvard University Press, 2000.

Sale, Maggie Montesinos. *The Slumbering Volcano: American Slave Ship Revolts and the Production of Rebellious Masculinity.* Durham, NC: Duke University Press, 1997.

Sansay, Leonora. *Secret History; or, The Horrors of St. Domingo and Laura.* Edited by Michael J. Drexler. Peterborough, ON: Broadview, 2007.

Schmitt, Carl. *Le categorie del "politico."* Translated by Pierangelo Schiera. Bologna: Mulino, 1972.

———. *The Nomos of the Earth in the International Law of the* Jus Publicum Europaeum. Translated by G. L. Ulmen. New York: Telos, 2006.

———. *Land and Sea: A World-Historical Meditation.* Translated by Samuel Garrett Zeitlin. Candor, NY: Telos, 2017.

Schomburg, Arthur A. "The Negro Digs Up His Past." In *The New Negro: An Interpretation,* edited by Alain Locke, 231–37. 1925; New York: Arno, 1968.

Schwartz, Seymour I. *Putting "America" on the Map: The Story of the Most Important Graphic Document in the History of the United States.* Amherst, NY: Prometheus, 2007.

Schwartz, Seymour I., and Ralph E. Ehrenberg. *The Mapping of America.* New York: Harry N. Abrams, 1980.

Sernett, Milton C. *North Star Country: Upstate New York and the Crusade for African American Freedom.* Syracuse, NY: Syracuse University Press, 2002.

Serres, Michel. *Rome: The Book of Foundations.* Translated by Felicia McCarren. Stanford, CA: Stanford University Press, 1991.

Shakespeare, William. *The Tempest.* Edited by Arthur Quiller-Couch and John Dover Wilson. Cambridge: Cambridge University Press, 1971.

———. *The Tempest.* In *The Complete Works,* edited by Stanley Wells and Gary Taylor, 1315–40. Oxford: Clarendon, 1986.

———. *The Tempest.* Edited by Frank Kermode. London: Routledge, 1988.

Shirley, Rodney W. *The Mapping of the World: Early Printed World Maps, 1472–1700.* London: Holland, 1983.

Showalter, Elaine. *Sister's Choice: Tradition and Change in American Women's Writing.* Oxford: Clarendon, 1991.

Sinha, Manisha. *The Slave's Cause: A History of Abolition.* New Haven, CT: Yale University Press, 2016.

Sklar, Kathryn Kish, and James Brewer Stewart, eds. *Women's Rights and Transatlantic Antislavery in the Era of Emancipation.* New Haven, CT: Yale University Press, 2007.

Slauter, Eric. "History, Literature, and the Atlantic World." *William and Mary Quarterly* 64.2 (April 2007): 251–54.

Smith, Andrew F. *The Tomato in America: Early History, Culture, and Cookery.* Urbana: University of Illinois Press, 2001.

Smith, Gerrit. "Address of the Anti-Slavery Convention of the State of New York Held in Peterboro, January 19th, 1842, to the Slaves in the U. States of America." In *The Rise of Aggressive Abolitionism: Addresses to the Salves,* by Stanley Harrold, 153–61. Lexington: University Press of Kentucky, 2004.

Sollors, Werner, ed. *Multilingual America: Transnationalism, Ethnicity, and the Languages of American Literature.* New York: New York University Press, 1998.

———. Introduction to *The Interesting Narrative of the Life of Olaudah Equiano, or Gustavus Vassa, the African, Written by Himself.* Edited by Sollors, i–xxxi. New York: Norton, 2001.

Solow, Barbara L., ed. *Slavery and the Rise of the Atlantic System.* New York: Cambridge University Press, 1993.

Spivak, Gayatri Chakravorty. "Can the Subaltern Speak? Speculations of Widow Sacrifice." *Wedge* 7.8 (Winter–Spring 1985): 120–30.

———. *The Postcolonial Critic: Interviews, Strategies, Dialogues.* Edited by Sarah Harasym. London: Routledge, 1990.

———. *A Critique of Postcolonial Reason: Toward a History of the Vanishing Present.* Cambridge, MA: Harvard University Press, 1999.

———. "World Systems & the Creole." *Narrative* 14.1 (January 2006): 102–12.

Stahl, William H. "Li riconoscerai dalle loro carte." In *Geografia e geografi nel mondo antico,* edited by Francesco Prontera, 17–46. Rome: Laterza, 1983.

Starobinski, Jean. "Le mot Civilisation." In *Le temps de la réflexion* N. IV (October 1983): 13–22.

Steedman, Carolyn. *Dust: The Archive and Cultural History.* Manchester: Manchester University Press, 2001.

Stepto, Robert B. "Storytelling in Early Afro-American Fiction: Frederick Douglass's 'The Heroic Slave.'" *Georgia Review* 36 (Summer 1982): 355–68.

Sternberger, Dolf. *Immagini enigmatiche dell'uomo.* Bologna: Il Mulino, 1991.

Stewart, Charles, ed. *Creolization: History, Ethnography, Theory.* Walnut Creek, CA: Left Coast, 2007.

Stowe, Harriet Beecher. *Uncle Tom's Cabin.* Boston: John P. Jewett, 1852.

———. *A Key to "Uncle Tom's Cabin": Presenting the Original Facts and Documents upon Which the Story Is Founded.* 1853; Bedford, MA: Applewood Books, 2015.

Strachey, William. "A True Reportory of the Wracke. . . ." In *Hakluytus Posthumus or Purchas His Pilgrimes,* by Samuel Purchas, 19:5–72. New York: AMS, 1965

Subrahmanyam, Sanjay. "Connected Histories: Notes towards a Reconfiguration of Early Modern Eurasia." *Modern Asian Studies* 31.3 (July 1997): 735–62.

———. *Explorations in Connected History: From the Tagus to the Ganges.* Oxford: Oxford University Press, 2005.

———. "Par-delà l'incommensurabilité: pour une histoire connectée des empires aux temps modernes." *Revue d'histoire moderne et contemporaine* 54.4 (2007): 34–53.

———. *Aux origines de l'histoire globale.* Paris: Collège de France / Fayard, 2014.

Sundquist, Eric J. *To Wake the Nations: Race in the Making of American Literature.* Cambridge, MA: Harvard University Press, 1993.

"Superb Gift Books: Books in Press." *National Era,* December 16, 1852, 5.

Symcos, Geoffrey, ed. *Repertorium Columbianum.* Turnhout: Brepols, 1993–.

Tanoukhi, Nirvana. "The Scale of World Literature." In *Immanuel Wallerstein and the Problem of the World,* edited by David Palumbo-Liu, Bruce Robbins, and Nirvana Tanoukhi, 78–98. Durham, NC: Duke University Press, 2011.

Taviani, Paolo Emilio. *Christopher Columbus.* Edited and translated by Luciano Farina. 3 vols. Rome: Italian Geographic Society, 2000.

Taylor, Eric Robert. *If We Must Die: Shipboard Insurrections in the Era of the Atlantic Slave Trade.* Baton Rouge: Louisiana State University Press, 2006.

Tenth Annual Report of the Board of Managers of the Mass. Anti-Slavery Society. Boston: Dow & Jackson's, 1842.

Thomas, Helen. *Romanticism and Slave Narratives: Transatlantic Testimonies.* Cambridge: Cambridge University Press, 2004.

Thoreau, Henry David. *A Week on the Concord and Merrimack Rivers, Walden, The Maine Woods, Cape Cod.* New York: Library of America, 1985.

Thiong'o, Ngũgĩ wa. *Decolonising the Mind: The Politics of Language in African Literature.* London: Currey, 1986.

Tibebu, Teshale. "On the Question of Feudalism, Absolutism, and the Bourgeois Revolution." *Review (Fernand Braudel Center)* 13.1 (Winter 1990): 49–152.

"To Booksellers and the Public in the Western States." *National Era,* March 3, 1852, 3.

Tomich, Dale, and Michael Zeuske. "Introduction, the Second Slavery: Mass Slavery, World-Economy, and Comparative Microhistories." *Review (Fernand Braudel Center)* 31.2 (20008): 91–100.

Tooley, R. V., and Charles Bricker. *Landmarks of Mapmaking: An Illustrated Survey of Maps and Mapmakers.* Dorset: Westminster Editions, 1981.

Trethewey, Natasha. *Native Guard.* Boston: Mariner, 2007.

Trivellato, Francesca. "Is There a Future for Italian Microhistory in the Age of Global History?" *California Italian Studies* 2.1 (January 2011). https://escholarship.org/uc/item/0z94n9hq. Accessed March 19, 2018.

Trouillot, Michel-Rolph. *Silencing the Past: Power and the Production of History.* Boston: Beacon, 1995.

Troutman, Philip. "Grapevine in the Slave Market: African American Geopolitical Literacy and the 1841 *Creole* Revolt." In *The Chattel Principle: Internal Slave Trade in the Americas,* edited by Walter Johnson, 203–33. New Haven, CT: Yale University Press, 2004.

TuSmith, Bonnie. *All My Relatives: Community in Contemporary Ethnic American Literatures.* Ann Arbor: University of Michigan Press, 1994.

Vespucci, Amerigo. *Letters from a New World.* Translated by David Jacobson. New York: Marsilio, 1992.

Walcott, Derek. *Collected Poems, 1948–1984.* London: Faber and Faber, 1992.

———. *The Antilles: Fragments of Epic Memory.* New York: Farrar, Strauss and Giroux, 1993.

Waldseemüller, Martin. *Cosmographiae Introductio.* Translated by Joseph Fischer and Franz von Wieser. Ann Arbor, MI: University Microfilms, 1966.

Walker, Michelle Boulous. *Philosophy and the Maternal Body: Reading Silence.* London: Routledge, 1998.

Wallerstein, Immanuel. *The Modern World-System.* Vol. 1, *Capitalist Agriculture and the Origins of the European World-Economy in the Sixteenth Century.* New York: Academic, 1974.

Warner, Marina. *Indigo; or Mapping the Waters.* London: Vintage, 1993.

White, Hayden. *Metahistory: The Historical Imagination in Nineteenth-Century Europe.* Baltimore: Johns Hopkins University Press, 1975.

Williams, Eric. *Capitalism and Slavery.* Chapel Hill: University of North Carolina Press, 1944.

Wilson, Ivy G. "On Native Ground: Transnationalism, Frederick Douglass, and 'The Heroic Slave.'" *PMLA* 121.2 (2006): 453–68.

———. *Specters of Democracy: Blackness and the Aesthetics of Politics in the Antebellum U.S.* New York: Oxford University Press, 2011.

Wilson, William J. "A Leaf from My Scrapbook." In *Autographs for Freedom,* edited by Julia Griffiths, 165–73. Rochester: Wanzer, Beardsley, 1854.

Winslow, Edward. *Good Newes from New England: A True Relation of Things Very Remarkable at the Plantation of Plimoth in New England.* Bedford, MA: Applewood Books, 1996.

Winthrop, John. "A Model of Christian Charity." In *The Norton Anthology of American Literature,* 3rd ed., 1:31–42. New York: Norton, 1989.

Wittgenstein, Ludwig. *Tractatus Logico-Philosophicus.* Revised ed., translated by C. K. Ogden. London: Routledge and Kegan Paul, 1974.

Woodward, David. "Maps and the Rationalisation of Geographic Space." In *Circa 1492: Art in the Age of Exploration,* edited by Jay Levenson, 83–88. New Haven, CT: Yale University Press, 1991.

Wynter, Sylvia. "Beyond Miranda's Meanings: Un/Silencing the 'Demonic Ground' of Caliban's Women." In *Out of the Kumbla: Caribbean Women and Literature,* edited by C. Boyce Davies and E. I. S. Fido, 358–66. Trenton, NJ: Africa World, 1990.

Yarborough, Richard. "Race, Violence, and Manhood: The Masculine Ideal in Frederick Douglass's 'The Heroic Slave.'" In *Frederick Douglass: New Literary and Historical Essays,* edited by Eric J. Sundquist, 166–88. New York: Cambridge University Press, 1990.

Zerubavel, Eviatar. *Terra Cognita: The Mental Discovery of America.* New Brunswick, NJ: Rutgers University Press, 1992.

Zeuske, Michael. *Amistad: A Hidden Network of Slavers and Merchants.* Translated by Steven Rendall. Princeton, NJ: Marcus Wiener, 2015.

———. "The Hidden Atlantic: Michael Zeuske Reflects on His Recent Research." Interview by Dorothea Fischer-Hornung. *Atlantic Studies: Global Currents* 15.1 (March 2018): 136–47.

———. "Out of the Americas: Slave Traders and the *Hidden Atlantic* in the Nineteenth Century." Translated by Dorothea Fischer-Hornung. *Atlantic Studies: Global Currents* 15.1 (March 2018): 103–35.

Zuniga, Jean-Paul. "L'Histoire impériale à l'heure de l'histoire global: Une perspective atlantique," *Revue d'histoire moderne et contemporaine* 54.4 (2007): 54–68.

Index

Note: Page numbers in *italics* refer to illustrations; those followed by "n" indicate endnotes.

Lightning Source UK Ltd.
Milton Keynes UK
UKHW040156300822
408023UK00003BA/974